297
Islam

Islam in world cultures
: comparative

Islam in
World Cultures

Islam in World Cultures

Comparative Perspectives

Edited by

R. MICHAEL FEENER

A B C ⬤ C L I O

Santa Barbara, California   Denver, Colorado   Oxford, England

Library of Congress Cataloging-in-Publication Data

Islam in world cultures : comparative perspectives /
R. Michael Feener, editor.
p. cm.
Includes bibliographical references and index.
ISBN 1-57607-516-8 (hardback : alk. paper)
ISBN 1-57607-519-2 (e-book)
1. Islam—21st century. 2. Islam and civil society.
3. Islam and state—Islamic countries. 4. Islamic countries—Civilization—21st century.
I. Feener, R. Michael.
BP161.3.I74 2004
297'.09—dc22
2004017397

08 07 06 05 04   10 9 8 7 6 5 4 3 2 1

This book is also available on the World Wide Web as an e-book.
Visit abc-clio.com for details.

ABC-CLIO, Inc.
130 Cremona Drive, P.O. Box 1911
Santa Barbara, California 93116-1911

This book is printed on acid-free paper.
Manufactured in the United States of America

*For Mom and Dad,
with love and gratitude*

Contents

Contributors

David Buchman is a cultural anthropologist who has traveled throughout the Middle East pursuing the study of Arabic, Persian, Islam, and the status of contemporary Sufism. He is an assistant professor of anthropology and Middle East studies at Hanover College in Indiana, and his publications include a translation of Abu Hamid al-Ghazali's (d. 1111) work *Mishkat al-Anwar* (Niche of the Lights, 1999).

Tim Carmichael teaches African History at the College of Charleston (South Carolina). He is online editor of *H-Africa,* associate editor of *Northeast African Studies,* and coeditor of *Personality and Political Culture in Modern Africa* (1998). His publications focus on Islam, politics, and culture in Ethiopia, Kenya, and Yemen.

Edward E. Curtis IV is assistant professor of religious studies at the University of North Carolina, Chapel Hill, and author of *Islam in Black America* (2002). He offers courses in both Islamic studies and African American religions and is currently at work on a history of religious life in Elijah Muhammad's Nation of Islam. He holds a doctorate in religious studies from the University of South Africa.

R. Michael Feener teaches religious studies and Southeast Asian studies at the University of California, Riverside. His research covers aspects of Islam in Southeast Asia and the Middle East from the early modern to the contemporary periods. He has published articles on topics ranging from Qur'anic exegesis to Sufi hagiography, and he is currently completing work on a monograph tracing the development of Muslim legal thought in twentieth-century Indonesia.

Anna M. Gade is assistant professor of religion at Oberlin College. She specializes in Islamic traditions and religious systems of Southeast Asia and is the author of *Perfection Makes Practice: Learning, Emotion, and the Recited Qur'an in Indonesia* (2004).

Dru C. Gladney is professor of Asian studies and anthropology at the University of Hawai'i at Manoa. His books include *Muslim Chinese: Ethnic Nationalism in the People's Republic* (1991); *Making Majorities: Composing the Nation in Japan, China, Korea, Malaysia, Fiji, Turkey, and the U.S.* (1998); *Ethnic*

Identity in China: The Making of a Muslim Minority Nationality (1998); and *Dislocating China: Muslims, Minorities, and Other Sub-Altern Subjects* (in press).

Adeeb Khalid is associate professor of history at Carleton College. He is the author of *The Politics of Muslim Cultural Reform: Jadidism in Central Asia* (1998) and is currently working on a book on the multifaceted transformation of Central Asia in the early Soviet period.

Robert Rozehnal is assistant professor in the Department of Religion Studies at Lehigh University. He holds a Ph.D. in Islamic studies from Duke University and an M.A. in South Asian studies from the University of Wisconsin–Madison. In addition to the history and practice of Sufism in South Asia, his research interests include ritual studies, postcolonial theory, and religious nationalism.

Gregory Starrett is associate professor of anthropology at the University of North Carolina at Charlotte. A graduate of Stanford University, he has written about Islamic literature, ritual interpretation, public culture, and religious commodities in Egypt and the United States. His book *Putting Islam to Work: Education, Politics, and Religious Transformation in Egypt* (1998) examines the historical and contemporary use of religious education programs in public schools and their connection to Islamist political movements. Current research projects address religious violence, the cultural and symbolic elements of national security, and the globalized production and consumption of Islamic intellectual goods, focusing on African American Muslims.

Abdulkader Tayob has worked on the history of Islam in the modern period in general and in South Africa in particular. He has published on the youth, religion, and politics during the apartheid and postapartheid eras. Presently, he is based at the International Institute for the Study of Islam in the Modern World and is working on modern Islamic identity and public life in Africa. His major publications include *Islamic Resurgence in South Africa* (1995); *Islam in South Africa: Mosques, Imams, and Sermons* (1999); and *Islam, a Short Introduction* (1999).

Chapter One

Islam

Historical Introduction and Overview

R. MICHAEL FEENER

For many people in the United States, the dramatic and tragic events of and following September 11, 2001, seem to have exploded into the world from out of nowhere. Over the weeks and months that followed, a new awareness of the roles of Islam in countries ranging from Afghanistan to the Philippines began to emerge. However, in the process, phenomena that have only recently come into mainstream American public consciousness via mass media coverage are often presented there without the kind of background materials that are helpful in analyzing and understanding such developments. Popular media reportage can only go so far in providing contexts for understanding current events in different societies around the world. The chapters in this book attempt to provide a deeper grounding for discussions of contemporary Muslim societies.

This short volume can provide only a critical selection of studies rather than comprehensive coverage of all Muslim societies. Thus we have been unable to include, for example, chapters on western Africa or eastern Europe. Nevertheless, the in-depth explorations of the societies that are discussed here can serve as introductions to the complexities of contemporary Islam as it is lived by Muslims in local as well as global contexts. In their discussions of race, language, politics, and piety in diverse Muslim societies, these chapters bring to light some of the most consequential issues affecting the interpretations of Islam and the experiences of Muslims in the modern world. In this introduction I will present an overview of Islam that highlights earlier historical developments that have shaped the tradition for centuries and that continue to inform debates and discussions in many Muslim societies today.

Muhammad and the Rise of Islam

Islam originated in the Mediterranean region in late antiquity (circa 250–700 C.E.). Its founding in seventh-century Arabia took place in a society that was coming into increasing contact with elements of Greek culture as well as with religious ideas from Judaism, Christianity, and other faiths. Though Islam shares much with the cultural legacy of the West, it has spread far beyond its region of origin. As it spread, it carried with it not only the idea of monotheism but also Aristotelian philosophy and tales of Alexander the Great far into Africa and Asia. Today, Islam is a religion with over a billion adherents, and Muslims constitute major segments of the population in countries ranging from Mali to Malaysia. It is also one of the three monotheistic religious traditions that are sometimes collectively referred to as the "Abrahamic" religions. Like Judaism and Christianity, Islam acknowledges a spiritual lineage through Abraham and teaches that one God has communicated to humanity through a succession of prophets.

Muhammad, the Prophet of Islam, lived in the Arabian peninsula, mostly in the two towns of Mecca and Medina, from approximately 570 to 632 C.E. For the last 1,400 years, he has been regarded by his followers as the last and greatest of God's prophets in a line that stretches back through Jesus and Moses to Adam. According to Muslim tradition, Muhammad was orphaned at an early age and raised under the protection of one of his uncles. As a young man, he developed a reputation for sincerity and trustworthiness while working in the camel-caravan trade based in Mecca. He eventually attracted the attention of and married Khadija, a wealthy woman some fifteen years his senior. Until she died, Muhammad married no other woman, and Khadija served as a source of tremendous support for him, even in the most trying of times.

It was Khadija who comforted and reassured Muhammad after he returned home in a frantic state from one of his visits to a cave outside Mecca where he was accustomed to seek solitude and meditate. On that day, Muslims believe, Muhammad was visited by the angel Jibril (Gabriel), who revealed to him the first verses of the Qur'an. As the divinely chosen recipient of this prophecy, Muhammad came to speak the very word of God. However, Muhammad is not deified in Islam, and he is not worshipped by Muslims. The Islamic tradition combines an intense love, respect, and desire to emulate Muhammad's behavior with an acknowledgment of the Prophet's humanity. Fittingly, Muhammad himself is believed to have said that the only miracle God granted him was the revelation of the Qur'an.

Muslims hold the Qur'an to be the word of God, revealed progressively in human history in verses that responded to the changing contexts of Muhammad's prophetic mission over the course of twenty-two years. Since the earliest days of Islam, although theological debates have been waged over the "uncreated" nature of the Qur'an, many Muslims have acknowledged some aspects of the historicity of their sacred text. One of the major arenas for this discussion was the traditional practice of Qur'anic interpretation that examined individual verses in relation to specific events recorded in the biography of Muhammad *(asbab al-nuzul)*. Traditional Muslim scholars have also maintained that the current written text of the Qur'an was not set before the death of the Prophet. Muslim tradition maintains that the verses recited by Muhammad were written down only after his death by his companion Zayd ibn Thabit and that they were not arranged into what became their standard order until the caliphate of Uthman (644–656). Even after that, variant readings persisted and have been regarded as acceptable by the community throughout the subsequent centuries of Muslim history. Thus, throughout the ages, Muslims have not been averse to an acknowledgment of change within the tradition, even at its very core. In fact, it could be argued that until the modern period, such issues have been less problematic for Islam than for some other religions, including Christianity. In the twentieth century, a number of Muslim scholars began revisiting these traditional models of contextual Qur'anic interpretation using modern historical methodology to develop readings of the Qur'an resonant with the needs of Muslims living in contemporary societies.

Moslems believe that the complete text of the Qur'an that we have today is made up of collected materials revealed piecemeal over twenty-two years of Muhammad's life (610–632). Its verses deal with law and salvation history, and they contain narrative material, apocalyptic imagery, and passages of great poetic beauty, all strung together in a way that has tended to seem jumbled, confused, and even unreadable to many Western readers—but not to Muslims or even to many non-Muslims undergoing processes of Islamization. In fact, in many conversion narratives preserved in the classical texts of the Arabic tradition as well as in a myriad of local cultures of Africa and Asia that have embraced Islam, the sublime beauty of the Qur'anic text in Arabic has been cited as a primary motivation to conversion.

In Muhammad's day, however, not everyone in Mecca was instantly won over to the new faith by the beauty of the revealed verses. Muhammad's prophetic challenge to the prevailing norms of polytheistic Arabian society was viewed as threatening by many, including the Quraysh tribe, who were custodians of the polytheistic shrine that made Mecca a widely recognized religious sanctuary. As Muhammad continued to preach and to call for the abandonment of this traditional cult, he faced increasing pressure from the Qurayshi Meccan establishment. In 622, Muhammad moved from Mecca to the agricultural oasis of Yathrib, later to be renamed Medina, "city [of the Prophet]." There he was welcomed as the new leader of the community for his ability to mediate in disputes between feuding tribes. This move, called the *hijra* in Ara-

4 ISLAM IN WORLD CULTURES

bic, is such an important event in the history of the Muslim community that the Islamic lunar calendar starts its year one from this point.

From his new position in Medina, Muhammad began to spread his message of belief in one God and the moral obligations it implied to a religious community that by the time of his death in 632 included almost all of the Arabian peninsula. The initial community that Muhammad formed at Medina comprised a confederation of Arab tribes, new Muslim converts, and Jewish groups, all of whom had agreed to accept Muhammad's leadership in the arbitration of disputes among themselves and with any outside parties. This agreement was formalized with the signing of the Constitution of Medina. This remarkable text from the lifetime of the Prophet includes such provisions as this one: "The Jews of the clan of Awf are one community with the Believers (the Jews have their religion and the Muslims have theirs)" (Ibn Ishaq 1997, 231–233). Similar stipulations were also made for the Jews affiliated with other local Arab clans.

These statements are preserved in the oldest surviving biography of Muhammad, that of Ibn Hisham (d. 833). As will become clear from the chapters of this volume, discussions of such formative texts continue to play important roles in the religious lives of contemporary Muslims. For example, in a recent book published in Jakarta, the Indonesian Muslim scholar J. Suyuthi Pulungan argued that examining the relationship between the various Jewish tribes of Medina and the Muslim community requires a renewed investigation of the meaning of *umma,* "community." To reconcile this statement with later Islamic tradition's generally accepted definition of the *umma* as a community bounded by religious affiliation, Pulungan makes it clear that the term *umma* can be used on two different levels simultaneously, one general and one specific, and then shows that both these understandings of the term have a solid foundation in the Qur'an itself (Pulungan 1994).

Since the late twentieth century, the Constitution of Medina has become the subject of other studies around the world, including one by the contemporary Turkish intellectual Ali Bulaç. He has argued that this first treaty negotiated by the Prophet sets forth a model of intercommunal relations based on a principle of participation rather than domination, "because a totalitarian or unitarian political structure cannot allow for diversities" (Quoted in Kurzman 1998, 174). As the chapters that follow show, diversity is a vital issue for Muslims not only in their interactions with other religious traditions but also in their management of differences within the community of believers. For throughout the fourteen centuries of Islamic history, the multiformity of interpretations of the Prophet's legacy has been the central dynamic for the growth and development of the tradition. Nevertheless, most Muslims have agreed that to a certain extent, in Islam, the politics of communal identity are not completely separated from religious concerns. Muhammad combined the roles of religious prophet and political leader, judging cases through a combination of a charismatic sense of divine guidance and an astute recognition of the needs and conditions of the society in which he lived.

The Five Pillars of Islam

Many writers, both Muslim and non-Muslim, discuss the foundational religious duties established by Islam in terms of "Five Pillars." However, in a recent essay, Ahmet Karamustafa has called into question the accuracy and usefulness of this standard model of defining Islam. In an attempt to move beyond static and essentializing formulations of Islam, he argues that

> there is utility in this formulaic definition, but only if it is embedded within a civilizational framework and used with care and caution. Islam *does* revolve around certain key ideas and practices, but it is imperative to catch the dynamic spirit in which these core ideas and practices are constantly negotiated by Muslims in concrete historical circumstances and not to reify them into a rigid formula that is at once ahistorical and idealistic. (Karamustafa 2003, 108)

This warning is important and useful and should be kept in mind as one reads both this historical introduction and the contextualized studies of local Muslim communities in the era of globalization in the chapters that follow.

The first of the Five Pillars is *shahada,* or "witnessing" to the faith. The *shahada* is more than simply a statement of belief; it also marks communal identification through a ritualized speech act. The text of the *shahada,* spoken with proper intention, determines one's position as a member of the Muslim community. One becomes a Muslim simply by pronouncing, with the proper intention, the words of an Arabic formula that translates as "There is no god but God, and Muhammad is his messenger." Conversion to Islam is thus rather easy, requiring neither elaborate rituals nor any formal institutional acknowledgment. But this "simple" act of embracing Islam implies an open-ended entry into ongoing processes of Islamization that lead to the other rights and responsibilities outlined in the remaining four "pillars" and in their extensive elaborations in the development of Islamic law over the past fourteen centuries. In the brief overview that follows, the remaining four pillars are discussed in general terms, sometimes with illustrative examples from a variety of cultural settings. However, these discussions are not intended as tests for determining "how Islamic" a given person or society is. Rather, they are intended only as an introduction to some of the areas of doctrine and practice in which Muslims have come to both define and debate the tradition in discussions among themselves and with others.

The second pillar of Islam, *salat,* is the obligatory daily prayers that Muslims perform at five set times each day: dawn, midday, mid-afternoon, sunset, and night. *Salat* may be performed alone or together with others, although according to Muslim tradition communal prayer is held to be more meritorious than individual prayer. The prayers consist of a standard set of verbal formulas recited in Arabic to which are added short readings from the Qur'an. The Qur'anic verses recited in the formal prayers of *salat* are chosen either by the individual, if he or she is praying alone, or by the leader of the group at prayer. This prayer leader is often referred to as an imam, and in this sense an imam is not an officer of any organized clergy. In fact, in many Muslim communities the leadership of communal prayer rotates among different individuals without any of them having any officially ordained status. Furthermore, in groups spontaneously formed by Muslims who just happen to find themselves together at prayer time, polite arguments can arise as each tries to persuade another to take up the honor of leading the prayer. However, the position of imam can take on more institutional associations, particularly in North America, where Muslim communities have been organizing themselves in ways that—largely unintentionally—follow the models of parishes and congregations that exist in this particular cultural setting.

However, beyond such local contexts, *salat* can also function to create a sense of unity across the global Muslim community, bridging space and shaping time in the day-to-day lived experience of Islam. At each prayer time, Muslims who do pray face Mecca, each looking toward the same reference point regardless of whether they are to the west, east, north, or south of Arabia. Furthermore, wherever they are, Muslims around the world often break up their day according to the rhythms of prayer. And in some places, such as Yemen, informal appointments and meetings with friends are often scheduled not by the hours of the clock, such as "for 4:00 P.M." but, rather, by the times of the daily prayers, such as "after mid-afternoon prayers, God willing."

The ultimate reliance on God's will expressed in such statements should not, however, lead us to think that Muslims are passive recipients of divinely decreed fate. For the sense of moral responsibility and the requirement to act in this world are crucial aspects of Muslim religious life. Indeed, the third pillar of Islam, *zakat* (almsgiving), is linked explicitly to the performance of *salat* in the Qur'an and is centrally concerned with Muslims' real-world responsibilities for the welfare of their communities. *Zakat* involves the redistribution of the material resources of Muslim communities for the physical and social benefit of the public at large.

Muslims who have more than they need for basic subsistence are obliged to give a portion of their surplus for the good of their neighbors. Thus, *zakat* might be seen as forming a complementary, "horizontal" axis of Muslim piety to the "vertical" orientation of *salat.* This metaphor reflects a traditional Muslim paradigm of viewing Islam in terms of two related sets of obligations: those to God *(hablun min Allah)* and those to one's fellow human beings *(hablun min al-nas)*. It is in the latter that one can most clearly recognize something of the potential social import of *zakat* for Muslim societies. In fact, since the 1990s, progressive reinterpretations of *zakat* have been advanced by such Muslim thinkers as the Indonesian Masdar F. Mas'udi in attempts to realize the potential of this third pillar of Islam as an instrument of social justice (Mas'udi 1993).

The actual transferal of resources associated with *zakat* are guided by a complex of Islamic legal rulings and also vary according to local practice across different Muslim societies. In many communities, however, Muslims make a payment of *zakat* during the last days of the Islamic lunar month of Ramadhan. That month is also the annual occasion for observing the fourth pillar of Islam, *sawm*. At a minimum, *sawm* entails abstaining from all food, drink, and other physical pleasures such as smoking and sex from sunrise to sunset each day of the month of Ramadhan. Beyond this, however, most Muslims stress the interior dimensions of the fast as being just as important as the physical discipline. For example, one will often hear Muslim sermons during Ramadhan that expound upon the need to control one's emotive states as much as one's sensual appetites—especially since some people may be a bit crankier than usual due to hunger or caffeine deprivation.

Despite such restrictions, however, Ramadhan is a very special time in Muslim communities, an occasion for both pious devotion and pleasant camaraderie. After sunset each day, people gather in homes and mosques to break the fast together. These nightly communal meals are often followed by prayers, readings from the Qur'an, and discussions of religious and other topics, although the foods eaten and the nature of conversations vary considerably across Muslim communities. The end of Ramadhan is marked with great celebration, with round after round of visits and feasting with family and friends beginning immediately after prayers on the first morning of the next month. These end-of-Ramadhan celebrations are one of the two major annual festivals of the Islamic lunar calendar. The other is observed at the culmination of the formal rites of the *hajj*.

Hajj, the fifth pillar, is the annual pilgrimage to Mecca during the lunar month Dhu'l-Hijja. Muslims consider it a good thing to visit Mecca at any time of the year, but only a pilgrimage during the appointed season is recognized as *hajj*. For more than fourteen centuries, the annual rites of the *hajj* have brought Muslims from different regions to Mecca to worship together as a community. Over the centuries, as Islam expanded beyond the Arabian peninsula and out of the Middle East, the pilgrimage brought together Muslims from widely diverse regions and cultures, helping foster ties between geographically far-flung areas of the Muslim world and cultivating a sense of com-

Hundreds of thousands of Muslims bowing their heads toward the Holy Kaaba in prayer on the streets of Mecca, March 1, 2001. More than 2 million pilgrims were expected to perform the annual hajj *that year. (Reuters/CORBIS/Adrees A. Latif)*

munity in Islam that ideally transcends differences of language, race, or ethnicity. When the African American Muslim Malcolm X performed the *hajj* in 1962, he perceived it in this way. As he relates the experience in his autobiography, on his journey to Mecca he was powerfully impressed to see that his fellow pilgrims were "white, black, brown, red, and yellow people, blue eyes and blond hair, and my kinky red hair—all together brothers! All honoring the same God Allah, and in turn giving equal honor to each other" (Malcolm X 1964, 323). However, other accounts of the modern *hajj* stress not Islam's universality but, rather, the marked differences between the different groups of Muslims gathered there, such as in the published *Letters and Memories from the Hajj* by the Indonesian author A. A. Navis:[1]

> Looking at the women from various countries here on the *hajj,* one sees that each nation has its own style of dress. In general, they cover almost their entire body except for their faces. When they don their special pilgrim's garb, the women cover their entire bodies except for their faces and the palms of their hands. However, even in this they do not all look the same. Some wear socks, and some do not. City girls, especially those from the chic Jakarta set, really pay attention to their looks. Their clothes are always something special, even when they are dressed as "humble" pilgrims. They wear special gloves that cover their wrists, while the palms of their hands are bare, and these gloves can be lacy. Young women from other countries, even Arabs, just wear simple clothes, which are not lacy or fancily decorated. Turkish or Iranian women wear cream-colored blouses with long sleeves, and they also wear a triangular scarf as a form-fitting head-covering so that no hair can become exposed. Women from central Africa tend to wear colorful clothing. (Navis 1996, 40–41)

Mecca is a sacred place for all Muslims, regardless of where they come from or what they are wearing. It is the place toward which they direct the daily prayers of *salat* and the birthplace of the Prophet Muhammad. Moreover, the rituals of the *hajj* point to even more ancient associations between this Arabian town and the missions of God's prophets, for most of the major rites of the *hajj* serve as reenactments of the drama of Muslim sacred histories of Abraham and his family, including the binding and near-sacrifice of his son and the banishment of Hagar and Ishmael. According to Muslim tradition, the proper performance of the rituals associated with these prophetic narratives were "reinstated" by Muhammad after he purified Mecca of its pagan religious practices from the pre-Islamic "Age of Ignorance" (*Jahiliyya*). As will be discussed below, the sense of difference constructed between *Jahiliyya* and Islam has become a powerful rhetorical device wielded by some modern Muslim reformists.

Transmitting and Interpreting the Way of the Prophet

According to a number of Muslim commentators on the Qur'an, in 632, on his last *hajj,* Muhammad received the following verse: "Today your religion has been perfected for you" (Qur'an 9:128). Many Muslim legal scholars hold this to mark the formal end to the text of revelation. However, historians, anthropologists, and other students of comparative cultures are left to look elsewhere for answers to just what this verse might mean. For the death of Muhammad shortly after this last pilgrimage left the nascent Muslim community with a still somewhat incomplete set of rules for believers to live by. Even the more detailed regulations for accomplishing the Five Pillars and the other duties and prohibitions of Islam were presented in the Qur'an in broad, general formulations rather than in fully explicated legislation.

The "classical" formulations of Muslim responsibilities came into being only two to three centuries after the Prophet's death. In fact, the entire history of the community from early times until today might be characterized as continuing developments in the unfinished business of Islamization—the working out of how believers follow and fulfill the teachings of the Qur'an and the example of Muhammad while living in times and places dramatically different from the seventh-century Arabia of the Prophet.

The rules Muhammad set for the community during his lifetime were taken as the foundation for establishing an authoritative "way," or *sunna,* that continued to serve as a guide for Muslims even after his death. Remembrance of the Prophet has been a powerful phenomenon in the history of the Muslim community, evidenced not only in the field of law but in expressions of personal piety and devotional poetry as well. For example, in the verses of Umm Assa'd bint Isam al-Himyari, a thirteenth-century Muslim poetess from Cordova, we read:

> I will kiss the Prophet's sculpted shoes if I cannot have the originals
> So that I may kiss him in paradise . . .
> Lovers of all times hang on the memory of those they love.
> (Quoted in al-Udhari 1999, 240)

The intense, emotional attachment to the memory of Muhammad evoked by lines like these reveal the deep personal and spiritual appeal of the way of the Prophet, an appeal that is often hidden from outside observers, who sometimes focus primarily on the legalistic legacy of the *sunna* in Islamic history.

At first the *sunna* was transmitted orally; later, the guidelines were collected and transcribed into the textual corpus of *hadith*. The *hadith* relate not only what Muhammad said and did but also what sorts of things he implicitly approved by his presence in certain situations. *Hadith* consist of two distinct parts: the text of the saying, story, or anecdote *(matn),* and the chain of authorities documenting the transmission of that information across the generations (isnad). During the ninth century, the myriad hadith that Muslims had come to transmit and discuss—a vast amount of oral material conveying both the isnad and the matn—were written down and compiled into a number of collections. Six of these compilations have since come to be regarded as especially authoritative by Sunni Muslims.

Although some of these six books boast titles that include the words "sound" or "authoritative" (sahih), throughout the centuries Muslims have continued to energetically discuss this material, how the authentication of various hadith is to be evaluated, and how they are to be applied to governing the lives of individuals and the community. The early twentieth century saw a resurgence of activity in the field of hadith criticism, especially in debates over the criteria for determining the authenticity of hadith texts through critical examinations of their chains of transmission (Juynboll 1969). Since the 1970s, however, such debates on the authentication of hadith have become more marginalized in Muslim discourses. Increasingly today, critical approaches to the authentication of hadith are met with hostility by those who adhere to modern understandings of the sunna that uncritically assert the collective "soundness" and authority of all the individual hadith in certain collections. This phenomenon is evidenced, for example, in the growing number of modern Muslim publications in Arabic and other languages that relate hadith by reproducing matn while at the same time omitting the accompanying isnad. Such texts excise the very part of the hadith that has traditionally been the focus of most activity in the field of Muslim hadith criticism. The use of such publications by contemporary Muslims has contributed to important changes in popular understandings of the sources of the tradition and in the way the Prophet's teachings are understood and interpreted in many parts of the world today.

Islam after Muhammad: Political Succession and the Formation of Tradition

Muhammad's charismatic career of religious, social, political, and military leadership was so remarkable that when he died, it is said, some of his followers could not believe he was mortal. The tradition records, however, that when his oldest companion, Abu Bakr, publicly announced the passing of the Prophet, he said, "Oh people, those who worshipped Muhammad [must know that] Muhammad is dead; those who worshipped God [must know that] God is alive [and] immortal" (al-Tabari 1990, 185). In this, we have a crystalline expression of what was undoubtedly the resolution of a much larger and more ambiguous dilemma centered on how, if at all, the movement was to continue after the Prophet's death and who would lead the Muslim community as his successor. Most Muslims were convinced that Muhammad had died not only without leaving sons but also without making any clear and undisputed statement on who was to succeed him or how the community was to be governed. Some, however, contended that in fact Muhammad had appointed a successor in a statement he made at Ghadir Khumm. This group claimed that the Prophet had designated his cousin and son-in-law Ali ibn Abi Talib to take his place as leader of the community. Those who argued for Ali as successor were to become known as the Shi'a ("partisans [of Ali]"), who have remained a minority in the broader Muslim population to this day.

Most Muslims, however, rejected these arguments for determining Muhammad's successor, contending that they had not been present at Ghadir Khumm and that they did not believe the event even took place. Thus they saw no reason to submit to Ali's leadership and instead were left to find other ways to determine the succession to Muhammad. Furthermore, some who had initially supported Ali's leadership of the community became disillusioned and split to form their own community, and they have come to be known as the Kharijites. The divisions between these various groups did not disappear when the immediate political struggles were resolved. Instead, the groups continued along parallel historical tracts, developing complex elaborations of ideas on the religious implications of their political histories and sometimes dividing even further among themselves over variant interpretations of these developments.

Today, Shi'ites form a ruling majority in Iran, and their place in the administration of a post–Saddam Hussein Iraq—where they also form a demographic majority—is yet to be determined. Most Shi'ites in both of those countries are of the Ithna'ashirite sect, which acknowledges a succession of twelve spiritual leaders (also referred to as imams) in the line of Ali. This group comprises the largest number of Shi'ites in the world today. However, there are also a number of other Shi'ite groups, including the Zaydis and various branches of the Isma'ilis, who comprise significant (but mostly minority) segments of the Muslim populations of Yemen, Pakistan, India, and a number of countries in sub-Saharan Africa. In East Africa, one finds populations of Ibadis as well, latter-day followers of the Kharijites who also form a ruling majority in contemporary Oman.

However, throughout the history of Islam, the majority of Muslims were not Kharijites or Shi'ites of any type. Rather, they were of the orientation that later came to refer to itself as "Sunni," or more properly, the *ahl al-sunna wa'l-jama'a,* "people of the way [of the Prophet] and the community." The Sunnis determined succession to leadership of the community not through familial descent but through a consensus of the leaders of the community. The first four successors chosen in this way were all personal friends and companions of Muhammad, and within the tradition, they came to be referred to collectively as the four "rightly guided caliphs."

When the third of these caliphs, Uthman, was murdered while at prayer, some members of his clan sought to institutionalize their position by creating the first hereditary ruling dynasty of Muslim history, the Umayyad Caliphate. The Umayyads continued the expansionist military campaigns of the earlier caliphs, and by the centennial anniversary of the Prophet's death, Islamic armies had extended their territorial control from what is today Pakistan to the neighborhood of Paris. We should, however, be aware that these military campaigns were not primarily about converting the populations of the conquered territories to Islam. In fact, some of the administrative and fiscal structures of the early empire were predicated upon maintaining divisions between the Arab Muslim military elite and the local populations. In this situation, the notion of preaching the Prophet's message as a vehicle for universal salvation seems to have been set aside, and in some places the conversion of conquered populations to Islam was frankly discouraged. Under this system, the Umayyads and their associates accumulated wealth and luxury undreamed of in the Bedouin Arabia of Muhammad's day. In this atmosphere, Muslims in their new courts and palaces sought out both the sophisticated intellectual cultures and the more worldly luxuries of the civilizations they overran around the shores of the Mediterranean.

Although some enjoyed the prosperity of the caliphal empire and the wealth and power it brought, other members of the community began to voice dissatisfaction with what they viewed as corruption. In search of alternatives to the excessive and decadent worldliness of the new Islamic order under the Umayyads, some pious Muslims turned to new appreciations of Islam's religious heritage, including to forms of religious asceticism. The term *zuhd* was used to refer to a range of ascetic physical disciplines and ritual practices that were pursued by various groups within the Muslim community and in particular by groups in Iraq from the early eighth century onward. Practitioners of *zuhd* imagined that by denying themselves some of the physical luxuries that had proliferated with the expansion of the Islamic empire, they could regain the pristine spiritual relationship between God and humankind that had been revealed through Muhammad in the Qur'an.

Sufism

The rise of Muslim ascetics can be viewed in relation to the development of a broader movement comprised of various traditionalist Islamic religious groups that have been referred to collectively by some historians as the "piety-minded" (Hodgson 1974, 252–256). The religious orientations represented by these groups together formed the basis for developments in almost every field of Islamic religious expression, from *hadith* and law to Sufism, or Muslim mysticism. Recognizing the interrelatedness and the overlapping methods of *hadith* study, law, and Sufism, we should be skeptical of the polemics of those who would set up Sufis as a group separate from and in opposition to the *ulama* who specialized in Islamic law. More often than not in the histories of Muslim societies, not only in the earliest days of the piety-minded but also in later centuries, an individual could be actively affiliated with both approaches to Islam simultaneously. For example, many modern-era Muslims, including the Wahhabis of contemporary Saudi Arabia, characterize the fourteenth-century Hanbali jurist Ibn Taymiyya as the model "anti-Sufi." However, in doing so, they deny much of the historical legacy of Ibn Taymiyya's religious experience, for he himself was a member of the Qadiriyya Sufi order, and his thought draws considerably on ideas developed within Sufi tradition (Makdisi 1974).

Early Sufism can also be seen as a complex of ways Muslims have attempted to create spaces for religion, culture, and community that would facilitate living according to their understandings of the spirit of the Qur'an and the *sunna* of the Prophet. However, many early Western scholars of Islam—and the modern Muslim reformists with whom they sometimes have much in common—have tended to focus in their discussions of Sufism on the ideas of major Sufi authors or ritual practices associated with organized Sufi orders. The term "Sufism" itself thus presents some problems of interpretation, for it has all too often been used indiscriminately to refer to phenomena ranging from mystical poetry and philosophical cosmology to the folk practices of shrine veneration.

One way to begin to understand the complexity of Sufism in Muslim societies is through a historical approach to the growth and development of Sufism's various traditions. Over the course of the ninth and tenth centuries, Sufism experienced rapid developments that distinguished it from the *zuhd* movement. In the process, Sufi teachings came to be defined according to certain schemes of systematization. This occurred first on a textual level as various Muslim writers tried to arrange their thoughts on mystical experience and a deepening relationship to God in coherent, codified writings. The institutional level eventually developed analogously, as the transmission of various ways (*tariqa*s) of teachers (*shaykh*s) more advanced on the spiritual path of Sufism became institutionalized for the instruction and benefit of their pupils and spiritual descendants.

In some Sufi traditions, these chains of successive teachers and students include women as well as men. Women's place in this history is recorded in medieval biographical dictionaries that contain entries on women such as Fatima bint Abbas, a fourteenth-century scholar who was described by Abd al-Ra'uf al-Munawi (d. 1621) as

> learned in the recondite intricacies and most vexing questions of *fiqh*. Ibn Taymiyya and others were impressed with her knowledge and unstinting in their praise of her brilliance, [and] her humility. . . . The swells of the ocean of her

learning roiled and surged. Her being a woman stood out in [people's] mention of her, but awareness of [that fact] was no detriment to her reputation. (Quoted in Renard 1998, 288)

The institutional forms and sets of ritual practices transmitted across some networks of Sufi students and teachers eventually took on the form of organized orders—also referred to in Arabic as *tariqa*s and often named after the purported founding *shaykh*. From the twelfth century on, various *tariqa*s created communities of Muslims centered on forms of association and ritual practice that institutionalized the teachings of particular *shaykh*s. The number of organized Sufi orders grew steadily, and many spread far from their local points of origin to establish branches throughout the Muslim world from North Africa to Southeast Asia.

In addition to the organized orders, there were also less-institutionalized Sufi schools of thought covering ritual practices and devotional exercises, and there were complex intellectual formulations by figures such as the thirteenth-century scholar of Muslim Spain, Ibn Arabi. Ibn Arabi is one of the most controversial figures in Islamic history, and debates over his legacy often extend beyond the polemics of Sufism to incorporate aspects of theology and philosophy. Many of Ibn Arabi's later Muslim detractors attacked him for espousing a model of the relationship between God and humankind that they saw as dangerous, potentially leading to the improper effacement of the distinction between creation and its Creator. Despite such criticisms, the thought of Ibn Arabi was never universally condemned by all Muslims. Even in the modern period, there was a renaissance of interest in his work among scholars such as those associated with the Akbariyya of late nineteenth-century Damascus. Abd al-Qadir al-Jaza'iri, a major figure in those circles, found in Ibn Arabi's thought tools for dealing in dynamic ways with the challenges of rationalism and modernity posed by the growing cultural and political hegemony of the West (Weismann 2001, 141–224).

Islamic Philosophy

The origins of Islamic philosophy can be traced to the vibrant and cosmopolitan intellectual atmosphere of the early Abbassid Caliphate at Baghdad (750–991), when the Arabic translation movement was introducing texts from classical Greek, Christian, and other "foreign" literatures into the conversations of educated Muslims. This material was selectively interpreted and represented in ways that seemed to address the concerns and interests of various groups of Muslims at that time. In the ninth century, Muslim "free thinkers," such as Ibn al-Rawandi and Abu Bakr al-Razi, dove into the pre-Christian phi-

Muslim mystics in the modern world; at a Sufi shrine outside Cape Town, South Africa.
(R. Michael Feener)

losophy of the ancient Greeks, sometimes placing themselves in open conflict
with the central conceptions of the religious authority in Islam (Stroumsa
1999). Others, such as the eleventh-century philosopher Ibn Sina (d. 1037;
known in the West by the Latinate name Avicenna), worked to integrate certain aspects of Greek philosophical method into complex systems of Islamic

religious thought. With the work of the Islamic philosophers, new issues came to the fore in debates over the relative authority of human reason and divine revelation in human knowledge. These discussions continued to develop over the centuries under the leadership of Muslim thinkers such as Ibn Rushd (d. 1198; known in the West as Averroës).

Many Western histories have appreciated the medieval Muslim philosophers for their role in developing and transmitting to late-medieval and Renaissance Europe the thought of Aristotle and other Greek philosophers, whose intellectual heritage had largely been lost to Europe during the dark days of the Middle Ages. However, the medieval Muslim philosophers are also important in their own right for their role in the history of Islam. Without their valuable contributions to knowledge, the famed accomplishments of medieval Muslims in science, medicine, ethics, and political thought would not have been possible. Since the 1980s, the Moroccan Muslim philosopher Mohammed Abed al-Jabri has called for a radical reappraisal of this rich tradition—not as a historical legacy to be transmitted as an inert artifact but, rather, as a spirit of rationality and realism that he identifies with the work of Ibn Rushd. Al-Jabri sees such a reappraisal as the best way to reanimate Islamic intellectualism in order to meet the new challenges and opportunities of life in the contemporary world (Al-Jabri 1999).

Islamic Theology

In the intellectual history of Islam, not all Muslims have been prepared to go as far in the application of human reason to religious issues as the philosophers. However, over the centuries, some Muslim thinkers became increasingly prepared to accept certain aspects of the methodology of the philosophers in their studies of religious subjects, provided there was an understanding that reason would, in this vein, remain subservient to revelation. These developments contributed to the further evolution of Islamic theology, which had begun in the eighth century with Muslim attempts to address issues of Qur'anic interpretation in debates over the relationship between the Creator (that is, God) and the created world. In the medieval period, Muslim theologians began to address not only other Muslims but also different groups of Christian thinkers. By this time, Christian theologians had an extensively developed theological enterprise, which was marshaled to advance sectarian arguments against both "pagan" philosophers and Christians belonging to other, rival churches. Muslims, in the process of developing their arguments—both internal and external—evolved their own schools of theological thought. The field of these debates of Islamic theology is referred to in Arabic as *kalam*.

Since the earliest developments of *kalam*, theological debates were often intertwined with important political power plays. The most often discussed instance of such entanglement is the *mihna,* perhaps the closest parallel to the Christian Inquisition that one can find in medieval Islam. The *mihna* began in the early ninth century when the caliph reigning at Baghdad attempted to impose one interpretation of Islamic theology—that of the rationalist school known as the Mu'tazila—as the official doctrine of his Islamic empire. In attempting to assert his authority to determine religious orthodoxy, he ordered that scholars who opposed him be stripped of their positions as teachers or judges, and he sometimes even had the recalcitrant imprisoned and tortured (Zaman 1997, 106–118). These policies were abandoned after about two decades, and the appeal of Mu'tazilite rationalism among Muslims was drastically diminished. Subsequently, other schools of *kalam* arose, most of them placing more reliance on revealed knowledge than on human reason in determining Islamic religious doctrine. Nevertheless, in the centuries following the *mihna, kalam* was rarely, if ever, the primary concern of most Muslim scholars, since for most of the medieval and early modern periods, theology was not as prominent in Islam as it was in Christianity.

The relative importance of *kalam* to other areas of Muslim thought and practice is evidenced in the work of many medieval Muslim theologians, such as that of the fourteenth-century Central Asian scholar Sa'd al-Din al-Taftazani, who spoke of *kalam* as "beneficial for this world insofar as it regulates the life [of humans] by preserving justice and proper conduct, both of which are essential for the survival of the species in ways that do not result in corruption" (quoted in Knysh 1999, 146).

Thus, like Judaism, Islam has generally tended to place greater emphasis on proper conduct regulated by religious law than on the abstract formulation of orthodox dogma as the central arena of religious and intellectual activity. Only in the twentieth century has Islamic theology once again come to the fore in public debates, both internally between different groups of Muslims and externally in the form of apologetics explicitly or implicitly arguing against the foil of modern Western thought.

Islamic Law

Alongside Sufism, Islamic philosophy, and *kalam,* another sphere of Islamic religious expression that has been central to the historical traditions of Muslim learning is law. Although the caliphates of the classical period claimed their authority to rule was based on succession from Muhammad, governance in their territories tended to be a continuation of practices long established by the absolutist empires of the pre-Islamic Middle East, especially Byzantium and Sasanid Persia. Feeling that such absolutist models of monarchy were contrary to the messages of humility and equality proclaimed by Muhammad, many Muslims sought rules to live by in the words of the Qur'anic revelation and the precedent of prophetic practice *(sunna)*. These sources were thus brought to bear on contemporary issues in a changing world, and the foundations of Muslim jurisprudence *(fiqh)* were constructed. Methodologies of legal reasoning were systematized both for interpreting the legal injunctions contained in scripture and for discovering ways of arriving at legal decisions in the many cases for which neither the Qur'an nor the *sunna* provides a clear ruling.

By the end of the ninth century, Islamic law was the queen of the sciences in the Muslim curriculum. By that time, a number of prominent teachers of Muslim jurisprudence had come to be viewed as especially authoritative, and their teachings formed the bases for diverse schools of Islamic legal thought. Each school *(madhhab)* conceived of itself as possessing a particularly effective mode of interpreting the primary sources of Islam—the Qur'an and *hadith*—in order to determine proper human understanding of God's law. After the tenth century, four of these schools eclipsed the others, and these four have since coexisted as equally authoritative approaches to jurisprudence in Sunni Islam. Teachers of Islamic law belonging to one of these four schools—the Hanafi, Shafi'i, Maliki, and Hanbali—make up the *ulama*, the scholars of Islam who are central to the transmission and development of Islamic learning.

For most of Islamic history, these scholarly processes of determining the law were the special preserve of the *ulama* as traditionally trained religious scholars. In the modern period, however, the *ulama*'s monopoly on such discussions has been broken. In the process, many new groups and individuals have taken it upon themselves to write on Islamic legal issues and even to issue their own legal opinions *(fatwa)*, whether or not they have the specialized religious training and traditional authority to do so. Contemporary examples of such challenges to the *ulama*'s authority run the gamut from the support for a progressive agenda for women's rights produced by the Malaysian group Sisters in Islam to Osama bin Laden's militant proclamations of global *jihad*.

In the early centuries of Islamic history, the law developed by the *ulama* for regulating individual and social practice grew in popularity, and Muslim states granted a degree of respect and recognition to the system. However, the law of Islam—the *shari'a*—was rarely the sole legal standard in Islamic lands, and it was applied at best selectively by most of the major Muslim empires and smaller states. Most medieval Muslim rulers, even if they had the will to do so, were unable to establish themselves as the sole authorities and arbiters of Islamic law (Gerber 1999, 43–54). This situation was exacerbated by the fact that the interpretation and application of Islamic law was increasingly being developed in institutions that were outside direct state control and whose jurisdictions sometimes complemented those of civil courts, addressing different issues, and sometimes, when both venues had significant claims on a case, conflicted with them. Consequently, for generations of independent Muslim religious scholars, Islamic law has been a powerful potential source of alternative authority and opposition to ruling regimes. In the early modern period, however, some Muslim states (such as the Ottoman Empire) began to bring together the administration of the *shari'a* and the offices of the state in new ways, forging paths that have been further pursued in a number of Muslim societies to this day.

Religious Scholars and Institutions of Learning

The histories of the *ulama* have been dynamic and complex across many Muslim societies throughout the medieval and modern periods. Some Muslim governments attempted to make the *ulama* subservient to state interests. In other Muslim states, the *ulama* policed their own ranks, reacting to perceived internal and external threats to Islam. Yet the space for independent thought and action by the *ulama* never completely disappeared. This fact was remarked upon, for example, by the eighteenth-century *hadith* scholar Shah Wali Allah al-Dihlawi, who had studied in both India and Mecca. In a critique of what he saw as the growing narrow-mindedness of some of his fellow *ulama,* al-Dihlawi described the typical scholar of his day as "a prattler and wind-bag who indiscriminately memorized the opinions of the jurists whether these were strong or weak and related them in a loud-mouthed harangue." However, he was also quick to add, "I don't say that this is so in all cases, for God has a group of His worshippers unharmed by their failure, who are God's proof on earth even if they have become few" (quoted in Hermansen 1996, 455).

A generation later, in Yemen, at least one of those "few" surviving, independent-minded scholars whom al-Dihlawi might have thought worthy was able not only to survive but to flourish. When Muhammad ibn Ali al-Shawkani was asked to accept the position of overseer of judges for the Qasimi state, he agreed to do so only when assured by the ruler that his judgments would be executed "whatever they may be and whomever [they concern], even if the imam himself was implicated" (quoted in Haykel 2003, 69). The continuing political and social importance of the *ulama* in many parts of the contemporary Muslim world has been persuasively argued in the recent work of Muhammad Qasim Zaman, who has noted that, for example, the number of students enrolled in *madrasa*s in the Punjab region of India has increased by more than a factor of ten over the past four decades (Zaman 2002, 2). This, he contends, speaks for the increasing relevance of the *ulama* as spokesmen for Islamic traditions in a world where notions of cultural authenticity have become global concerns.

Since the eleventh century, *ulama* teaching law according to one of the es-

Public well in the Wadi Hadhramawt, Yemen. In many parts of the Muslim world, waqf *have traditionally funded such public wells and water fountains. (R. Michael Feener)*

tablished schools had come to occupy the highest positions in a new kind of educational institution that was to spread from Baghdad throughout the Muslim world—the *madrasa*. The earliest *madrasa*s were established for the teaching of Islamic law according to one of the established Sunni schools (Makdisi 1961). By the fourteenth century, under the rule of the Mamluk dynasty in Syria and Egypt, many of the most prominent *madrasa*s were being built in a cruciform style in order to house teachers from all four of the schools simultaneously, one in each of the four wings of the building. The accommodation of all four schools within a single institution is a remarkable testament to the openness to religious opinions and the complex dynamics of Muslim unity and diversity in the premodern period.

Madrasa institutions stood largely outside direct state control, for they were privately founded and funded through *waqf,* a special type of religious endowment through which a person could set aside a portion of his wealth to fund mosques, schools, hospitals, or other institutions of social welfare. Once a Muslim had formally established a *waqf,* he or she could not impose any further conditions on the use of the funds, a stipulation that ensured a considerable amount of freedom—academic and otherwise—to the teachers attached to the *madrasa*s. *Waqf* were also important in providing one of the major avenues for women's participation in public religious and political life in some Muslim

A modern permutation of the public fountain waqf, *street-side charity in Istanbul, Turkey.*
(R. Michael Feener)

societies. Indeed, a number of the major Muslim architectural monuments in Middle Eastern cities were built to house institutions founded on *waqf* bequests by wealthy women during the period of the Ottoman and Safavid Empires (Ruggles 2000). Such arrangements had the double benefit of providing the wealthy with a way to secure their property in perpetuity while at the same time providing important income and resources to the ranks of religious scholars who constructed the regulations of this system and thus avoided subservience to the state.

However, the freedom idealized in the classical formulations of *waqf* regulations proved not to be completely unassailable, and later Muslim authorities took various means to exert control over religious scholarship, which they saw as an important sphere of potential opposition. For example, in the seventeenth century, the Ottoman Empire promulgated new "official" legal codes aimed at standardizing Islamic law in their territories (Voll 1982, 19). In the early nineteenth century, the modernizing programs of Muhammad Ali in Egypt brought more centralized administration and even the outright dissolution of Muslim institutions that had previously found their sources of funding and social autonomy in privately endowed *waqf*. The financial support of *ulama* associated with Egyptian *madrasas* was progressively eroded, first by the taxation of *waqf* in 1809 and then by the state confiscation of *waqf* properties in 1814 (Marsot 1984, 66, 143). Similar programs were often also taken up by European powers in the Muslim societies that came under their colonial control in the late nineteenth century, as well as by the independent postcolonial governments of many Muslim countries. Khaled Abou El Fadl has cited these trends toward centralized control of *waqf* as contributing to the disruption of civil discourses of disagreement among traditionally trained Muslim scholars and to the subsequent rise in popularity of more narrowly imagined religious authoritarianisms (Abou El Fadl 2003, 46).

In the medieval and early modern periods, the establishment of the *madrasas* and the system of *waqf* that supported them had provided mechanisms for social mobility and cultural continuity during times when the great Muslim empires of the Middle East and South Asia appeared to be crumbling. Following the devastating disruptions of the thirteenth-century Mongol invasions of the Middle East and the consequent shattering of large-scale state institutions in the region, the *ulama* associated with the *madrasas* provided a means not only to preserve the traditions of Islam but also to spread them into areas beyond the limits of earlier Muslim movements into Europe, Africa, and Asia. As *madrasa* institutions proliferated throughout the expanding Muslim world, they fostered the formation of networks of *ulama* who read and commented on the same texts and shared a cosmopolitan cultural tradition that paralleled that of the royal courts.

Movements for Renewal and Reform

These later expansions of Islam did not follow on the heels of military conquest. Rather, Islam spread through generally peaceful penetration of ever-widening frontiers along global and regional trade routes. Throughout the medieval period, many of the most important sea lanes and overland caravan routes in Asia and Africa were dominated by Muslim merchants. After the thirteenth century, Arab and Persian Muslims from the Central Lands of Islam increasingly traveled to seek their fortunes, and they even established families in newly Muslim lands far from the tradition's historical centers in the Middle East. At that time, the leading edges of this expansion were rapidly moving southward along both the east and west coasts of Africa, northeastward into Central Asia, and southeastward through India and into the Indonesian archipelago. Among the growing number of Muslim travelers in this period were merchants and scholars, some of whom were often also members of Sufi orders. However, the spread of Islam along these avenues was in no way an organized movement like modern Christian missionary enterprises. Rather, the spread of Islam into Asia and Africa most often occurred through gradual and informal processes, such as the formation of business partnerships and political affiliations, as well as through intermarriage. Thus, increasingly closer ties were forged between local populations of the frontiers and the Muslims who had come there during the expansion of Islam in the late medieval period.

It was only later, if at all, that organized Islamic religious associations played a significant role in the further Islamization of some areas already at least nominally converted, both within the Middle East and farther afield. In the eighteenth century, a new stream of developments in the history of Sufi orders, a phenomenon that some modern scholars have referred to as neo-Sufism, contributed to these developments. A number of Sufi orders were transformed through organizational restructuring and through an increasingly activist orientation. Much of this energy was directed toward reestablishing Sufism as the "way of Muhammad" *(tariqa Muhammadiyyah)*.

This reformation of Islamic mystical tradition involved various means of deepening one's personal relationship to the Prophet of Islam in order to arrive at a more certain type of religious knowledge. Sometimes this knowledge came from visionary experiences or dreams in which Sufi masters were given special teachings by the Prophet Muhammad himself. The institutional frameworks of the new Sufi orders then helped spread these teachings across wide areas of the Muslim world, thus playing an important role in the development of Islamic reformism in the eighteenth century.

During that period of Islamic history, movements for religious reform were of many types, both Sufi and non-Sufi. The one that is best remembered today is that of the Wahhabis, a movement of scripturalist reformism that came to political power in the Arabian peninsula. It originated with Muhammad ibn Abd al-Wahhab (d. 1792), who grew up at Nejd in the Arabian peninsula. His writings on reforming Islam drew considerably on the works of medieval Hanbali scholars such as Ibn Taymiyya; however, he claimed to be an independent reformer who derived his arguments directly from the Qur'an and *hadith*. He called for a radical reform of society to free Islam from what he viewed as the accretion of "ignorant" and "pagan" traditions, including the traditional Muslim jurisprudence of the four established schools of law, as well as such local customs as the veneration of shrines dedicated to Sufi "masters" *(awliya Allah)*.

These agendas were significantly advanced in Arabia after the Wahhabi movement for religious reform came together with the political and military energies of the local Sa'ud clan. For much of the second half of the eighteenth century, campaigns both of words and of blunter weapons were waged by the Wahhabi-Saudi forces until the establishment of the first Saudi state and the Saudi and Wahhabi conquest of Mecca in 1806. Through their control of the cities of Mecca and Medina, the influence of Wahhabi doctrine spread beyond the Arabian peninsula to all parts of the Muslim world, following pilgrims on the *hajj* as well as itinerant Muslim scholars and students who came from all over Asia and Africa to study in Islam's holiest city. The Wahhabis were known, then as now, for their sharp criticism of Muslim ideas and practices that they deemed to be un-Islamic. This criticism often extended to many teachings and practices associated with Sufism as well as to the institutions and ideas that had dynamically managed the differing Muslim scholarly opinions that had animated religious developments in earlier centuries of Islamic history.

However, Wahhabism was not unopposed. In this period, one of the most important early critics of Wahhabism was a North African scholar named Ahmad ibn Idris, who wrote a treatise defending the rich traditions of Muslim learning and religious experience established in Islamic history against the Wahhabi reformism that sought to discard these legacies:

> As for you [the Wahhabis]—God bless you—you are familiar with texts entitled *The Rudiments* and *Basic Principles,* and you imagine that knowledge of the Book (i.e., Qur'an) and the Sunna (as related through *hadith*) consists of what is contained in such summaries. This is compound ignorance! . . . If you were cognizant of the accommodating religious learning which others possess, the realities would be apparent to you and you would proceed along the clearest path. But you have imposed restrictions on yourselves and the roads have become narrow for you. You have reduced Islam to what you are aware of and you claim that you are the saved ones, whereas all others shall perish. This amounts to narrowmindedness and the hardening of accommodation. But God guides us and guides you! (Quoted in Radtke et al. 2000, 197–198)

These remarks reveal sharply the major points of debate over Islamic reform in the modern period. They show the lines between those who would bring new life to Islam in the lives of contemporary Muslims through attempts at both broadening and deepening Muslim appreciation and understanding of the richness of their tradition, and those who would pursue the same goal through programs of policing newly imposed borders around one particular brand of Islam both on library shelves and in the lives of individual believers.

In many parts of the world today, a form of latter-day Wahhabism is a significant force in public debates over the interpretation of Islam. One hallmark of such an orientation is a tendency to view "Islam" as one monolithic entity with a "pure" essence that must be preserved and protected from the "pollution" of cultural and historical change. However, even in the face of the spread of such fundamentalist visions of Islam, other Muslims argue for more subtle and adaptable approaches to defining their religion. For example, the contemporary Iranian intellectual Abdol Karim Soroush argues:

> There is no such thing as a "pure" Islam, or an a-historical Islam that is outside the process of historical development. The actual lived experience of Islam has always been culturally and historically specific, and bound by the immediate circumstances of its location in time and space. If we were to take a snapshot of Islam as it is lived today, it would reveal a diversity of lived experiences which are all different, yet existing simultaneously. (Quoted in Noor 2002, 15–16)

This volume presents a series of such snapshots of contemporary Islam in geographical and cultural contexts around the globe in order to present some sense of its richness and variety. The chapters that follow prompt us to move beyond simplified essentializations of Islam to ask the who, what, where, and when of Islamic expressions in working toward understandings of both historical and contemporary phenomena. An exposure to such a comparative perspective helps us see why abstracted or essentialized claims that Islam (or Christianity or Buddhism for that matter) "says this" or "does that" should be viewed critically, especially when they are uttered in politically charged public discourses.

Political and Social Change in the Modern Period

One of the leading scholars of modern Islamic history, John Voll, has written of three major themes visible in the eighteenth century: political decentralization, a reorientation of Sufi traditions, and religious revivalist movements (Voll 1982, 34–38). The first of these can be seen in the development of the Ottoman, Mughal, and Safavid Empires that came to power in the Middle East and southern Asia after the collapse and fragmentation of the Abbasid Caliphate. In the eighteenth century, these large, agrarian states witnessed a decentralization of political control and reconfigurations of their basic economic structures. This economic disruption was to some degree the result of European influence on commerce in the Middle East and southern Asia, which had begun to make itself felt even before European imperialism and colonial expansion in those regions were fully developed politically and militarily. These changes tended to decrease the central power of the empires, which in turn fostered the growing autonomy of local and regional rulers.

At the same time as the political and economic spheres were evolving, significant changes were occurring in Muslim religious life. A number of Sufi orders and other religious revivalist movements took on new doctrinal positions that favored modes of purification of Islamic doctrine over adaptation to local cultural practices. As has been mentioned already in connection with the Wahhabi and neo-Sufi movements, much of the Islamic reformism during this period was aimed at pursuing the social and moral reconstruction of Muslim societies through a renewed emphasis on and stricter adherence to the teachings of Islam in the Qur'an and *sunna*. At times, these new visions of a reformist Islamic moral order clashed with the policies of the major Muslim empires of the period, which revealed aspects of the historical split between Muslim officials in the service of various states, on the one hand, and the independent religious scholars, on the other. Challenges to the authority of the state increasingly met with new government measures designed to extend bureaucratic control over the *ulama* and their associated institutions, a strategy that later European colonial regimes and the independent governments of the postcolonial period also followed.

As the nineteenth century progressed, these developments constituted a broad trend across the Muslim world, a trend that found manifestations in a wide range of cultural and political settings and included armed Muslim resistance to the French in North Africa, the British in India, the Russians in Chechnya, and the Dutch in Indonesia. Over time, more and more Muslims began to feel that their interests—political and economic as well as religious—were being imperiled by the spread of European colonialism in their societies. The religious impetus for revival and reform that had earlier been directed toward internal critiques of corruptions of Islam was redirected and reenergized in opposition to the external threat of European imperialism. Moreover, during the nineteenth century, the improvements in transportation and communication brought to these regions by Western colonial powers contributed even further to the spread of reformist Islam in modernizing Asian and African societies.

Islamic Modernism

One of the first major figures in the development of Islamic modernism was Sayyid Jamal al-Din "al-Afghani" (d. 1897), whose career as a Muslim reformist and anticolonial activist in many ways set a new paradigm for Muslim leadership. Jamal al-Din's origins remain to a considerable degree obscure, and it appears that he deliberately kept them thus. By mid-life, however, he had emerged as a highly visible and globally mobile individual working for the advancement of Islamic political agendas in places like London and Paris as well as Cairo and Istanbul. During Jamal al-Din's lifetime, rapid progress in travel and communications technologies were increasingly allowing Muslims to receive and locally reinterpret ideas originating elsewhere. These exchanges of ideas and innovations fostered the creation of a wide variety of new conceptions of what it means to be Muslim in the modern world.

Primary among Jamal al-Din's causes were the unification of Muslims worldwide in a pan-Islamic movement of resistance against European imperialism, and demonstration of the compatibility of Islam with modern science (Keddie 1983). Jamal al-Din's agenda of promoting rationalism in modern Islamic thought was more elaborately developed in the works of the Egyptian reformer Muhammad Abduh (d. 1905). Abduh called for a radical reappraisal of Islam's religious and intellectual heritages, and he became a proponent of a new wave of religious thought that championed a return to the foundational sources of the Qur'an and *sunna,* combined with a renewed emphasis on the place of human reason in their interpretation. As Abduh expressed it in a fragmentary autobiography, he saw his mission as one aimed at understanding

> religion as it was understood by the elders of the community before dissension appeared; to return, in the acquisition of religious knowledge, to its first sources, and to weigh them in the scales of human reason, which God has created in order to prevent excesses or adulteration in religion, so that God's wisdom may be fulfilled and the order of the human world preserved; and to prove that, seen in this light, religion must be accounted a friend to science (Quoted in Hourani 1993, 140–141).

His ideas became known throughout the Muslim world through the publication of influential periodicals under his editorship: *Urwa al-Wuthqa* (which he published with Jamal al-Din in exile at Paris in 1884) and later *al-Manar,* on which he collaborated with his younger Syrian colleague, Rashid Rida (d. 1935).

Rida's reformism, however, was somewhat more conservative than that of Abduh and is often associated with the Salafi movement. During the late nineteenth century in Rida's native Syria, an active group of Salafi *ulama* attracted to the radical reformist thought of the fourteenth-century Hanbali scholar Ibn Taymiyya were already developing aspects of his medieval reformist ideas in new, more modern directions (Commins 1990). Rida's own place in the further development of modern Salafism signaled a new turn in which Islamic modernism became more open to influences from a revived twentieth-century Wahhabism (Voll 1982, 130, 159). Rida added to Abduh's modernist project a Salafi understanding of "returning to the Qur'an and *sunna*" that has since become influential in the development of the Egyptian Muslim Brotherhood and other Islamist movements all across the Muslim world in the twentieth century. In the lands of the former Ottoman Empire and beyond, Salafis set themselves up as strident critics of what they viewed as the weakening of Islam in the face of incursions from the modern West, which they perceived in the persons of "secularizing" Muslims as well as in the institutions of European colonial governments in the lands of Islam. Further discussions of these developments and their implications for Islam in the contemporary Middle East can be found in Chapter 2 in this volume, Gregory Starrett's "Islam after Empire: Turkey and the Arab Middle East."

Islam in a Postcolonial World

In the twentieth century, Muslims attempted to find new ways to modernize in order to live in a rapidly changing world. During the century's first decades, some Muslims favored more secularizing and "Westernizing" visions of modernization, believing such means to be the only way to become strong enough to achieve true independence from the West. The most radical example was the establishment of the modern nation of Turkey in 1924, when Kemal Atatürk assumed control over the core of the swiftly unraveling Ottoman Empire and introduced a new, modern model of militarized politics to further his programs for the forced secularization of Turkish society. His measures designed to obliterate the public symbols of Islam prominent under the Ottomans—such as banning the wearing of head scarves for women and ordering men to abandon the fez in favor of Western-style brimmed hats—led to an artificial dichotomy between Islam and secularism that continues in the country to this day and that is increasingly reflected in other societies as well.

Other Middle Eastern nations born in the twentieth century, such as the second Saudi state, which came to power in 1926, asserted themselves as autonomous Islamic realms defined by the stringent application of a revived Wahhabi style of Islam. With the discovery of oil and its sharp rise in importance for the world economy in the later twentieth century, the Saudis found themselves with the financial means not only to impose a Wahhabi-style Islam at home but also to export it abroad. Saudi influence has fostered the globalization of one particular vision of religion and its place in modern societies, a vision that some have come to refer to as "petro-Islam." Thus, even in countries where the implementations of such formalist interpretations of Islam are not supported by the state, groups advancing Wahhabi-inspired agendas continue to attract people who support a firmer establishment of Islam in their communities. In some cases, the forces mobilized by such movements can be as strong or stronger than state-supported Islamization in the transformation of modern Muslim societies. This has especially been the case in some of the new majority-Muslim nation-states that have emerged in former European colonies. For in such contexts, more formalist conceptions of Islam sometimes came to be seen as more culturally authentic responses to the perceived hegemony of Western ideas and institutions.

The era of formal European imperialism largely came to an end after World War II, when global instability so disrupted the institutions of colonial power that most Western powers were unable to reassert control of their Asian and African territories at war's end. In the decade following the end of the fighting, many former colonies asserted themselves as sovereign countries according to a Western model of modern nation-states. However, despite these formal revolutions bringing local Muslims to power in various countries, the European colonial legacy in the new states had a deep impact on many Muslim societies, an impact that continues to be felt, even though half a century or more has passed since much of the Muslim world was under the direct political control of Western powers.

Nevertheless, after World War II, a number of the new postcolonial states sought to maintain at least some nominal recognition of Islam, even when imported Western ideologies were the official bases for their constitutional models and state systems. Such, for example, was the case in the later years of Soekarno's warming to socialist and communist politics under the banner of *Pancasila,* the Indonesian state ideology whose first principle was "belief in one God." Although in the early part of the twentieth century a number of Islamist movements were established in the Indonesian archipelago, over the later part of the twentieth century, programs for the further Islamization of Indonesian society underwent a major shift to more explicitly depoliticized cultural strategies of both liberal and scripturalist bents. Together, these two tendencies, referred to in general terms as *pembaharuan* and *da'wa,* respectively, provided the dynamics for a broad-based resurgence of Islam in contemporary Indonesian society. Since Suharto's thirty-three-year rule of Indonesia ended in 1998, some Muslims associated with both of these movements have turned toward a renewed emphasis on politics as a means for advancing the further Islamization of society. Some of the implications of these developments are further discussed in this volume in Chapter 7, "Muslim Thought and Practice in Contemporary Indonesia," by Anna Gade and R. Michael Feener.

Countries like Indonesia had culturally based programs of Islamization; other twentieth-century majority-Muslim countries attempted to elaborate their visions of Islam in more explicitly political terms. One example is Pakistan, which separated itself from newly independent India in 1947. There, the idea of a separate Muslim state in southern Asia gained support by appealing to sentiments stirred by modern Muslim writers of the subcontinent, both poet/philosophers like Muhammad Iqbal (1877–1938) and Islamist ideologues like Mawlana Mawdudi (1903–1979). Mawdudi held an activist vision of Islam that demanded the formal implementation of the *shari'a* in order to be truly fulfilled. Thus, he argued, in order for Islam to live up to its true ideals, it needed to be made the foundational law of society through the establishment of an Islamic state, albeit one constructed around modern rather than medieval Muslim institutions (Nasr 1996, 80–106). Mawdudi's ideas have been an important—but by no means the only—influence on understandings of the role of Islam in contemporary Pakistani society. The development of alternative visions of Islam there are discussed in Chapter 4, Robert Rozehnal's "Debating Orthodoxy, Contesting Tradition: Islam in Contemporary South Asia."

Alongside Mawdudi, perhaps the most influential thinker of twentieth-century Sunni Islamist revivalism was Sayyid Qutb (d. 1966) of the Egyptian Muslim Brotherhood. After an early career as a journalist and literary critic, Qutb became the most prominent voice of the Brotherhood in the 1950s. He wrote extensively, producing short treatises as well as a full-length commentary on the Qur'an, and his works remain popular among many Muslims around the world. One of the major themes of his writings is the idea that Islam is a complete way of life: a totalizing system that should ideally govern all actions of individuals in society. Although such a vision of Islam appeals to many Muslims today, others, such as the Muslim scholar and former Indonesian president Abdurrahman Wahid, reject it, advocating models of Islam more integrated into contemporary society.

Given the wide variety of religious ideas, governmental forms, and social theories that have flourished in Muslim societies during the twentieth and early twenty-first centuries, we are faced with complex questions of just what "Islam" means to different groups and individuals around the world. To address such questions, the essays collected in this volume approach their subjects from an array of perspectives and disciplines, including history, anthropology, and the academic study of religion. In doing so, they present readers with a variety of styles of discussion, ranging from the histories of religious teachings and ethnographic descriptions of local communities to considerations of geopolitics and international economics. The varied nature of these studies, both in terms of subject matter and angle of approach, is emphasized in this volume in order to communicate something of the range of issues involved in attempting to understand the complexities of Islam in contemporary societies.

The chapters that follow are intended as a series of explorations that highlight the diversity of responses to modernity in different Muslim communities. For some, as we shall see in Chapter 3, David Buchman's "Shi'ite Islam in Contemporary Iran: From Islamic Revolution to Moderating Reform," conceptions of the nation-state were at the heart of debates over Islam and its role in contemporary society. In other settings, modernity and Islam met in cultural contexts where race had become a primary locus for debates, as discussed in the chapters by Abdulkader I. Tayob (Chapter 9, "Race, Ideology, and Islam in Contemporary South Africa") and Edward E. Curtis (Chapter 10, "Peril and Possibility: Muslim Life in the United States"). Elsewhere, issues of Islam in relation to identity formation shaped up along different fault lines, such as that of ethnicity, as can be seen in the contributions by Adeeb Khalid (Chapter 5, "Islam in Contemporary Central Asia") and Dru C. Gladney (Chapter 6, "Islam in China: Accommodation or Separatism?"). Tim Carmichael, in Chapter 8, "Religion, Language, and Nationalism: Harari Muslims in Christian Ethiopia," examines issues of language and history among the Muslim Harari minority of Ethiopia through the lenses of national language policies and popular publications circulating within that community. All of these various phenomena have factored into the ways Muslims experience the world, and they therefore are important elements to be considered in examining the place of Islam in world cultures.

Islam in Contemporary Societies

Although they deal with a wide range of cultural and geographical regions, the chapters in this text share a common concern with examining the ways new conceptions and understandings of Islam have developed in relation to modernization. In many Muslim societies, these developments might be viewed in terms of Islamization. For the purposes of this book, "Islamization" refers not just—or even primarily—to the conversion of non-Muslims. Rather, it refers to the myriad ways Muslims throughout history have attempted to adapt to an ever-changing world by envisioning and implementing ever-new ways to make themselves "better Muslims." This perspective on Islamic civilization follows a model of Muslim history that Marshall Hodgson referred to as "the venture of Islam": a continuous unfolding and exploration of Muslim understandings of their religion across vast stretches of time and space (Hodgson 1974). Seen in this way, the recent history of, and contemporary developments in, Muslim societies can be examined as phenomena in which processes of Islamization and modernization do not necessarily function as competing visions for the future but, rather, are interrelated in complex ways.

However, in many instances, the interdependence of modernization and Islamization in contemporary societies is obscured. This problem has been exacerbated both by the rhetoric of Western ideas of a "clash of civilizations" (Huntington 1996; cf. Qureshi and Sells 2003) and by that of Islamist ideologues who posit Islam as the antithesis, in every way, to the "barbaric igno-rance" *(jahiliyya)* of non-Islam. Most readers of this book will probably be fa-miliar with the former through their exposition in the U.S. media, and there is little need to extensively elaborate them here. However, something does need to be said of the latter in relation to the Islamic resurgence that has manifested itself in societies around the world since the 1970s. In such developments, one can see something of the complexity of relations between political and cul-tural aspects of Islamization in contemporary societies and the difficulty of completely separating them.

For example, the modern history of Libya illustrates one of the ways Islam came to be understood as a culturally authentic source of authority. As Dirk Vandewalle notes, Mu'ammar Qadhafi's early policies of radical cultural de-colonization—such as "[the] prohibition of alcohol, attempts to contain the influence of the West and its presence within the region, the closing of nightclubs, the conversion of churches into mosques, the adoption in princi-ple of Islamic punishment—preempted many of the issues that became the foci of Islamist movements elsewhere" (Vandewalle 1998, 132–133). Never-theless, Qadhafi himself increasingly grew wary of other Libyan political Is-lamists, whom he saw as threatening his own hold on power. For the Islamic revivalism that he promoted in Libya still takes for granted the basic unit of the nation-state—a concept of modern, Western, historical lineage. How-ever, since the late 1980s, such Islamic variants of religious nationalism have had to confront challenges from more radical movements of a new, global-ized Islamism, whose agendas do not correspond as neatly to the borders of nations.

The term "Islamism" was coined by scholars to refer to certain late modern developments and thus should not be confused with, or used as a synonym for, "Islam," Islam as a whole. The French scholar Olivier Roy defines Islamism as "the perception of Islam more as a political ideology than as a mere religion. . . . In this sense Islamism is a modern movement, the last wave of an anti-imperialist mobilization that dates back to the last century" (Roy 2001, 199). Islamism's more immediate origins, however, might be traced back to the late 1970s, when the experiences of many in the Muslim world reflected a sense summed up by Patrick Gaffney's description of this period in Egyptian history as "a time of growing unrest and uncertainty, with rising social, eco-nomic and political expectations on a collision course with limited opportuni-ties and resources" (Gaffney 1997, 263).

Such conditions led some Muslims to turn toward more "revolutionary" forms of Islamism in the Middle East and elsewhere. The most dramatically successful such movement was the Iranian Revolution of 1979. Following this watershed event, the 1980s witnessed the rapid spread of new Islamist move-ments. Often these movements were mobilized under the leadership of charis-

matic individuals, such as Muhammad Husayn Fadlallah of the Lebanese
Shi'ite group Hizbullah, a group that rose to prominence in the wake of the Israeli invasion of Lebanon in 1982 (Kramer 1997). A number of these movements turned increasingly to the use of violence and even terrorist attacks
upon civilians as the means to further their agendas. For many Americans before September 11, 2001, this type of militant Islam was most often associated
with the Palestinian *intifada*—the "uprising" against the Israeli occupation of
the West Bank and the Gaza Strip. Indeed, Islamic activists and ideologues like
the leader of Hamas, Shaykh Ahmad Yasin, have masterfully manipulated Muslim sentiments to make Palestine "the symbolic, if not the actual, center of
worldwide Islamist resistance" (Abu-Amr 1997, 242). Suicide bombers and the
terror they inspire have exploded on front pages and newscasts worldwide
since the 1980s with stories and gruesome images of militant Muslims killing
Jews and Christians. However, some Islamist movements directed their violence not only toward non-Muslims but also toward Muslims whose politics did
not agree with their own.

For example, in 1981 President Anwar Sadat of Egypt was assassinated by
members of the Islamic Jihad. During the shooting, one of the gunmen
shouted, "I have killed Pharaoh!" referring to the Qur'anic symbol of the great
antagonist of Moses (Kepel 1993, 192). During the Iran-Iraq War of
1980–1988, some Iranian Shi'ite clerics preached that the issue was a battle
against the "Great Enemy" of Islam in the person of Saddam Hussein. The government of the Islamic Republic of Iran also ordered an official boycott of the
hajj from 1987 to 1990 in protest against the policies of the Saudi state. The
year after the Iranian boycott ended, Saddam Hussein himself took a new turn
toward Islamic politics, picking up the baton of self-righteous indignation
against the Saudis to criticize their cooperation with the "infidel Americans"
during the first Gulf War in 1991 (Piscatori 1991).

One of the most visible trends in Islam in the late twentieth and early
twenty-first centuries has been its increased ideologization and politicization
in many parts of the world. However, there has never been any consensus on a
unified model of Islamic politics, and contestations over the place of Islam in
state institutions have thus continued to be played out in myriad different
ways in different places, dependent on local cultural contexts and on the
modern histories. In Sudan, for example, a military coup in 1989 brought to
power an Islamist government whose policies are directed by the Western-
educated Hassan Turabi (Esposito and Voll 2001, 134). On the other hand, in
1992, when Islamists had made significant gains in electoral politics in Algeria, the military staged a coup to prevent the Islamists from gaining power
there, igniting waves of horrendous violence that decimated the country for
nearly a decade (Willis 1996, 233ff.). In Malaysia, a nonviolent Muslim opposition movement led by the moderate Anwar Ibrahim was stifled when he was

arrested on trumped-up charges of corruption and sexual misconduct, effectively moving the political contestation out of the public and into the personal sphere.

For many today, however, the example of Muslim politics that most immediately comes to mind is that of the Taliban in Afghanistan. Although the images of bearded men and burqa-clad women lead some to see the Taliban as a harkening back to the Middle Ages, upon closer investigation, one finds very little about them that can be seen as "traditional." Indeed, many scholars of religion characterize "fundamentalism" as a distinctly modern development. Fundamentalism, a particular configuration of ideology and organizational resources, originated in Protestant Christianity and shares a number of characteristics across confessional divisions in the modern period (Almond, Appleby, and Sivan 2003, 14). One group of contemporary scholars has coined the term "strong religion" to refer to the shared characteristics of comparative fundamentalisms across different religious traditions ranging from Judaism to Hinduism. These include emphasis on conceptions of "purity," selective readings of their respective religious traditions, and a concern with bolstering the authority of the contemporary guardians of the faith (ibid., 17–21).

The immediate origins of the Taliban as an Islamic fundamentalist movement were in the depressingly modern setting of refugee camps on the Pakistani border, which were fertile recruiting grounds for radical Islamists. The Taliban's rise to power involves issues of both modern geopolitics and Muslim piety, for much of the Taliban's leadership was drawn from the ranks of the *mujahidin* (literally, "those who wage *jihad*") who were active in Afghanistan in the 1980s and early 1990s (Maley 2001, 15). The cause of the *mujahidin*, framed as a battle against the godless forces of an occupying Communist army, caught the attention and garnered the support of a number of parties, including wealthy adventurers like Saudi-born Osama bin Laden. The *mujahidin* were also actively supported and even armed by the U.S. government (Nojumi 2002, 197) and were hailed in the United States as "freedom fighters" struggling against the Soviet occupation of Afghanistan. By the turn of the twenty-first century, however, many of the same individuals engaged in those campaigns had been targeted by the U.S. government as the world's most-wanted terrorists (Weaver 2000, 228). The foreign policies of the United States and other Western powers have been important factors contributing to the evolution of shifting alliances, revolutionary movements, and repressive regimes in many majority-Muslim countries in recent decades (Esposito 1999, 271). The complex dynamics of such developments are thus, some would argue, as much if not more important than any study of Islamic scripture or medieval Muslim theology for understanding current events in the Muslim world today.

Since September 11, 2001, the U.S.-led "War on Terror" has already had widely diverse and extremely complex effects, particularly among Muslim communities. Among the dozen or so nations whose citizens have been marked by U.S. immigration authorities for closer scrutiny, all but one (North Korea) have a majority Muslim population. Furthermore, Muslim minorities have come under increased scrutiny and sometimes even violent attack by the national governments of states like China and Russia, which believe that the United States will now look the other way if they call their actions part of a crackdown on terrorism. Since 2001, U.S. troops have been deployed in Iraq, Afghanistan, and in Muslim regions of the southern Philippines, bringing far-flung areas of the Muslim world into the Western media spotlight to an unprecedented degree.

However, it is important that we not allow the constant media coverage of Islamic militant movements around the globe to be our only source of information in trying to understand Islam in contemporary societies. For beyond the headline-grabbing terrorists, there exists a great diversity of Muslim experiences. These include some remarkable developments among scholars and activists working toward more liberal or progressive visions of Islam to accommodate the rapidly changing needs of contemporary societies. In the course of your reading in this book, you will be briefly introduced to some of these scholars, ranging from Ebrahim Moosa of South Africa to the Indonesian Nurcholish Madjid. For those interested in exploring the works of such Muslims, there are considerable resources available in English. Many Muslim scholars and activists, both "liberal" and "conservative," now regularly write in English, which has come to serve as a language of international Muslim discourse in the era of globalization. In the suggestions for further reading in Chapter 11, you will find books originally in English by Farid Esack and Anwar Ibrahim as well as collections of shorter pieces, such as those in the volume recently published by Omid Safi (2003). Beyond these sources, more material translated into English from a wide variety of other languages can be found in Charles Kurzman's anthology *Liberal Islam* (1998).

Many people now want to learn more about Islam and about Muslim cultures. The chapters in this volume explore the religious, political, social, and cultural dynamics of contemporary Islam in a number of societies where Muslims form either a majority or a minority of the population. As you read through this book, you will be introduced to a range of histories and cultural phenomena, from the interaction of Islam and secular nationalist ideals in Uzbekistan to issues of race and gender in the United States. In taking this approach to detailed, contextual studies of Islam in different societies, this book is meant to be an aid in moving beyond the headlines and sound bites of current-events reportage and to serve as an introduction to the multiplicity of Muslim experiences in the modern world.

Notes

I would like to thank Merlin Swartz, Hal Nevis, Henk Maier, and Mayuko Feener for their helpful comments on earlier drafts of this essay and Angela Predisik for her help with the preparation and formatting of this manuscript.

1.   This selection was translated in collaboration with Anna Gade.

References

Abou El Fadl. 2003. "The Ugly Modern and the Modern Ugly: Reclaiming the Beautiful in Islam." In *Progressive Muslims on Justice, Gender, and Pluralism,* edited by Omid Safi, 33–77. Oxford: Oneworld.

Abu-Amr, Ziad. 1997. "Shaykh Ahmad Yasin and the Origins of Hamas." In *Spokesmen for the Despised: Fundamentalist Leaders of the Middle East,* edited by R. Scott Appleby, 225–256. Chicago: University of Chicago Press.

Almond, Gabriel A., R. Scott Appleby, and Emmanuel Sivan. 2003. *Strong Religion: The Rise of Fundamentalisms around the World.* Chicago: University of Chicago Press.

Commins, David Dean. 1990. *Islamic Reform: Politics and Social Change in Late Ottoman Syria.* New York: Oxford University Press.

Dawood, N. J., trans. 1999. *The Koran.* London: Penguin Books.

Esposito, John. 1999. *The Islamic Threat: Myth or Reality?* 3rd ed. New York: Oxford University Press.

Esposito, John, and John O. Voll. 2001. *Makers of Contemporary Islam.* New York: Oxford University Press.

Gaffney, Patrick D. 1997. "Islamic Fundamentalist Preaching and Islamic Militancy in Upper Egypt." In *Spokesmen for the Despised: Fundamentalist Leaders of the Middle East,* edited by R. Scott Appleby, 257–293. Chicago: University of Chicago Press.

Gerber, Haim. 1999. *Islamic Law and Culture, 1600–1840.* Leiden: Brill.

Haykel, Bernard. 2003. *Revival and Reform in Islam: The Legacy of Muhammad al-Shawkani.* New York: Cambridge University Press.

Hefner, Robert W., and Patricia Horvatich, eds. 1997. *Islam in an Era of Nation-States.* Honolulu: University of Hawai'i Press.

Hermansen, Marcia, trans. 1996. *The Conclusive Argument from God: Shah Wali Allah of Delhi's Hujjat Allah al-Baligha.* Leiden: Brill.

Hodgson, Marshall G. S. 1974. *The Venture of Islam: Conscience and History in a World Civilization.* Vol. 1, *The Classical Age of Islam.* Chicago: University of Chicago Press.

Hourani, Albert. 1993. *Arabic Thought in the Liberal Age, 1798–1939.* New York: Cambridge University Press.

Huntington, Samuel P. 1996. *The Clash of Civilizations and the Remaking of World Order.* New York: Simon and Schuster.

Ibn Ishaq. 1997. *The Life of Muhammad: A Translation of Ibn Ishaq's "Sitat Rasul Allah."* Translated by A. Guillaume. Karachi: Oxford University Press.

Iqbal, Allama M. 1968. *The Reconstruction of Religious Thought in Islam.* Lahore: Ashraf Press.

Al-Jabri, Mohammed A. 1999. *Arab-Islamic Philosophy*. Translated from the French by Aziz Abbassi. Austin: University of Texas Press.

Juynboll, G. H. A. 1969. *The Authenticity of the Tradition Literature: Discussions in Modern Egypt*. Leiden: Brill.

Karamustafa. 2003. "Islam: A Civilizational Project in Progress." In *Progressive Muslims on Justice, Gender, and Pluralism,* edited by Omid Safi, 98–110. Oxford: Oneworld.

Keddie, Nikki R. 1983. *An Islamic Response to Imperialism: Political and Religious Writings of Sayyid Jamal al-Din "al-Afghani."* Berkeley and Los Angeles: University of California Press.

Kepel, Gilles. 1993. *Muslim Extremism in Egypt: The Prophet and Pharaoh.* Translated by Jon Rothschild. Berkeley and Los Angeles: University of California Press.

Knysh, Alexander D. 1999. *Ibn 'Arabi in the Later Islamic Tradition: The Making of a Polemical Image in Medieval Islam.* Albany: State University of New York Press.

Kramer, Martin. 1997. "The Oracle of Hizbullah: Sayyid Muhammad Husayn Fadlallah." In *Spokesmen for the Despised,* edited by R. Scott Appleby, 83–181. Chicago: University of Chicago Press.

Kurzman, Charles, ed. 1998. *Liberal Islam: A Sourcebook.* New York: Oxford University Press.

Makdisi, George. 1961. "Muslim Institutions of Learning in Eleventh-Century Baghdad." *Bulletin of the School of Oriental and African Studies* 24: 1–56.

———. 1974. "Ibn Taimiya: A Sufi of the Qadiriya Order." *American Journal of Arabic Studies* 1: 118–129.

Malcolm X. 1964. *The Autobiography of Malcolm X.* New York: Grove Press.

Maley, William, ed. 1998. *Fundamentalism Reborn: Afghanistan and the Taliban.* New York: New York University Press.

Marsot, Afaf Lutfi al-Sayyid. 1984. *Egypt in the Reign of Muhammad Ali.* Cambridge: Cambridge University Press.

Mas'udi, Masdar F. 1993. *Agama Keadilan: Risalah Zakat (Pajak) dalam Islam.* Jakarta: P3M.

Nasr, Seyyed V. R. 1996. *Mawdudi and the Making of Islamic Revivalism.* New York: Oxford University Press.

Navis, A. A. 1996. *Surat dan Kenangan Haji.* Jakarta: Gramedia Pustaka Utama.

Nojumi, Neamatollah. 2002. *The Rise of the Taliban in Afghanistan: Mass Mobilization, Civil War, and the Future of the Region.* New York: Palgrave.

Noor, Farish. 2002. *New Voices of Islam.* http://www.isim.nl/files/paper_noor.pdf.

Piscatori, James. 1991. "Religion and Realpolitik: Islamic Responses to the Gulf War." In *Islamic Fundamentalisms and the Gulf Crisis,* edited by James Piscatori, 1–27. Chicago: American Academy of Arts and Sciences.

Pulungan, J. S. 1994. *Prinsip-Prinsip Pemerintahan dalam Piagam Madinah Ditinjau dari Pandangan Al-Quran.* Jakarta: Rajawali.

Qureshi, Emran, and Michael A. Sells, eds. 2003. *The New Crusades: Constructing the Muslim Enemy.* New York: Columbia University Press.

Radtke, Bernd, John O'Kane, Knut S. Vikor, and R. S. O'Fahey, trans. 2000. *The Exoteric Ahmad ibn Idris.* Leiden: Brill.

Renard, John, ed. 1998. *Windows on the House of Islam: Muslim Sources on Spirituality and Religious Life.* Berkeley and Los Angeles: University of California Press.

Roy, Olivier. 2001. "Has Islamism a Future in Afghanistan?" In *Fundamentalism Reborn: Afghanistan and the Taliban,* edited by William Maley, 199–211. New York: New York University Press.

Ruggles, D. Fairchild, ed. 2000. *Women, Patronage, and Self-Representation in Islamic Societies.* Albany: State University of New York Press.

Safi, Omid, ed. 2003. *Progressive Muslims on Justice, Gender, and Pluralism.* Oxford: Oneworld.

Stroumsa, Sarah. 1999. *Freethinkers of Medieval Islam.* Leiden: Brill.

Al-Tabari. 1990. *The History of al-Tabari.* Vol. 9, *The Last Years of the Prophet.* Translated by Ismail K. Poonawala. Albany: State University of New York.

Al-Udhari, Abdullah. 1999. *Classical Poems by Arab Women: A Bilingual Anthology.* London: Saqi Books.

Vandewalle, Dirk. 1998. *Libya since Independence.* Ithaca, NY: Cornell University Press.

Voll, John O. 1982. *Islam: Continuity and Change in the Modern World.* Boulder, CO: Westview Press.

———. 1987. "Linking Groups in the Networks of Eighteenth-Century Revivalist Scholars." In *Eighteenth-Century Renewal and Reform in Islam,* edited by N. Levtzion and J. O. Voll, 69–92. Syracuse, NY: Syracuse University Press.

Weaver, Mary Anne. 2000. *A Portrait of Egypt: A Journey through the World of Militant Islam.* New York: Farrar, Straus and Giroux.

Weismann, Itzchak. 2001. *Taste of Modernity: Sufism, Salafiyya, and Arabism in Late Ottoman Damascus.* Leiden: Brill.

Willis, Michael. 1996. *The Islamist Challenge in Algeria: A Political History.* New York: New York University Press.

Zaman, Muhammad Q. 1997. *Religion and Politics under the Early Abassids: The Emergence of the Proto-Sunni Elite.* Leiden: Brill.

———. 2002. *The Ulama in Contemporary Islam: Custodians of Change.* Princeton, NJ: Princeton University Press.

Chapter Two

Islam after Empire

Turkey and the Arab Middle East

Gregory Starrett

> *. . . over weeping sounds now*
> *We hear the beats of drums and rhythm.*
> *They are storming his forts*
> *And shouting: "We will not stop our raids*
> *Until you free our lands."*
>
> —Osama bin Laden, Ramadhan 1422/November 2001

"Why do they hate us?" This was one of the most frequent questions asked by journalists and ordinary citizens after the terrorist attacks in the United States of September 11, 2001. The political and cultural issues that surround the question have in various ways shaped the contexts in which the chapters in this book have been written, and these issues will still be relevant as you read them. However, the key terms in the question are not what they may at first seem to many of "us." In order to understand Islam in the contemporary Middle East, we need to focus not on the alleged sources of one emotion or another—and certainly not of hatred, in any case—but on the complex intersections between the terms "they" and "us." Even without considering the vexing problem of Israel, the intersections between the heartland of Islam and "the West" are extraordinarily complex. After a terrorist cell whose members were mostly Saudi and Egyptian brought about such a catastrophic loss of property and human lives in lower Manhattan, the United States attacked Afghanistan in reprisal. There, a Saudi millionaire who had supported the U.S. effort to expel the Soviet occupying forces of the 1980s was now supporting a brutal Pashtun regime and directing anti-American paramilitary actions around the world with the help of a largely Arabic-speaking militia. So, who are "they"? Saudi Arabia and

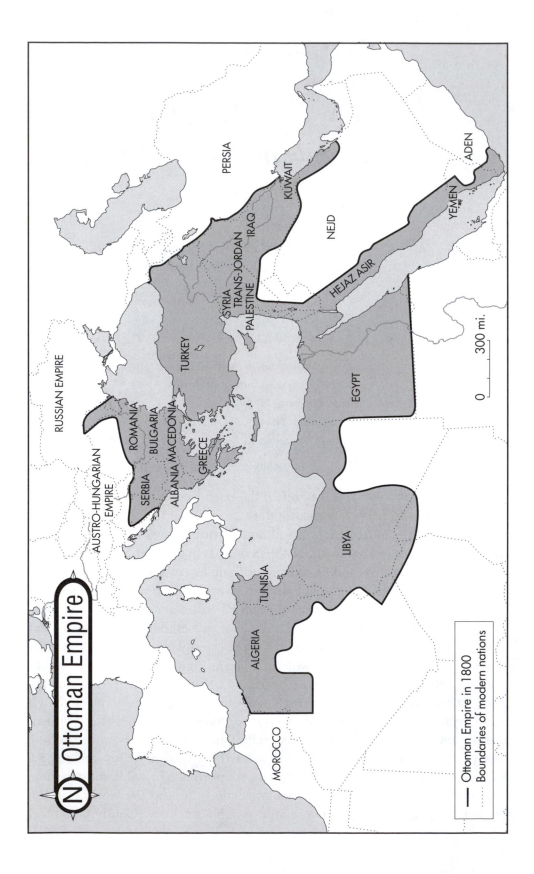

Egypt remain two of the closest U.S. allies in the region, despite the violent actions of their citizens and despite the fact that neither has the democratic credentials of Iran, against whom the United States supported Iraqi dictator Saddam Hussein after his invasion of that country in 1980. In the years that followed, the United States gave missiles and other military aid to the Afghan *mujahidin* (literally "those who engage in jihad"), encouraged the graduates of militant Pakistani Islamic religious schools, and sold weapons to Iran, which supported Shi'ite groups who were kidnapping Americans in Lebanon. What does this twisted history say about the "us" and about the values we think "we" hold dear? The brutal play of international power politics in the region is inseparable from the ways Middle Easterners understand and debate their historical, cultural, and religious heritage, and it is inseparable from their understanding of their place in the world. And for virtually the whole of the last two centuries, that play has held little benefit and more than enough pain and frustration for many people of the Middle East.

As you read this chapter, then, think not about a system of theology or a traditional lifestyle called "Islam," lying like an ancient carpet from the Atlas Mountains in the west to the Zagros Mountains in the east. Think instead about the historical events during which the experiences of Islam have been formed, so that the image becomes one of a thousand looms weaving threads old and new, tattered and whole, into a constantly changing pattern in which no panel of cloth entirely matches the ones around it. The world wars of the twentieth century; the anticolonial struggles of new nations; the sudden renaissance of art, architecture, and literature in the Middle East; and the base greed and conspicuous consumerism triggered by the late twentieth-century oil economy have all shaped the life, thought, and action of Muslims living in the region. Think about what "civilization" and "tradition," "duty" and "virtue" mean at the beginning of the twenty-first century, because these are the things Muslims in the Middle East and elsewhere have been thinking about, too. Islam, either as a religious tradition or as a personal experience, is about living concerns, about making sense of change and discomfort and fear as well as of joy and tradition, comfort and love.

Also as you read this chapter, think about the institutional and cultural atmosphere in which we apprehend Islam, the Middle East, and religion in general, because our own concerns and preoccupations shape our perception of the preoccupations of others. This does not mean we are always looking into a mirror; rather, it means we are looking through a window in which our own reflection colors what we see beyond it. Many of us tend to be much less forgiving of the imperfections of others than we are of our own, and one of the chief errors we as humans make in viewing other cultures is to compare "our" own high ideals with other people's very imperfect realities. Comparisons should, of course, harness identical types, comparing our realities with theirs, their ideals with ours.

God, the Qur'an says, is closer to you than your jugular vein (50:16). That immanent presence impels pious Muslims to think seriously about God's intentions for individuals and for humanity as a whole, about his expectations of thought and conduct, passions and plans. Since the late eighteenth century, and increasingly in the years leading up to the twenty-first century, Islam's place in people's daily lives has been in a state of accelerating change. As are our own lives, the lives of Muslims around the world are increasingly defined by global markets, instant communication, changing family forms, and the continued pressures of economic inequality, the growth and decay of empires, and the specters of genocide and cultural dissolution. Because of the facts of geography and history, all these things are felt more keenly today in the Middle East than they are in the United States. But crisis can bring creativity, as it often does in periods of global integration, whether Greek or Arab, Mongol or Ottoman. The crisis of what we call "modernity" has meant, for Muslims, thinking more and more about the rights and responsibilities of common people—and not just of the traditional elites of wealth or education or political power—in forging, nurturing, and protecting Islamic society. This is the element of Islam in the contemporary Middle East that will be emphasized in this chapter.

Both the Middle East and North Africa are historically urban societies. Although two out of every five people in the region still live in rural areas, urban civilization as a social structure—defined by cities as centers of power, literacy, manufacture, and trade—is older in this part of the world than anywhere else. The cultural traditions of countryside and city are separate but interconnected, as are the fragments of social class within cities. Separations of family and class, occupation and residence, educational attainment and gender, have always helped pattern the way Islamic ideas and practices were elaborated in the social world. But from the mid-nineteenth century to the beginning of the twenty-first, the Islamic traditions in the region have been undergoing a long, slow transformation as large-scale economic, political, and social changes have encompassed countries from Iraq to Morocco.

Modernization in the Ottoman Empire

Between the sixteenth and the early twentieth centuries, most of the region was part of the Ottoman Empire, one of the most expansive state structures the world had seen since the time of ancient Rome. By the turn of the nineteenth century, that vast empire had begun to fragment, weakened by war with Russia, nationalist and tribal movements in southeastern Europe and Arabia, the complicated internal problems of administering its own enormous territory, and the new economic and military threat of an industrializing western

Europe. Ottoman responses to these challenges were varied. They included both a restructuring of the military and a series of legal and administrative reforms that sought to transform a disjointed feudal social and political order into a centralized modern state.

These reforms, called the *tanzimat,* or "reorderings," affected the central elements of the Ottoman bureaucracy as well as the subsequent course of Islamic legal and political development in Ottoman territories. In particular, these legal reforms set the stage for a comprehensive revision in traditional methods of legal and religious training and are in part responsible for contemporary calls for the application of *shari'a,* or Islamic law. *Shari'a* had traditionally revolved around a complex set of educational institutions in which men committed to memory a hierarchy of sacred texts and their commentaries, beginning with the Qur'an and the *sunna* of the Prophet, as witnessed by his contemporaries and transmitted through specific lines of intellectual descent. A deep familiarity with these texts as well as with later works of jurisprudence, or *fiqh,* qualified one to render opinions, or *fatwa*s, on points of correct practice relevant to ritual, commercial, or personal activities. The institutional structures through which *shari'a* was applied consisted of courts, mosques, and schools manned by a corps of professional men of learning, who, as Albert Hourani has argued, acted as both administrative and moral links between the Ottoman sultan and his subjects throughout the empire.

As part of the Ottoman *tanzimat,* committees of scholars and bureaucrats were charged with reordering the practice of *shari'a.* Their goal was to forge scattered principles of legal decisionmaking—formerly embodied in the individual jurists, whose authority rested on their personal mastery of the legal tradition—into an abstract and systematized European-style legal code. Theoretically, such a code was to be applicable in a standardized way across the vast geographical reaches of the empire, without differences of emphasis or opinion on the part of individual judges. The practice of law would thus no longer require the informed interpretation of a traditionally trained scholar. Instead, the flexible traditional system of adjudication and advice in which each scholar could potentially render a different decision based on distinct traditions of textual interpretation—and in which a questioner could potentially ignore one scholar's interpretation in favor of another, equally authoritative one—would be forced into a new institutional framework, to become the monovocal voice of a centralizing state.

It is ironic that today, the call by contemporary Islamic activists to rid their countries of Western influence by applying *shari'a,* or Islamic law, comes at the very time that "Islamic law" is increasingly conceptualized as a list of behavioral rules "composed in a manner which would be sufficiently clear so that anyone could study it easily and act in conformity with it," a cultural standard devised by Western European legal theorists (Messick 1993, 55–56). Such codes take the form of numbered articles in an internationally standard legislative format rather than in the forms used by traditional Islamic legal manuals, which were sometimes written as rhymes for easy memorization by legal scholars. Whereas traditional forms of Islamic legal reasoning and writing—including discussion of previous commentaries on legal principles, their difficulties, and the multiple and sometimes contradictory positions taken by other authorities in the past—were highly decentralized, these modern codes remove "the authorship of law . . . from the hands of individuals such as imams and virtuoso jurists and [make it] instead the collective responsibility of drafting committees and legislative bodies" (Messick 1998, 5). In both form and application, such practices seem ever less "traditionally" Islamic. Since the mid-twentieth century, many Middle Eastern governments have enshrined Islam in their state constitutions (yet another institution imported from the West) as the official religion of the state. Consequently, the common Western perception that "Islam" is a monolithic and unquestionable set of ideas and practices is at least as much an artifact of contemporary political organization as it is of a medieval Islamic heritage (Starrett 1998).

By the early twentieth century, Ottoman educational policy had transformed the way Islam was conceived of and taught in the region's schools. Traditionally throughout the Middle East, the earliest phase of formal education consisted of study—or, more precisely, memorization—of the text of the Qur'an. Although taking place in a group, instruction was individualized. With the help of a local teacher, students (mostly boys, but sometimes girls as well) would listen to and repeat the rhythmic cantillation of the scripture, learning to reproduce it exactly while at the same time acquiring the skills of reading and writing. Even in Arabic-speaking countries, students whose own dialect differed from the classical Arabic of the Qur'an did not necessarily comprehend the text. The effort to learn the meaning of the text was postponed to later years, when the academically talented boys might travel to a *madrasa*, where they would learn, eventually, the sciences of textual interpretation and legal reasoning.

The Ottoman government's establishment of a new system of schools brought a revolutionary change in curriculum. New textbooks, new subjects, and new classroom activities began to stress, in new ways and from the earliest grades, the government's concern with directly regulating the personal behavior of its subjects. This transformation incorporated the notion that the modern social order demanded of each student individual responsibility and effort to live an ordered life. Hygiene; patience; duty to parents, scholars, and officials; and loyalty to the Ottoman state were explicitly inculcated and linked to new formulations of the Islamic character of society. These changes, identical to those wrought by British and indigenous educators in nearby Egypt at the same time, resulted in a long-term change in the ways the mass of Muslim students thought about the essentials of their faith, history, and the social world. As Benjamin Fortna phrases it, "Combining morals with chemistry and French derives from a very different tradition from the one that linked grammar, logic, theology, and jurisprudence" (2000, 381). Thus, the intellectual moorings of Islamic life were being transformed.

Programs of Reform in the New Nation-States

Although the Ottoman Empire was dismembered by the European powers after the end of World War I, its modernizing reform programs nevertheless had lasting effects on the new nationalizing elites in its former territories. One of the most important of these legacies was the Ottomans' mid-nineteenth-century conviction that in order to compete politically, economically, and militarily in the new world order and in order to free themselves of foreign domination, they would have to incorporate into their societies unfamiliar Western ideas and institutions that could help their cultures flourish even as they changed. According to this line of thought, Islam, as an important part of those cultures, would have to change as well.

The paths of change taken by the central Ottoman lands in Asia Minor and by the Arabic-speaking lands to its south and east differed substantially. The new state of Turkey retained its independence following World War I under Mustafa Kemal, a general who through a mixture of charisma and brute force revolutionized the way his country would construct its future, earning him the name Atatürk, "Father of the Turkish Nation." However, at the same time, the former Ottoman territories of North Africa, along with the Levant, parts of Arabia, and Mesopotamia, became or remained European dependencies until the latter half of the twentieth century.

In these peripheral lands of the Ottoman Empire, substantially new ways of thinking about Islam had begun to emerge during the latter half of the nineteenth century. These new ways of thinking responded to the growing imperial power of the European nations by adopting Europe's own political ideologies and intellectual tools. These tools, the most important of which were the school and the newspaper, led to the emergence of a new kind of spokesperson for Islamic tradition in the region. French and Italian instructors who had been brought to the Ottoman court in the late eighteenth century had by the 1830s helped found a generation of intellectuals familiar with European languages and ideas. Soon thereafter, Arabic- and Turkish-speaking student delegations returned from residence in Paris with new understandings of both modern military tactics and the political philosophies of Jean-Jacques Rousseau and Montesquieu, who wrote about the unique souls of nations and the necessity of popular participation in government. These returning students became teachers in turn, and a number of them worked to establish institutes for the translation of European works into local Middle Eastern languages. Others among them, including the Egyptian Rif'at al-Tahtawi, also edited newspapers and periodicals and wrote textbooks and new "national" histories. Tahtawi and his intellectual successors advanced the idea that the *ulama,* or scholars of Islamic religious sciences, could advise their rulers wisely only if they also understood the rapidly changing conditions of the modern world. This, of course, would imply yielding some of their authority in the fields of engineering, medicine, agriculture, and other modern arts and sciences to experts in those areas. At the same time, these reformers proposed that the general public, girls as well as boys, should be educated in schools so that they could contribute to national economic and technological progress by appropriating the best of modern Western science and technology to advance the public welfare of Muslim societies.

Similar developments took place in Tunisia, Lebanon, and Syria, as educated men began to debate the nature of Islam and Arabic culture in the modern world. These discussions raised such issues as the balance to be struck between local and national loyalties, the regional and transregional identities of language and religion, and the opportunity to reach outside the boundaries of the Islamic tradition to appropriate relevant ideas and developments from elsewhere. Key to these debates was Jamal al-Din, widely known as "al-Afghani" ("the Afghan"). Jamal al-Din was a gifted teacher who called for pan-Islamic solidarity in the face of increasing European expansionism in the late nineteenth century. Arguing that Islamic civilization was in decline because it had lost the values of its golden age, he saw the possibility of renaissance through the achievement of political and cultural solidarity and through faith in the power of human reason to mold both individuals and countries. According to Jamal al-Din, the revelations of Islam were identical with the truths of philosophy and the findings of modern science, and for him the essence of Islam was the active participation of Muslims in applying their reason both to the world and to sacred scripture.

Islamic Modernism

Jamal al-Din's travels, from south central Asia to Cairo, India, Istanbul, Persia, Russia, Paris, and London, are a map of the political fault lines he tried to transcend. The reaction of both European and Middle Eastern elites to his international contacts, his founding of secret societies (he formed one in Paris with disciple Muhammad Abduh, which published an influential but short-lived Arabic newspaper), and his anti-imperialist rhetoric appears to have been similar in some ways to suspicions of the charismatic, pan-Islamic organizers in our own day. Jamal al-Din's thought and career, as the founder both of modern pan-Islamic ideology and of Islamic modernism, illuminate a pattern of response common to many later Islamist figures of the twentieth century. On the one hand, he eagerly sought ways to discuss the benefits of modernity in Islamic terminology, arguing, for example, that the Qur'an, read properly by an enlightened mind, provided hidden references to the findings of modern science and to modern political forms like parliamentary legislatures (Hourani 1983, 127). In his view, it was science as such, rather than any inherent superiority of Western culture or civilization, that was responsible for the dominance of European civilization in the modern era:

> Thus I say: If someone looks deeply into the question, he will see that science rules the world. There was, is, and will be no ruler in the world but science. . . . The English have reached Afghanistan; the French have seized Tunisia. In reality this usurpation, aggression, and conquest have not come from the French or the English. Rather it is science that everywhere manifests its greatness and power. Ignorance had no alternative to prostrating itself humbly before science and acknowledging its submission. (Jamal al-Din, quoted in Keddie 1968, 102–103)

Scientific thought was to be seized for the benefit of Muslims. On the other hand, Jamal al-Din was critical of the materialism of contemporary European intellectuals, and especially of their ideas that nature was spiritually empty raw material whose movement was the result of blind impersonal laws and that mankind could find its way unaided by revelation. For as a Muslim reformer, al-Afghani maintained that there could be no knowledge, no justice, and no virtue without the enveloping presence of divine will and wisdom.

These ideas were developed by Jamal al-Din's Egyptian student and collaborator Muhammad Abduh and then by Abduh's own contemporaries and followers. Prominent among them were Qasim Amin, who argued in 1899 for the emancipation of women, and Mustafa Abd al-Raziq, who, like Abduh, worked to reform religious education in Egypt. The key theme in much of their Islamic modernist writings was education and the power of formal instruction in science, philosophy, history, and religion to mold thought and behavior, transforming both students and society into dynamic sources of material and cultural progress. The ultimate goal of these modernists was to revitalize Islamic thought and practice by consciously using Islam to solve contemporary problems while using modern measures of public welfare to determine which elements of Islamic thought were relevant in the modern world.

Abduh and his Syrian colleague Rashid Rida, in particular, stressed the idea that the modern Muslim community should directly follow the example of the early Muslim community, the *salaf,* rather than "blindly" imitating the example of each previous generation of Muslim scholars. Key to their project was a series of critiques both of the entrenched interests of the traditional *ulama* and of many of the popular practices of Sufi orders, peasants, and the urban poor, which were condemned for being based on superstitions and as having neither a rational nor an Islamic scriptural foundation. Abduh drew attention to the difference between those elements of Islam—mostly having to do with worship— that were eternal and those having to do with social, political, economic, and family life, which were sensitive to cultural and historical difference and change. The latter, he argued, needed to be continually interpreted anew in changing circumstances. Some modernist thinkers had the opportunity to put their ideas into practice, as advisers to the government or as rectors of al-Azhar University, the premier institution of Islamic study in the Arabic-speaking world. Other reformers served as teachers, writers, and journalists, building what has come to be known in the twentieth century as a "public sphere," a metaphorical space where ideas could be exchanged, debated, criticized, and developed.

Secularization in Modern Turkey

Two events of the 1920s altered the way the public sphere would develop in the Middle East for the remainder of the century. In 1924, as part of his effort to build a nation-state out of the remains of the Ottoman Empire, Mustafa Kemal (Atatürk) abolished the institution of the caliphate, the historical succession of men who, under different dynasties, had claimed to follow the Prophet Muhammad's role in the leadership of the world's Sunni Muslim community. Claimed by the Ottoman sultan since the sixteenth century, the caliphate had long been an office impotent practically but powerful symbolically. It was an emblem of Sunni unity and a link to the golden age of Muslim prosperity and power. Its severance marked a rupture in the way many Muslims thought about the temporal political order and a shift in the way Turks saw their place in the region. No longer masters of an empire, the Turks, newly constituted as the Turkish nation, were breaking with the past and with the Arabic-speaking neighbors whom Turkish reformers considered irredeemably backward—an evaluation that Arab intellectuals turned with equal vehemence on their former rulers.

Turkey in the 1920s and 1930s embarked on a long and troubled road to becoming a self-proclaimed "modern" and "secular" state in which religious expression was pushed out of public life. The dress styles of the Ottoman religious elite were banned by law in 1925, and a decade later, women were forced to remove their head scarves in public. Muslim religious schools were forcibly closed, and the scholars who had formed the bulk of the old Ottoman bureaucracy were summarily removed from ministries, from teaching posts, and from the court system. Islamic law was officially replaced by a combination of civil and criminal codes inspired by those of Switzerland and Italy. Polygamy was abolished, Sufi orders were prohibited from taking part in politics, and in a final blow to Turkey's connection with the rest of the Muslim world, the script in which the Turkish language was written was changed from Arabic letters to Roman letters. In turning away from public manifestations of its Islamic heritage, Turkey's new elites were confident that they were joining what they saw as the "modern" world. In Atatürk's words, "There is no second civilization; civilization means European civilization, and it must be imported with both its roses and its thorns" (quoted in Lewis 1968, 236).

In speeches to the public on these matters, Atatürk emphasized the sense in which public displays of religiously significant symbols belonged to the past rather than to the future:

> Gentlemen . . . it was necessary to abolish the fez, which sat on the heads of our nation as an emblem of ignorance, negligence, fanaticism, and hatred of progress and civilization, to accept in its place the hat, the headgear used by the whole civilized world, and in this way to demonstrate that the Turkish nation, in its mentality as in other respects, in no way diverges from civilized social life. (Quoted in Lewis 1968, 268)

> In some places . . . I have seen women who put a piece of cloth or a towel or something like it over their heads to hide their faces, and who turn their backs or huddle themselves on the ground when a man passes by. What are the meaning and sense of this behavior? Gentlemen, can the mothers and daughters of a civilized nation adopt this strange manner, this barbarous posture? It is a spectacle that makes the nation an object of ridicule. It must be remedied at once. (Quoted in Lewis 1968, 270)

Curiously, though, in banishing religious symbols and practices from public view, Turkey's new secular elites were not removing them from politics. For their actions, instead, placed religion at the very center of politics, as something to be tamed, managed, administered, controlled, and domesticated by the national government. The 1926 Turkish Criminal Code, for example, announced penalties for those

> who, by misuse of religion, religious sentiments, or things that are religiously considered as holy, in any way incite the people to action prejudicial to the security of the state, or form associations for this purpose. Political associations on the basis of religion or religious sentiments may not be formed. (Quoted in Lewis 1968, 412)

Far from denying the importance of religion, the state acknowledged its utility as a political ideology and recognized the efficiency of religious institutions and organizations like the ancient Sufi orders as centers of political mobilization. In effect, the state claimed for itself a monopoly on the legitimate politicization of religion. Turkey's secularism took the form of an official anticlericalism based on the notion that modernly educated elites should transform traditional Islam into a private religion of personal spiritual development that could be harnessed to the national interest. Basic necessities, such as the training of religious functionaries who could lead prayers in mosques, were handed over to a national Ministry of Religious Affairs in 1924. The official purpose of this government ministry was "to cleanse and elevate the Islamic faith, by rescuing it from the position of a political instrument, to which it has been accustomed for centuries" (quoted in Lewis 1968, 264).

For Turks, religion was now to be considered an internal matter, a question of faith and of personal worship, albeit worship guided by a new kind of centrally administered state religious bureaucracy. Political action motivated by nonstate religious organizations was outlawed, so that the public performance of such Islamic religious duties as prayer no longer signified membership in the local or worldwide community of Muslims. Rather, public religious practice was forcibly recast as nothing more than the aggregate of individual parishioners expressing their private faith at the same time. In his drive to "Europeanize" Turkey, Atatürk at one point considered replacing prostration and chanting during prayer; worshipers would sit on pews and sing liturgical music, as in a Christian church. This idea, however, was never implemented.

The Muslim Brotherhood

The growth of a modern secular elite—a class of people versed in history and literature, politics and geography, mathematics and the sciences, rather than in the religious learning taught in traditional Islamic schools—does not automatically entail the withering away of religion. For the preeminence of a secular rather than a religious elite often serves instead to change the forms religion takes in social and personal life. Four years after the abolition of the caliphate, Hasan al-Banna, an Egyptian schoolteacher, founded a social movement that changed the face of Middle Eastern Islam. Formally named the Society of Muslim Brothers, al-Banna's movement grew rapidly in the 1930s and 1940s. By the end of that decade, it had half a million members and perhaps a million more sympathizers in Egypt. The movement soon spread to Syria, Jordan, and other countries as well. What distinguished the Brotherhood from other Islamic reform movements was its organization. It consisted of a hierarchy of administrative levels and bodies overseen by a general guide and a consultative assembly, who oversaw sections dealing with issues faced by families, labor groups, peasants, students, and professionals as well as special sections dedicated to *da'wa,* sports, publications, and translation work. The Brotherhood founded hospitals, schools, and other social service institutions; sponsored meetings and conferences; and trained lay Muslim preachers. Its thoroughly modern administrative apparatus and its social, cultural, and political activism were broadly popular among urban Egyptians, particularly schoolteachers, clerks, lawyers, physicians, police, civil servants, and students. But despite its wide range of social activities, al-Banna always reminded followers of the broader purpose of the movement:

> Brethren, you are not a benevolent organization, nor a political party, nor a local association with strictly limited aims. Rather you are a new spirit making its way into the heart of this nation and revivifying it through the Qur'an; a new light dawning and scattering the darkness of materialism through the knowledge of God; a resounding voice rising and echoing the message of the Apostle. . . . We are calling you to Islam, which was brought by Muhammad. . . . government is part of it, and freedom is one of its religious duties. If someone should say to you: This is politics! say: this is Islam, and we do not recognize such divisions. (Al-Banna, "Between Yesterday and Today," translated in Wendell 1978, 36)

The Brotherhood's political goals were to rid Egypt of the British, to transform the Egyptian government into an Islamic one, and to initiate changes in the *umma* that would eventually result in the reestablishment of the caliphate. In the view of the Muslim Brotherhood, the moral and political bankruptcy of such Western ideologies as liberal capitalism and communism—the first seen as a kind of Christian imperialism and the second as an equally belligerent missionary atheism—was clear. The years following the horrors of World War I saw cultural critics in both the West and the Middle East commenting on the failures rather than the successes of European civilization. The American poet Ezra Pound, for example, wrote of the modern West as "an old bitch gone in the teeth . . . a botched civilization" (Pound 1920). For al-Banna, writing during the Great Depression of the 1930s,

> the civilization of the West, which was brilliant by virtue of its scientific perfection for a long time, and which subjugated the whole world with the products of this science . . . is now bankrupt and in decline. Its foundations are crumbling, and its institutions and guiding principles are falling apart. Its political foundations are being destroyed by dictatorships, and its economic foundations are being swept away by crises. The millions of its wretched unemployed and hungry offer their testimony against it, while its social foundations are being undermined by deviant ideologies and revolutions which are breaking out everywhere. Its people are at a loss as to the proper measures to be taken and are wandering far astray. (Al-Banna, "Toward the Light," translated in Wendell 1978, 106).

According to al-Banna and the Muslim Brotherhood, the proper response was to abandon "the path of fleshly desires and vanities—the path of Europe" and follow Islam, the perfect system of social organization (al-Banna, "Toward the Light," translated in Wendell 1978, 124). In this way, political community was to be defined not by territory or race or power but by creed:

> O our people, we are calling out to you with the Qur'an in our right hand and the Sunna in our left, and with the deeds of the pious ancestors of the sons of this *umma* as our example. We summon you to Islam, the teachings of Islam, the laws and guidance of Islam. . . . Muslims, this is a period of creation: create yourselves, and your *umma* will thereby be created! (Al-Banna, "Toward the Light," translated in Wendell 1978, 75, 84)

The organization's public activities drew positive attention from much of the public, but the Brotherhood worried the government, not only because of its growing power but also because within the organization was a secret military wing that engaged in political violence. In late 1948, the Egyptian prime minister banned the organization and was assassinated by a member of the secret apparatus. Hasan al-Banna was assassinated in retaliation, and thousands of Brotherhood members were imprisoned, a cycle of action and reaction that has been repeated each decade since as the Egyptian government and the Brotherhood (and its more radical offshoots) have struggled over issues of activism, change, and restraint.

These recurrent waves of arrests, imprisonments, and executions of Islamic activists have had a deep effect on the ideologies and organizational forms of Islamic movements in the Middle East. Political repression has confirmed in the minds of the members of various Islamic movements the view that the governments under which they live are persecuting "true Muslims" in the name of secularism, communism, or some other Western ideology, and the interaction has radicalized many Muslim groups. Prisons have been valuable recruiting grounds and sites of ideological development for activists' political stance, just as contacts with the West have been formative for their moral and cultural ideas. Al-Banna's ideological successor, Sayyid Qutb, had both experiences at his disposal.

Sayyid Qutb

Sayyid Qutb and Hasan al-Banna were exact contemporaries, each born in 1906. But the two had very different career paths as Islamic activists. Al-Banna entered the world of Islamic organizing early. He attended anti-British rallies and later attended the circle of Muhammad Abduh's collaborator Rashid Rida.

Al-Banna was founding activist organizations with other students as early as his preparatory school years. Qutb's path was a more complex, circuitous one. Like al-Banna, he was trained as a teacher at the Dar al-Ulum (the House of Sciences), a modern teacher-training college, and worked as a teacher in the public schools and as a school inspector for the Egyptian Ministry of Education. All the while, he was also writing as a journalist, poet, novelist, and literary critic, becoming involved in political criticism only after World War II. In 1948, Qutb's life was transformed when the Ministry of Education sent him on a mission to the United States to observe the U.S. educational system. However, instead of being attracted by the U.S. way of life, Qutb was repulsed. The greed, promiscuity, and racism of U.S. society revived Qutb's attachment to his own heritage, and in 1951, after returning to Egypt, he joined the Muslim Brotherhood.

Qutb quickly rose to leadership positions within the organization, but he also suffered for that, for in 1954 and again in 1965 he was arrested, tortured, and (in 1966) executed along with other Muslim Brothers who were implicated in real or imagined conspiracies against the Egyptian president, Gamal Abdel Nasser. During his time in prison, Qutb wrote his most famous works, a multivolume commentary on the Qur'an and a small but important volume called *Signposts along the Road.*

Signposts was one of the most widely read and controversial Arabic books of the twentieth century. Using the Indian jurist Mawlana Mawdudi's concept of *jahiliyya,* the idea that contemporary society is indistinguishable from the era of pagan ignorance before the revelation of the Qur'an, Qutb argued against earlier thinkers like al-Afghani and Abduh, who had attributed Muslim weakness to the careless imitation of previous generations of Muslims, which had resulted in the slowing and eventual stultification of thought and society. Instead, Qutb saw the cause of Muslim weakness as the careless imitation of foreign moralities and philosophies, the rendering of sovereignty unto men who elevated themselves over others as rulers and lawmakers:

> We are today immersed in *jahiliyya,* a *jahiliyya* like that of early Islam, but perhaps deeper, darker. Everything around us expresses *jahiliyya:* people's ideas, their beliefs, habits, traditions, culture, art, literature, rules and laws. Even all that we have come to consider Islamic culture, Islamic sources, philosophy and thought are *jahili* constructs. This is why Islamic values have not taken root in our souls, why the Islamic worldview remains obscured in our minds, why no generation has arisen among us equal to the calibre of the first Islamic generation. (Qutb, *Signposts,* quoted in Euben 1999, 57)

In this view, any society that does not worship God alone is *jahili.* The only true social freedom and equality are freedom from human oppression and the equality of universal submission to God:

When the highest authority is God alone—and is expressed in the dominance of divine law—this sovereignty is the only kind in which humans are truly liberated from slavery to men. Only this is "human civilization," because human civilization requires that the basis of rule be the true and perfect freedom of man and the absolute dignity of each individual in society. There is no true freedom and no dignity for men, or for each and every individual, in a society where some individuals are lords who legislate and others are slaves who obey. (Qutb, *Signposts*, quoted in Euben 1999, 63–64)

Qutb's solution to this dilemma was to point to the shortcomings of movements that sought merely to preach. The material forces of power responsible for the protection and perpetuation of *jahili* society had to be confronted with direct action. First, Muslims should abandon the ideas and practices of "ignorance" to take a divergent path and, in effect, secede from the larger society. No longer working from within the established political system, this growing movement would become an independent Islamic society in practice, and from a position of separation, it would battle contemporary paganism by all necessary means, including violence. The political system would thus have to be overthrown.

Islamist Movements in the Modern Middle East

The culture of imprisonment in Nasser's Egypt and the ideological guidance of *Signposts* radicalized a new generation of Egyptian youth. During the 1970s, a string of small militant groups formed and disbanded, preached and organized in secret, carried out attacks on government targets and were arrested and destroyed, only to return again in different forms. Some of them developed Qutb's ideas in far more explicit form, arguing that militant *jihad*—not just the struggle for moral self-mastery incumbent upon every Muslim—was as central a feature of Islamic practice as were prayer and fasting. Meanwhile, the Egyptian president, Anwar Sadat, released hundreds of jailed Islamists and allowed their sympathizers to organize on university campuses in order to counterbalance socialist political groups, which Sadat wished to control.

Egypt's defeat in the 1967 war with Israel had deepened the nation's sense of dejection and its disillusionment with Nasser's socialism. The economy was stagnant, public services were beginning to suffer, population and urbanization were growing, housing was in short supply, and employment opportunities for educated youth were disappearing. To make matters worse, Sadat had concluded a controversial peace treaty with Israel, which had occupied Jerusalem. A new set of crises loomed. And on October 6, 1981, Sadat was assassinated by a member of a group called Jihad as he was watching a military

Campaign poster for the Muslim Brotherhood in Cairo, Egypt. (Gregory Starrett)

parade file past the Tomb of the Unknown Soldier, a monument commemorating Egypt's military power. The tomb was built in the mid-1970s in the shape of a pyramid, the symbol of Egypt's ancient pagan kings. Drawing potently on this *jahiliyya* symbolism, Sadat's assassin shouted, as the echoes of gunfire died, that he had killed Pharaoh.

Other Arab countries have experienced the growth of modern Islamic activist groups as well. In Morocco, Tunisia, Lebanon, Palestine, and Yemen, the symbolic vocabulary of Islam has replaced that of Marxism as the idiom in which the largest and most successful political opposition groups voice their ideologies. Some of these groups encourage direct confrontation against corrupt governing structures while others, like the reconstituted Muslim Brotherhood in contemporary Egypt and Jordan, work for reform both within the political system and in open activities in society at large, continuing the tradition of Hasan al-Banna in providing educational programs, clinics, and recreational facilities in poor neighborhoods. Such services benefit the poorest segments of society and attract supporters both among clients and among professionals who volunteer their time, money, and energy to improve their societies.

Other groups, such as the Palestinian Hamas (literally, "Zeal," but also an Arabic acronym for "Islamic Resistance Movement"), are active on both political and military fronts. With a dual structure, Hamas has a military wing that carries out attacks against Israelis and a civil wing that provides public services to populations under Israeli military occupation in the West Bank and the Gaza Strip. Hamas's social programs are so efficient and respected by the population of the territories that at various times, international humanitarian agencies have funneled relief supplies through them rather than through the official but corrupt secular governing structures. Hamas was founded in 1987, during the first Palestinian *intifada,* or revolt against Israel. Its leaders were members of the Muslim Brotherhood of Gaza, which had run an Islamic center in Gaza City since 1973. As is the case with most important Islamic groups in the contemporary Middle East, the founders and most important members of the Muslim Brotherhood of Gaza do not fit the standard stereotypes of Muslim fundamentalists as poor, uneducated, and backward. Present at its small founding meeting were a pharmacist and a physician, a teacher and a schoolmaster, an engineer and a university staff member. The group's leader, Ahmad Yasin, was a former schoolteacher who had studied English in Cairo in the 1960s (Abu-Amr 1994).

Similar profiles of movement leaders and members—teachers, civil servants, and professionals—can be found in the ranks of Islamist movements throughout the region. In Morocco and Algeria, Islamist movements have been particularly popular among students and recent graduates both at the university and high school levels. As an Algerian student said in 1990,

In this country if you are a young man . . . you have only four choices: you can re-main unemployed and celibate because there are no jobs and no apartments to live in; you can work in the black market and risk being arrested; you can try to emigrate to France to sweep the streets of Paris or Marseilles; or you can join the Islamic Salvation Front and vote for Islam. (Quoted in Munson 1993, 173–174)

Political repression, stale economies, and a pervasive sense of hopelessness make the bright promise of a moral and prosperous Islamic future attractive to youth who were raised during a century in which Islam was framed not only as a tradition of worship but also as a social philosophy in a modern sense, com-parable and even superior to capitalism or socialism, fascism, nationalism, or secularism. Such views of Islam are reinforced by the conversion of leaders from secularist philosophies to Islam, a common occurrence throughout the region during the 1970s and 1980s. Heads of unions, journalists, and others who rediscovered Islam brought with them the cadences of revolutionary so-cialism, whether of the French or the Eastern Bloc variety. Concern for the plight of the poor, opposition to hereditary monarchy, and the image of the West as a source of political repression and moral corruption animate the writ-ings of some Islamic activists, who see Islam as a radical doctrine. Note the in-terplay of Islamic and Marxist vocabulary in this 1981 manifesto of the Moroc-can group Islamic Youth:

Our present and our future are caught between the hammer of American Impe-rialism and the anvil of its agents represented by the corrupt monarchial regime. . . . [We are], God willing, in the vanguard of an authentic Islamic revo-lution in Morocco; a revolution that enlightens the horizons of this country and liberates its people to bring them back to the Islam of Muhammad . . . not the Is-lam of the merchants of oil and the agents of the Americans. (Quoted in Mun-son 1993, 159)

But popular Islamic movements are not always strident, violent, or explicitly revolutionary. As more and more ordinary, educated Muslims take the time to read, think, and talk about their religious heritage, they come to appreciate its achievements, its depth, and its relevance to their daily lives. Most Islamic or-ganizations are, in fact, explicitly nonviolent, focused solely on religious edu-cation, virtuous action, and spiritual growth (Mahmood 2001a, 2001b; Hirschkind 2001a, 2001b). Many are relatively small and loose-knit networks of teachers, friends, and students that manage to avoid the attention of repres-sive governments, rather than highly visible hierarchical organizations like the Muslim Brotherhood (Wiktorowicz 2000). Others, outgrowths of Sufi organi-zations, stress personal piety and reflection on God. Despite the suspicion and contempt that many educated Middle Easterners have for traditional Sufism, which is increasingly stereotyped as a movement of peasants and the working classes, prominent Islamists sometimes have backgrounds that involved various elements of Sufi thought and practice. Ayatollah Khomeini in Iran, Hasan al-Banna in Egypt, and popular leaders and cultural critics Fqih Zamzami and Abd al-Slam Yasin of Morocco all had roots in Sufism. In Lebanon, on the other hand, the Ahbash Sufi order has energetically organized to oppose politically active Sunni Islamic groups. The Ahbash reject the ideology of Sayyid Qutb and call for pacifism and moderation, even while entering electoral politics to counterbalance groups linked with Saudi and Egyptian Islamist radicals. Paradoxically, they maintain good relations with Hizbullah, the Shi'ite group that became internationally notorious in the 1980s for its attacks on Israel and its kidnapping of foreigners in Beirut during the civil war that followed the 1982 Israeli invasion. In Lebanon as well as in other countries where Sufism is a popular practice, the Shi'ite veneration of the Prophet Muhammad and his family is attractive to Sunni Muslims as well and can act as a devotional bridge between the two communities (Hamzeh and Dekmejian 1996; Hoffmann-Ladd 1992).

Electoral ventures such as that of the Ahbash are not rare in countries where limited political participation is allowed. In Egypt and Jordan, members or sympathizers of the Muslim Brotherhood have run for and won election to seats in Parliament and have been appointed to the judiciary. But the boundaries of toleration are always uncertain and are constantly shifting. In 1982, President Hafez al-Asad of Syria ordered the massacre of 10,000 people in the town of Hama as part of an attack on Syria's Muslim Brotherhood. Elsewhere, relative degrees of freedom to form political parties and participate in elections for local or national offices alternate with cycles of repression, vote fixing, and political arrests. The Egyptian government still periodically cracks down on the Muslim Brotherhood, as it did in 1995 when it claimed to possess evidence of Brotherhood involvement in an assassination plot against President Husni Mubarak. Days before an election for the lower house of Parliament, Egyptian police arrested hundreds of Muslim Brotherhood members, as well as leftists, human rights advocates, and others.

In 1991, as Algeria's Islamic Salvation Front (FIS) was poised to win a round of national elections, those elections were canceled when the country's military seized control of the government and outlawed the FIS. This action precipitated a decade of obscene violence in which tens of thousands of Algerians died. The military claimed that FIS's entry into the political arena was a platform for the permanent seizure of power through the cancellation of future elections, since some Islamist activists claim that human legislation through parliamentary democracy is contrary to the rule of divine law. This is, of course, a fundamental contradiction of modern liberalism: that people might freely elect those who would deprive them of freedom. But the military's action, although popular with many Algerian secularists, infuriated Islamist organizations and others who saw that the popular will was being overturned. These voices contended that the electoral process was not, in fact, free if it could be canceled. Riots and protests turned to bloodshed. Groups claiming Islamic identity—sometimes as a proclamation of ideological justification, but sometimes only as a thin cover for such criminal acts as rape, robbery, and revenge—murdered ordinary people in villages and cities, shot unveiled women in the streets, and assassinated artists and politicians, while threatening and harassing the remainder of Algerian society. In turn, secularist paramilitaries and the Algerian police and army massacred Islamists, tortured suspected members of a bewildering number of radical groups, and shot veiled women in the streets. The incalculable suffering of Algeria in the 1990s has only gradually begun to burn itself out. Both sides described the conflict as being between the Islamic and European heritages of the country, which had been a French possession since the 1830s. But every faction—and there were many more than two—took pains to present themselves as victims and their foes as barbarians.

Women in Contemporary Islam

The role of women as targets of violence in the Algerian conflict—and in any number of conflicts worldwide, not just in the Islamic Middle East—points to the important role that women play as symbols of culture. As Lisa Pollard, Beth Baron, and other historians have pointed out, women often act as symbols with which men envision the political order. States and nations are often portrayed as female, as are such concepts as justice, wisdom, and liberty and more intimate values like nurturing, family, and social continuity. In Algeria, women's dress was used by secularists as a badge either of freedom or of fanaticism and by religious groups as a sign either of piety or of wickedness.

There is probably no symbol of Islam more viscerally engaging to Europeans and Americans than the veil, whether the simple head scarf of a Turkish schoolgirl or the enveloping burqa of the Afghan widow. Why this is so has largely to do with the particular cultural understandings in the United States of the relationship between personhood and display. For Americans, personhood is marked by the idea of autonomy, and autonomy is linked to such concepts as physical comfort, sexual activity, and the overcoming of socially imposed restrictions on behavior.

To many Muslim women, by contrast, personhood is a more complex balance between autonomy, on the one hand, and understandings of status, responsibility, and control over social interaction, on the other. Veiling, a traditional part of women's dress in the Mediterranean since at least ancient

Greek times, is a complex symbolic system that women and men have used and understood in different ways throughout history. By the 1920s, French-educated upper-class Muslim women in Egypt had begun to argue that face-veiling (the expected form of public dress for the urban upper and middle classes) was a sign of women's oppression. Led by Hoda Sha'rawi and others, women of the upper classes began to remove their veils and to organize women's associations, agitating for changes in the laws dealing with marriage and divorce and encouraging the mandatory education of girls. Whereas in Turkey, women unveiled under legal compulsion, in other parts of the Middle East, the practice generally began with women high in the social scale and then gradually worked its way downward until, by the 1950s, one would not have found more than a handful of older women in major cities who covered their hair at all. At that time, *hijab,* or modest dress, was perceived as a mark of cultural and personal backwardness. In the Gulf countries, such developments never took place, and modest dress, complete with the face veil, has been enforced by both tradition and law. But in the early 1970s, with the growing influence of Islamic political movements in universities, some young women in other parts of the region began again to cover their hair, their arms, and their legs with full-length garments. A few began wearing face veils and gloves as well. Today, the majority of Muslim women in most Middle Eastern countries where the veil had been discarded in midcentury—and increasingly even in secularist strongholds like Turkey—have since adopted various forms of modest dress.

Their motivations are diverse. For some, pressure from brothers, husbands, fiancés, or fathers involved in Islamist movements has been a deciding factor. For others, modest dress is an adaptation to the stresses of crowded cities in which unveiled women experience sexual harassment or receive unwanted attention from strangers. Veiling, in these contexts, allows a woman to signal that she is virtuous, visually marking a separation between herself and others in situations—a crowded city bus, a university classroom—where physical separation is impossible. Particularly for women who work outside the home, modest dress is a way of marking concern with traditional values of family and domesticity. For some women, modest dress becomes a fashion competition, for the styles have become brighter, more complex, and open to more creative possibilities than in the past. For other women, the veil is an expression of deepening piety. Several Egyptian women I know began veiling in the 1980s against the express wishes of their husbands, who feared they would be accused of pressuring their wives into modest dress and that clients, coworkers, or others would suspect them of involvement in Islamist movements. One of the most interesting developments with regard to the veil, though, is a gradual narrowing of its meaning. Traditionally donned when a girl reached puberty and was thus marriageable, modest dress is spreading to younger and younger girls. Its former marking of age is beginning to vanish, so that gender becomes an even more significant factor in its symbolism.

The social and intellectual context of women's participation in Islamic practice is changing. Traditionally encouraged to fulfill their religious duties at home, Middle Eastern women, from Morocco to Oman, are increasingly taking advantage of new opportunities for study, for worship, and for participation in formal and informal Islamic organizations in the public sphere. Women organize prayers and study circles in both public and private mosques, and religious lessons for women are becoming popular for working-class women as well as for those of the middle class. Growing rates of literacy and increasing educational attainments as well as the economic necessity of working outside the home to support their families has increased urban women's mobility and their connectedness with broader intellectual and cultural currents. New understandings of Islamic values are drawn not only from conversations with colleagues, friends, families, and neighbors but from mass media as well. The ready availability of Islamic literature, old and new, at newsstands, the growing frequency of religious broadcasts on radio and television, and their widespread dissemination on cassette tapes are all altering the outlines of Islam at a popular level.

Islam in an Era of Globalization

These new technologies and media have contrasting effects. On the one hand, they alter the way people apprehend the Islamic past by tending to minimize appreciation of historical disagreements and variant interpretations of important topics. But on the other hand, they provide the material for new sorts of discussions and creative uses of Islamic thought. In Yemen, for example, where both modern Islamist movements and resurgent Sufi organizations coexist with traditional tribal structures, groups argue about what sorts of verbal styles are appropriate for Islamic cassettes. Should they convey merely live recordings of sermons, or is it better to use the flexibility of the medium more creatively, mixing sermons with commentary and religious songs set to popular music (Miller 2000)? In Egypt, television specials broadcast during Ramadhan have contributed to a Christmas-like commercialization of the holiday (Armbrust 2002). Mass media can homogenize the forms in which culture is reproduced, even when deployed with the intention of maintaining or amplifying cultural difference.

Even in the most homogeneous and conservative countries in the Middle East, the complexities of contemporary life bring the outside world in and distribute members of the nation far and wide internationally. Take, for example, Egyptian political scientist Mamoun Fandy's recent description of Saudi Arabia:

> [The] eastern province is dominated by a Shi'a population, an oil industry, and an obvious American influence. Highways, shopping malls, and expatriate communities give the impression that one is in an American city, especially when one sees the number of American soldiers and civilians in Dhahran, Damam, and Khobar. Except for scattered and sometimes diffuse native cultural practices of closing shops for prayers and veiling women, these cities are a microcosm of global creolization. Even when one examines the local, one discovers that hijabs and abayahs (local dress) are made in Taiwan and Hong Kong, as well as designer abayahs prepared in Paris and London. Prayer rugs with a compass indicating the direction of Mecca are made in Japan. Moreover, the local Shi'ism transcends Saudi territories to reach Bahrain, Lebanon, and Iran. Even the holy places [to the west] in Mecca and Madina are not immune to the global effect. Almost all religious icons sold outside the Prophet's mosque in Madina are made outside the country and sold to foreigners as if they were Saudi. Foreign workers, estimated to equal the population of natives, add to the peculiarity of the Saudi state. Saudi children are raised by Asian and European nannies and are frequently bilingual. (Fandy 1999, 125–126)

Islamist groups that criticize government corruption, political oppression, or dependence on U.S. mercenary troops nevertheless themselves use fax machines, computers, photocopiers, the Internet, cassette tapes, and other modern technologies to spread their ideas both at home and abroad. Some opposition groups make available toll-free telephone numbers that people can call for updates, and they rely on the recruitment of Saudi students studying abroad in the freer informational climate of the United States or Europe. The Saudi government and royal family, for its own part, use the same technologies of persuasion, reaching far beyond the country's borders through elaborate financial and informational infrastructures in London, Washington, and elsewhere.

The Middle East, then, is a thoroughly internationalized place with long histories of inter- and intraregional migration. Saudi and Sudanese students travel to Beirut and Cairo, Lebanese and Turkish businessmen cut deals in Rabat and Doha, Moroccan and Syrian pilgrims voyage to Mecca and Najaf, and Egyptian, Pakistani, Filipina, and Palestinian workers make their way to Kuwait and Bahrain. People, resources, and ideas flow constantly across national borders, blurring the lines between local and international debates about Islam. There is seldom a clear line between what is authentic and what is imported, what is traditional and what is modern. In parts of southern Yemen, for example, a revival of local Sufi orders is opposed by groups supported by the Saudis, whose Wahhabi Puritanism forms the ideological basis of the Saudi state.

Islamic calligraphy and Disney decals on sale in Cairo, Egypt. (Gregory Starrett)

The pioneer of this puritanical stream of modern Islam was Muhammad Ibn Abd al-Wahhab, an eighteenth-century reformer and client of the Sa'ud family. Al-Wahhab denounced what he saw as the superstitious reverence for saints in the Sufism of his day, as well as the social inequality inherent in the practice of discipleship to the families of charismatic Sufi leaders. Following his lead, present-day Yemeni Wahhabis denounce and sometimes disrupt rituals at the graves of local Sufi saints. In doing this, they hearken back, like Salafis everywhere, to their own constructed vision of the authentic practices of the Prophet's companions, which, they argue, have been corrupted over time. But unlike other Muslim movements of similar orientation, such as the Muslim Brotherhood, Wahhabis in Yemen do not emphasize charitable activities, the use of technology, education, or scriptural interpretation. Contemporary Sufi orders, on the other hand, maintain Sufi rituals but downplay its mystical theology, stressing instead the continuity of their local history, in contrast to that of the Salafis. They claim that their tradition is not ruptured from the immediate past but, rather, maintains an unbroken line of authentic tradition stretching through previous generations to the first Muslims, a different way of claiming authentic historical practice. They criticize the Salafis as being foreign inspired and focus on the legacy of charity and outreach work of local Sufi families, using to that end all the media technology and educational practices usually associated with modernists (Knysh 2001).

The constant crossing and transcending of boundaries and categories and the reformulation of Islamic culture in new forms by new populations occurs in official as well as unofficial institutions. In Egypt, and in most other countries in the region, Islam is the official religion of the state. This means that Middle Eastern governments take responsibility for basic Islamic education, the maintenance of some portion of the countries' mosques, the employment of preachers, and the administration of financial structures that support religious causes. Until the late nineteenth century, this was very rare in the states of the region. Traditionally, mosques, shrines, *madrasa*s, and charitable organizations in the Middle East had been supported by private endowments called *waqf*. These were tax-exempt bequests of land or other wealth for the support of religious institutions, usually administered by members of the family who donated them. Religious scholars made their livings variously as teachers, scribes, Qur'an reciters, or *mufti*s. Over the course of the nineteenth and twentieth centuries, most Middle Eastern governments have encroached on this "private sector" of religious institutions and taken over the responsibility of administering *waqf* properties and the institutions, individuals, and activities they fund. Because of governments' new roles in relation to the regulation of religion and society, conflicts of political interest expose them to sharp criticism by Muslims who oppose particular policies or practices perceived as being un-Islamic. Popular targets of such critiques include the governmental sanction of such things as the availability of alcohol, sexual content in the media, reform of divorce laws, or treaties with countries that abuse local Muslims.

Significantly, such criticisms often come from the state's own religious personnel as well as from independent organizations and individuals. Some of Egypt's state-trained religious scholars ally themselves with the Muslim Brotherhood or, occasionally, even with small splinter militant groups. Shaykh Umar Abd al-Rahman, currently in a Minnesota prison for conspiracy in the 1993 World Trade Center bombing case, is one such example. The independence of Egypt's judiciary allowed for Islamist judges to gain considerable influence in guiding cultural and political policy in disputes between secularist and Islamist groups. Ironically, the century-long process of enhancing programs of religious education in government-funded public schools and the more recent efforts of states to respond to Islamist challenges with religious propaganda of their own have increased rather than diminished the tendency of major political groups to promote their positions in Islamic terms. Particularly where there is social fragmentation due to tribal differences, such as in Jordan or Yemen, or sustained geographical mobility in the form of refugees or populations relocated in programs of urban renewal, other sorts of social and cultural identities have had trouble taking hold. Islam thus becomes a common language of protest and political mobilization for a broad range of groups.

This is even true of Turkey's continued use of both Muslim ethnic identity and political secularism in the construction and maintenance of its modern national identity. For decades, the country has experienced periods of democratization punctuated by military coups as the army responds to perceived threats from communist or Islamist sources. As far back as the 1950s, though, the government began to reintroduce religious studies to secular schools, and it later allowed the rapid expansion of a parallel set of religious schools known as Imam-Hatip institutions. In the 1970s, anticommunist concerns led the government to support Islamic organizations, and the market-oriented reforms of the 1980s saw politicians realizing that "state planning of religious and moral life was . . . the prerequisite for promoting a national culture that could secure unity of purpose and homogeneity of ideas" (Sakallioglu 1996, 245). In 1991, General Kenan Evren, president of the Turkish Republic from 1982 to 1989, explained the reasoning behind the state's interest in religious education:

> [R]eligious education cannot be given to children by every family. In fact, even if the family tried to do so, this would be improper since it may be taught wrongly, incompletely or through the family's own point of view. I asked you before not to send your children to illegal Qur'anic courses. Thus, we made this a provision of the constitution. In this way, religion will be taught to our children by the state in state schools. Are we now against the cause of secularism or serving it? Of course we are serving it. Secularism does not mean depriving Turkish citizens of reli-

gious instruction and exposing them to exploiters of religion. (Quoted in Sakallioglu 1996, 246).

By the 1990s, a new Islamic force had successfully entered Turkish politics. The Refah (Welfare) Party, founded in 1983, gained enough electoral strength to win the plurality of votes in general elections in 1995, allowing a coalition government that, for the first time, placed an Islamic activist, Necmettin Erbekan, in the prime minister's office. The party was abolished by the Turkish courts in 1998 as an illegitimate intrusion of religion into politics, but its victories were part of a long-term change in the basis of support for Islamic politics. As Turkey's economy has globalized, its earlier-established political and economic elites have lost ground relative to the small entrepreneurs, professionals, and new urban workers who have no links or loyalty to standing power structures (Gulalp 2001). These groups have tended to support the Welfare Party and its successor, the Virtue Party, in part because of its Islamic message, but also in part due to these parties' skillful use of newly deregulated television markets and other mass media. Working with a professional marketing firm, they portrayed themselves in campaign advertisements as modern, broad-based, issue-oriented movements seeking unity in diversity and justice in an atmosphere of economic exploitation and corruption (Oncu 1995).

But the Welfare Party's victory hardened the secular establishment's resistance to the growing public interest in discussing contemporary social issues in Islamic terms. When a number of young female Turkish medical students wore scarves on their hair to examinations in January 1998, they were turned away and prevented from attending further classes. The rector of Istanbul University reiterated its long-standing ban on head scarves for women, and an economics professor and administrator of the university remarked, "The head scarf is a symbol which represents an ideology. . . . Many people who like to see the scarves would also like to see a regime like the one in Iran. That suggests a totalitarian approach which does not recognize any alternative" (quoted in Kinzer 1998). The university's own restriction on choice is intended to mark the line between legitimate and illegitimate religious activity in a country that tries ever harder to merge political secularism with its heritage as the last caliphal state of Islam (Kaplan 2002). In an age where individual participation in the interpretation of history, scripture, and identity is becoming ever more important, the drawing of these sorts of official lines becomes increasingly difficult.

In a broader sense, the drawing of any sorts of lines at all, any way to distinguish between authentic values and counterfeit ones, is beginning to seem like a utopian dream. Karl Marx's characterization of the modern world as one in which "all that is solid melts into air" has never seemed more appropriate than now. The conceptual lines between technology, science, religion, and politics are fading quickly as Muslim intellectuals and businesspeople use the Internet, satellite broadcasting, book publishing, and other modern media as never before. What does it mean to have the pan-Islamic, anti-imperialist ideology of Jamal al-Din disseminated with technologies and organizational forms invented and developed in the West? In the contemporary environment, who can authoritatively speak for the Islamic heritage? How can Muslims sort out the ravings of technically proficient lunatics or self-aggrandizing powermongers from the considered opinions of people who understand the complexities of scripture and history? Who can we, as outsiders, trust to tell us what Islam is really about?

Such questions are important not only in the abstract. They can have literally life-and-death consequences for Muslims and non-Muslims alike. Although there have always been local and national political leaders around the world ready to use religious ideas and religious institutions to further their own goals, the globalization of media means that we confront them far more often and far more immediately than we used to. Protestant mobs attack Roman Catholic schoolgirls in Northern Ireland; Hindus burn mosques in India; Serbs rape and murder Croats and Muslims in Sarajevo. Even before Osama bin Laden drew the world's attention as the patron of the events of September 11, 2001, he alarmed many Muslims and non-Muslims by deploying his light smattering of Islamic education to issue statements he claimed were *fatwas*, or rulings on points of Islamic law. These often took the form of political proclamations rather than informed judgments, such as his 1998 declaration that "[t]he ruling to kill Americans and their allies—civilian and military—is an individual duty for every Muslim who can do it in any country in which it is possible to do it, in order to liberate the al-Aqsa Mosque and the holy mosque [Mecca] from their grip" (Bin Laden 1998).

Bin Laden has an undergraduate degree in civil engineering rather than in religious sciences, although he has taken for himself the title *"shaykh."* Throughout the Middle East, actual *muftis*—men who are judged by their instructors and peers to be competent to issue Islamic legal opinions—have any number of views on the matter, but most disagree with the main lines of bin Laden's statement. On September 13, 2001, Shaykh Yusuf al-Qardawi wrote in response to the World Trade Center destruction that "Islam, the religion of tolerance, holds the human soul in high esteem and considers the attack against innocent human beings a grave sin. . . . I categorically go against a committed Muslim's embarking on such attacks. Islam never allows a Muslim to kill the innocent and the helpless" (quoted on U.S. Department of State Office of International Information Programs Web site). And the next day, the head of al-Azhar University in Egypt and the country's former official *mufti*, Shaykh Muhammad Sayyid al-Tantawi, told Agence-France Presse that "[a]ttacking innocent people is not courageous; it is stupid and will be punished on the day of judgment. It's not courageous to attack innocent children, women, and civilians. It is courageous to protect freedom; it is courageous to defend oneself and not to attack" (ibid.).

Endless contemporary examples of the polyvocality of Islamic law could be cited. Does Islam, traditionally suspicious of representational art, allow photography? Some scholars see no problem; after all, everybody needs an ID card. But others class it with the evil of idol-worship. Music? Some say the Prophet forbade it; others merely see it as frivolous; others even support it as a means of *da'wa*. Democracy? Some claim that it misappropriates legislative power from God; others see the Qur'an and the *sunna* approving it in the form of consultation between ruler and ruled and decisionmaking through community consensus, on the model of the activities of the Prophet's early companions. But neither the continuity of Islamic scholarship—nor the rather different tradition of wealthy warlords like Osama bin Laden claiming religious credentials—represents the main trend of change in Middle Eastern Islam.

The main trend of change is the expansion of education and the consequent entry of increasing numbers of citizens and subjects into informed discussion and debate of Islamic ideas and practices. In Egypt, the leftist physician Mustafa Mahmud rediscovered Islam in the late 1960s and gained a following over the succeeding decades by writing Qur'anic commentaries, novels, and articles blending Islam, science, and everyday experience. Since he has been the host of a television series called *Science and Faith,* his following has continued to grow, allowing him to found a large private mosque along with a clinic and other social service institutions in one of Cairo's western suburbs (Salvatore 2001). The Syrian civil engineer Muhammad Shahrur studied in both Moscow and Ireland before publishing, in 1990, a bestseller called *The Book and the Qur'an,* in which he reinterpreted sacred scripture without serious reference to the preceding fourteen centuries of scholarship, bypassing earlier work as irrelevant to the modern condition. In a more recent work, his *Islamist Charter,* Shahrur writes that

> Islam is a covenant between God and the whole of humanity, and . . . faith is a covenant between God and the believers who specifically follow Muhammad's prophecy. Hence we declare ourselves as Muslims first, and second as believers trusting in God, a conscious trust free from compulsion. This leads us to talk about freedom, knowledge, and legislation. No one has the right to claim a monopoly or exclusive possession of them, because these concepts belong to all the peoples of the world, and without them any given society would descend to the level of beasts. Hence what distinguishes human society is knowledge, legislation, ethics, [and] freedom as described in the Qur'an as viceregency and trust. All these are God's gifts to mankind. (Shahrur 2000)

What Mahmud and Shahrur have articulated in the contemporary Arab world, Bediuzzaman Said Nursi articulated some decades before in Turkey. As did Jamal al-Din and Muhammad Abduh before him, Nursi insisted on being able to read the sacred text with some flexibility of interpretation, and—vitally—he insisted on understanding the relationship of the text to the reader. "Since the Qur'an," he wrote, "proceeds from all-encompassing knowledge, all its [literal as well as allegorical] meanings may be intended. It cannot be restricted to one or two meanings like man's speech, the product of his limited mind and individual will" (quoted in Voll 1999, 255–256). In opposition to approaches that seek single and exclusively true interpretations of divine intent, this sort of approach emphasizes pluralism. For Shahrur as well,

> [c]hange and flux are . . . one of God's laws of nature. Human societies are evolving societies. From this derives the necessity constantly to reinterpret the legislative verses of the Qur'an in order to embody these principles as accurately as possible in reality.
>
> Since the interpretation of legislative verses and their application is a human activity, it is fallible and can only be relatively right. What is valid for one era may be irrelevant to another in spite of the fact that the sanctity of the legislative verses is eternal. For this reason, no human interpretation or practice ought to be accepted without discussion as it carries relative historical characteristics and will vary from one period to another, and differ from one society to another. (Shahrur 2000)

As a general philosophy of applying revelation to human life, this approach is not terribly different from either those of Muhammad Abduh in the nineteenth century or those of the original schools of legal thought developed during the eighth and ninth centuries, all of which faced the necessity of adapting existing knowledge to new circumstances. What is new is the issue of personnel.

In the twentieth and twenty-first centuries, the Middle East and the wider Islamic world are experiencing a reformation of thought and practice in which pious engineers, physicians, literature scholars, government employees, and others can bring to the public new insights, new questions, new issues, and new interpretations of their religious heritage. That this results in conflicts both physical and intellectual is not surprising. After all, the century after the Protestant Reformation in Europe was also a confused, troubled, and sometimes bloody time. But the widening of interpretive horizons and the growing participation of ordinary people in self-conscious discussions and negotiations over the meaning and significance of Islam in the modern world can bring convergences as well. Whether the future of Middle Eastern Islam belongs to those who believe democracy is a corrupt philosophy that marginalizes God or to those who see it, rather, as part of God's own plan for humanity, whether it belongs to women deepening their understanding and piety in study circles or to men who see their duty as bloody martyrdom, whether it belongs to Muhammad Shahrur or to Osama bin Laden, depends not just on indigenous events and currents of thought. It certainly depends very little on what the scriptures of Islam "really" say, since, even when people pay attention to scripture, the issue of their meaning is one of the major points of contention, just as it is for Christians, Jews, and adherents of other religious traditions. It depends, rather, on whether the international order becomes one of justice and respect or one of hypocrisy and exclusion, whether the global economy distributes wealth fairly or not, whether the wealthy and militarily powerful nations of the world encourage freedom and self-determination or support repressive political structures who traffic in class, gender, ethnic, or confessional repression. It depends on where all of us, regardless of our respective religious traditions or lack thereof, decide to guide this new century.

References

Abu-Amr, Ziad. 1994. *Islamic Fundamentalism in the West Bank and Gaza: Muslim Brotherhood and Islamic Jihad.* Bloomington: Indiana University Press.

Armbrust, Walter. 2002. "The Riddle of Ramadan: Media, Consumer Culture, and the 'Christmasization' of a Muslim Holiday." In *Everyday Life in the Muslim Middle East,* edited by Donna Lee Bowen and Evelyn Early, 335–348. Bloomington: Indiana University Press.

Bin Laden, Osama. 1998. "Jihad against Jews and Crusaders. World Islamic Front Statement." February 23. http://www.fas.org/irp/world/para/docs/980223-fatwa.htm.

Euben, Roxanne Leslie. 1999. *Enemy in the Mirror: Islamic Fundamentalism and the Limits of Modern Rationalism.* Princeton: Princeton University Press.

Fandy, Mamoun. 1999. "CyberResistance: Saudi Opposition between Globalization and Localization." *Comparative Studies in Society and History* 41, no. 1: 124–147.

Fortna, Benjamin C. 2000. "Islamic Morality in Late Ottoman 'Secular' Schools." *International Journal of Middle East Studies* 32, no. 3: 369–393.

Gulalp, Haldun. 2001. "Globalization and Political Islam: The Social Bases of Turkey's Welfare Party." *International Journal of Middle East Studies* 33, no. 3: 433–448.

Hamzeh, A. Nizar, and R. Hrair Dekmejian. 1996. "A Sufi Response to Political Islamism: Al-Ahbash of Lebanon." *International Journal of Middle East Studies* 28, no. 2: 217–229.

Hirschkind, Charles. 2001a. "Civic Virtue and Religious Reason: An Islamic Counterpublic." *Cultural Anthropology* 16, no. 1: 3–34.

———. 2001b. "The Ethics of Listening: Cassette-Sermon Audition in Contemporary Egypt." *American Ethnologist* 28, no. 3: 623–649.

Hoffman-Ladd, Valerie J. 1992. "Devotion to the Prophet and His Family in Egyptian Sufism." *International Journal of Middle East Studies* 24, no. 4: 615–637.

Hourani, Albert. 1983. *Arabic Thought in the Liberal Age: 1798–1939*. Cambridge: Cambridge University Press.

Kaplan, Sam. 2002. "Din-u Devlet All Over Again? The Politics of Military Secularism and Religious Militarism in Turkey following the 1980 Coup." *International Journal of Middle East Studies* 34, no. 1: 113–127.

Keddie, Nikki, ed. 1968. *An Islamic Response to Imperialism: Political and Religious Writings of Sayyid Jamal ad-Din "al-Afghani."* Berkeley and Los Angeles: University of California Press.

Kinzer, Stephen. 1998. "Culture Clash Flares Anew: Turkey Again Confronts Divide between Secularism, Religion." *Charlotte Observer,* March 18.

Knysh, Alexander. 2001. "The Tariqa on a Landcruiser: The Resurgence of Sufism in Yemen." *Middle East Journal* 55, no. 3: 399.

Langohr, Vickie. 2001. "Of Islamists and Ballot Boxes: Rethinking the Relationship between Islamisms and Electoral Politics." *International Journal of Middle East Studies* 33, no. 4: 591–610.

Lewis, Bernard. 1968. *The Emergence of Modern Turkey*. Oxford: Oxford University Press.

———. 1998. "License to Kill: Usama bin Ladin's Declaration of Jihad." *Foreign Affairs,* November/December.

Mahmood, Saba. 2001a. "Feminist Theory, Embodiment, and the Docile Agent: Some Reflections on the Egyptian Islamic Revival." *Cultural Anthropology* 16, no. 2: 202–236.

———. 2001b. "Rehearsed Spontaneity and the Conventionality of Ritual: Disciplines of Salat." *American Ethnologist* 28, no. 4: 827–853.

Messick, Brinkley. 1993. *The Calligraphic State: Textual Domination and History in a Muslim Society*. Berkeley and Los Angeles: University of California Press.

———. 1998. "Written Identities: Legal Subjects in an Islamic State." *History of Religions* 38, no. 1: 25–52.

Miller, W. Flagg. 2000. "Invention (Ibtidaa') or Convention (Ittibaa')? Islamist Cassettes and Tradition in Yemen." New Media and Information Technology in the Middle East Web site. http://www.georgetown.edu/research/arabtech/wp/papers/fmiller.htm.

Munson, Henry. 1993. *Religion and Power in Morocco*. New Haven: Yale University Press.

Oncu, Ayse. 1995. "Packaging Islam: Cultural Politics on the Landscape of Turkish Commercial Television." *Public Culture* 8, no. 1: 51–72.

Pound, Ezra. 1920. *Hugh Selwyn Mauberly*. London: Ovid Press.

Sakallioglu, Umit Cizre. 1996. "Parameters and Strategies of Islam-State Interaction in Republican Turkey." *International Journal of Middle East Studies* 28, no. 2: 231–251.

Salvatore, Armando. 2001. "Mustafa Mahmud: A Paradigm of Public Islamic Entrepreneurship?" In *Yearbook of the Sociology of Islam* 3, edited by Armando Salvatore. New Brunswick, NJ: Transaction Publishers.

Shahrur, Muhammad. 2000. "Islamist Charter: Proposal for an Islamic Covenant." Translated by Dale F. Eickelman and Ismail S. Abu Shehadeh. Islam 21 Web site. http://www.islam21.net/pages/charter/may–1.htm.

Starrett, Gregory. 1998. *Putting Islam to Work: Education, Politics, and Religious Transformation in Egypt*. Berkeley and Los Angeles: University of California Press.

U.S. Department of State. Office of International Information Programs. Web site http://usinfo.state.gov/products/pubs/terrornet/print/quotes.htm.

Voll, John O. 1999. "Renewal and Reformation in the Mid-Twentieth Century: Bediuzzaman Said Nursi and Religion in the 1950s." *Muslim World* 89, nos. 3–4: 245–259.

Wendell, Charles, trans. and ed. 1978. *Five Tracts of Hasan al-Banna (1906–1949)*. Berkeley and Los Angeles: University of California Press.

Wiktorowicz, Quintan. 2000. "The Salafi Movement in Jordan." *International Journal of Middle East Studies* 32, no. 2: 219–240.

Chapter Three

Shi'ite Islam in Contemporary Iran
From Islamic Revolution to Moderating Reform

DAVID BUCHMAN

Of the 66 million people in Iran today, in 2004, 98 percent are Muslims and of those 90.5 percent are Twelver Shi'ite (Held 2000, 488). Shi'ite teachings play a major role in peoples' actions and worldviews, but Iran is also a modern, industrialized nation, with an economy, polity, and educational system based upon Western models. In contemporary Iran, secular values, ideas, institutions, and behaviors mix with religion in sometimes paradoxical manners (Boroujerdi 2001, 13–17). The contentious interplay of these realities in the modern period has brought about increased politicization of religion in Iran. This chapter first presents an overview of basic Twelver Shi'ite beliefs and practices. Then it outlines the political history of the Shi'ite Muslim clergy in Iran, variously called *ulama, mullah, ruhani,* and *akhund.* During the modern period, the political function of the clergy increased from being merely critics or legitimizers of the monarchical governments to establishing and running an institutionally modern (Abrahamian 1994) but ideologically theocratic (Arjomand 2000) nation-state, the Islamic Republic of Iran, following the Iranian Revolution of 1979. Religious thinkers reinterpreted Islam in modern terms, giving rise to the clergy's increased politicization. Today, society and culture in the Islamic Republic of Iran is a conglomeration of both religious and secular ideas and institutions, run by a modern totalitarian state, which uses a radical political interpretation of Shi'ite Islam to legitimize its rule. However, recently a new generation of Iranian intellectuals is challenging the legitimacy of the state by reinterpreting Islam in even more modern terms than before.

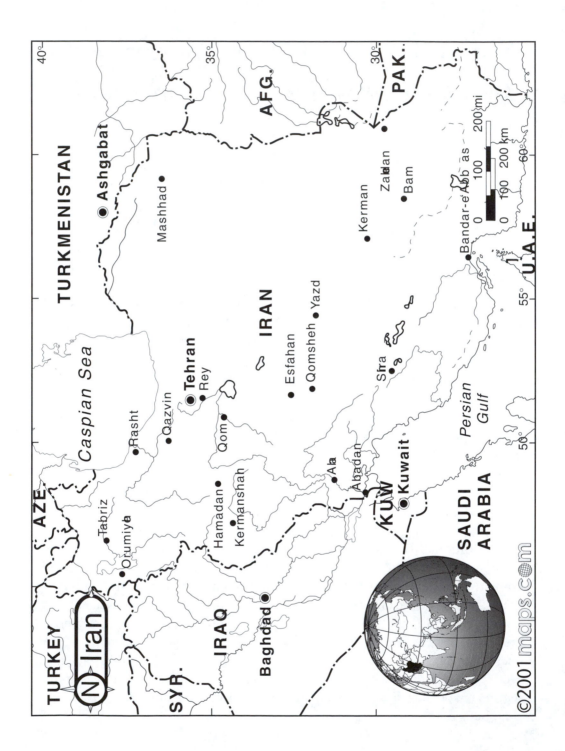

TURKEY

Iran

TURKMENISTAN

AZE.

Tabriz
Orumiye

SYR.

IRAQ

Baghdad

Caspian Sea

Rasht

Qazvin

Hamadan
Kermanshah

Tehran
Rey

Qom

Ahvaz
Abadan

KUW.
Kuwait

Ashgabat

Mashhad

IRAN

Esfahan

Qomsheh Yazd

Shiraz

Persian
Gulf

SAUDI
ARABIA

AFG.

Kerman

Zahedan

Bam

Bandar-e 'Abbas

U.A.E.

PAK.

200 mi

200 km
100
100

©2001 maps.com

Twelver Shi'ite History, Belief, and Popular Ritual Practice

The English words "Shi'ite," "Shi'ism," and "Shi'a" come from the Arabic *shi'atu Ali*, "partisans or party of Ali," the cousin and son-in-law of the Prophet Muhammad. Twelver *(ithna ashari)* and other forms of Shi'ism differ from Sunni Islam on the issue of the succession to Muhammad as leader of the Muslim community after his death in 632 C.E. The partisans of Ali argued that leadership of the Muslim community should go to a member of the family of the Prophet because they inherited from Muhammad special spiritual knowledge and abilities to help them to better lead the Muslim community. In the Shi'ite view, Ali was designated by the Prophet as his caliph, or successor, but this position was refuted by other Muslims, who argued that succession should be determined by the traditional *(sunni)* political method of consensus among the community's leaders. Ali eventually became the fourth caliph in 656 C.E., inheriting a position already saddled with great political and social problems, which eventually lead to his murder in 661 C.E. by disgruntled former supporters.

After Ali's death, his followers designated his progeny as the true caliphs and called them imams (from the Arabic *imam*, "leader"); in principle they are vested with both religious and political authority. The Twelver Shi'ites are so-called because they recognize a succession of twelve Imams who are regarded as sinless and infallible and so the only ones worthy to lead the community (Halm 1999). However, after Ali, none of these twelve Imams ever became political ruler of the Muslim empire. Instead, they kept to their own Shi'ite religious circles and taught those around them. In the struggles for leadership of the Muslim community after Ali's death, the political caliphate passed into the hands of Mu'awiya, the governor of Damascus, who established a hereditary dynasty from the Umayyad branch of the Quraysh tribe. He pensioned off Hasan, the second Shi'ite Imam (who retired in Medina), and made his own son Yazid caliph, so as to secure dynastic succession. Upon Hasan's death, his brother Husayn was recognized as the third Imam and was urged by his followers to retake the leadership of the community from Yazid. The Umayyad forces put an end to the revolt by killing Husayn and most of his family and supporters on the desert plain of Karbala, in Iraq.

Nine consecutive Imams came to head the Shi'ite community after Husayn's death. The sixth Imam, Ja'far Sadiq (d. 757), codified Twelver Shi'ite law and recommended that the Imam should be a religious teacher and not concern himself directly with running a government (Arjomand 1984, 34). The twelfth and last Imam entered a hidden state of existence called "occultation" in 939 C.E. This last Imam is believed by the Twelvers to be still alive and to appear secretly to select pious Muslims. This unseen dimension of the imamate has a cosmological function, for the twelfth Imam stands as an intermediary between God and the world, giving blessings to all (Tabataba'i 1977,

214). Twelvers believe that near the end of history, he will appear again as the Mahdi, the Rightly Guided One (*al-mahdi*), who is expected to return with Jesus to reestablish a just community, defeating the forces of evil and injustice that have taken over since the Prophet's death (Arjomand 1984, 39–40). For Twelver Shi'ites, the teachings of these twelve Imams are absolutely necessary to understand and follow Islam correctly. Both Sunni and Shi'ite Muslims follow the Qur'an and *hadith* of the Prophet, but Shi'ites add to these sources the teachings of the Imams, codified in special collections of their own *hadith* and books. While the twelfth Imam is hidden, the Shi'ite clerics, as will be discussed below, function to guide the people. But before discussing the clerics, a brief sketch of important Shi'ite rituals related to the Imams is necessary because these rituals are still carried out by Iranians today, and some of them have been manipulated by clerics for political ends.

Three major contemporary social Shi'ite rituals are found throughout Iran today: the annual passion plays *(taziyeh)* (Chelkowski 1979) reenacting Husayn's martyrdom; the frequent preaching on Husayn's character and significance for personal salvation after death; and the recurrent visitation to the tombs of the Imams and saints to ask for God's blessing and help. Husayn's death has cosmic, soteriological, and political significance for the Shi'ite community. Cosmically, his death is believed to have been foretold from all eternity, when before the creation of the world God gathered before him all the prophets and saints, asking who among them would be willing to drink the cup of sorrows of humanity's sins. Husayn drank down the whole cup, doing what the others were incapable of doing, and so God destined that Husayn would willingly face an unjust death at Karbala as a recompense for all people's sins. Having voluntarily sacrificed himself for others, Husayn earned the right to intercede to God on the Day of Judgment on behalf of anyone who has faith in his sacrifice (Ayoub 1978). Acknowledging this event means recognizing that although an injustice was done to Husayn, it was a necessary evil to allow purification of humanity's sins. On a more spiritual level, to remember what happened on the plain of Karbala is to be reminded of the personal injustice all Muslims do to themselves and each other by not following the teachings of the Qur'an, the *hadith,* and the Imams.

Remembrance of Karbala is a constant source of inspiration to strive to perfect one's sincerity in religion. In order to reinforce this motivation, rituals of remembrance developed, such as the *taziyeh,* or passion plays, of Husayn's martyrdom, which occur during the beginning of the Muslim month of Muharram, through the tenth day, Ashura. *Taziyeh* are performed throughout Iran, many times accompanied by parades. In the *taziyeh,* people are designated to play the various roles in a public forum, and sometimes the crowds become so excited that the man who plays the killer of Husayn must be protected from angry spectators. An especially poignant ritual during Ashura processions is

Shi'ite Muslims practicing self-flagellation as part of Muharram observances in Karbala, Iraq. (Getty Images)

the self-flagellation or beating done by groups of men and boys, who do this as a type of repentance for what happened to Husayn and, more important, for their own sins. Nowadays, the government discourages the more extreme forms of these acts, where actual blood is spilt. Aside from spectacular annual dramas, the events of Karbala are also remembered in sermons, which are given daily, weekly, and "on occasions of death memorials, religious commemorations, and communal gatherings" (Fischer 1980, 11) in homes, mosques, and other gathering places called Husayniya. Audiences sometimes shed tears, so as to share with Husayn his pain, repent from their own sins, increase sincerity in religion, and hopefully receive his intercession for salvation after death (Fischer 1980, 100).

Visitation to the tombs of saints and the Imams is another popular devotional activity. A pilgrim is someone who leaves the safety of home to travel to a sacred place, such as the tombs of the Imams. Pilgrimage purifies, brings the person closer to God, and achieves divine blessings. Many of the well-visited tombs of the Imams have become mosque and religious school complexes. The largest pilgrimage site in Iran is the tomb of the eighth Imam, Reza, the only one of the Twelve buried in Iran. The site is located in the northwest province of Khorasan, in Mashhad, a large, modern city with the tomb complex at its center. Tens of millions of pilgrims visit each year, and since the Revolution in 1979 this complex has grown tremendously, expanding to include schools, dozens of acres of beautifully tiled squares, a major library of Shi'ite studies, bookstores, and two large museums of art and cultural history. People from all segments of Iranian society visit the Mashhad site.[1] The area around the tomb has become a central tourist site, where people, when coming to visit the Imam, buy clothes, jewelry, and specialty foods as part of a vacation-pilgrimage. Hundreds of hotels do brisk business, especially during the summer pilgrimage season, when as promotions they provide their guests with gifts—prayer carpets, prayer stones, and rosaries with the hotel logo on the packaging—and supply small instructional books on how to properly visit the shrine, the history of Shi'ism, the life of Imam Reza, and the complex itself. Thus, a "sacred vacation" mixes together a family holiday atmosphere with the blessedness of the Imams. This mixing is embodied by the mile-long two-storied covered Reza Bazaar that stands right next to the shrine complex.

Public and Private Islam

Despite the widespread practice of these religious rituals, Iranians today are also very much affected by non-Islamic beliefs and practices. Like many Muslim countries that have modernized using European secular values and institutions as models, Iran, until the Revolution of 1979, had a diversity of religious and nonreligious ways of life derived from Western secular philosophies and Eastern religions in addition to Shi'ite Muslim worldviews. Since the Revolution, much of this multiplicity is still very much alive, but it has been greatly privatized and limited to people's homes, where the government control of the clerics cannot reach. For the past twenty-two years, the regime, as a modern totalitarian police state, has publicly enforced a single, extremist brand of Shi'ite Islamic law in the form of political ideology.

In Tehran nowadays we find a modern industrial society with stores, industries, occupations, and institutions like those in any contemporary European country, but with people in public behaving and dressing according to strict state codes of behavior. Inside people's homes, especially among young people, there is defiance against the regime-enforced public Islam, and so some people drink alcohol, watch satellite television with Western movies and programs, have Internet connections, dress in thoroughly Westernized fashions, enthusiastically discuss popular Western culture and music, and in general live a life that rejects the state's version of Islam (Yaghmaian 2002). Many Iranians love God, the Prophet, and the Imams but see that their government has failed to combine Islamic ideas and values with the realities of the modern world in a just, harmonious, peaceful, and loving way. They demand from the government moderating reforms, which conservative forces are currently doing their utmost to prevent.

The Clergy in Iranian Society

This unsatisfactory situation in Iran arose as a result of the increasing politicization of the clergy during the modern period, culminating in the maneuverings of a powerful cleric, Ayatollah Ruhollah Khomeini (d. 1989), who brought about the present Islamic Republic of Iran in 1979. To understand Islam in contemporary Iran necessitates retelling the story of the politicization of the clergy. The clerical class consists mostly of men educated in traditional schools *(madrasas),* whose primary pre-Revolution function was the nonpolitical role of transmitting all dimensions of Islamic teachings and practices to the less educated. About 140,000 people today have had some degree of *madrasa* training. The *madrasas'* curriculum focuses primarily on the field of Islamic law, but the fields of theology, philosophy, and mysticism may also be studied. Once male students reach a certain stage of learning, they may wear special clothes in public: a turban, cloak, and slippers. Clergy can be rich or poor, and many are dependent on alms for their livelihood. The poorer clergy could run mosques and traditional schools, taking fees for teaching and preaching. Others could have great wealth, through owning businesses and land. Since the Revolution, about 10,000 clergy are employed in all sorts of government positions, holding the power and drawing the wealth that such occupations offer.

In pre-Revolution Iran, no single person, school—whether physical or intellectual—or institution controlled what type of Twelver Shi'ism was taught and lived. Thus, no single person had the religious and temporal authority to speak definitively on and enforce such matters. Rather, rich debate and dialogue coupled with grassroots consensus among learned and laity determined the types of Islamic beliefs and practices of the community. The premodern governments of Iran did not enforce Islamic law. Because Islamic law is actually ethics and morality coupled with a desire for innate sincerity to submit to God, as well as a means of regulating interpersonal behavior within the community, the people themselves, in the form of families and neighborhoods, saw to it that the law was followed; the clerics gained their authority not through political means but because as a collectivity, they spoke for the Imam while he was in occultation. However, a cleric could gain greater moral authority than other clerics by becoming a *marja-e taqlid,* literally, "source of emulation," embodying a living source of Islamic law. The concept of following a living cleric derived from the unique interpretation of Islamic law found only in Twelver Shi'ism. Shi'ites follow the rulings of a living expert on law, called a *mujtahid* (literally, "someone who has struggled" in learning and piety), some of whose reputations were so great they become *marja-e taqlids.*

This notion of *mujtahid* developed out of Shi'ite scholarly debates in the seventeenth through nineteenth centuries over the role of the clergy in propagating and interpreting religious teachings. On the one side were the Akhbaris, who argued that the role of the clergy was to memorize and transmit the *akhbar,* "news" or teachings, of the Imams and the Prophet, not to come up with new teachings. On the other side were the Osulis, who argued that through using the *usul,* "roots" or principles, derived from what the Prophet and the Imams had said and done, and through *ijtihad,* literally "self-struggle," people could come up with new rulings and so could act on behalf of the Hidden Imam. The Osulis argued not that every ruling of a *mujtahid* (one who is qualified to do *ijtihad*) was a valid interpretation of what the Hidden Imam would say but, rather, that in general, all the *mujtahid*s as a collective group could potentially make decisions as representatives of the Imam (see Arjomand 2000, 13–14; Fischer 1980, 30). Another title of more recent origin is *ayatollah,* literally "signs of God," which is a term of respect given usually, but not all the time, to a cleric of *mujtahid* standing. They are so named because through their teachings and practices such people make knowledge of God apparent to others. Unfortunately, as *marja-e taqlid*s die today, fewer and fewer individuals qualify to take over their positions.

Politics and the Twelver Clergy

Twelver clergy first appeared in Iran in the sixteenth century when the Safavid dynasty (1501–1722) made the Twelver form of Islam the new state religion. Before that time, people in the region were Sunni Muslims or non-Twelver Shi'ites. By the end of the Safavid period, most of the Twelver Shi'ite clergy had become a distinct social class, albeit one with little economic or political autonomy from the Safavid kings, who supported them. The next major dynasty to appear after the fall of the Safavids and a period of disunity were the Qajars. During the Qajar dynasty (1797–1925), the clergy obtained the right to own land and an increasingly institutionalized control over special tax revenues. This control enabled them to gain greater economic and political autonomy from the monarchy, which complemented their moral authority among the population. As a result of these developments, the clerics eventually came to play a check-and-balance role on the authorities of the Qajar state: When a king was unjust, leading clergy would admonish him; when just, the clergy would legitimize his rule as being properly Islamic. Despite the common perception nowadays that Islam is applicable to all aspects of life, there tended to be a de facto separation between the religious clergy and the secularly oriented monarchical government in the premodern period (Arjomand 1984, 36). The monarchs ruled politically; the clerics, religiously; and both waited for the return of the Hidden Imam, in whose hands both political and religious leadership would once again be united.

The balance between clerical religious power and governmental political power began to break down in the nineteenth and twentieth centuries as a consequence of European imperial interests in the region. By combining the economic and political might wrought by the Industrial Revolution with the bureaucratic structure of the modern nation-state, the European powers and Russia became imperialists, seeking raw goods and markets within the Iranian world. The Qajars lost land to Russia, and lucrative concessions were given to Western European interests, such as the exclusive right to grow and sell to-bacco in Iran, a privilege that hurt local peasants and landowners. The clerics moved to check this injustice in what is now called the Tobacco Protest of 1891–1892. They used their religious influence and ruled that smoking to-bacco was against Islamic law, thus leading the way for a general boycott and opposition to the product, which eventually ended the concession.

As the twentieth century progressed and imperial interference increased in Iran, clerical protests and checks were no longer adequate to curb Qajar cor-ruption and European influence. In response to these conditions, Western-educated Iranians realized that to fight this trend, a new type of political con-sciousness, also taken from Europe, should arise: a national government based upon a constitution. The clergy tended to be the most expedient social class around which to rally nascent nationalist tendencies. Although the populace did feel culturally Iranian, this cultural ethnic identity did not directly lead to collective state political action. Whether wealthy merchant or poor peasant, all saw themselves as Twelver Shi'ite Muslim, so Islam became the central ideas and its representatives, the clergy, became the central class behind which a na-tionalist collective feeling in the modern sense arose to curtail Qajar misrule and end Western imperialism.

In these contexts, Shi'ite teachings were reinterpreted by the clerical class in contemporary political terms to be used as powerful social-binding metaphors to protest against the Qajars. Semisecret societies arose proposing liberal nationalist reform, claiming religious legitimacy by stating that Imam Husayn had set the precedent by forming such groups himself. The political rhetoric of the clergy followed the Shi'ite teachings on the usurpation of the caliphate, drawing upon symbolic language to call attention to unjust rulers oppressing sincere Muslim followers. But now, instead of being politically qui-etist, clerics demanded reform, just as Ali and Husayn had demanded reform of the Umayyads. Hence, "[s]ermons proclaimed the danger to Islam and compared the tyranny of the Qajars to that of the Umayyads, who had mar-tyred the Imam Husayn" (Esposito 1998, 84). What had before been a story about injustice to inwardly motivate individuals to be better Muslims was rein-terpreted as an agenda for social change. Just as the Umayyads were corrupt and needed Husayn to fight them, so also the Qajars were corrupt and needed to be fought against. Major protests arose against Qajar policy, riots broke out, the merchants closed downed their markets, and the clergy kept up their rhetoric at Friday sermons. When government forces came to apprehend the clergy and merchant leaders, thousands went to the mosques and the tombs of saints for sanctuary, thus politicizing what had before been places for more privately oriented personal spiritual growth.

The Constitutional Revolution

Eventually the Qajars agreed to establish a constitution based upon European constitutional monarchies, guaranteeing basic human rights through parliamentary legislation. This incident became known as the Constitutional Revolution of 1905–1911, and it was the first time the clergy were forced to confront issues of the compatibility between a modern secular democratic government and Islamic law (Dahlen 2002, 108). A National Consultative Assembly was established, made up of both laity and clergy, to determine and implement a constitutional system. A series of questions arose that Iranians today are still debating: How does a society of people who desire to follow Islamic law institute a modern nation-state based on the secular model of constitutional legislation? What role does Islamic law take in such institutionalization, and who has the authority to determine its rulings? If the clerics are to assume this degree of power, then how is their power to be checked? Is democracy as a modern form of political system compatible with the spirit and law of Islamic teachings? Can a Muslim society be governed by a democracy run by people who know little about Islam?

Two major points of view arose among clergy on the question of democracy as a form of government to run an Islamic society, yet many at that time did not actually understand the modern notions of democracy and so the arguments remained inconclusive (Martin 1989). Two well-known clerics took opposing sides. Shaykh Fadlullah Nur (1842–1909) said that a democratic constitution is an "innovation and down right aberration because in Islam no one is allowed to legislate"; only God had that privilege. Furthermore, he argued that "constitutionalism is against the religion of Islam. . . . It is not possible to bring this Islamic country under a constitutional regime except by abolishing Islam" (quoted in Esposito 1998, 88). However, other clergy saw that a constitutional monarchy could be the foundation of an Islamic society just as well as an absolutist monarchy could. Shaykh Muhammad Husayn Naini (1860–1936) argued that since the twelfth Imam is hidden, complete implementation of Islamic law is not possible. And since a constitutional monarchy prevents absolutist power, it is preferable as a check to the king's power. Nevertheless, he argued, this government should have an advisory assembly to make sure the laws implemented follow Islamic legal rulings (Esposito 1998, 89).

In earlier periods, these questions were not an issue because there was a clear separation between the religious teachings of the clerics and the political functions and actions of the monarchy. In the premodern system, the rule of Islamic law was local, and the clergy as a whole guided people religiously and provided checks to the monarch's power through their moral influence over the population. However, the governments of modern nation-states extend their control to take over and eliminate such systems of grassroots local rule. Unlike earlier states, whose power was checked by an autonomous class outside the government, a modern nation-state's all-encompassing rule has tended to internalize mechanisms of checks and balances. In some streams of modern Western political traditions, the solution to the problem of checking the state was to be found in a constitution that provided for three branches of a democratic government, the judicial, executive, and legislative, as checks to each other's power. However, in some Muslim societies, this model was complicated due to the issues relating to the authority of Islamic law. New questions arose in these contexts: Since the modern government is so all-encompassing, should it thus incorporate the enforcement of Islamic law? Or should there be a de facto separation, as was found in premodern polities? Is such a separation even possible? In the premodern system such a separation worked because low levels of technology and personal institutions prevented total state control over people's lives. However, with a modern nation-state that has fixed borders; all-encompassing, impersonal institutions; enforced law; and ability to control people's behavior, how is Islamic law to be implemented? Indeed, are "modern" state systems and Islamic law even compatible?

The Pahlavi Dynasty

After the Constitutional Revolution, due to fighting among the clergy and other groups over this and other issues, the government became impotent, and Russia and Great Britain stepped in and divided the country into two spheres of influence, Russian in the north, British in the south. For the next ten years, the Qajar constitutional monarchy was under Russian influence, and during this time various tribal factions were warring with each other throughout the country, and little centralized authority was in place. Iran's first experiment in Western democracy failed to either keep out imperial influence or prevent national divisiveness. These crises of centralized authority ended in 1921 when an Iranian military leader of the Russian Cossack Brigade, Reza Khan, seized power. Through a series of deft moves to gain control of the army and the sources of government wealth, he eventually had the Qajar dynasty ended by parliament in 1925 and had himself proclaimed shah (from the Persian for "king"), taking on a new name, Pahlavi, that was reminiscent of the pre-Islamic empire of Persia. Reza Shah Pahlavi had the support of many of the Constitutionalists, who saw that a strong monarch was the only way to unite the country. Reza Shah knew that the best way to consolidate his power was to win over the clerics, so he supported government-run religious rituals, met with many major *mujtahid*s to allay their fears that the government would become anti-Islamic, and in general promised that his rule would preserve "the principles of the religion and strengthen its foundations because [he] consider[ed] the complete reinforcing of religion one of the most effective means of achieving national unity and strengthening the spirituality of Iranian society" (speech by Reza Shah, quoted in Arjomand 2000, 62–63, 81).

However, after consolidating his power, Reza Shah began establishing modernized and secularized institutions that disenfranchised the clerical class. He took away the checks and balances the clerics had over his power by centralizing the government's control over clerical juridical and educational institutions and over the land trusts that were the source of the clergy's wealth. He also made secular education mandatory, making it difficult for clerics to teach in traditional schools, and he modernized the court system into a single, government-run system that ended separate clerical jurisdictions. Reza Shah's totalitarian policies prevented any political liberalization or local autonomy, which greatly upset both the secularist liberals and the Shi'ite clergy. During World War II, he also alienated the Allied powers, which removed him from command, replacing him with his twenty-two-year-old son, Muhammad Reza, who continued the earlier Westernizing, centralizing, and secularizing practices of his father.

In the 1950s, Muhammad Reza's policies of kowtowing to the demands of Great Britain and the United States made him lose favor among the clerical and merchant classes, paving the way for various groups to unite under a new party, the Nationalist Front, headed by Mohammad Mosaddeq. After coming to power as prime minister, Mosaddeq attempted to bring about major economic and political reforms that eventually exiled Muhammad Reza Shah and nationalized the lucrative monopolistic Iranian oil company, which up till then was run by the British. Mosaddeq's rise to power and reforms from 1950 to 1953 ended up scaring not only the West but also the clerics, because both feared that his socialist tendencies would give rise to Communist rule in Iran. The U.S. Central Intelligence Agency (CIA) maneuvered the overthrow of the Mosaddeq rule and returned the shah, much to the delight and support of various powerful ayatollahs (Arjomand 2000, 81), some of whom contended that rule by a king was more Islamic than rule by a socialist government or even a republic.

Upon his return to power, Muhammad Reza Shah continued to implement modernization policies in an absolutist manner, and he encouraged foreign, non-Muslim influences to enter into Iranian life. For example, his White Revolution of 1963 advocated modern programs for land reform and women's suffrage. The land reform once again threatened the clergy, who lost the land that supported their institutions, and many clerics saw women's suffrage as a means of destroying basic family structure, which is the basis of Muslim society. In reaction to the shah's policies, people who had never been political partners joined together against him. The "discontent with the fast pace of the modernization and imperial autocracy contributed to the expansion of a religio-cultural alliance of traditional religious leaders and lay intellectuals that had developed during the 1960s and 1970s" (Esposito 1998, 197). More important, the clerics "became irreconcilably alienated from the Pahlavi state" (Arjomand 2000, 81), and their growing popularity among the people kept increasing their political role as critics of the shah's government.

The Politicization of Modern Shi'ite Thought

The 1960s and 1970s saw the rise of many radical thinkers among both clergy and laity who reinterpreted Shi'ite Islamic teachings in light of modernity to challenge the policies of the shah. The most influential nonclerical thinker of this period was Ali Shariati (1933–1977), whose public lectures and published essays criticized the regime by using Islam as a political ideology to appeal to anti-shah, Western-educated religious individuals. Shariati was educated in Mashhad and Paris and was influenced by both Shi'ite thought and the ideas of Jean-Paul Sartre and Frantz Fanon. He reinterpreted Shi'ite teachings in political terms, using the thought of Karl Marx, mixing Islam with radical socialist notions of change, and saying that to be a Muslim means to revolt against a repressive regime (Shariati 1979, 1980; Dahlen 2002, 150). Shariati criticized the imperial influence of the Western nations in Iran, the Shi'ite clerical class's traditional quietism as well as outdated notions of religion and politics, and a purely secular lifestyle. His ultimate goal was not the traditional religious one of getting to heaven in the next world or of reaching inward perfection in this life but, rather, a social reform movement to create a "classless, repressionless, and antityrannical" religious society (Dabashi 1995, 66; see also Shariati 2000). Shariati's thought appealed to both the religious people, who wanted divine justification for rebellion, and the secular revolutionists, who saw the power of religion to motivate the masses for change. However, he never explicitly promoted the idea that the clergy should run the government.

The lay thinker Jalal Al-i Ahmad (1923–1969), Shariati's contemporary, was born into a clerical family. He is best known for making popular in his public lectures a Persian neologism, *gharbzadagi*, "plagued by the West" or "Occidentosis" (Al-i Ahmad 1984). This term came to symbolize the notion that Western technology, institutions, and values are a disease that Persian culture must slough off so as to create a better society for itself. Al-i Ahmad's ideas were not sociologically revolutionary, nor did they bring in religious ideas. Nevertheless, his phrase became a ubiquitous catchword among many of those discontented with the shah's policies.

Two other non-clerical thinkers were Sayyid Abdol-Hasan Bani Sadr (b. 1933) and Mehdi Bazargan (1907–1995). Bani Sadr added to the Islamic ideological rhetoric by discussing the economic problems of the country under the Pahlavi regime, using the theological idea of *tawhid,* "divine unity," to critique the already-established modern economy and then to create an "Islamic" one within it. Bazargan was an engineer whose political writings and teachings were inspired by those of Mohandas Gandhi's movement in India. He was a deputy prime minister in the Mosaddeq government in the early 1950s, founded the Freedom Movement of Iran in the 1960s, and was first interim prime minister after the Revolution. Bazargan maintained, as had Shariati, that clergy should be proactive in governmental change, and he wrote on the relationship between scientific investigation and Islam, arguing that Islamic ideas are thoroughly grounded in modern science (Dahlen 2002, 150–151; Esposito 1998, 200). Bazargan is noted for being among the earliest thinkers to employ the term "ideology" for Islam in the political sense, arguing that Islamic ideology is better than such secular ones as Marxism (Dahlen 2002, 151).

Although the teachings of Shariati and Bazargan enabled Iranians to reinterpret Shi'ite teachings in a distinctly modern manner in order to justify political action, it was the presence and teachings of Ayatollah Khomeini that became the main catalysts for the Revolution. Being much more learned in traditional Shi'ite thought than the secular thinkers, Khomeini was able to politicize Shi'ite teachings even more than Shariati was, justifying the creation of a theocratic clerical ruler with unlimited authority within a modern nation-state. Khomeini, a *marja-e taqlid* from Qom, was the most outspoken clerical critic of the shah's policies. In the early 1960s, he argued against the shah on three counts: (1) that he was an autocratic ruler, ignoring the people's true needs, (2) that he was a pawn of the West, having close ties to the United States, (3) and that he was corrupting the morality of the country through his secularizing laws (Arjomand 2000, 86). In 1964, Khomeini's followers staged massive demonstrations, which the shah brutally crushed, culminating in Khomeini's exile in 1964 to Iraq and later to Paris. From 1964 to 1979, Khomeini became the exiled religious spokesperson for the different anti-shah groups, providing Shi'ite legitimation for rebellion, revolution, and the creation of a modern state governed by Shi'ite clergy. In 1970, Khomeini wrote a book in Persian entitled *Velayat-e Faqih: Hokumat-e Islami* [The Guardianship of the Jurist: Islamic Government] (Khomeini 1978), in which he argued that since the twelfth Imam is hidden, only the clergy, by reason of their religious knowledge, are qualified to have direct governmental rule over the people, rather than serving as advisers to the rulers, as was the case in premodern forms of governments. This interpretation of *velayat-e faqih* was considered a radical reinterpretation, which later thinkers are now challenging (Sachedina 2001, 1988).

Other Shi'ite clerics also emerged during this time period, such as Murtaza Mutahhari (1920–1979) and Sayyid Mahmud Taleqani (1910–1979), who employed Shi'ite thought in their writings and sermons to overthrow the shah. Whereas Shariati was highly critical of certain clergy and mixed Marxist and Islamic ideas to legitimize social change, Mutahhari argued that Marxist and liberal ideologies were not needed to bring about transformation of society and that people must turn away from Western secular ideologies and look toward Islamic philosophy for inspiration on legitimizing social change (Mutahhari 1986). Taleqani, like Mutahhari, also battled Marxist and liberal ideologies, expressing his political message within his Qur'anic commentaries (Taleqani 1983). Both Taleqani and Mutahhari were influenced by the great Shi'ite cleric Allamah Tabataba'i (1903 or 1904–1980), who wrote seminal works in all areas of Muslim learning, especially philosophy and Qur'anic commentary. He was conversant with modern European philosophy and wrote a well-known book refuting the claims of Marx and Sartre, but through Islamic philosophical principles (Tabataba'i 1977, 24, 239). However, unlike Mutahhari and Taleqani, Tabataba'i remained apolitical in both his life and his writings.

The Revolution and Khomeini's Islamic Republic

The shah's poor economic and political policies, oppressive police force, weak leadership, and failing health combined with decreasing support from the United States to produce growing discontent in Iran during the 1970s. By January 1979, the political and religious climate in Iran reached a breaking point, culminating in the shah's departure. Within a month, Khomeini arrived in Tehran, after years of exile, inaugurating the Islamic or Iranian Revolution. Although Islam did play an important ideological role in the Revolution, many of its supporters within the intelligentsia had secular justifications for governmental change. In the spirit of Shariati and other lay thinkers' politico-Islamic ideological teachings combined with the religious figurehead of Khomeini, Iranians of all classes united to bring about the Revolution. Khomeini used deeply entrenched religious messages to justify his overthrow of the shah. Khomeini drew on the idea of the Hidden Imam returning to dethrone the unjust rulers of the world, and he came to be seen as the destroyer of evil and restorer of justice, paralleling the actions of the twelfth Imam.

After returning to Tehran, Khomeini used his moral authority to implement a new vision of government, and he eventually came to run the new government as an absolutist monarch. His revolutionary vision was not a religious "fundamentalist" return to premodern modes of government, nor did it reject modern technology and secular institutions. On the contrary, according to one observer, his political actions were similar to those of the secular leftist revolutionaries who led the modern populist revolts of recent South American history (Abrahamian 1993, 26–32). Khomeini, especially after writing *Velayat-e Faqih,* openly exploited class antagonisms in order to mobilize the poor and the oppressed to revolt against the oppressors, which came to include the shah, his supporters, and all foreign—especially Western—powers. Khomeini also made remarkable use of such modern technology as tape recorders to spread his message from exile to the people of Iran. His revolution was not to bring about total dissolution of class difference, as liberal Marxists hoped, or to install premodern institutions of rule and technologies, as some people might define a religious "fundamentalist" program. Rather, after the Revolution, he upheld class differences, utilized modern technology, and implemented even greater state control by expanding the secular institutions of government and economy created by the shah. Just as the leaders of certain successful, popularly supported revolts in South America ended up keeping the status quo as new dictators, so also Khomeini, after the departure of Muhammad Reza, became the latest despot, over a police state even more brutal than the shah's. Ostensibly, what made Khomeini's revolution Islamic was the modernized religious ideology that backed it, the installation of clergy in positions of power, and the enforcement of an extremist form of Islamic law, all of which were and continue to be contested by many Iranian intellectuals as measures that contradict the spirit and form of Muslim teachings.

It took a few years for Khomeini to eliminate the opposition and accomplish these tasks. During the first year of the Revolution, politically diverse parties hotly debated the role of Islamic teachings and the Shi'ite clergy in the new government. In 1979, a multiparty interim government composed of both lay and clerical members began the task of writing a constitution for the newly established Islamic Republic of Iran. The first draft of this document was based on European constitutions, which organized the government into legislative, executive, and juridical branches as checks and balances to power and provided for a democratically elected term president and parliament. Many people in the interim government, such as Bani Sadr and Prime Minister Bazargan, wanted a secular Iranian state based upon those of European nations, keeping clergy and most of the government separate (Sick 2001, 193). However, before the constitution was completely ratified, the clergy, with Khomeini's tacit approval, revised and added to the constitution articles 107–112 (Algar 1980, 66–69), giving the clergy enormous power based upon Khomeini's interpretation of *velayat-e faqih.* To the dismay of moderate clergy and secularists, two positions of authority were created: a supreme leader and a Guardian Council. The supreme leader is to be a cleric of the highest religious knowledge and impeccable character, a *marja-e taqlid;* he oversees the whole governmental process for life. His word is assumed to represent the will of the Hidden Imam and thus possesses potentially unlimited political and religious authority. The Guardian Council is also composed of clerics, whose main duty is to make sure that all branches of government follow their version of Islamic law. The juridical branch is also composed of clerics appointed by the supreme leader. This version of the constitution enables the clergy to control all three branches of the government, keeping the president and parliament subservient to clerical wishes. Hence, the government is both an absolutist theocracy and a democratic republic, with the former holding sway over the latter.

Khomeini combined the totalitarian nature of the modern nation-state with an extreme interpretation of the Shi'ite imamate. Many *mujtahid*s, such as the well-loved and respected *marja-e taqlid* Ayatollah Khoie (1899–1992), cited Khomeini's system as anti-Shi'ite (Sachedina 2001, 128). Opposition was ruthlessly persecuted into silence. During Khomeini's reign, tens of thousands of men and women, young and old, were imprisoned and executed, and many were tortured into giving public recantations of their beliefs, which were broadcast on radio and television (Abrahamian 1999). The regime's brutality was considered greater than that of the shah's government (Abrahamian 1999, 124–138, 167).

Khomeini was made supreme leader, and he ruled until his death in 1989. His word was broadcast as reflecting the will of the Hidden Imam. Indeed, he was referred to as "Imam"—an epithet only previously used for the Twelve Imams of early Shi'ite history. Observers now agree that the position of supreme leader as originally conceived was tailored for Khomeini, who was the only person with enough charisma to bring together the roles of *marja-e taqlid* and supreme executive leader of a modern state (Sachedina 2001, 142). Once the state was equated with religious authority, any person who argued against the government's interpretation of Islam—a process of debate that has been natural and endemic to Islam since its inception—was now considered an enemy of Islam and of God, and he or she could be imprisoned and killed with religious legitimation.

Khomeini's vision turned Iran into a police state run by conservative clergy and backed by a less educated and poorer class of people. The government entered into the private and personal lives of Iranians, destroying "all independent forms and institutions of social and cultural life" (Yaghmaian 2002, 143). Radio, television, and newspapers were directly controlled by the government. Iranians were forced to pray, dress, and act a certain way in public. For example, women were compelled to veil their hair and cover their bodies to their ankles and wrists with dark scarves and an overcoat. Men were allowed to wear loose fitting, dark-colored Western-style clothes that reached the ankles and wrists. They were greatly discouraged from wearing ties, which was a symbol of the West and its secular values, and so Western-style shirts were buttoned to the top. While women were allowed in public and held all the jobs they had before the revolution, unrelated men and women were forced to be segregated in most public circumstances, such as walking on the streets and riding buses and trains, which had special gender-divided sections (Esfandiari 2001).

The modern family laws and courts established in the shah's regime were abolished and replaced by those enforcing official government interpretations of Islamic law. Although at the beginning of the regime, the plan was to re-duce women's presence in the public sphere, this never happened, for women have successfully asserted their rights using Islamic teachings to challenge the state (Esfandiari 2001). In other areas, people were forced to pray and attend mosques during prayer time, music was prohibited, and even laughing in pub-lic was considered inappropriate Muslim behavior (Yaghmaian 2002, 49). To enforce these rules, people were harassed in public by local government "com-mittees," volunteer youth brigades, and the Revolutionary Guards, who roamed the streets on the lookout for deviants to punish. For example, unre-lated men and women walking on the street who were caught by these police would be brought before a judge to be married or to be punished by a fine, whipping, or a jail sentence.

Observers of Iranian politics and religion (Dahlen 2002; Abrahamian 1999) note ironically that in the Islamic Republic, the nature, use, and imple-mentation of Islamic law is more modern than traditional in its institutional form (see Arkoun 1994, 13). In premodern times, Islamic law was never en-forced by a state. Rather, it was practiced and mutually enforced by people on the local, face-to-face level of society (see Abou El Fadl 2001, 5–6). The im-personal state was responsible for protection from outside invaders and for peace within its borders, not for making those living within its borders follow any particular interpretation of Islamic law. Moreover, Islamic law was never legislated or produced in the modern sense that contemporary positive law is, and the clergy were not in the positions of political authorities or rulers. Rather, they were consulted by people when needed as cases arose. In con-trast to this, laws in modern states are codified statutes based upon positive law, determined by case studies and precedents that have a utilitarian func-tion in society. In traditional *ijtihad,* the clergy do not make rulings based upon statutes and codes or previous case studies, but they use certain princi-ples and analogies to come up with rulings for each case. As one observer notes, Islamic law in the premodern sense "is not considered to be legislated or produced but discovered, understood and formulated" (Dahlen 2002, 350). The Islamic Republic of Iran modernized Islamic law by codifying it and enforcing it by a state government, and so it was fixed in an artificial way for all, which goes against the traditional practice of local probity coupled with a diversity of rulings and dialogue with other clerics and the public. The Islamic Republic is thus in form actually a modern state with modern codes mandating an extreme version of Islamic law, not a return to a premodern "Islamic" form of government in a society of Muslims.

One might, then, wonder how it is that this repressive regime has managed to maintain power for more than two decades. One factor that helped Khomeini keep power was the almost immediate start of the Iran-Iraq War (1980–1988), which helped him rally nationalist support of some who would normally have rebelled. The war devastated families and towns, killing a million people and preventing economic growth, which called for immense sacrifices among the population. All of this kept the population too unnerved to fight the regime. The government used religious rhetoric to legitimize itself in the trying circumstances, likening the death of Iranian soldiers to Husayn's martyrdom, thus guaranteeing them Paradise. Khomeini also kept his power by promoting a rhetoric demonizing the West, which first started with the taking of the U.S. embassy hostages soon after the Revolution. Many of his advisers were perplexed and argued against this action because it would alienate a powerful country that otherwise might help the new government. Khomeini blamed the United States for many of the social, economic, moral, and political problems found in Iran. Iranians were still angry at the United States for having had the CIA reinstate the now-defeated shah, so Khomeini's rhetoric was quite appealing to the masses, who needed a new enemy and needed to stay focused on the Revolutionary program now that the shah was gone. By calling the United States the "Great Satan," Khomeini mixed politics and deeply held religious values and so prevented any dissenting moderate voices from arising. Both Bani Sadr and Bazargan were ousted from their positions because they did not agree with such a clergy-run government; they were accused of being sympathetic to the West and thus "demonic." Indeed, all Eastern and Western ideologies, even those, such as socialism and Marxism, that had helped in overthrowing the shah, were demonized by Khomeini and his regime as enemies of Islam. "Death to America" has thus been the slogan around which the Islamic Republic regime defines not only its foreign policy but also itself.

Reforming the Revolutionary Regime

As Khomeini's death approached and the Iran-Iraq War ended, the government realized that without their charismatic leader or the debilitating distraction of battle, people's support for the state might wane, especially under the poor economic conditions that plagued the postrevolutionary state. As a way to hold off such discontent, the government shifted its focus from implementation of ideological Islam to enacting pragmatic political, social, and economic reforms. They also rewrote the constitution to give the clerics even more power than before. Khomeini's charisma gave the office of supreme leader more power than was allocated in the constitution, so with his passing, the clergy saw themselves losing authority to people in the democratically elected positions. In 1988, these clergy and Khomeini amended the constitution, giving the position of supreme leader the de jure power that Khomeini held de facto. They abolished the position of prime minister, weakened the power of the president by giving presidential authority to the supreme leader, and lowered the religious qualifications required for clergy to be eligible for the position of supreme leader.

Upon Khomeini's death, a low-level cleric, Hojatolislam Khamenei, who was not a *marja-e taqlid,* was made supreme leader, and he remains so today. Some observers feel that he is a figurehead for the powerful conservative clergy on the Guardian Council. In 1989, a neoliberal, pragmatic economic policy was put in place by Khamenei and President Ali Akbar Hashemi Rafsanjani, then a cleric. Due to the war and the economic sanctions enforced by the United States after the hostage crisis, the economy was extremely weak, with many Iranians living below the poverty line. In order to boost the economy, reforms were implemented to free the financial system from state control: Laws allowing private ownership and foreign investments were passed, the local currency was floated on the free market, and people were encouraged to purchase commodities (Khajehpour 2001). Although the local "committees," which prowled the streets looking for people who broke the moral law, remained ubiquitous, some of the public restrictions, such as the prohibition of traditional music, were abolished. These reforms were not successful, and by the late 1990s, the discrepancy between rich and poor was even greater than it had been before. The value of local currency continued to decline, and personal, cultural, and political freedoms remained restricted (Yaghmaian 2002, 157).

Since the 1980s, Iranians have lived through a devastating war, a faltering economy, a repressive totalitarian regime, and the strictures of a state-sponsored religious extremism. A whole generation of disenfranchised youth—over 70 percent of the country is under thirty years old—have lived most of their lives under these conditions and are ready for moderating reforms, the end of the anti-West rhetoric, and greater political, religious, and social freedom (Yaghmaian 2002). These voices have voted into power moderate reformist clergy and lay parliamentarians. In 1997 and 2001, a moderate cleric and former minister of culture who promoted the growth of the arts and women's rights, Muhammad Khatami, received a landslide victory in the presidential election, mainly because of his promised reforms in both domestic and foreign policy. Khatami promoted the notion of "dialogue of civilizations" as a way to open the door to the alienated Western nations and also shrewdly argued against the "death to America" and anti-West rhetoric of the conservative powers in the government. He also reinterpreted dominant religious ideology—saying that "civil society," "democracy," "basic human rights," and "right of law" are all Islamic notions—and allowed reformist presses to be opened. At the same time, he increased government funding of artistic endeavors and curbed the state's control of people's behavior (see Khatami 1997, 1998). As a result, women do not veil as strictly as in the earlier years of the Islamic Republic, and unrelated men and women can walk together without fear of being jailed. People would like to see further changes and reforms to the government, such as a more balanced view of Islamic law and a lessening of the powers of the office of supreme leader and the Guardian Council. As for economic reform, people would like to see a restructuring of government policy on how wealth is spent so as to make it transparent to public scrutiny. Finally, a more open journalism, less state oppression and control, and an acceptance of certain aspects of Western culture would be welcomed. Many of Khatami's initial supporters feel he is not reforming the government quickly enough. The conservative forces within the government have put up obstacles to these reforms by closing down dozens of the presses, imprisoning antigovernment writers and reformist students who have staged public protests. Most recently, Supreme Leader Khamenei is trying to have the judiciary branch of the government make it illegal to promote reconciliation with the United States.

Under Khatami's administration, moderate thinkers have begun to appear, challenging the government by reinterpreting Islam once again. For example, one recently jailed cleric, Mohsen Kadivar, has published and given talks on varying interpretations of the central justification of the conservative branch of the government, *velayat-e faqih*. He has argued publicly what many other Iranians think privately, that the doctrine of *velayat-e faqih* does not necessarily entail direct governmental power for clergy. Rather, such a position should be supervisory, not executive, within a government. Because of the outspoken nature of this interpretation, which threatens the religious legitimacy of the current regime, Kadivar has been imprisoned. While Khatami implicitly agrees with Kadivar, Khamenei does not (Milani 2001, 48).

Since the late 1980s, Abdol Karim Soroush, a popular lay thinker, has been giving public talks and publishing writings radically reinterpreting the meaning of Islam in light of modern philosophical notions of rationalism and postmodern thought (Dahlen 2002). He argues that Islam is innately compatible with tolerance, pluralism, and democracy, and so his ideas have appealed to many who would like to see such political reform couched in Islamic terminology (Vakili 2001, 173–176). Soroush is conversant in and highly influenced by European philosophers, especially Immanuel Kant, and by traditional modes of *madrasa* knowledge, which includes Islamic law, philosophy, theology, and the spiritual teachings of the famous medieval Persian poet Jalal ad-Din Rumi. In 1997, Soroush left his teaching post because of threats of violence.

However, Soroush has not always been known as a "liberal." At the beginning of the Revolution, he was an important state ideologue, running the council that controlled Islamic pedagogy at universities, and so was responsible for much of the oppression and persecution of dissident student groups. After Khomeini's death, Soroush began to speak out against the state's absolutism in the interpretation of Islam and enforcement of religious law. Using modern notions of rationality, Soroush takes a radical stance, saying that Islamic law must be totally reformed because it is a relative affair dependent on the times, and not a timeless measure of God's will for ultimate human happiness. Using Kant's speculations on the use and power of reason, Soroush argues in his well-known work *The Contraction and Expansion of Religious Law* that traditional Muslim jurisprudence is a product of the times of the Prophet. Contemporary times are governed by a modern scientific, rational, and secular worldview and so have different social problems than those confronted by the earliest Muslim communities. In order to maintain its relevance, Islamic law must engage the issues of today and develop accordingly.

By saying that Islamic law as traditionally formulated is no longer valid for the modern world, Soroush does not disregard Islam altogether, but he does, instead, argue that religion in the modern world should be primarily a type of inward personal faith or spirituality divorced from law. Since he separates faith from premodern conceptions of religious law, he then argues that if Islam is inner faith, then enforcing a religious law will do nothing to build that inner faith, and so the actions of the Islamic Republic of Iran are philosophically and religiously wrong. Rather, Soroush argues that the best way to create a modern state that allows religion to flourish is through a democracy in which the people themselves use modern rational analysis to decide what their laws should be, and if enough people are religiously motivated in this, then they will all vote for a government that allows their faith to be cultivated and expressed in civil society (Vakili 2001, 155).

Soroush also argues that a state should not use ideology to make society religious, and so he distinguishes between an ideological society and a religious society, saying that

> [i]n an ideological society, the government ideologizes the society, whereas in religious societies, the society makes the government religious. In an ideological society, an official interpretation of ideology governs, but in a religious society, [there are] prevailing interpretations but no official interpretations. In an ideological society, the task of [the formulation of] ideology is relegated to the ideologues. In a religious society, however, the issue of religion is too great for it to be relegated solely to the hands of the official interpreters. In a religious society, no personality and no *fatwa* is beyond criticism. And no understanding of

Young Iranian women looking at election leaflets in front of Tehran University at the beginning of Friday prayers, February 2004. (Morteza Nikoubazl/Reuters/Corbis)

religion is considered the final or most complete understanding. (Quoted in Vakili 2001, 158)

This quotation, although apparently pro-religion, actually undermines the importance of a premodern notion of Islamic law from what one observer has called a postmodern perspective (Dahlen 2002). Postmodernism is a philosophical position that arose in Europe in the 1970s as a way of deconstructing theoretical systems to show that all so-called truths are actually relative to one's history and current sociocultural circumstances. This quotation reflects Soroush's postmodern interpretation of Islam, by saying that Islamic law is relative to the times and that no single conception of it is final or complete. According to this perspective, there are no "official interpreters" of Islam; all can participate in the process of redefining Islam in contemporary society. On the surface, this argument appears to follow the Osuli argument that all law must constantly be rethought and reformulated by qualified *mujtahid*s. However, unlike the traditional Osuli system, which argues that only a *mujtahid* is qualified, this "postmodernist" relativistic reading extends to include in these debates all people who can put forth a rational argument.

Soroush's ideas lessen the importance of the clergy as the legitimate representatives of Islam and puts religious interpretation into the hands of laity. Is a *mujtahid*'s legal opinion, based upon years of studying the religious texts, to be considered equal to that of a lay person, who may have only a cursory knowledge of such matters? In Soroush's system, it might very well be. Hence, Soroush has been called the Martin Luther of Islam (Soroush 2000, xv). Just as Luther challenged the legitimacy of the Catholic Church as the only representative of Christianity, so Soroush's ideas contest the authority of the clergy by arguing that *ijtihad* is an outdated mode of knowledge, based upon premodern modes of thinking no longer valid in today's rational world. As one observer notes, Soroush's philosophy, if implemented, would create a profoundly secular society, in which Islam would be a personal faith different for all and religious law would be a relative affair dependent upon democratic vote of diverse individuals (Dahlen 2002).

In the early twenty-first century, proclamations from the United States claim that Iran is among those nations promoting terrorism, and so is part of an "axis of evil." These statements surprise many Iranians, especially since President Khatami has made great overtures to the United States by opening up lines of communication, fostering progressive developments in cultural and academic fields, and condemning the tragedy of September 11, 2001, and the form of Islam promoted by the Taliban. In its provocative labeling of Iran as an abode of evil, the U.S. government appears to have overlooked some of the remarkable developments toward democratization in Iran during the 1990s. These remarks certainly ignore the fact that most Iranians have come to reject both terrorism and religious extremism. Many consider the Islamic revolutionary regime to have been both a religious and a political failure. The majority of the people in Iran want to reconcile Islam with the contemporary world outside the regime's extremist religious ideology and want to slough off such fanaticism and embrace a future in which they have greater freedom, justice, and prosperity than they do now.

Summary and Conclusions

The modern period in Iran has brought about an increased politicization of the Shi'ite clergy, which culminated in Khomeini's creating a totalitarian modern Islamic state whose institutional forms are derived from totalitarian secular nations. Even Iran's version of Islamic law is a modern form of state-enforced behavior that does not adhere to a traditional understanding of the *shari'a*. On a day-to-day basis, Iran has experienced the problem of Islam and modernity in intimate and, for many, frightening terms. Is Islam compatible with the modern world? Are the only answers to the mixing of modernity and Islam a political conundrum of a totalitarian theocratic "republic" of enforced extremist Islamic law or a paradoxically secularized democratic Islam, where everybody, regardless of religious qualifications, can give a respected opinion about law? Or is the answer to go back to the de facto check and balance of the separation of state and clergy?

Regardless of what the future holds for Islam in Iran, it is clear that due to the government's policies, Twelver Shi'ism has for some become a religion of wrath. As one former prisoner of the regime characterized it, "Islam is a religion of care, compassion, and forgiveness. This regime makes it a religion of destruction, death, and torture" (Abrahamian 1999, 140). When I asked people in Tehran about the difference in religious practice and inward sincerity and faith before and after the Revolution, one person replied, "Before the revolution, we would go out, drink, not follow the law, and then we would come home, close all the shades, repent and do our prayers. Nowadays, when we go out, we don't drink, but are forced to pray, and then when we come home, we close our shades and then drink." Or as another said, "Many people stopped doing their prayers when the truth of this government came to light."

Nevertheless, the love and devotion that Iranians have for God, his Prophet, and his Imams are still extremely strong and are not likely to diminish anytime soon. Islam in Iran today is a living, vibrant faith. Whether established through a totalitarian regime, in the heart of a sincere, crying repentant at a *taziyeh,* or by a postmodern interpreter, the many forms of Shi'ite Islam remain a powerful, deep, and seminal reality in the lives of the people of Iran as they continue to struggle with how to live as sincere Muslims in a secularized contemporary world suffused with tremendous social, political, and economic problems.

Notes

1. These observations on the Imam Reza complex are based upon research that I carried out in Iran for five weeks during the summer of 2000.

References

Abou El Fadl, Khaled. 2001. *Speaking in God's Name: Islamic Law, Authority, and Women.* Oxford: Oneworld Publications.

Abrahamian, Ervand. 1993. *Khomeinism: Essays on the Islamic Republic.* Berkeley and Los Angeles: University of California Press.

———. 1999. *Tortured Confessions: Prisons and Public Recantations in Modern Iran.* Berkeley and Los Angeles: University of California Press.

Algar, Hamid. 1980. *Translation from the Persian of Constitution of the Islamic Republic of Iran.* Berkeley, CA: Mizan Press.

Al-i Ahmad, Jalal. 1984. *Occidentosis: A Plague from the West.* Translated by R. Campbell. Berkeley, CA: Mizan Press.

Arjomand, Said Amir. 1984. *The Shadow of God and the Hidden Imam: Religion, Political Order, and Societal Change in Shi'ite Iran from the Beginning to 1890.* Chicago: University of Chicago Press.

———. 2000. *The Turban for the Crown: The Islamic Revolution in Iran.* Bridgewater, NJ: Replica Books. Originally, Oxford: Oxford University Press, 1988.

Arkoun, Mohammed. 1994. *Rethinking Islam: Common Questions, Uncommon Answers.* Translated and edited by Robert D. Lee. Boulder, CO: Westview Press.

Ayoub, Mahmoud. 1978. *Redemptive Suffering in Islam: A Study of the Devotional Aspects of Ashura in Twelver Shi'ism.* The Hague: Mouton.

Boroujerdi, Mehrzad. 2001. "The Paradoxes of Politics in Postrevolutionary Iran." In *Iran at the Crossroads,* edited by John L. Esposito and R. K. Ramazani, 13–28. New York: Palgrave.

Chelkowski, Peter, ed. 1979. *Ta'ziyeh: Ritual and Drama in Iran.* New York: New York University Press.

Dabashi, Hamid. 1995. "Shi'i Islam." In *The Oxford Encyclopedia of the Modern Islamic World.* Vol. 4: 55–68. New York: Oxford University Press.

Dahlen, Ashk. 2002. *Deciphering the Meaning of the Revealed Law: The Surushian Paradigm in Shi'i Epistemology.* Acta Universitatis Upsaliensis. Studia Iranica Upsaliensia 5. Uppsala, Sweden: Uppsala University Library.

Esfandiari, Haleh. 2001. "The Politics of the 'Women's Question' in the Islamic Republic, 1979–1999." In *Iran at the Crossroads,* edited by John L. Esposito and R. K. Ramazani, 75–92. New York: Palgrave.

Esposito, John L. 1998. *Islam and Politics.* 4th ed. Syracuse, NY: Syracuse University Press.

Fischer, Michael M. J. 1980. *Iran: From Religious Dispute to Revolution.* Cambridge, MA: Harvard University Press.

Halm, Heinz. 1999. *Shi'a Islam: From Religion to Revolution.* Translated from the German by Allison Brown. Princeton: Markus Wiener Publishers.

Held, Colbert C. 2000. *Middle East Patterns: Places, Peoples, and Politics.* 3rd ed. Boulder, CO: Westview Press.

Huntington, Samuel P. 1996. *The Clash of Civilizations and the Remaking of World Order.* New York: Touchstone Books.

Jahanbakhsh, Forough. 2001. *Islam, Democracy, and Religious Modernism in Iran (1953–2000): From Bazargan to Soroush.* Leiden: Brill.

Khajehpour, Bijan. 2001. "Iran's Economy: Twenty Years after the Revolution." In *Iran at the Crossroads,* edited by John L. Esposito and R. K. Ramazani, 93–122. New York: Palgrave.

Khatami, Mohammad. 1997. *Hope and Challenge: The Iranian President Speaks.* Binghamton, NY: Institute of Global Cultural Studies. Binghamton University.

———. 1998. *Islam, Liberty, and Development.* Binghamton, NY: Institute of Global Cultural Studies. Binghamton University.

Khomeini, R. 1978. *Velayat-e Faqih: Hokumat-e Islami* [The Guardianship of the Jurist: Islamic Government]. Tehran.

Loeffler, Reinhold. 1988. *Islam in Practice: Religious Beliefs in a Persian Village.* Albany: State University of New York Press.

Martin, Vanessa. 1989. *Islam and Modernism: The Iranian Revolution of 1906.* London: Tauris.

———. 2000. *Creating an Islamic State: Khomeini and the Making of a New Iran.* London: Tauris.

Milani, Mohsen M. 2001. "Reform and Resistance in the Islamic Republic of Iran." In *Iran at the Crossroads,* edited by John L. Esposito and R. K. Ramazani, 29–58. New York: Palgrave.

Mutahhari, Ayatullah Murtaza. 1986. *Social and Historical Change: An Islamic Perspective.* Translated from the Persian by R. Campbell. Berkeley, CA: Mizan Press.

Sachedina, Abdulaziz. 1988. *The Just Ruler in Shi'ite Islam: The Comprehensive Authority of the Jurist in Imamite Jurisprudence.* New York: Oxford University Press.

———. 2001. "The Rule of the Religious Jurist in Iran." In *Iran at the Crossroads,* edited by John L. Esposito and R. K. Ramazani, 123–148. New York: Palgrave.

Shariati, Ali. 1979. *On the Sociology of Religion: Lectures by Ali Shariati.* Translated from the Persian by Hamid Algar. Berkeley, CA: Mizan Press.

———. 1980. *Marxism and Other Western Fallacies: An Islamic Critique.* Translated by R. Campbell. Berkeley, CA: Mizan Press.

———. 2000. *Religion vs. Religion.* Chicago: Kazi Publications.

Sick, Gary. 2001. "The Clouded Mirror: The United States and Iran, 1979–1999." In *Iran at the Crossroads,* edited by John L. Esposito and R. K. Ramazani, 191–210. New York: Palgrave.

Soroush, Abdolkarim. 2000. *Reason, Freedom, and Democracy in Islam: Essential Writings of 'Abdolkarim Soroush.* Translated, edited, and with a critical introduction by Mahmoud Sadri and Ahmad Sadri. New York: Oxford University Press.

Tabataba'i, Allamah Sayyid Muhammad Husayn. 1977. *Shi'ite Islam.* Translated from the Persian, edited, and with an introduction and notes by Seyyed Hossein Nasr. 2d ed. Albany: State University of New York Press.

Taleqani, Seyyed Mahmood. 1983. *Islam and Ownership.* Translated from the Persian by Ahmad Jabbari and Farhang Rajaee. Lexington, KY: Mazda Press.

Vakili, Valla. 2001. "Abdolkarim Soroush and Critical Discourse in Iran." In *Makers of Contemporary Islam,* edited by John L. Esposito and John O. Voll, 150–176. New York: Oxford University Press.

Yaghmaian, Behzad. 2002. *Social Change in Iran: An Eyewitness Account of Dissent, Defiance, and New Movements for Rights.* Albany: State University of New York Press.

Chapter Four

Debating Orthodoxy, Contesting Tradition

Islam in Contemporary South Asia

ROBERT ROZEHNAL

In the aftermath of September 11, 2001, Islam has fallen under an intense and unrelenting mass media spotlight. Newspapers, television, and cyberspace inundate us with a daily stream of images, arguments, and innuendo. Much of this information views religion through the prism of ideology, blurring the boundaries between piety and politics. With rare exceptions, the modern Muslim world is portrayed as a fossilized monolith: Arab, patriarchal, rigid, violent, and utterly at odds with modernity. As the chapters in this volume illustrate, however, contemporary Islam is simply not so easy to encapsulate; its complexity belies reductive stereotypes and sound-bite summaries. A study of history shows that Muslims have always evolved with the times, evoking remarkably different beliefs, practices, and cultural symbols in response to changing local realities. From Morocco to Indonesia to the United States, Islam is as diverse and dynamic as the cultural continuum it inhabits. In pursuit of a more nuanced understanding of Islam's place in today's world order, therefore, we need to get beyond politics and polemics to explore the tradition as a lived religious encounter, rooted in a sacred past, inscribed in texts and embodied in ritual practices within localized contexts. In few places is the Muslim world's heterogeneity more apparent than in its contemporary demographic center, South Asia.

The Legacy of Partition

Islam today has a global reach, but above all it is a pan-Asian religion centered in South Asia. At first, this may seem paradoxical. It certainly challenges the

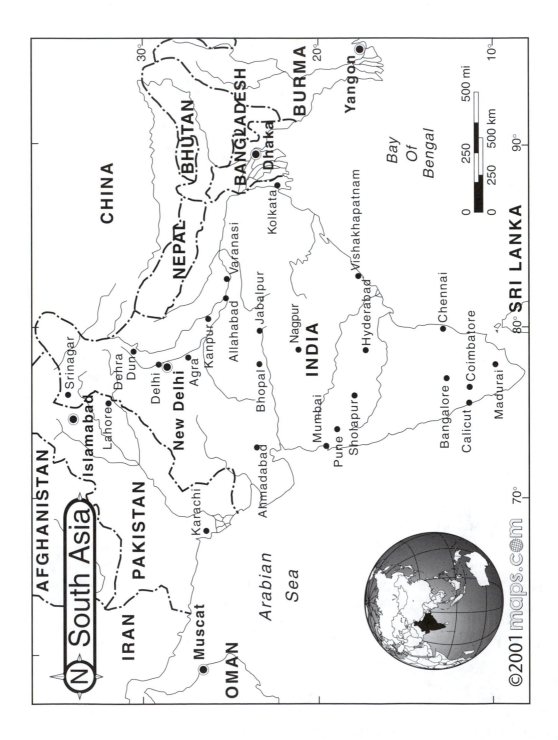

South Asia

N

AFGHANISTAN

IRAN

OMAN

Muscat

PAKISTAN

Islamabad

Lahore

Karachi

Ahmadabad

Arabian
Sea

Srinagar

Dehra Dun

Delhi

New Delhi

Agra

Kanpur

Bhopal

Mumbai

Pune

Sholapur

CHINA

NEPAL

BHUTAN

BANGLADESH

BURMA

Varanasi

Allahabad

Jabalpur

Nagpur

INDIA

Hyderabad

Vishakhapatnam

Dhaka

Kolkata

Yangon

Bay
Of
Bengal

Bangalore

Calicut

Coimbatore

Madurai

Chennai

SRI LANKA

30°

20°

10°

90°

80°

70°

0   250   500 km
0   250   500 mi

©2001 maps.com

prevalent stereotype that situates Islam primarily in the Middle East. Yet today, in 2004, more than 360 million of the world's approximately 1.2 billion Muslims live in three South Asian countries: Pakistan, Bangladesh, and India. Islam's encounter with South Asia has a long and storied past, a complex history of conquest, colonialism, and exchanges among civilizations. Arab traders first reached the west coast of India in the eighth century, and Indo-Muslim empires ruled north India continuously from the eleventh century through nineteenth century. Muslim power and the unique Turko-Persian Islamic culture that it created reached its zenith under the Mughal dynasty (1526–1858) before being eclipsed by the rise of the British Raj. With the birth of India and Pakistan in 1947 and the subsequent formation of an independent Bangladesh in 1971, the Subcontinent was partitioned along cultural and religious fault lines. To this day, religious nationalism plays a pivotal role in regional politics. As the destabilizing war in Afghanistan, the continued conflict between India and Pakistan over Kashmir, and the divisive communal violence in Ayodhya and Gujarat illustrate, the politics of religion pervades modern South Asia.

For the diverse Muslim communities of South Asia, public debate now more than ever centers on the complex relationship between religious and national identities. Faced with regional instability and the threat of internal implosion, politicians, religious leaders, and ordinary people alike grapple over Islam and, by extension, over religion's proper role in the ideology and institutions of the state. What is Islam, and who speaks for the tradition? Is Islam itself compatible with modernity, or, as some suggest, is there a fundamental "clash of civilizations" that creates an unbridgeable gulf between the values of Islam and the West? What exactly does it mean to be an Indian, Pakistani, or Bangladeshi Muslim? Within the complex cultural milieu of today's South Asia, Muslims are separated by issues of language, ethnicity, education, class, and culture—as well as by contested political boundaries and competing national identities. In the face of this immense diversity, where is the ground for Muslim unity? At a time of immense upheaval, answers to these vexing questions have assumed a renewed urgency and have profound implications for Muslims across the globe. With the dawn of the twenty-first century, South Asian Muslims stand as the heirs to the rich legacy of Indo-Muslim political power and cultural achievement. At the same time, as members of independent nations, they struggle to respond to the legacy of British colonialism and the shifting local, regional, and global landscape.

South Asian Muslim Responses to Modernity

Although South Asia's social, cultural, and political environment has continued to change over the past two centuries, many of the most basic issues facing

Muslims in the region have not. In the wake of the violent but short-lived Mutiny of 1857, the East India Company was abolished, and the British Crown assumed direct administration of the Indian Empire. For the Muslims of South Asia—the scions of 700 years of Indo-Muslim rule—this final eclipse of political power and authority occasioned a deep crisis of faith. Over the century that followed, the colonial encounter, combined with a new and vigorous wave of Hindu religious revivalism, dealt a powerful blow to the Muslims' sense of cultural pride while undermining long-standing institutions and social networks.

Engulfed by what world historian Marshall Hodgson calls the "Great Western Transmutation" (Hodgson 1974, vol. 3: 176–196)—the bureaucratization, rationalization, technicalization, and systemization of every dimension of life—South Asia's Muslims were forced to reevaluate their own history, faith, and practices in the interest of cultural survival. They did so in a variety of ways. Some responded to this crisis of identity by adopting European ideas, institutions, and cultural norms as a panacea for the decline of Muslim power. Others decried the dilution of Muslim values and ritual practices as nothing less than cultural suicide and embraced a broad palate of social reforms, from the restoration of traditional civic and educational institutions to the direct and literal application of Islamic law *(shari'a)* to all aspects of social and political life. The Khilafat movement (1919–1924) crystallized anti-British sentiments among Indian Muslims, who rallied behind an attempt to preserve the Ottoman sultan as the spiritual and temporal leader (caliph) of Islamdom. Drawing the support of Mohandas Gandhi and his noncooperation movement, it marked the height of Hindu-Muslim cooperation and the promise of a unified Indian nationalist movement. Its failure, however, spurred the rise of communal politics that culminated with the partition of India and Pakistan in 1947.

This chapter offers a brief and highly selective survey of the wide range of Muslim responses to the challenges of colonialism and modernity, focusing on three discrete categories of thinkers: traditionalists, modernists, and revivalists. Although this typology is a convenient heuristic device, it is admittedly less than foolproof. It is important to recognize from the outset that both between and within these schools of thought there was (and is) a remarkable latitude of ideas, opinions, and discourse. Much of this elasticity stems from the slippery concept of "tradition" itself. For Muslims everywhere, tradition serves as a key organizational principle, an inspirational rallying cry, and a blueprint for social action. By integrating individuals within a broader, more inclusive, trans-historical community, shared notions of sacred history and genealogy provide a sense of orientation, meaning, and purpose. Especially in the midst of unsettling change, a faith in a direct and unbroken link with the past provides a vital sense of continuity. Muslims universally look to the Qur'an, the recorded teachings of the Prophet Muhammad *(hadith),* and the dictates of Muslim law for guidance and inspiration. The key question, however, is how to actualize these traditions in order to make this sacralized past meaningful, here and now. Despite claims to a timeless universalism, opinions have always diverged over the interpretation and implementation of the tenets of Islamic faith. Tradition, in short, has proven to be a malleable construct, subject to constant reinvention.

Within the complex geopolitical landscape of modern South Asia, political actors continue to wrestle over the mantle of Islamic authority and authenticity. Since the nineteenth century, this contestation has involved a complex process of bargaining, protest, accommodation, and conflict. In the public sphere, numerous movements for social reform were typically dominated by urban male elites. However, as Gail Minault's monograph *Secluded Scholars: Women's Education and Muslim Social Reform in Colonial India* (1998) illustrates, Muslim women also played vital roles as writers, educators, intellectuals, and activists, making strong and enduring contributions along the religious and political spectrum. From the rise of British colonialism through Partition and down to the present day, the competition between Muslim traditionalists, modernists, and revivalists over the message and meaning of Islam has profoundly influenced the contours and trajectory of South Asian society.

Traditionalists

Muslim traditionalists—the religious scholars *(ulama)* whose authority derives from their knowledge of the Qur'an, *hadith,* and the science of interpreting Islamic law *(usul al-fiqh)*—find solace in Islam's past glory. Historically, the *ulama* maintained the prerogative of defining and defending "tradition," mediating between the religious and political realms. Under the impact of modernity, however, their monopoly on the status of arbiters of Islam has been increasingly challenged by a host of new social actors who challenge entrenched notions of political, social, and cultural authenticity. As their power and prestige has eroded in South Asia, Muslim traditionalists have struggled to maintain their status as cultural spokesmen and the defenders of Islamic orthodoxy. By reifying a golden-age past, they erect an essentialized, normative Islam as a bulwark against pervasive societal change.

In South Asia, a wide range of *ulama* leaders have sought to define Islam on the public stage. Debating openly with one another, and against their Christian and Hindu counterparts, they often employ new technologies such as print media to help spread their message. Their efforts have helped frame public debate and establish select Islamic symbols as key markers of social and cultural identity. During the nineteenth century, many *ulama* worked to establish networks of religious schools *(madrasas)* across the Subcontinent in an effort to safeguard tradition and defend their own intellectual turf. Foremost among these was the Dar al-Ulum *madrasa* at Deoband, a small town northeast of Delhi. Established in 1867, Deoband became a major center for the active reassertion of Sunni orthodoxy and a locus for conservative opposition to the growing spread of Western thought and institutions. Its founders, a dedicated group of scholars and reformists, were deeply influenced by the famous eighteenth-century Sufi leader, Shah Wali Allah of Delhi (1703–1762). A spiritual master *(shaykh)* in the Naqshbandi Sufi order and a prolific scholar, Shah Wali Allah advocated a return to the fundamentals of the *shari'a* in an attempt to purify South Asian Islam. Embracing the legacy of their Mughal predecessors, the founders of Deoband accepted the mystical elements of the Sufi intellectual tradition but vehemently rejected ritual practices associated with prevalent local customs, including such popular rituals as listening to devotional music *(sama')* and pilgrimages to the shrines of Sufi saints.

The Deoband school's founders and early leaders—among them Muhammad Qasim Nanautawi (1833–1877), Hajji Imdadullah (1817–1899), and Rashid Ahmed Gangohi (1829–1905)—each combined the roles of religious scholar, teacher, and spiritual guide. The Deoband *madrasa* coupled a Western-style university format (with faculty, formal exams, and fund-raising) with a traditional Islamic curriculum (focusing on the study of Qur'an, *hadith,* and the methodology of the Hanafi school of law). The school aimed to return Indo-Muslim society to its own cultural and religious roots by training teachers, prayer leaders, and scholars to disseminate proper moral and religious guidance.

The Deobandi leadership was deeply distrustful of Western influences and was dedicated to revitalizing Muslim society through the revival of traditional religious learning and the values it imparted. Beyond the *madrasa*'s classrooms, Deobandis actively engaged in public discourse, using the printing press to disseminate legal opinions *(fatwas)* and polemical pamphlets. One of the movement's most prolific intellectuals, Ashraf Ali Thanawi (1864–1943), is best known for his influential book *Bihishti Zewar* [Heavenly Ornaments]. A practical guide to religious propriety and social etiquette for Muslim girls, Thanawi's text stands as a primer to Deobandi reformist ideology. Describing the motivation for the book, he wrote,

> Thanks to divinely guided insight, experience, logic and learning, I realized that the cause of this ruination is nothing other than women's ignorance of the religious sciences. This lack corrupts their beliefs, their deeds, their dealings with other people, their character, and the whole manner of their social life. . . . [F]aulty belief leads to faulty character, faulty character to faulty action, and faulty action to faulty dealings that are the root of the disquietude of society. (Thanawi 1990, 48)

Thanawi and his Deobandi cohorts saw religious education and moral reform—for both men and women—as an essential precursor to the reformation of Indo-Muslim social, cultural, political, and religious life. Though highly influential, Deoband did not speak for all South Asian traditionalists, and numerous other groups of *ulama* emerged to challenge their reformist agenda. The Ahl-i Hadith, for example, favored a direct and literal use of the Qur'an and *hadith* and rejected the authority of any particular school of law. They also were severely critical of Sufi institutions and practices and prohibited all ritual practices associated with Sufi tomb cults. With a following of mostly educated urbanites, the Ahl-i Hadith embraced the legacy of the famous Hanbali jurist Ibn Taymiyya (d. 1328), and they distinguished themselves by their dress and style of prayer. In contrast, the Barelwi movement rose to the defense of local practices associated with the Sufi tradition. Led by the scholar and Qadiri Sufi master Ahmad Riza Khan Barelwi (1856–1921), the Barelwi *ulama* embraced Hanafi law, emphasized the status and role of the Prophet, and defended the important place of Sufi saints as patrons and intercessors. The Barelwis blamed both British colonial rule and the influence of reformist Muslims for the decline of the community, and they sought to preserve intact the foundations of Islamic identity rooted in local cultural practices. Identifying themselves as the *ahl al-sunna wa'l-jama'a* ("people of the way [of the Prophet] and the community"), the Barelwis championed themselves as the true heirs to the legacy of the Prophet Muhammad.

In the twentieth century, and in particular after the traumatic events of Partition, South Asian traditionalists diverged even further among themselves over issues of national and religious identity. The Jamiat Ulama-i Hind, for example, was formed in 1921 by a coalition of Deobandi *ulama* and actively supported the Indian Congress Party. They rejected the demands for Partition in favor of a vision of an independent India in which Muslims would control their own educational, legal, and religious institutions. When the Subcontinent was ultimately divided in 1947, this group adopted the idea of a secular Indian state, and today they continue to urge Indian Muslims to support the government in Delhi. The Jamiat Ulama-i Islam, on the other hand, followed a more conservative line. Linked closely with Deoband, the members of this group became staunch supporters of the Muslim League's campaign for Partition. This urban-based group remains politically active in contemporary Pakistan, where it controls a large number of local mosques and *madrasa*s. Its authority, however, was challenged in turn by the Jamiat Ulama-i Pakistan, a largely rural-based group formed by Barelwi *ulama*. Though also supportive of the movement for a separate Pakistan, this group argued for the orthodoxy of traditional local practices. Despite the marked diversity of ideologies and agendas, however, South Asian traditionalists have remained united in their sense of the importance of Islamic tradition as an antidote to challenges of modernity.

Afghan refugee boys at a window in one of several madrasas *at the Shamshatu refugee camp near Peshawar, Pakistan, December 6, 2001. (REUTERS/Corbis/Haider Shah)*

In Pakistan, the second half of the twentieth century witnessed the rapid proliferation of independent, self-styled religious parties, and along with it, an explosion of urban sectarian violence. As the journalist Ahmed Rashid documents in his book *Taliban: Islam, Oil, and the New Great Game in Central Asia* (2000), the marked rise of militant Islam in the region is, in large measure, the direct result of the Afghan war of the 1980s. In one of the last theaters of the cold war, the Pakistani government, with active support from both the United States and Saudi Arabia, backed disparate groups of *mujahidin* soldiers in the fight against the Soviet Union. During this proxy war, the military regime of President Zia al-Haq actively funded a broad network of *madrasa*s within Pakistan. Diverse in ideology and institutional structure, these religious institutions offered young Pakistanis and Afghan refugees food, shelter, a free education, and military training. Throughout the 1980s, the Jamiat Ulama-i Islam (JUI), under the leadership of Maulana Fazlur Rehman, established hundreds of *madrasa*s in the Pashtun ethnic belt along the North-West Frontier Province and Baluchistan. In 1993, with the return to power of the Pakistan People's Party under the leadership of Benazir Bhutto, the JUI began to receive state support and entered the official circles of power. At the same time, dozens of breakaway, extremist factions emerged out of the mainstream JUI. Among them was a group led by Maulana Samiul Haq, whose *madrasa*, the Dar al-Ulum Haqqania, became a major training ground for the leadership of a radical new political movement that filled the power vacuum in Afghanistan following the Soviet withdrawal in 1989: the Taliban.

The Taliban emerged from the city of Kandahar in southern Afghanistan in 1994, sweeping rapidly north to capture the capital, Kabul, in 1996. Made up of the majority Pashtun ethnic group, the Taliban espoused an extremist form of Deobandism, a neofundamentalist radicalism unprecedented in Islamic history. As Ahmed Rashid illustrates, many of the Taliban were born in Pakistani refugee camps, educated in Pakistani *madrasas* and trained to fight by *mujahidin* parties based in Pakistan. Under the leadership of Mullah Muhammad Omar—and with the financial support of Osama bin Laden's al-Qaeda organization—the Taliban provided a safe haven and arms for some of the most radical Sunni extremist groups in the region. Virulently anti-Shi'a and anti-American, such groups continue to advocate the overthrow of Pakistan's ruling elite and the establishment of an Islamic state. A number of these groups are also involved in the militant *jihad* movement against the Indian military forces in the disputed territory of Kashmir. With the fall of the Taliban and its al-Qaeda allies under the U.S.-led military campaign in 2002, the international spotlight has now shifted to Pakistan's internal political landscape. President Pervez Musharraf, who swept to power in a military coup in 1999, now walks a dangerous political tightrope, trying to maintain domestic order and international support while reining in Pakistan's religious parties.

Modernists

In contrast to the approach of the traditionalists, Muslim modernists propose to rescue Islam from cultural stasis and political implosion through a program of adaptation and accommodation. The roots of Islamic modernism can be traced to the Salafi movement of nineteenth-century Egypt and to the legacy of such key figures as Jamal al-Din "al-Afghani" (d. 1897) and his disciples, Muhammad Abduh (d. 1905) and Rashid Rida (d. 1935). In their encounters with colonialism and the challenges of modernization, these influential thinkers focused on a central question: How can Muslims be true to the enduring values of their own past while living in the modern world? Embracing the ideas of *islah* (reform), *tajdid* (renewal), and *ijtihad* (independent legal reasoning), the modernists promoted Muslim unity and resistance to Western cultural hegemony by adopting the fruits of science and technology while overhauling Muslim educational, legal, and political institutions.

In South Asia, the modernist school of thought was embodied by Sayyid Ahmad Khan (1817–1898). Born into a conservative, well-connected family, Sir

Sayyid became both a loyal British supporter and a staunch Muslim nationalist. Tracing his own intellectual heritage to Shah Wali Allah, he argued that the Qur'anic worldview was entirely compatible with science and rational thought. Sir Sayyid was convinced that the survival of South Asia's Muslims demanded both the incorporation of Western ideas and accession to British rule. To this end, he embarked on a broad campaign of intellectual and institutional reform. His efforts to persuade South Asian Muslims to adopt modern scientific methods, acquire new technological skills, and embody the spirit of European liberalism culminated in the establishment of such progressive institutions as the Scientific Society (1863), the All-India Muslim Educational Conference (1886), and, most important, the Mohammaden Anglo-Oriental College (1876), later known as Aligarh Muslim University. Through his writings and institution building, Sir Sayyid struggled to meet the challenges of modernity by appropriating Western education and ideology while giving new direction to Muslim social, educational, and religious ideals.

In twentieth-century South Asia, the figure of Muhammad Iqbal (1877–1938) also looms large among Muslim modernists. Educated in Lahore, London, and Munich, Iqbal was a true renaissance man: a poet, philosopher, lawyer, writer, and activist. Inheriting the legacy of both Shah Wali Allah and Sir Sayyid, Iqbal fluidly combined Western and Islamic thought. Throughout his philosophical magnum opus, *The Reconstruction of Religious Thought in Islam* ([1934] 1982), Iqbal describes his vision of Islamic history as a dynamic, creative, and adaptive tradition. He views the *shari'a* as the cultural backbone of the Islamic community, arguing that it provides both an anchor of stability and a blueprint for adaptive change. Iqbal's famous poem "Shikwa" [Complaint], ends with an emotive, nostalgic call for the reform of Indo-Muslim culture via a return to the foundational paradigm of Prophetic tradition:

> *Let the lament of this lonely bulbul [nightingale] pierce the hearts of all,*
> *Arouse the hearts of the sleeping, with this my clarion call.*
> *Transfused with fresh blood, a new compact of faith we'll sign.*
> *Let our hearts thirst again for a sip of the vintage wine.*
> *What if the pitcher be Persian, from Hijaz [the region in Arabia where the*
> *   Prophet Muhammad was born] is the wine I serve.*
> *What if the song be Indian? It is Hijazi in its verse.* (Iqbal 1981, 58)

In Iqbal's mind, Islam's essential dynamism had been corrupted and ossified by the *ulama*, sequestered behind the walls of their *madrasa*s. Rejecting the closing of the doors of *ijtihad*, therefore, he called for an end to conservatism, inflexibility, and intellectual stasis. And it was Iqbal who first articulated the idea of an independent homeland for South Asian Muslims—a movement that gained rapid momentum and culminated in 1947 with the creation of the Islamic Republic of Pakistan under the leadership of Muhammad Ali Jinnah (1876–1948).

More than half a century has passed, but the legacy of these modernist intellectuals and activists continues to influence new generations of Muslim thinkers, in South Asia and beyond. Fazlur Rahman (1919–1988), a prominent philosopher, educator, and spokesman for a liberal, reformist Islam, championed Islam's relevance in the modern world. As the director of the Institute of Islamic Research in Pakistan and later as a professor at the University of Chicago, Rahman urged modern Muslims to study the Qur'an for themselves in order to discover the spirit behind its message. Equally critical of the *ulama* traditionalists for their intellectual stasis and of the revivalists for their scriptural literalism, he embraced an open, dynamic, and adaptive faith. Like Iqbal, Rahman called for the revitalization of the sciences of legal interpretation and devoted himself to educational reform.

In a similar fashion, Shabbir Akhtar (b. 1960) has evoked the spirit of Sir Sayyid and Iqbal in his book *A Faith for All Seasons* (1990). A Pakistani educated in Canada and living in England, Akhtar challenges his fellow Muslims to re-think their own faith and practices in order to confront the current challenges of secularism, atheism, religious pluralism, Marxism, and global capitalism. In Akhtar's assessment, Islam is a progressive and responsive faith suitable for all times and places. Like his intellectual predecessors, he also embraces *ijtihad*, philosophical reasoning, and a dynamic, open interpretation of faith, asserting that it is indeed possible to be both piously Muslim and progressively modern.

Revivalists

Islamic revivalists, or Islamists, seek to revitalize and reinvigorate tradition. In their view, the proper response to social decay and political weakness is an aggressive cultural renewal, and they vehemently reject the ideologies of modernism and nationalism as well as the traditional authority of the *ulama*. Championing themselves as the defenders of God against a corrupt modern world, revivalists promise to restore Islam's lost glory through a systematic program of social, religious, and political activism. Most significantly, they interpret Islam as a comprehensive ideological system embracing the spiritual and political, the private and the public realms. For revivalists, Islam offers a panacea for cultural decline and spiritual malaise.

In many ways, the wave of Islamic resurgence in the twentieth century was a direct response to endemic economic stagnation, cultural alienation, educational decline, and political impotence. Islamic revivalism is grounded on the concepts of *nahdah* (renaissance), *thawrah* (revolution), and *awdah* (a return to foundations). Across the cultural spectrum, Islamists envision a utopian social and political order grounded on the fundamental doctrine of *hakimiyya* (the absolute sovereignty of God). In this paradigm, the Qur'an serves as both a religious and political standard-bearer and as a measuring stick for personal and public behavior. As activists and ideologues, Islamic revivalists claim the sole prerogative to interpret and institutionalize the dictates of sacred scripture. Employing the instruments of modernity—political institutions, propaganda, mass media—and a remarkable organizational acumen, revivalists attempt to answer the challenges of Western dominance through a renewal *(tajdid)* of the values and institutions of an idealized Islamic past.

In South Asia, Muslim revivalism is nearly synonymous with the name of Mawlana Abu al-A'la Mawdudi (1903–1979). An activist, writer, and politician, Mawdudi lived through turbulent times, and his legacy has had a deep impact throughout the Muslim world. Born into a highly conservative family, he received a traditional Islamic education before attending Aligarh Muslim University, the bastion of modernist thinking. Following the failure of the Khilafat movement, Mawdudi's thinking took a decidedly conservative turn. Disillusioned with nationalism, modernization, and Western values, he embraced a radically exclusive communalism, effectively dividing the world into "Muslim" and "Other." Throughout his broad corpus of writings, Mawdudi called upon Muslims to abandon static interpretations of the faith and the outmoded teachings of the *ulama* in order to return directly to the message of the Qur'an and *hadith*.

Mawdudi's scripturalist style views Islam as a totalizing system, a complete way of life. In his assessment, the *shari'a* is nothing less than timeless, immutable divine law, encompassing every dimension of human existence. In his famous treatise *Towards Understanding Islam,* Mawdudi wrote,

> This law [*shari'a*] is eternal. It is not based on the customs or traditions of any particular people and it is not meant for any particular period of human history. It is based on the same principles of nature on which man has been created. And as that nature remains the same in all periods and under all circumstances, the law based on its unalloyed principles should also be applicable to every period and all circumstances. (Mawdudi [1940] 1970, 177)

For Mawdudi, as for his Islamist counterparts elsewhere in the Muslim world, the lessons of Islamic sacred history impart timeless truths applicable to every age. Rejecting the separation of religion *(din)* and the state *(dawla),* he envisioned the establishment of a "theo-democracy" as the basis of a utopian Islamic state. Beyond his voluminous writings, Mawdudi's most enduring legacy was the creation of a political organization, the Jama'at-i Islami, in 1941. Although the Jama'at's success at the ballot box has proved less than spectacular, the dedication of its membership and the impact of its message stand as an abiding tribute to Mawdudi's revivalist vision. On the whole, however, Mawdudi was more concerned with the imperative for individual moral reform than with the details of political and institutional reconstitution.

Mawdudi's ideology struck a chord throughout the Muslim world, having an impact on prominent European and American converts as well. Maryam Jameelah is a Jewish American convert to Islam who, on the invitation of Mawlana Mawdudi, moved to Pakistan in 1962. Born Margaret Marcus in 1934 in New Rochelle, New York, Jameelah felt deeply alienated from U.S. culture from a young age. Significantly, her own spiritual journey to Islam was deeply influenced by yet another Jewish convert to Islam: Muhammad Asad (1900–1992). Asad (born Leopold Weiss) was an itinerant writer, activist, and diplomat. Born in Austria, he too became disillusioned with Judaism and Western civilization as a young man. Leaving home, he traveled widely in the Muslim world, living for extended periods in Saudi Arabia, India, and Pakistan, where he eventually served as a civil servant and diplomat to the United Nations. As a journalist and scholar, Asad wrote everything from newspaper articles and political tracts to an English translation of the Qur'an. He is perhaps best known, however, for his famous spiritual autobiography, *The Road to Mecca* (Asad [1954] 2000).

As a convert and political activist, Muhammad Asad offered an alternative model for a socially engaged, internationalist Islam. Maryam Jameelah was clearly inspired by Asad's story of disillusionment, spiritual searching, and political engagement. As a prominent ideologue in her own right, Jameelah's voluminous writings offer a conservative defense of Islamic tradition and a sharp indictment against materialism, secularization, and the mores of Western modernity. Jameelah is equally critical of Islamic modernism, which she views as a total betrayal of Islamic teachings. In her view, Islam prescribes a complete way of life, and she insists that practices such as veiling, polygamy, and *purdah* (gender segregation) are mandated by the Qur'an and *sunna* of the Prophet. Maryam Jameelah still lives in Lahore, and her influence continues to have an important impact on the development of revivalist thought throughout the Muslim world.

The Tablighi Jama'at offers another model of South Asian revivalism. Founded in 1926 by the Deobandi scholar and Naqshbandi Sufi Maulana Muhammad Illyas Kandhlawi (1885–1944), it has rapidly expanded into a global grassroots Islamic movement. In many ways, the Tablighi ideology parallels the neotraditionalism of the Deobandis. Critical of such popular expressions of religion as the veneration of Sufi saints and the visiting of saint's shrines, Tablighis champion a purified Islam based on a strict adherence to the *sunna* of the Prophet and the dictates of the *shari'a*. What distinguishes the Tablighi Jama'at, however, is its staunchly apolitical stance and unique organizational framework. Focusing on missionary work *(dawa),* the movement calls for a reawakening of Muslim religio-cultural identity through individual moral reform.

Tablighi religious education is carried out through active proselytization rather than formal study in a *madrasa*. Taking their message directly to the masses, teams of Tablighi volunteers live and travel together for extended periods of time, preaching the fundamental beliefs and ritual practices of Islamic faith. Women participate in these popular outreach programs as well, working among other women and on occasion traveling along with their husbands and sons on longer tours. The Tablighi model is itself a striking break with tradition, effectively undermining the authority of the *ulama* by asserting that preaching is the duty of every pious Muslim. The rapid growth of the Tablighi Jama'at in South Asia and throughout the Muslim world marks a new stage and style of Islamic activism.

Sufism in Contemporary Pakistan

Sufism—the inner, or "mystical," dimension of Islam—stands as an alternative nexus of Islamic piety and practice. Neither a sect nor a cult, it is best understood as a spiritual quest. Pushing the borders of normative Islam, Sufis strive for a direct, intimate, and unmediated experience of the Divine. Sufi adepts tend to emphasize the inward over the outward, intuition over intellect, spiritual contemplation over scholarly debate, and ecstatic poetry over legalistic prose. Since the twelfth century, Sufi institutional orders—discrete spiritual "paths" *(tariqas)*—have proliferated throughout the Muslim world. Though they vary in their teachings and techniques, most Sufis strictly follow the dictates of the Qur'an and the *shari'a* and model their behavior on the example of the Prophet Muhammad *(sunna)*. With their bold claims to experiential knowledge and authority, however, Sufis have often found themselves in the midst of controversy.

Within the combative public sphere of contemporary Pakistan, Sufism is a particularly emotive, multivalent, and contested tradition. In an intense debate over the parameters of religious orthodoxy, competing groups—Islamists, modernists, secular intellectuals, *ulama,* and Sufis themselves—evoke Sufi doctrine, piety, and practice to either defend or decry their Islamic credentials. Throughout South Asia, the lives of Sufi saints are deeply woven into local poetry and legends, and their shrines remain vital centers of popular pilgrimage. Even so, many of the activities and groups associated with Sufism are viewed with intense ambiguity and suspicion, particularly by revivalist groups that denigrate Sufism as an impure, un-Islamic tradition. With a population around 145 million, Pakistan is today the second largest Muslim country in the world. It is also a society deeply divided along ethnic, linguistic, economic, and sectar-

Sufis at a shrine in Srinagar, Kashmir. (Paula Bronstein/Getty Images)

ian fault lines. Amid this social and cultural heterogeneity, Islam itself is argued and contested. And when it comes to Sufism, the lines of these debates
are deeply drawn.

Sufism in Pakistan is found in the popular practices surrounding the tomb
complexes of long-dead saints and in the ecstatic poetry of premodern literary

luminaries. But beyond these public manifestations of a distant past, it also remains a dynamic, living teaching tradition. As a personal spiritual discipline, Sufism is communicated in the intimate exchange between master and disciple and experienced through ritual performance. In South Asia, the Chishtiyya has remained the most prominent and prolific Sufi order since the twelfth century. With its doctrine of social equality, tolerance, and spiritual discipline, the Chishti Sufi order spread rapidly eastward from its roots in Afghanistan. Under the guidance of charismatic spiritual leaders (*shaykhs* or *pirs*) who embodied Islamic doctrine through their piety and practice, Sufism helped endear Islam to the indigenous population. Versed in local customs and vernacular languages, Chishti *shaykhs* established centers of learning and hospices (*khanaqas*) that offered intensive spiritual training for their initiates, solace for the local inhabitants who visited them for spiritual blessings (*baraka*), and food and shelter for the wayfarers and mendicants who survived on their charity. Upon their death, the legacy of many Chishti *shaykhs* often led to the development of elaborate shrine complexes (*dargahs*) to which devotees continued to flock in search of spiritual power to alleviate their worldly troubles. As centers of sacred geography and fonts for public social welfare, these regional Chishti shrines still thrive as pilgrimage sites and symbols of local Muslim culture and identity.

The Chishti Sufi order has two main genealogical branches. Breaking from the lineage of the predominant Nizami branch in the thirteenth century, the eponymous founder of the Chishti Sabiri subbranch, Ali Ahmad Sabir (d. 1291), initiated an alternative model of spiritual asceticism and withdrawal from public, urban life and from the alluring royal courts. From the beginning, the Chishti Sabiris were much less visible than their Chishti Nizami counterparts. Renowned for their intense, awe-inspiring personalities, Chishti Sabiri *shaykhs* stuck to more rural locales, made fewer public appearances, trained fewer devotees, wrote fewer books, and avoided building large shrine complexes.

In the colonial era's heightened atmosphere of polemics and competition, however, certain Chishti Sabiri leaders increasingly came to view silence and withdrawal as untenable. Mounting the public stage to defend their tradition from its critics, prominent *shaykhs* called for social reform; they founded educational institutions and published a broad range of texts. Yet even as South Asia's changing social, cultural, and ideological landscape forced a radical rethinking of the order's public posture, the discipline of Sufi ritual practice remained the enduring bedrock of Chishti Sabiri identity. In today's Pakistan, spiritual masters of the order continue to guide their followers along the Sufi path, armed with a spiritual genealogy (*silsila*) that links them directly to the authority and legacy of the Prophet Muhammad. Given this continuous—but contested—tradition, the reemergence and reconstitution of the Chishti

Sabiri order on the public stage of postcolonial Pakistan offers a fascinating case study of Islam's ongoing debate with modernity.

Three Pakistani Sufi Masters

For contemporary Chishti Sabiri disciples, three spiritual masters set the standard for Sufi piety and practice: Muhammad Zauqi Shah (1877–1951) and his two principal successors, Shahidullah Faridi (1915–1978) and Wahid Bakhsh Rabbani (1910–1995). These modern Sufi exemplars embodied the complexity of their times, and their lives paralleled the birth and development of Pakistan itself. Zauqi Shah was educated at Aligarh Muslim University and pursued a career in journalism and politics before emigrating to Pakistan and devoting himself to his spiritual duties as a Chishti Sabiri *shaykh*. His designated successor, Shahidullah Faridi, was the son of a wealthy London industrialist. Born John Gilbert Lennard, he converted to Islam along with his elder brother in 1937 and traveled widely throughout the Muslim world in search of spiritual knowledge. After becoming a disciple of Zauqi Shah in Hyderabad, India, he married his *shaykh*'s daughter and then moved to Pakistan with them following Partition. Shahidullah spent the last thirty years of his life in Karachi immersed in the Sufi path, guiding his own devoted corps of disciples. Wahid Bakhsh Rabbani was born and raised in the southern Punjab and educated at the Officers Indian Military Academy in Dehra Dun. He was commissioned in the Bahawalpur State Forces in 1933 as an infantry officer in the British Indian Army before moving with his regiment to Malaysia at the outbreak of World War II. Retiring from military service after being charged with insubordination for refusing to cut his beard and wear shorts, he returned to South Asia, where he joined the Civil Secretariat. During his tenure in the British military and civil service, Wahid Bakhsh Rabbani immersed himself in Sufi practice under the guidance of his mentor, Zauqi Shah. For the last three decades of his life, he too committed himself to a life of scholarship and spiritual discipline as a Chishti Sabiri teaching *shaykh*.

Collectively, the experiences of these contemporary Chishti Sabiri leaders provided them with a unique perspective on Sufism and its relation to colonial and postcolonial structures of authority, knowledge, and power. Unlike their *ulama* counterparts, they were all educated in Western-style universities rather than in traditional *madrasa*s. Multilingual, urban, and mobile, they moved fluidly in multiple cultural complexes and epistemological universes. Acquainted with (and profoundly disillusioned by) direct engagement with the instruments and ideology of modernity, these *shaykh*s appropriated and critiqued the language of science, nationalism, and secularization. As teachers, writers, and political activists, they each defended the orthodoxy of Sufi thought and praxis and championed a reconstructed Pakistani cultural identity that was simultaneously Muslim, mystic, and modern.

Writing Sufism

In many ways, the contemporary Chishti Sabiri model of a socially engaged Sufism parallels that of their nineteenth-century predecessors. Hajji Imdadullah and Rashid Ahmed Gangohi—key players, as we have seen, in the foundation of the Deoband *madrasa*—were themselves Chishti Sabiri *shaykh*s, and their legacy stands as an enduring model. The reformist agenda of Muhammad Zauqi Shah, Shahidullah Faridi, and Wahid Bakhsh Rabbani, however, was focused not on institution building but on the written word. Combining spiritual pedagogy and practice with literary acumen, these contemporary masters grounded Pakistani Sufism in a distinctly modern idiom. Writing in both Urdu and English, each of them valorized Chishti Sabiri identity as a defense against the tradition's critics and as a barrier against Western cultural encroachment and political hegemony. Addressing a diverse Pakistani and international audience, they employed technical and scientific vocabulary in combination with mass media (from the printing press to cyberspace) to demonstrate the enduring relevance of the doctrinal teachings and ritual practices at the heart of Sufi identity.

Zauqi Shah drew on his experiences and expertise as a journalist to inscribe a new vision of Chishti Sabiri identity through a diverse range of publications. The *shaykh* went even further in his political activism. Attending the first meeting of the Muslim League in Karachi in 1907, he formally joined the organization in 1940 and went on to serve as vice president for the district of Ajmer. A confidant of Muhammad Ali Jinnah, Zauqi Shah wrote a series of letters in English to Pakistan's future leader. This lengthy and lively correspondence has recently been published by the order in a book entitled *Letters of a Sufi Saint to Jinnah* (Muhammad Zauqi Shah 2000). Among contemporary Chishti Sabiri disciples, Zauqi Shah is remembered for both his high spiritual status and his political clout as an early Pakistani nationalist. In *Tarbiat al-Ushaq*, a compilation of the *shaykh's* discourses (*malfuzat*), Wahid Bakhsh Rabbani wrote:

> This matter is not generally known by the people, but the elect know it: while Qaid-e Azam [Muhammad Ali Jinnah] was the outward founder of Pakistan, Hazrat Muhammad Zauqi Shah was its inward, spiritual founder. The fact is that from ancient times Chishti saints have played a major role in the conquest of Hindustan. . . . That is why Hazrat often used to say, "Hindustan is the inheritance of the Chishtis." (Rabbani 1983, 76–77)

In this retelling of Indo-Muslim history, the Chishti Sabiri historiographical project deviates radically from that of their Islamist counterparts. Here, Sufi saints are anything but marginalized mystics. Instead, Chishti spiritual masters are placed firmly at the forefront of both religious and political life, guiding and sanctifying the teleological evolution of South Asian Islam from the Delhi sultanate through the birth—under the spiritual direction of Muhammad Zauqi Shah himself—of the "Land of the Pure" (Pakistan).

Though he wrote comparatively less than his mentor, Shahidullah Faridi also published numerous tracts. One of his most accessible texts, *Inner Aspects of Faith* ([1979] 1986), contains a series of essays on a broad range of topics, from Islamic theology to Sufi psychology. Without a doubt, though, it was Wahid Bakhsh Rabbani who inherited the literary mantle and political legacy from Zauqi Shah. Rabbani produced a voluminous body of texts, in both Urdu and English. Encompassing a massive collection of letters to his disciples, numerous translations of pre-modern Persian biographical texts, treatises on ritual practice, and polemical pieces defending the Chishti Sabiri tradition from its detractors, his writings are remarkably diverse in content and form.

In his work entitled *Islamic Sufism* (1984), for example, Rabbani responds directly to both Euro-American Orientalist scholars and his Islamist detractors in a spirited defense of the Sufi tradition. In a broad and nuanced exposition, he challenges the assumptions, methodologies, and conclusions of Sufism's critics with a critical eye and a sharp tongue. The book's format and style mirrors the models of Orientalist scholarship, complete with technical vocabulary, an index, bibliography, glossary, and graphs, as well as a full-page color photograph of the *shaykh*. A true bibliophile, Rabbani moves easily between multiple languages and diverse epistemologies. Yet throughout, there is never any doubt about his fundamental loyalties and commitments. Though he is fluent in the language of modernity, his book remains firmly grounded in Islamic idioms and a Sufi worldview. *Islamic Sufism,* in short, presents an old message through a new medium.

Nothing more lucidly encapsulates contemporary Chishti Sabiri imaginings of Sufi identity and its role in the legacy of South Asia, however, than an eclectic book Rabbani wrote late in his life, *The Magnificent Power Potential of Pakistan* (2000). This is a weighty text, more than 550 pages long in both its Urdu and English manifestations. Its scale is equaled by its scope, which ranges from a comprehensive analysis of early Islamic military history to a detailed survey of the legacy of Indo-Muslim culture. The book culminates in a frank assessment of Pakistan's position (and, as the title suggests, "power potential") in the contemporary global order. It is a unique and in many ways atypical work in a Pakistani market glutted with religious literature, much of it ideological and highly polemical. Even for Rabbani, whose literary pursuits embraced multiple genres in diverse registers, this work stands out as unique. Throughout the book, he employs a scholarly narrative voice to place Pakistan in its historical and geopolitical contexts, but the book has a subtle, subversive twist that places Sufism at the very center of both Islamic thought and practice and Pakistani national identity and ideology.

Echoing a theme that resounds throughout the Chishti Sabiri literary corpus, *The Magnificent Power Potential of Pakistan* champions Chishti Sabiri history, doctrine, and practice as a defense against Sufism's critics and as an antidote for widespread societal malaise. Much like his Islamist counterparts, Rabbani embraces the instruments of modernity—science, technology, mass media—while rejecting its pervasive values and ideology. He is particularly critical of secularization, arguing that God must not be marginalized from human affairs. In the twilight of the cold war, he views the world through polarized, essentialized lenses, dividing the globe into two predominant civilizational fracture zones: a mechanized, secularized, materialistic, Godless "West" and a traditional, communal, spiritualized Muslim "East." Looking back to a reified golden age, he calls for a return to the fundamental values and foundational institutions of the earliest Islamic community. In effect, he champions a revitalization of Islamic orthodoxy as an antidote to the profound identity crisis plaguing South Asian Muslims faced with an aggressive, expansionist West. But for Rabbani, this is an orthodoxy with Sufism as its foundation. In his mind, it is the destiny of the Muslims of Pakistan to lead an Islamic global resurgence, reviving and then modernizing Islamic military, cultural, and political traditions in order to stake their rightful claim in the emerging new world order. For Rabbani, Pakistan is rightfully both an Islamic and a *Sufi* republic.

Experiencing Sufism

Sufis write books, but the heart of the tradition is rooted in ritual performance. The Sufi path centers on techniques of mental and bodily discipline—a complex system of routinized and rigorous ritual practices grounded in a comprehensive psychology. Beginning with the normative requirements incumbent on all Muslims, Sufis intensify their spiritual devotions in an effort to control the selfish ego that binds human beings to the world and distances them from God. For Chishti Sabiri disciples (*murids*), spiritual practice involves a program of supererogatory prayers, reciting of the Qur'an, fasting, ritual chanting (*dhikr*), and meditation (*muraqaba*). In the end, disciples assert, progress rests primarily on an individual's attention to his or her own spiritual homework. In the words of a senior male disciple:

> A serious person on the Sufi path is recommended to do spiritual work four to
> five hours a day, in addition to their job and daily routine. Two to three hours in

the morning after *fajr* [morning prayer], and one to two hours after *isha* [evening prayer]. It is all about your intention. It all comes down to your serious- ness. A student studying for A-level examinations studies this much! But it affects your ability to socialize. You're cut off from outsiders, even family. Your guest list just drops off.[1]

To say the least, the discipline of Sufi practice demands personal dedica- tion, vigilance, and sacrifice. For today's Chishti Sabiri practitioners, it is the continuity of embodied and enacted rituals that links them to their sacred past and imbues their lives with a sense of meaning and purpose in the face of con- stant change.

Chishti Sabiri teachings demand a strict and sober adherence to the dictates of the *shari'a*. In the words of one *murid,* a conservative, middle-aged woman who lived for twenty years in both Saudi Arabia and Turkey and who now runs an informal *madrasa* for women in Lahore:

> Our Prophet (peace be upon him)was the greatest Sufi. Self-negation in every- thing, that was his way. But, at the same time, he was so disciplined. Each moment of his life was within the *shari'a*. What is Sufism? It is self-negation, controlling your self, controlling your ego [*nafs*]. And what is *shari'a*? *Shari'a* is there to guide you, to keep you within bounds. Sufism has kept the Prophet's life, his role model alive. If you take the *ulama,* if you take those people who are just practicing the *shari'a* without the spirit of it, Islam is just dry. The spirit of *shari'a* is Sufism.

This is a typical refrain among contemporary Chishti Sabiri disciples. Far from being a seen as a peripheral, un-Islamic tradition, Sufism is repositioned at the very heart of Muslim history, belief, and practice. Time and again in inter- views, Chishti Sabiri *murid*s highlighted the distinction between the outer, or exoteric *(zahir),* and inner, or esoteric *(batin),* dimensions of knowledge and experience. As the "science of the heart," they assert, Sufism aims at a balance between these two realms—a purification of the inner self, which in turn man- ifests itself in external behavior *(adab).*

In private, many Chishti Sabiri disciples condemn their coreligionists, whose narrow focus on outward displays of piety, they say, veils a woeful igno- rance of Islam's deeper meanings. Predictably, they are especially critical of contemporary Deobandis, who in their view have perverted the original teachings of their Chishti Sabiri founders. This critique, often couched in an- ecdotes of direct personal confrontation, also extends to the Ahl-i Hadith, Wahhabis, the Jama'at Islami, and the Tablighi Jama'at—all groups that dis- miss Sufism in public discourse. A quote from a conversation about the in- creasing "Talibanization" of Pakistani society with a senior male *murid* encap- sulates this counter-polemic:

The Taliban see themselves as reformers, a movement to restore past glory. The logic is we must become exactly like the Sahaba [the early community surrounding the Prophet Muhammad]. But you can not be like that. The Prophet and the Sahaba are not coming back. This is just shallow imitation *(taqlid),* nothing else. Imitating them without their purification and perfection. You see, a focus on outward display is an easy way out for something that is simply not so easy. The *sunna* of the Prophet is beyond the capacity of any Muslim. I think it's incumbent on all Muslims to try to follow the *sunna* of the Prophet in all areas. But there is a difference between imitation and *sunna.* The outward becomes mere imitation.

What we have here is nothing less than a battle over the definition of Islamic orthodoxy itself, a public wrangling over authority and authenticity, a debate about *who knows* and about who has a right to speak for Islam. For the Chishti Sabiri practitioners, the answer is unambiguous: only the *awliya Allah* (the Sufi masters, the "friends of God"), with an authority forged through self-discipline and experiential knowledge, carry the mantle of the Prophet. In the words of another senior male disciple:

Our group is not like the Jama'ati Islami and others. You are not told that you should behave in this or that manner. It is just the way you feel inside. If someone is sleeping during prayer time, let him sleep. In the Tablighis, however, you couldn't imagine not praying at the exact times! We reject all elements of compulsion or force. There is a saying of Hazrat Shahidullah Faridi that you simply can not do *dawa* without permission. Until you are explicitly given permission, you are just a student, you have no business doing *dawa.* So many of these *maulvis* [preachers] give passionate speeches. People leave in tears. But people don't change. It's because these *maulvis* do not have permission to speak. The *shaykhs* do not say a word, but people's lives are profoundly changed. That is because they have the express permission to do *dawa.*

As this quote suggests, Chishti Sabiri Sufis find revivalist attempts to reify, synthesize, codify, and systematize Islamic piety and practice highly dubious. True knowledge, they assert, must be *earned* through a disciplined journey along the Sufi path under the watchful tutelage of a spiritual master. In the absence of individual moral and spiritual reform cultivated under the discipline of daily worship, channeled through strict adherence to *shari'a,* and grounded in the rigors of Sufi ritual practice, any attempt to institutionalize top-down social reforms is doomed to failure. Such rhetoric, Chishti Sabiris argue, is nothing more than political posturing.

Upon entering the Chishti Sabiri order, a disciple is forced to relinquish personal autonomy, surrendering selfhood to the will of a teacher. To quote a

The dargah *of Shaykh Wahid Bakhsh Rabbani during the* urs *of 2001, Allahabad, Pakistan.* (Robert Rozehnal)

well-known adage, the *murid*'s surrender to the *shaykh* must be total and uncompromising, "like a corpse in the hands of a washerman." In practice, however, the dynamic and intensely personal relationship with a spiritual mentor demands a careful and constant balancing act. The Sufi adept must combine submission to hierarchical authority with an enduring imperative for individual action and moral responsibility. It is the *shaykh* who guides the novice disciple through the twists and turns of the Sufi path, but progress is impossible in the absence of individual acquiescence, determination, and discipline.

Though an individual's spiritual progress ultimately depends on personal effort, disciples provide their peers with a vital support system. Together, they share experiences; clarify doubts, ambiguities, and anxieties; and participate in collective ritual activities. In addition to their own individual spiritual practices, Chishti Sabiri disciples gather four times a year to commemorate the death anniversaries *(urs)* of important Sufi masters in their spiritual lineage. On the occasions of these *urs* celebrations, *murid*s travel from all over Pakistan and beyond, gathering together for several days of communal worship at key Sufi tomb complexes. On these annual occasions, disciples benefit from the knowledge and experiences of their peers through a complex nexus of story telling. Between prayers, meditation, and recitation of the Qur'an, disciples can be found sitting together in small groups where they recall personal experiences—dreams, visions, doubts, and fears—and narrate legends about past spiritual masters and the lives of their own *shaykh*s. In the words of a young male novice:

> A lot of guidance comes indirectly as well through these group activities. I missed three or four *urs* because of my job. The recent urs in Allahabad [the shrine of Wahid Bakhsh Rabbani] was one of the first I've been able to attend for two years. I was amazed at the amount of things I picked up, and realized I was missing, just by living with the other *murid*s. If you as a *murid* had sat with the *shaykh* three years ago and heard him say something, you would narrate that. Or you'd say that you read something in a book and then discussed it with him, and his interpretation was this or that. We keep learning in this way.

In short, *urs* provide Chishti Sabiri disciples with a vital forum in which to share collective wisdom and learn about the tradition's roots directly from each other.

Although there are prominent exceptions to the rule, the contemporary followers of the Chishtiyya-Sabiriyya-Zauqiyya *silsila* fit a general profile: educated, middle-class, mobile urban professionals. Although Chishti Sabiri *shaykh*s, in keeping with tradition, are exclusively male, many of the order's most active and highly respected disciples are women. Most *murid*s move fluidly between multiple cultural universes, and many of them have extensive networks of family and friends living abroad in the Gulf, England, Canada, and the United States. Though well acquainted with the instruments and ideology of modernity, many disciples also come from families with a long history of Sufi affiliations. Regardless of their personal background, however, without exception they stress the centrality of their Sufi identity and practice in their busy, complex lives.

Shaykh Siraj Ali, the order's current teaching *shaykh*—the successor *(khalifa)* of Shahidullah Faridi—is himself the embodiment of this dominant Chishti Sabiri pattern. A fourth-generation Chishti Sabiri, he was a graduate of the prestigious Pakistani Air Force College and the senior pilot for Pakistan International Airlines until his recent retirement. He is multilingual and a computer expert, and he travels frequently both within Pakistan to visit his own disciples and abroad to see his sons and daughters currently living in the United States. Significantly, the backgrounds both of the *shaykh*s and of the bulk of the disciples in this order entirely contradict the prevalent stereotypes about South Asian Sufism. Eager to explain away the ubiquity and continuity of Sufi allegiances and practices, critics of the tradition—Islamists and secularists alike—typically portray Sufis as rural and uneducated Muslims. The background and experiences of today's Chishti Sabiris, however, illuminate a much more complex reality.

Life in today's Pakistan is full of difficulties and challenges. Faced with the increasing demands of career and family life, along with the incessant worries brought on by political instability, how can a person still follow the Sufi path? For Chishti Sabiri disciples, the contingencies of modern, urban life have forced a reassessment of how best to balance the demands of the mundane world with the discipline (and rewards) of the spiritual quest. Acknowledging that the social landscape has changed, today's disciples look back on their premodern predecessors with a palpable sense of envy and nostalgia. They regretfully acknowledge, however, that the days of the traditional *khanaqa*—the premodern Sufi hospice memorialized in classical texts—have come and gone.

Accepting the pressing need to respond to the realities of modernity, there is a constant refrain that a new time demands a new paradigm for Sufi practice. Sufism, Chishti Sabiri disciples maintain, must be adapted to suit the needs of the day. In the words of a senior male *murid*:

> I think that the saints have concluded that it's not possible now to have a *khanaqa* where everyone could live together in one place. Because of the times, the requirements of jobs with everyone living such a fast pace of life. This is why we see a totally different type of emphasis now. It's how Sufism deals with the modern age. The thing which is emphasized is not to give up your spiritual exercises, even as you remain fully engrossed in the day-to-day workings of the modern world. In previous times, people had to do a lot of *mujahida* [spiritual work] to get even a little spiritual growth. Today, even staying away from TV is a *mujahida*.

Although Chishti Sabiri ritual practice has been modified to accommodate contemporary realities, there remains a striking continuity in the logic and mechanics of the Sufi path. In today's Pakistan, Chishti Sabiri Sufism is imagined and inscribed anew in texts, even as it is continuously performed in ritual contexts.

Conclusion: South Asian Islam after September 11, 2001

The events of September 11, 2001, have profound implications for all of us, Muslims and non-Muslims alike. The fallout from the terrorist attacks in the United States has already begun to alter the geopolitical balance of power, reconfigure global security arrangements, redefine international foreign policy, and test every nation's commitment to freedom and civil liberties. For the world's 1.2 billion Muslims, the impact has been even deeper and more direct. Across the globe, the vast majority of Muslims have responded to 9/11 with horror and disgust. The violent acts carried out by the radical followers of

Osama bin Laden are widely seen as a violation of the most sacred tenets of the faith, a gross distortion of the spirit of the Qur'an and the legacy of the Prophet Muhammad. Yet even as most Muslims vehemently reject Osama bin Laden's call for holy war, they are left to face the repercussions: a barrage of mass media images that only enforce distorted stereotypes and a global imbalance of power that is seen to only perpetuate political and economic iniquities. As Muslims continue to confront the backlash from 9/11, they will certainly turn to their own faith, to its sacred texts and history, in search for answers. As we have seen, the modern Islamic world is remarkably complex, diverse, and dynamic, and it is likely that the response of individual Muslims to the new local and global realities of the post-9/11 will be so as well.

I was in Pakistan on September 11, 2001. From my apartment in Lahore, I watched live television coverage of the fall of the World Trade Center's twin towers in New York, half a world away. Throughout that night and the following days, my telephone rang constantly as Pakistani friends called to express their horror, disbelief, and grief. In those sad and surreal days, they also talked about their own sense of fear and foreboding. Pakistanis, after all, now live with the bitter legacy of the Afghan war of the 1980s: waves of refugees, the explosion of drug and smuggling operations, burgeoning economic debt, the spread of militant Islam, and the rise of a culture of guns and violence. Not surprisingly, many of my Pakistani friends were therefore wary of the prospect of renewed U.S. involvement in the region and distrustful of U.S. foreign policy initiatives, even as they grieved for America's losses. When and how would the United States retaliate against the Taliban and al-Qaeda? How would the fragile government of President Pervez Musharraf respond? Would Pakistan's pro-Taliban religious parties strike against the government in Islamabad? What were the long-term social, political, and economic implications for the region? In the following weeks, Pakistanis spoke of little else in public and in private. While there were protests and demonstrations, they were sporadic, isolated, and small. Images of burning U.S. flags and sounds of anti-American slogans played again and again in the international media, but on the ground I saw none of this as I continued to move around the city. The sense of fear, however, was palpable.

In the aftermath of 9/11, Pakistan now finds itself at a crossroads as the struggle between the state and a wide array of religious groups continues to intensify. The renewed saber rattling with India over Pakistan's support for militant *jihadi* groups fighting in Kashmir has only added more fuel to the fire. As the world moves into the new millennium, the two South Asian giants once again teeter on the brink of war, divided by national and religious ideology and armed with nuclear weapons. Yet even as the political stakes continue to rise, Islam remains a stabilizing, unifying force in the lives of many of the region's Muslims. As always, the call to prayer is heard five times a day, reminding the believers of their spiritual and social duties in the presence of God. In the face of constant change and new challenges, Islamic faith and practice still serve as a powerful and enduring source of guidance and inspiration for the diverse Muslim communities of South Asia, even as Muslims continue to debate orthodoxy and contest tradition.

Notes

1.   The following quotations are drawn from interviews with Chishti Sabiri disciples during fourteen months of research in Pakistan (September 2000–November 2001). This fieldwork was conducted under the auspices of fellowships from the Social Science Research Council and the American Institute of Pakistan Studies. At the request of senior figures in the Sufi order, I have withheld the names of individual respondents in the interest of anonymity and privacy.

References

Ahmad, Mumtaz. 1991. "Islamic Fundamentalism in South Asia: Jamaat-i Islami and the Tablighi Jamaat of South Asia." In *Fundamentalisms Observed,* edited by Martin E. Marty and R. Scott Appleby, 457–530. Chicago: University of Chicago Press.

Akhtar, Shabbir. 1990. *A Faith for all Seasons: Islam and the Challenge of the Modern World.* Chicago: Ivan Lee.

Asad, Muhammad. [1954] 2000. *The Road to Mecca.* Louisville, KY: Fons Vitae.

Bose, Sugata, and Ayesha Jalal. 1998. *Modern South Asia: History, Culture, Political Economy.* London: Routledge.

Buehler, Arthur F. 1998. *Sufi Heirs of the Prophet: The Indian Naqshbandiyya and the Rise of the Mediating Sufi Shaykh.* Columbia: University of South Carolina Press.

Ernst, Carl W. 1997. *The Shambhala Guide to Sufism.* Boston: Shambhala Publications.

Ernst, Carl W., and Bruce B. Lawrence. 2002. *Sufi Martyrs of Love: The Chishti Order in South Asia and Beyond.* New York: Palgrave Macmillan.

Esposito, John L., and John O. Voll. 2001. "Maryam Jameelah: A Voice of Conservative Islam." In *Makers of Contemporary Islam,* 54–67. New York: Oxford University Press.

Ewing, Katherine Pratt. 1997. *Arguing Sainthood: Modernity, Psychoanalysis, and Islam.* Durham, NC: Duke University Press.

Faridi, Shahidullah. [1979] 1986. *Inner Aspects of Faith.* Karachi: Mahfil-e Zauqia.

Gimartin, David. 1988. *Empire and Islam: Punjab and the Making of Pakistan.* Berkeley and Los Angeles: University of California Press.

Hodgson, Marshall G. S. 1974. *The Venture of Islam: Conscience and History in a World Civilization.* Vol. 3, *The Gunpowder Empires and Modern Times.* Chicago: University of Chicago Press.

Iqbal, Allama Muhammad. [1934] 1982. *The Reconstruction of Religious Thought in Islam.* Lahore: Ashraf Press.

————. 1981. *Shikwa and Jawab-i Shikwa, Complaint and Answer: Iqbal's Dialogue with Allah.* Translated by Khushwant Singh. Delhi: Oxford University Press.

Jalal, Ayesha. 2000. *Self and Sovereignty: Individual and Community in South Asian Islam since 1850.* London: Routledge.

Jameelah, Maryam. 1976. *Islam and Western Society: A Refutation of the Modern Way of Life.* Lahore: Muhammad Yusuf Khan.

Khan, Sayyid Ahmad. 1997. *Causes of the Indian Revolt.* Compiled and edited by Salim al-Din Quraishi. Lahore: Sang-e-Meel Publications.

Lawrence, Bruce B. 1999. "The Eastward Journey of Muslim Kingship: Islam in South and Southeast Asia." In *The Oxford History of Islam,* edited by John L. Esposito, 394–431. Oxford: Oxford University Press.

Lelyveld, David. 1978. *Aligarh's First Generation: Muslim Solidarity in British India.* Princeton, NJ: Princeton University Press.

Liebeskind, Claudia. 1998. *Piety on Its Knees: Three Sufi Traditions in South Asia in Modern Times.* Delhi: Oxford University Press.

Malik, Jamal. 1996. *Colonization of Islam: Dissolution of Traditional Institutions in Pakistan.* Lahore: Vanguard Books.

Masud, Khalid, ed. 2001. *Travelers in Faith: Studies of the Tablighi Jama'at as a Transnational Islamic Movement for Faith Renewal.* Leiden: Brill.

Mawdudi, Sayyid Abu'l A'la. [1940] 1970. *Towards Understanding Islam.* Translated and edited by K'urshid Ahmad. Lahore: Idara Tarjuman-ul-Qur'an.

Metcalf, Barbara Daly. 1982. *Islamic Revival in British India: Deoband, 1860–1900.* Princeton, NJ: Princeton University Press.

Minault, Gail. 1998. *Secluded Scholars: Women's Education and Muslim Social Reform in Colonial India.* New York: Oxford University Press.

Muhammad Zauqi Shah. 2000. *Letters of a Sufi Saint to Jinnah.* Lahore: Talifaat-e Shaheedi.

Nasr, Seyyed Vali Reza. 1995. *Mawdudi and the Making of Islamic Revivalism.* New York: Oxford University Press.

————. 2001. *Islamic Leviathan: Islam and the Making of State Power.* Oxford: Oxford University Press.

Rabbani, Wahid Bakhsh. 1983. *Tarbiyat al-'Ushshaq.* Karachi: Mehfil-e Zauqiyya.

————. 1984. *Islamic Sufism.* Lahore: Sufi Foundation.

————. 2000. *The Magnificent Power Potential of Pakistan.* Translated by Muhammad Asghar. Lahore: Al-Faisal Publishers.

Rahman, Fazlur. 1982. *Islam and Modernity: Transformation of an Intellectual Tradition.* Chicago: University of Chicago Press.

Rashid, Ahmed. 2000. *Taliban: Islam, Oil, and the New Great Game in Central Asia.* London: Tauris.

Sanyal, Usha. 1996. *Devotional Islam and Politics in British India: Ahmad Riza Khan Barelwi and His Movement, 1870–1920.* New York: Oxford University Press.

Schimmel, Annemarie. 1963. *Gabriel's Wing: A Study into the Religious Ideas of Sir Muhammad Iqbal.* Leiden: Brill.

————. 1975. *Mystical Dimensions of Islam.* Chapel Hill: University of North Carolina Press.

Thanawi, Ashraf Ali. 1990. *Perfecting Women: Maulana Ashraf 'Ali Thanawi's "Bihishti*

Zewar. "Translated and with commentary by Barbara Daly Metcalf. Berkeley and Los Angeles: University of California Press.

Van der Veer, Peter. 1994. *Religious Nationalism: Hindus and Muslims in India.* Berkeley and Los Angeles: University of California Press.

Wali Allah, Shah. 1996. *The Conclusive Argument from God: Shah Wali Allah of Delhi's Hujjat Allah al-Baligha.* Translated by Marcia K. Hermansen. Leiden: Brill.

Werbner, Pnina, and Helene Basu, eds. 1998. *Embodying Charisma: Modernity, Locality, and the Performance of Emotion in Sufi Cults.* London: Routledge.

Zaman, Muhammad Qasim. 1999. "Religious Education and the Rhetoric of Reform: The Madrasa in British India and Pakistan." *Comparative Studies in Society and History* 41, no. 2 (April): 294–323.

Chapter Five

Islam in Contemporary Central Asia

ADEEB KHALID

Once, waiting in line at a cafeteria in Tashkent in 1991, in the last months of the Soviet era, I fell into a conversation with two men behind me. They were pleased to meet anyone from the outside world, to which access had been so difficult until then, but they were especially delighted by the fact that their interlocutor was Muslim. My turn eventually came, and I sat down in a corner to eat. A few minutes later, my new acquaintances joined me unbidden at my table, armed with a bottle of vodka, and proceeded to propose a toast to meeting a fellow Muslim from abroad. Their delight at meeting me was sincere, and they were completely un-self-conscious of the oddity of lubricating the celebration of our acquaintance with copious quantities of alcohol.

This episode, unthinkable in the Muslim countries just a few hundred kilometers to the south, provides a very powerful insight into the place of Islam in Central Asian societies at the end of the Soviet period. What did it mean to be a Muslim after seventy years of Soviet rule? How have things changed in the decade of independence? The Soviet Union collapsed in 1991, and since then, Central Asia, like the rest of the former Soviet Union, has seen a considerable religious revival. Islam has become more visible in Central Asia, and indeed, this visibility has given rise to alarmist visions of rampant fundamentalism threatening the existing secular regimes. Nevertheless, the seemingly paradoxical combination of pride in being Muslim (and curiosity about the broader Muslim world) with scant disregard for the strictures of Islam as a religion remains.

This chapter seeks to resolve this paradox. I will argue that the explanation of this paradox lies in the social, cultural, and political transformation of Central Asia during the seven decades of Soviet rule. During this period, the Muslim societies of Central Asia experienced sustained attempts by the Soviet state at secularization and the inculcation of ethno-national identities. As a result of

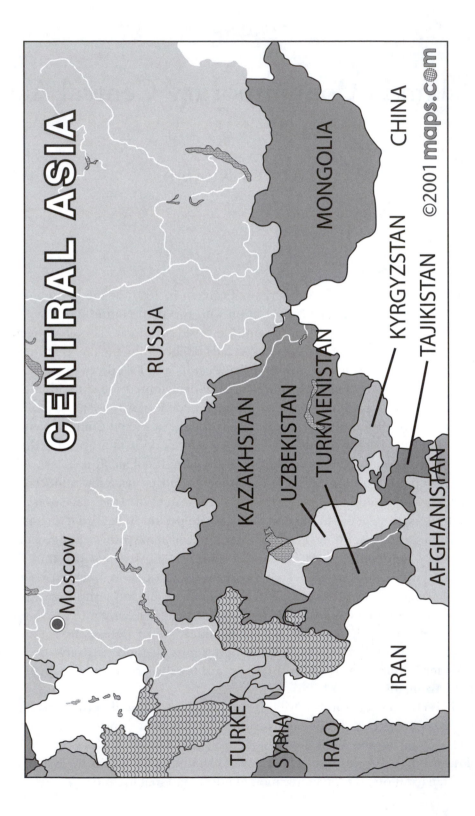

CENTRAL ASIA

Moscow

RUSSIA

KAZAKHSTAN

MONGOLIA

UZBEKISTAN

TURKMENISTAN

KYRGYZSTAN

TAJIKISTAN

AFGHANISTAN

CHINA

IRAN

TURKEY

SYRIA

IRAQ

©2001 maps.com

these policies, new meanings of Islam and of being Muslim emerged in Central Asia: Islam became a facet of national identity even as Islamic norms of behavior lost their authority over the public realm. This represents a new chapter in the very long history of Islam's presence in Central Asia. It also provides a very important contrast to other traditionally Muslim societies, where Islam interacts with nationalism and modernity in different ways.

Islamization of Central Asia

Central Asia has long been an integral part of the Muslim world. Arab armies conquered the cities of Transoxiana in the early eighth century, turning the region into the frontier of the Muslim world. Over the next two centuries, the urban population, mostly speakers of Persian, converted to Islam, and the cities very soon became connected to networks of Muslim culture and of Islamic learning. Indeed, some of the most important figures in Islamic civilization originated from Transoxiana. After the Qur'an, the second most important source of Islamic law are the *hadith*, the written traditions of the Prophet. Sunni Muslims hold six compilations of *hadith* to be authoritative. Two of the six compilers, Imam Abu Isma'il al-Bukhari (810–870) and Abu Isa Muhammad al-Tirmidhi (825–892), were from Transoxiana, as were the influential jurists Abu Mansur Muhammad al-Maturidi (d. circa 944) and Burhan al-Din Abu'l Hasan al-Marghinani (d. 1197). So too were the great scientist Abu Nasr al-Muhammad al-Farabi (d. circa 950), known as "the second teacher" (after Aristotle), and the rationalist philosopher Abu Ali Ibn Sina (known in the West as Avicenna, 980–1037)—all of them figures of central importance in the history of Islamic civilization in its so-called classical age. They were part of broader networks of travel and learning, which served to make the cities of Transoxiana part of the heartland of the Muslim world. This position was further cemented by the emergence, at the end of the tenth century, of Bukhara as the seat of the independent Samanid dynasty, which patronized the development of "new Persian" (written in the Arabic script) as a literary language (Frye 1965).

The surrounding steppe, with its largely Turkic-speaking nomadic population, remained a borderland. Conversion to Islam was a gradual process that lasted into the eighteenth century, although the fourteenth century was of crucial importance. Conversion to Islam on the steppe was the work of Sufi masters who made Islam meaningful to the population by synthesizing Islamic themes with nomadic myths of origin. Observers have conventionally held this syncretism to be evidence that steppe nomads were only "superficially Islamized" or that they were Muslims in name only. This view has resurfaced forcefully after the collapse of the Soviet Union and is sometimes applied to all

Central Asians. At its base lies the questionable assumption that "real" Muslims are those who practice Islam in the same way as it is practiced in the Middle East. This argument has been convincingly dismantled by the recent work of Devin DeWeese (1994) and a number of other scholars, who have shown that the syncretism worked both ways and that the native worldviews and myths of origin were thoroughly Islamized. The evidence of steppe epic tradition, narrative history, and hagiography shows that for steppe Muslims, Islam became the ancestral religion, and conversion to Islam came to be seen as the founding moment of the community as such. Islamic, ethnic, and communal identities were completely intertwined in local sacred history. Islam was thus absolutely central to nomadic conceptions of identity. If Islam was the ancestral religion, however, it followed that local customs (as the legacy of the ancestors) were ipso facto Islamic. These customs were Islamized, to be sure, but their meaning was specifically local.

The dichotomy between the cities and the steppe should not be overdrawn. The same processes of Islamizing local culture by localizing Islam can be observed among the sedentary population. The Turkic-language chronicle *Firdaws ul-Iqbal* (The Paradise of Fame), compiled in Khiva in the late eighteenth and early nineteenth centuries, also asserted that the people of Khorezm, as descendants of Japheth, the son of Noah, had been Muslim since creation. Along the way, various generations had lapsed into infidelity, but they had been brought back to the path of Islam by divinely guided ancestors, the last of whom was Oghuz Khan (a mythical figure). In dispensing with the historical narrative of the Arab conquest of Central Asia and the process of conversion, the *Firdaws ul-Iqbal* asserted that the people of Khorezm were innately Muslim (Munis and Ogahiy 1999; see also Khalid 1999).

The difference between the cities and the steppe lay in the different forms the transmission of Islam took in each, and even here the two were interconnected. In the cities, the transmission of Islam revolved around *madrasa*s (institutions of higher education roughly the equivalent of seminaries) or in Sufi lodges *(khanaqa*s). Bukhara, in particular, was renowned for its *madrasa*s, whose proliferation after the sixteenth century gave the city legendary status as "Bukhara the Noble." At the turn of the twentieth century, the city was supposed to have 300 *madrasa*s and 360 mosques, one for each day of the year. The actual numbers were much smaller (lectures were given in 22 *madrasa*s in those years), but the city attracted students from all over Central Asia and beyond. For our purposes, the important thing to note is that *madrasa*s as well as *khanaqa*s were patronized by rulers and other benefactors through the use of endowed property *(waqf)*. This patronage created a large and influential group of scholars *(ulama)* as the authoritative interpreters of norms of Islam as it was locally understood. On the steppe, this group was absent. Religious authority was much more diffuse and was not connected to the interests of an influential group in society. These differences have had important consequences during the modern period.

Reform and Modernism

Practices associated with the transmission of Islam survived the Russian conquest. Painfully aware of the thinness of Russian rule in the area and of its distance from Saint Petersburg and supremely confident of the superiority of the European civilization they brought to Central Asia, Russian administrators embarked on a policy of disregarding or ignoring Islam, assuming that without state support, it would simply decay. *Madrasa*s continued to exist and even thrived; indeed, they extended their influence to the steppe, where more scripturalist forms of religiosity began to spread by the late nineteenth century. The Kazakh elites, however, early began sending their sons to Russian schools in substantial numbers, so that by the turn of the twentieth century, a sizable secular Kazakh intelligentsia existed. This group, fluent in Russian and comfortable in the political ideas of the Russian intelligentsia, began to formulate a Kazakh national identity that had little place in it for Islam as anything but a marker of cultural identity.

The Russian conquest also brought in its wake printing, the telegraph, and the railway, which together began to change patterns of intellectual authority and cultural transmission. One result of this was the emergence of a movement for cultural reform built around the advocacy of the *usul-i jadid,* the new (that is, phonetic) method of teaching the Arabic alphabet. Called Jadidism, this movement shared a great deal in common with other modernist movements in the Muslim world at that time (Khalid 1998). Faced with the challenge posed by the loss of sovereignty to Russian rule and with the perceived threat of cultural and economic marginalization, proponents of reform called upon their compatriots to acquire modern knowledge. Not only was such knowledge completely congruent with the "true" teachings of Islam, it alone could allow Muslims to meet the demands of the age and thus ensure their survival. However the Jadids believed that the "true" teachings of Islam had been obfuscated by centuries of interpretations that had led Muslims astray. Although many of the most prominent Jadids (as the proponents of reform came to be called) came from learned families, Jadidism rejected the authority of traditional *ulama* to interpret Islam. Instead, the Jadids argued for a return to the textual sources of Islam.

This was a radically new way of understanding Islam, since it pulled Islam away from its moorings in local customs and traditions. Indeed, the Jadids denounced many local customs as un-Islamic. However, the Jadids' emphasis on meeting the "demands of the age" and on progress and enlightenment shifted the focus back to the community: Islam could be safeguarded (against both theological and geopolitical incursions) only if Muslims achieved success in this world. Islam thus became the defining characteristic of the nation; indeed, it *became* a nation. "Muslims" were now a community located in history and geography and existing alongside other communities. "Islam" became a commonly used term, denoting not just a religion but also the community and its members.

As with any other nation, the Muslim nation of Central Asia existed alongside many others; its essence was political rather than religious. In many Jadid writings, the distinction between Islam as a faith and Muslims as a community disappeared entirely. Thus, Mahmud Xo'ja Behbudiy, the leading Jadid author of Samarqand, could urge his compatriots to educate their children to become "judges, lawyers, engineers, teachers, the supporters and servants of the nation" so that they "would work for the true faith of Islam" (Behbudiy 1913, 155). The true faith, the nation, and progress blended very easily to produce what could be called a secular Muslim nationalism (Zürcher 1999). Islam was still connected to a communal identity, but the relationship had been reversed. The automatic connection between Islam and local custom was questioned, while the Jadids' fascination with progress undermined respect for custom. At the same time, the Jadids' fascination with progress allowed them to find all modern innovations completely congruent with Islam (and indeed demanded by it). Although the Jadids disconnected Islam from local custom, they tied it back to the community through its political and economic interests. The implications were of fundamental importance: If Islam were conceived as a community, it could exist without explicit reference to Islamic behavior. The implementation of Islamic law was never an issue in the politics of the Muslim nation (the question of the Islamization of law belongs to a later generation of Islamic thought). In Central Asia (as indeed in much of the Ottoman world), it was thus possible in the early twentieth century to be agnostic or even an atheist and yet retain a strong Muslim national identity. Recent crises in the Balkans have forced us to recognize that such forms of identity continue to exist among Balkan Muslims; we need to remember how widespread the phenomenon was in the early parts of this century.

Islam under Soviet Rule

The Russian Revolution and the resulting conquest of power by the Bolsheviks transformed the political and social context in which Islam was reproduced and transmitted. The new regime had an agenda completely different from that of its imperial predecessor, which had been content to ensure order through minimal interference in society. The Bolsheviks were committed to a utopian program of radical social and cultural change to remake society and the individual, a program that flowed directly from certain basic premises of Marxist thought as interpreted by the Bolsheviks. Socialism could be built in an "advanced" society that had experienced fully developed capitalism and the cultural achievements associated with it (universal literacy, secularization, and the like). However, Russia did not fit this description; its "backwardness" had to be overcome, and since a socialist government already held power, the battle with backwardness could not be left to capitalism but was to be the assigned task of the state. If Russia was backward, Central Asia, with low levels of literacy and an economy entirely dependent on agriculture, was especially so. Indeed, in the Bolsheviks' Eurocentric scheme of things, Islam itself was a sign of backwardness. In Central Asia, therefore, the cultural revolution of the 1920s involved an attack on Muslim education and its replacement by a network of modern schools, campaigns against illiteracy, an orthographic revolution that resulted in the adoption of a Latin alphabet for all Turkic languages of the Soviet Union in 1928 (the same year as in Turkey), and attacks on traditional practices in general.

Two aspects of this program were of particular importance to our concerns here: first, a radical transformation of society, attacking the property and status of old elites (many of whom had already suffered huge blows by the economic crisis of the civil war) and creating new elites; and, second, a frontal assault on religion in all its manifestations. In 1927, the Communist Party launched the *hujum*, or assault, on the traditional way of life. Its main focus was the veil—thousands of women unveiled in public acts of defiance of tradition—but it was a basic metaphor for the state's relationship to local customs and traditions, which it sought to recreate on a "more rational" plane. In the short run, the *hujum*, with its excesses, was unsuccessful and indeed counterproductive: The very customs it attacked became highly valued markers of local identity against an aggressive and oppressive state (Massell 1974; Kamp 1998; Northrop 1999). But in the long run, many of its goals were achieved; the veil disappeared, allowing large numbers of women to join the labor force, especially in the brutal cotton sector of the economy (Tokhtakhodjaeva 1995).

The assault on religion was motivated by a number of factors. At the political level, the Bolsheviks feared any axis of loyalty and mobilization beyond their control. But the ideological motivation, rooted in Enlightenment rationalism, of freeing the human mind from all dependence on the supernatural and all forms of "superstition" should not be lost from sight. Beginning in the late 1920s and continuing through the 1930s, hundreds of *madrasa*s and Sufi lodges were closed down (some destroyed, most turned to other uses, a few saved as "architectural monuments"); mosques were closed and in many cases destroyed; endowed property was confiscated; and the *ulama*, who became the enemies both of reason and of "the people," were mercilessly persecuted:

many executed, others exiled to forced-labor camps across the Soviet Union, yet others deprived of their livelihood and driven underground (Keller 2001). These policies dealt a deathblow to older means of reproducing Islam. Moreover, as the Soviet Union receded into a paranoid isolationism, links with the outside Muslim world were cut off. Central Asian Islam was forced into isolation, cut off from developments in the rest of the Muslim world.

Soviet Islam was thus localized and rendered synonymous with tradition. With Muslim educational institutions abolished, the ranks of the carriers of Islamic knowledge denuded, and continuity with the past made difficult by changes in script, the family became the only site for the transmission of Islam. At the same time, since no new religious texts could be published and since oral chains of transmission were often destroyed, the available religious knowledge was vastly circumscribed.[1]

These developments coincided with another very significant phenomenon: the emergence and consolidation of strong ethno-national identities in Central Asia. The Soviet Union presided over the largest project of nation-building in human history (Suny 1994; Slezkine 1994). From the very beginning, "nation" (and the related concepts of "nationality" and "the people," all rendered by *khalq* in Central Asian languages) was a constitutive part of the Soviet political system. While "Soviet internationalism" and "the friendship of peoples" remained constants in official rhetoric, they were premised on the assumption that every individual belonged to a nation. Nations were created (or "recognized") and equipped with territorial homelands, and policies of affirmative action were installed to promote native elites to positions of power within the political system (Martin 2001; Edgar 1999). Throughout the Soviet Union, new national identities were created along a template that emphasized language as the key marker of national identity. The old administrative boundaries of Central Asia were redrawn along ethno-national lines in 1924–1925, creating two (eventually five) national republics that entered the Union of Soviet Socialist Republics as members of the federation.

Each nation also had its own national history and its own national heritage, comprising of a pantheon of positive (that is, "progressive" and "secular") cultural heroes, a national literature, national dress, and national customs. The notion that everyone belongs to a nation—defined by language, history, custom, heritage, and common descent—became a commonplace. The keeper of the national heritage was the national intelligentsia, which in Central Asia was itself a creation of the Soviet regime. Its members found employment in an extensive network of universities, institutes, and academies, generously funded by the state. To be sure, nationalist chauvinism could not be expressed in official discourse, which had to stay within fairly strict limits and had to emphasize the "friendship of peoples," "Soviet internationalism," and "the leading role of the Great Russian people, the elder brother." Nevertheless, in the last three decades of the Soviet period, nationalist intelligentsias in each of the five Central Asian republics articulated a confident national identity. The golden age of the national intelligentsias was undoubtedly the Brezhnev era (1964–1982), when Soviet society at all levels came to prize stability above all else. The tumultuous decades under Joseph Stalin (in which the massive sacrifices of World War II compounded the murderous fury of the purges) were succeeded by the equally chaotic years of Nikita Khrushchev. When Khrushchev was ousted from power in 1964, the leadership wanted nothing more than stability. During this period, Soviet republics were effectively run by national party elites based on political mechanisms that had little resemblance to the formal, official rhetoric of the state. As long as the republican leaders kept fulfilling their economic obligations to the center and kept political demands under strict control, they were left with a great deal of leeway in running local affairs. For Central Asia, that meant fulfilling its assigned role as a cotton plantation—although considerable industrial growth took place, cotton monoculture dominated the economies of all the republics, with the partial exception of Kazakhstan. On this monoculture was built the façade of a new indigenous political class, well ensconced in the Soviet system. Leonid Brezhnev's rule as first secretary of the Party (and hence de facto head of state) coincided with equally long spells in office by Sharaf Rashidov in Uzbekistan and Dinmuhamed Kunaev in Kazakhstan.

But Soviet power was never so absolute as to supplant all local solidarities with purely Soviet ones. Indeed, the lowest level of state and Party organizations often coincided with traditional nodes of local society. In the cities, for instance, state and Party organizations were based on the *mahalla,* the residential neighborhood, which had long been the site of reciprocal social bonds and of collective memory and which continued to function as such in its Soviet guise. In the countryside, collective farms became sites of similar networks of kin-based solidarities (Roy 1997; Fathi 1997). This structure, combined with Soviet policies that from the mid-1920s emphasized the "nativization" *(korenizatsiia)* of the local apparatus of power, meant that power at ground level remained in local hands. Party leaders such as Rashidov and Kunaev presided over a political machine based on highly localized solidarity networks.[2]

It was these solidarities that provided the base for the transmission of Islam in Soviet Central Asia. Thus, every collective farm seems to have had a mosque, which was officially registered as a storage room or community hall; similarly, the imam received a salary as a tractor driver or a mechanic. Rituals were performed by men who claimed locally esteemed lineages and who transmitted the knowledge, usually quite slender, in the family (Roy 1997, 226). Other forms of observance also continued, while new forms of ritual arose to circumvent official restrictions. Visits to tombs and shrines had long been a part of Central Asian Islam; with the *hajj* not a real possibility, they now became a common expression of piety (Basilov 1970; Subtelny 1989). Sufi practice was also widespread. The supervisory apparatus of the state, itself not immune to these networks of solidarity, left much of this practice alone as long as it remained discreet, and it was left to the professional propagandists of atheism to bemoan the continuing hold of religion and tradition on the population.[3]

But if local solidarities supported Islam in the Soviet period, they also marked it in very significant ways. Although there is no question that religious observance continued and was widespread, it was not what was most important about being a Muslim. Rather, belonging to Islam now became a marker of national identity, for which no personal piety or observance was necessary. Islam came to be seen as an indispensable part of national customs and traditions that served to set Central Asians apart from outsiders. These customs and traditions included circumcision for boys (which was frowned upon as unhealthy by Soviet medical science, and hence its observance also had an aura of national opposition to Soviet dictates), the maintenance of patriarchal kinship networks, and the celebration of life-cycle rituals. Indeed, the feasts *(to'y)* connected with these rituals (especially circumcisions and weddings) acquired a central place as national customs in the Brezhnev period. The *to'y* served several purposes. Most clearly, they marked Central Asian Muslims as different from others living in their midst while at the same time affirming status within the national community. Conspicuous consumption and conspicuous possession of scarce consumer goods were the most important ways of asserting status and influence in this context (Koroteyeva and Makarova 1998), and the *to'y* were the most suitable occasions for this. The *to'y* were nearly universally observed, including by members of the Party. But these very same ceremonies were also awash in a sea of vodka, drinking that also became a part of national custom. Similarly, the vast majority of Central Asians, including Communists, were buried according to Islamic ritual in Muslim cemeteries; yet many Muslim graves were topped by busts of the deceased in the typical Soviet style. Tradition was malleable: Many were invented, and others were imbued with an importance they had not previously had. But what is important is that traditions as such became a central aspect of how national identities were conceptualized in the Soviet context.

Islam was subordinated to these national identities. Central Asians were Muslims by tradition and civilization, but they were also part of the modern world. In the late Soviet period, being Muslim was a very important source of identity, for it served to demarcate Central Asians (or "natives") as Muslims from Europeans or Russians (who were deemed "outsiders"). The primary emphasis of this identity was on custom and way of life. "Islam" was understood as a form of localism, with little or no basis in Islamic dogma or strictures. It was most emphatically not "pan-Islamic": Muslims from other parts of the world who did not share Central Asian customs were not included in these bound-

Muslims praying at a government-sponsored mosque in Tashkent, Uzbekistan, July 2, 2002. (Photo by Scott Peterson/Getty Images)

aries of "Muslimness" (Schoeberlein-Engel 1994, 222–244). Indeed, the rhetoric of Muslimness did not exclude the possibility of antagonism with other "peoples" of Central Asia, let alone with Muslims abroad. While Muslimness distinguished locals from outsiders in the Soviet context, most Central Asians did not see being Muslim as counterposed to being Soviet. The Soviet government presented Tashkent to the Third World, especially the Muslim world, as a showpiece of Soviet achievements in overcoming underdevelopment. It was a common destination for large numbers of foreign students, many of them Muslim. Yet there was little love lost between these foreign Muslim students and their hosts precisely because their common Muslimness meant little to the hosts. Indeed, most Central Asians at that time took great pride in being citizens of a superpower and of a state that stood against colonialism and oppression. Similarly, when Central Asians went abroad, especially to other Muslim countries, they went as Soviet citizens proud of being "more advanced" than other Muslims. Central Asians also served in large numbers in the Soviet forces in the war in Afghanistan.

Not only was Islam localized and "nationalized," it now existed in a radically de-Islamized public space. As we have seen, the official rhetoric of the Soviet regime was framed in terms of universal human progress, defined in entirely nonreligious terms. Religion was seen as a human construct corresponding with a certain (primitive) stage in the development of human society. More-over, the ideological function of religion as the "opiate of the masses" was con-stantly emphasized. Official channels of socialization, most importantly the school system and the army, reached very deep into society. Islamic practice now took place in an environment that was hostile to all religions.

Islam in the Soviet period was intertwined with the nation, but in a way very different from what had been the case with the Jadids. For the Jadids, belong-ing to Islam had become a form of national identity. But their attitude toward Islam was thoroughly reformist. The nation's survival depended upon a thor-ough reform of Islam itself. Practicing "true" Islam, accessible through mod-ern education and a recourse to Islam's original textual sources, shorn of the mediation of generations of commentary and supercommentary, necessitated jettisoning numerous customary practices. The Jadids were especially critical of the *to'y*, which they saw as wasteful and also as not sanctioned by Islam. They also criticized visits to shrines and tombs and Sufi practices in general (Khalid 1998, 142–147). During the Soviet period, these very practices were elevated to the status of national customs that alone differentiated Central Asians from outsiders. Islam now was part of the civilizational and cultural heritage of a na-tion imagined as an ethnic entity. Instead of requiring the transformation of customary practices, Islam was now synonymous with them. And because these customary practices were so firmly ensconced in Soviet institutions and the So-viet way of life, Islam was politically quiescent.

Islam in Contemporary Central Asia

The collapse of the Soviet Union in 1991 has transformed this situation in many ways, although, as the rest of this chapter will argue, fundamental conti-nuities with the Soviet period remain. Islam in post-Soviet Central Asia is marked by several important features that differentiate it from Islam in the rest of the Muslim world.

Mikhail Gorbachev's promotion of openness and restructuring ushered in an era of religious revival in Central Asia, a revival that has continued since the collapse of the Soviet Union. Disused mosques have been brought back into operation, and many new ones have been built; thousands of pilgrims perform the *hajj* every year; public expressions of piety have increased; and consider-able publishing activity has put many Islamic texts in print. Religious educa-tion is allowed again. But while the existence of this revival cannot be denied, its extent and its political import can easily be exaggerated. Indeed, the reli-gious revival has already caused a great deal of controversy, as many observers in Central Asia, Russia, and farther afield have written of an "Islamic threat" to the region. This view, which dominates opinion among state elites in Central

Asia and has been quite influential abroad, assumes that the revival of religious activity will inexorably lead to the emergence of Islam as a political force that will threaten the established secular regimes and destabilize the entire region. A closer look at the nature of the revival and its relation to deeper social and cultural forces, on the one hand, and to state power, on the other, leads one to conclude that such alarmist prognoses overstate the case.

Today's Islamic revival originated in the context of the open assertion of national identity that took place throughout the former Soviet Union in the late 1980s as glasnost broke old taboos. Nationalist discourses were now free to explore national and cultural legacies beyond the constraints placed on them by the Soviet regime. For Central Asians, that freedom meant rediscovering Islam and Muslim culture and reestablishing links with the broader Muslim world that had been severed by Soviet xenophobia and the downplaying of historical links with non-Soviet nations. There was, in addition, a search for old spiritual and moral values that many felt had been lost during the Soviet period. The religious revival in this sense is profoundly national, one aspect of reclaiming and asserting national identity. None of this was unique to Central Asia. Indeed, the religious revival in Russia itself has been more spectacular than in Central Asia: The Russian Orthodox Church has a secure place in official function, churches in Moscow's Kremlin are fully functional, and many new ones have been built. The religious revival has also encompassed the large numbers of non-Muslims living in Central Asia—mostly settlers from European parts of the former Soviet Union.

The most ubiquitous sign of the re-Islamization of society has been the availability of what one might call "religious commodities" (see by way of comparison Starrett 1995) in Central Asia. These range from plaques and stickers bearing prayers in Arabic and calendars with dates of Islamic holidays to posters bearing the photographs of the holy sites in Mecca and Medina and new editions of the works of "classical" Muslim authors of Central Asia. Yet the life of these religious commodities is different from what it is elsewhere in the Muslim world: In the cities of Uzbekistan, they often share shelf space with foreign liquor and tobacco, the most palpable symbols of the "opening" of the region to the outside world.

All the same, the publishing scene has been transformed, and many more Islamic texts are available now than was even conceivable until 1988. "Islamic" books have appeared in substantial numbers since the 1990s. Nevertheless, publishing in Central Asia is very different from publishing in the Middle East or South Asia. A brief survey of the new "Islamic" books and their place on the publishing scene will serve to highlight the peculiarities of contemporary Central Asian Islam.

In terms of content, the new Islamic books concentrate on introducing the basic tenets of Islam or on providing basic Islamic knowledge that was lost during the Soviet period (for example, Bo'riev 1992). In addition, there are new, Cyrillic-script editions of older texts. These are also seen as introductions to Islam and are published without any scholarly apparatus or explication. Such texts include Jadid primers and other works that were popular in the print market on the eve of the revolution. The choice of titles seems to be quite random, depending primarily on what older texts are at hand; some titles published in this manner are Tatar or even Ottoman in origin. The transcription in these texts usually sticks very close to the original text, even though the language is often markedly different from contemporary literary Uzbek and is not easily accessible to today's readers. Beyond the language, several other aspects of these works (the unstated assumptions of their authors and the cultural and intellectual milieu in which they were written) remain distant from their contemporary readers (for example, Samarqandiy 1995). One can also find facsimile reprints of lithographed texts from before the revolution, also chosen seemingly at random and often without any introduction or other scholarly apparatus. These seem to be aimed at acquainting the reader with the Arabic alphabet.

Also available are "classic" texts transcribed into Cyrillic and presented with some scholarly apparatus. Although these works' content is derived from earlier Islamic traditions in the region, their publication is located in the tradition of Soviet Orientalism. Now they serve to retrieve the cultural and spiritual heritage of the nation, although they are, of course, open to purely "religious" use. The last decade has seen the publication of some texts by al-Bukhari and Rabghuzi (the author of the most popular compilation of tales of the Prophets) and the first Uzbek translation of the Qur'an, which was, significantly, done not by an *alim* (a traditionally trained Islamic scholar) but by an Arabist from the Institute of Oriental Studies in Tashkent. In the same tradition are reprints of works by tsarist-era Russian Orientalists on Central Asian Islam and society, which now provide access to hitherto taboo aspects of history. Finally, one finds popular texts about the region's Islamic past, focusing on figures such as al-Bukhari, Baha'uddin Naqshband, and Temur (known in English as Tamerlane), all of whom are also part of the official canon of Uzbek cultural heroes. While the promotion of these figures as Uzbek heroes relocates Uzbek identity in a more Islamic domain, it also keeps Islam firmly Uzbek.

What does this range of topics tell us about the nature of the Islamic revival in Central Asia? Clearly missing from the repertoire are works of contemporary Islamic thought, works about Islamic law or jurisprudence or about Muslim figures not connected with Central Asia, or manuals of Islamic conduct, all of which appear in great numbers in countries such as Pakistan, Egypt, or Turkey. Moreover, the new Islamic books look exactly like those of the Soviet period, except that they are slimmer and usually not as well produced. This is in marked contrast to the "new Islamic books" in Egypt, for instance, which are illustrated and come with attractive covers (Gonzalez-Quijano 1998). Publishing practices have not changed very much since the Soviet era, and the actual production is still done by a few mammoth concerns that own most printing presses. Large numbers of small-scale publishers, like those that dominate the market for popular literature in Pakistan (Hanaway and Nasir 1996), are not to be found in Uzbekistan. Moreover, much of the impact of the easing of ideological constraints has been mitigated by a severe economic crisis that hit publishing especially hard.

The one sphere of life where the Islamic revival has had some effect is that of gender roles, where the rhetoric of cultural authenticity seeks a rehabilitation of traditional, "properly Islamic" norms for women's lives. There is a new emphasis on traditional roles for women, accompanied by a debate on whether the *hujum* (and, by implication, all it represented) was "necessary." But even here, the emphasis on reclaiming national traditions far outweighs concern with the Islamization of everyday life that accompanies political Islam elsewhere. Of the small number of manuals on proper behavior for women that have appeared in print, most are translations of turn-of-the-century reformist tracts from Central Asia (and in at least one case, from the Ottoman Empire [see Nazimo 1994]). Finally, the disappearance of large numbers of jobs resulting from the economic dislocation of the Soviet collapse feeds the rhetoric of redefining women's place in society (Tokhtakhodjaeva 1995).

The Post-Soviet Political Field

The Islamic revival is thus a grassroots movement, an example of nonstate groups asserting their presence in the public realm. How have relations between religion and the state, on the one hand, and between religion and the discourses of national identity, on the other, been changed since the collapse of the Soviet Union?

In all five countries of Central Asia, the states remain the dominant players in politics and society. The Brezhnev-era patterns of politics survived the transition to independence. The transition was not entirely smooth. Brezhnev's successor Yuri Andropov (in office 1982–1984) and Gorbachev himself tried to shake up the entrenched networks in the name of combating corruption. Although the anticorruption campaign dislodged many incumbents from their offices, it did little to alter the nature of the politics, and indeed, it served to arouse nationalist sentiment in the republics, especially in Uzbekistan, which was hit hardest by the anticorruption campaign (Critchlow 1991, 39–54). Nevertheless, independence came as a surprise to Central Asia—support for the dissolution of the Soviet Union was lower in Central Asia than anywhere else in the union—and the Party elites managed to stay in power as Soviet republics became sovereign states overnight. Not only are the regimes in control of public life, their attitude to Islam has changed only slightly from what it was in the Soviet period. In making the transition, they appealed to the idea of national identities as they had developed in the Soviet period. As such, they may be termed "nationalizing regimes" (Brubaker 1996; see also Bohr 1998). This phenomenon repays greater attention.

In Uzbekistan, President Islom Karimov has fashioned himself as the leader of a state that promises to build a great Uzbekistan in the future. The slogan *O'zbekiston, kelajagi buyuk davlat,* "Uzbekistan, the great state of the future," is ubiquitously displayed in public spaces. Independent Uzbekistan continues a great tradition of "Uzbek statehood" *(O'zbek davlatchiligi),* whose roots lie in the mists of Central Asian antiquity, that was rudely interrupted by Russian and then Soviet imperialism. The apogee of "Uzbek statehood" was reached under the Turco-Mongol conqueror Temur (1336–1405), who has been turned into the father of the nation. The Uzbek "state tradition" also produced a "golden heritage" *(oltin meros)* that the regime celebrates (Adams 1999). Islam is a significant part of this heritage, and the ruling elite has moved quickly to claim its stake in the re-Islamization of the country. The regime celebrates the Islamic cultural heritage of the region and invokes the moral and ethical values stemming from it. Sufism has been adopted as an example of the humanist traditions of the Uzbek nation, just as old mosques are celebrated as "architectural monuments." The *hajj* is now officially sponsored, and President Karimov has himself traveled to Mecca. Thus, the government has honored such figures as al-Bukhari, al-Maturidi, and al-Marghinani—as well as later Turkic figures such as the poet Mir Alisher Navoiy and the prince-astronomer Mirzo Ulug'bek—with lavish celebrations.

In Turkmenistan, the president (and former first secretary of the Turkmenistan branch of the Communist Party) Saparmurat Niyazov has sought to base legitimacy in tradition in an altogether different way. Instead of celebrating a continuous tradition of statehood, the regime celebrates the tribal traditions of the Turkmen people. Niyazov has taken for himself the title of "Türkmenbashï," literally "the head Turkmen," the chief of all Turkmen tribes. However, this traditionalizing move takes place in a state equipped with modern technologies of policing and surveillance; the cult of personality surrounding Niyazov is directly descended from that surrounding Stalin. In Niyazov's scheme of things, Islam has a certain place as an aspect of Turkmen history, but since Turkmen identity is supposed to predate Islam, that place is not central.

In Kazakhstan and Kyrgyzstan (which provides a partial exception to the rule of native Party elites claiming power effortlessly in 1991), too, the rhetoric of the recovery of an interrupted national development exists, but in both nations it is tempered by the political realities of needing to accommodate large, often-vocal Russian minorities (northern Kazakhstan has a Russian majority that has expended considerable energies in seeking union with the Russian Federation). The regime in Kazakhstan has tried to turn the shrine of Ahmet Yesevi, the great Sufi master and founder of the Yesevi order in Turkistan, into a pan-Turkic icon, but beyond that, the presence of Islamic symbols or figures in official discourse is rather limited.

Finally, the case of Tajikistan calls for particular attention. The country suffered a devastating civil war between 1992 and 1997—the only bloody conflict in Central Asia after the collapse of the Soviet Union—that was highly destructive of an already-weak economy. The two sides in the war were routinely labeled as "Communists" and "Islamists," leading many to believe that "Islamism" or "Islamic fundamentalism" had arrived in Central Asia. However, as several authors have convincingly argued, these labels were very misleading. The basic issues in that war were regional and clan based, and there was little to distinguish the two sides in terms of their allegiance to political Islam (Atkin 1994; Dudoignon 1997; Roy 1997, 212–217). The incumbent elites were challenged by groups from the region of Kulob, which had been marginalized in the power configurations of the Soviet era. This group was led in many instances by local *mullah*s, men who were locally influential, and therefore the group was labeled "Islamist" by its opponents as a convenient way of disparaging it. In practice, the whole of Tajik society, regardless of positioning in the civil war, was undergoing a process of "Islamization" in which symbols from the region's Islamic past were invoked. There is little to suggest that the program of the "Islamists" had any similarities with Islamist movements in the rest of the Muslim world. The civil war sputtered to an end in 1997, when a peace accord was reached around a formula giving the so-called Islamists a share in power. The subsequent development of politics in Tajikistan does not indicate any attempt by the Islamists to Islamize the state.

All Central Asian regimes are wary of Islamist activism and are committed to remaining in firm control of Islamic expression. To this end, they use Soviet-era tactics. The Spiritual Directorate of Muslims in the Asian Regions (SADUM) did not survive the fall of the Soviet Union. First, an unprecedented public demonstration in Tashkent in 1989 called for the resignation of the old leadership (the revolt was ultimately successful in achieving this goal). Next, the regional scope of the organization was destroyed, as its various national wings seceded. By 1992, each new country had its own religious administration. The Soviet-era official *ulama*, most of whom were modernists vaguely in the Jadid tradition, lost positions of authority and were replaced by formerly "unofficial" *ulama*, most of whom are much less prone to advocate reform (Roy 1997, 238–239). The new boards function as organs of state, firmly under the control of the regimes. Although governments in all Central Asian countries keep the religious establishment on a tight leash, the case in Uzbekistan is the most extreme.

150   ISLAM IN WORLD CULTURES

SADUM was renamed the Muslim Directorate of Uzbekistan (O'zbekiston Musulmonlar Idorasi). It has a monopoly on religious instruction and on the organization of contacts with the rest of the Muslim world. New *madrasas* have appeared under its auspices, and it organizes the *hajj* for several thousand citizens every year. It also controls all mosques and their personnel in the country. Mosques not controlled by the Muslim Directorate, on the other hand, are deemed illegal and have in many instances been closed (Human Rights Watch [HRW] 1998). The Karimov regime has long waged a battle against all manifestations of Islam beyond the control of the local Muslim Directorate. With a new leadership installed, the Muslim Directorate has been turned into a body loyal to the regime. Firm state bureaucratic control over Islam is hardly unusual in the Muslim world, as the different cases of Turkey (Kaplan 1996), Egypt (Starrett 1998), and Indonesia (Hefner 2000) show; what is unusual about Uzbekistan is the sheer intensity of the repression and the fact that the state acts from a position located almost entirely outside the realm of Islamic sensibilities.

The De-Islamized Public Sphere

All public discourse in the Soviet period was explicitly cast in materialist terms deriving from Marxism as a philosophy of universal *human* progress, in which human fulfillment entailed the conquest of religion and superstition. All public claims were validated by appeals to universal laws of history and to socialist construction, which created its own moral imperative. Islam, along with all other religions, was excluded from the public realm. Under Gorbachev, the rhetoric of "universal human values" gained some currency in Soviet discourse, without in any way admitting Islam back into public discourse. This marks Central Asia as different from almost all other parts of the Muslim world (with the possible exception of the Muslim states of the Balkans), where Islam and Islamic values (locally construed, to be sure, but "Islamic" nevertheless) are present to some extent or another, if only as a generally recognized pattern of moral values that frame public debate. Such is not the case in Central Asia. The religious revival that began during perestroika made Islam more visible. Nevertheless, the site for the reproduction of Islam has not been transformed significantly. Islam is still reproduced in the private realm, at home and during private lessons, or in carefully controlled official institutions. Its absence from public life is striking. Public discourse does not make use of any references to Islam; indeed, Islam itself has to be justified with reference to other discourses (of national identity and destiny, progress, enlightenment, and so on).

This is clearly evident in the post-Soviet literature on Sufism. This literature consists mostly of brochures and pamphlets that introduce readers to the basic tenets of Sufism or of a particular Sufi author. Most of this literature is produced by people trained in philology or history and is aimed at an audience that lacks many of the most basic concepts about Sufism (which are learned in most other Muslim societies in childhood). Thus, both producers and consumers of this literature stand outside the field of reference of Sufism. While these texts serve to provide a basic introduction to Sufism, the subject is framed very differently than it is in traditional Sufi tracts. Contemporary Central Asian writing extols Sufism as an indigenous tradition of humanism, a part of the national heritage that accords with universal human values and that contributed to a universal human civilization (Schubel 1999). There is little emphasis on the miracles associated with the Sufis. Sufism and Islam in general are cast in a consciously ecumenical and cosmopolitan frame of reference, as merely a local variant of a universal phenomenon, namely, religion. What marks Islam as important is, of course, its connection to national heritage.

The Islamic revival in post-Soviet Central Asia remains largely a phenomenon of cultural rediscovery; it shows little sign of affecting everyday life. There is little concern with observing Islam's basic prohibitions against alcohol and even pork. The rhythms of everyday life remain secular in a way that is inconceivable in, say, Turkey. Indeed, as Bruce Privratsky's field research shows, in Kazakhstan, most people call their religious life *musïlmanshïlïq*, literally "Muslimness," or *taza jol*, "the clean path," rather than "Islam." As he notes, "this reflects discomfort with the abstraction of Islam as an ideology and a preference for Muslim life as an experience of the community" (Privratsky 2001, 78). The community's experience of Islam need not be grounded in textual authority. Rather, as Privratsky shows, for most Kazakhs, being Muslim is intertwined with cults of saints and holy places. Saints act as guardians of the *taza jol* for the whole community, while holy places (such as shrines and mosques) serve to render Muslim the very territory on which Kazakhs live. The community is ipso facto Muslim, and as long as some people (in practice, the elderly and certain descent groups) fulfill the ritual requirements, the rest of the population is excused from them. Indeed, Privratsky records low levels of knowledge of Islam. Pilgrims at the shrine of Khoja Ahmet Yesevi associate it with Islam but seldom with Sufism. They know the figure of Ahmet Yesevi only in the vaguest terms as the man who "opened religion" in the region (Privratsky 2001, 54–57). Few Kazakhs know even the ritual affirmation of faith in Arabic and content themselves with the Kazakh phrase *Al-hamdulillah musïlmanmïn,* "Praise be to God, I am a Muslim" (ibid., 90–92).

This "religious minimalism" does not mean, however, that Kazakhs do not see themselves as Muslims; rather, they see Islam as an integral part of the way Kazakhs live. Since the collapse of the Soviet Union, such understandings of Islam have been challenged by more rigorous expressions of piety. Particularly in Uzbekistan and Tajikistan, the expression of Islam has diversified as new sects have appeared, largely as a result of contacts with foreign Muslims. The impact of such contacts can easily be overstated, however. Not only are the governments not happy, but there is also a general sentiment that deprecates foreign Muslims (whether Arabs, Pakistanis, or Turks) who preach rigorous observance of Islam. Such approaches to Islam are seen as foreign and as not suited to the temper of Central Asians.

At the same time, the school system remains resolutely secular, with no religious instruction whatsoever in any country. This, again, is in marked contrast to Turkey, where the laicist regime nevertheless ensures that Islam, in an approved and properly "nationalized" form, remains part of the moral education of all pupils (Kaplan 1996). In Central Asia, religious instruction continues in the private realm, although now it is not persecuted. A remarkable feature of the cultural landscape since the 1990s has been the emergence into the open of *otins*, women who teach children the basic tenets of faith, largely orally (Fathi 1998). Similarly, there has been a revival of Sufi orders, with *shaykhs* recruiting disciples openly. Yet it is clear that instead of being a return to some kind of "pure" Sufism, this phenomenon is redefining Sufism itself. As an Uzbek scholar has pointed out, the adepts' knowledge of the intricacies of Sufi ritual is often superficial, while older practices about initiation are widely disregarded (Bobojonov 1998; see also Privratsky 2001). Contacts with Sufi fraternities abroad has been reestablished, and the renovated shrine of Baha'uddin Naqshband outside Bukhara receives large numbers of visitors from far afield, but national differences and language barriers have proved to be very real.

The revival of Islamic vocabulary in a public sphere that remains de-Islamized often produces incongruous results. In 2001, the press secretary of the Türkmenbashï took adulation to a new level when he wrote, "Saparmurat Türkmenbashï is a national prophet, sent to the Turkmen people in the third millennium" (quoted in Arzybov 2001). The statement is blasphemous for the vast majority of Muslims, but it is nevertheless amusing: Its combination of the Stalinist rhetoric of Niyazov's cult of personality with Soviet-style nationalism and Islam transforms an apparatchik into a *national* prophet sent to the Turkmen people for the third millennium of the Christian era!

The Politics of Antifundamentalism

Such (attempted) use of Islamic rhetoric remains unusual, however. Far more typical today is the regimes' use of "the Islamic threat" (usually glossed as "Muslim extremism" or "Wahhabism") to justify authoritarian policies. The most extreme case is that of Uzbekistan. While the government of Uzbekistan

Muslims at a shrine in Bukhara, Uzbekistan. (Charles and Josette Lenars/CORBIS)

asserts its respect for the spiritual heritage of the nation, it also makes no bones about its opposition to the danger posed by the wrong kind of Islam. It holds that such Islam is not part of the nation's traditions; denotes backwardness, obscurantism, and fanaticism; and is bound to knock the nation from its path to progress. Karimov is keen "to make clear the difference between the spiritual values of religion and certain ambitions—political and other aggressive goals—which are far from religion" (Karimov 1998, 20). At other times, he can be more blunt. On May 1, 1998, in a speech broadcast live on radio, Karimov told the parliament of Uzbekistan, "Such people [Islamic extremists] must be shot in the head. If necessary, I'll shoot them myself" (HRW 1998). Since December 1997, the Karimov government has routinely resorted to repression of those it accuses of "Islamic extremism" (and indeed of all political opposition). The identification of such dangers allows the government to restrict religious activity itself. In January 1998, the Muslim Directorate outlawed the use of loudspeakers in mosques since their use is not "one of the fundamentals of Islam." Any expression of Islam or worship conducted outside the control of the Muslim Directorate is now illegal (and hence punishable) by definition, and thousands of people have been arrested on charges of "extremism," which in many cases amounts to possession of religious literature not approved by the Muslim Directorate, praying in an unofficial mosque, or simply sporting the wrong kind of beard (HRW 2001). The government also established a center for reviewing all religious literature and audio and videotapes entering the country from abroad. As an official stated matter-of-factly, "no non-state organization or state organization has any right to do anything concerning religion without the knowledge of our state" (HRW 1999, 307). Strict visa controls also keep suspected Muslim activists out.

How valid are these fears? On February 16, 1999, six bombs, aimed at crucial government buildings, exploded in the center of Tashkent, killing sixteen and injuring hundreds. The government quickly blamed the outrage on "extremists," and in the ensuing months, it arrested hundreds of alleged extremists (while many others were extradited from Turkey, Ukraine, Kazakhstan, and Kyrgyzstan) and duly found them guilty in courts of law. Hundreds of people were arrested, and several suspects were extradited while other trials continued. Then, during the summer of 1999, an armed band belonging to the Islamic Movement of Uzbekistan (IMU) attempted to cross from Tajikistan into Uzbekistan via Kyrgyzstan. After a hostage-taking drama involving Japanese citizens, the band retreated, only to reappear the following summer. Clearly, there is a militant movement in Uzbekistan that strives for the Islamization of law and the state and for the enforcement of Islamic norms as law. The scope of its ambitions, the resources it commands, and the support it enjoys among the population are, however, all open to question. Uzbekistan and the rest of Central Asia remains outside the flows of texts, personnel, and capital that have been instrumental in establishing political Islam as a transnational phenomenon. Censorship has not disappeared, and governments closely monitor contacts with Muslim organizations in the Middle East.

Nevertheless, these campaigns have placed the struggle against "extremism" at the forefront of the political agenda in Uzbekistan. The Karimov regime long ago borrowed the term "Wahhabi" to denote undesirable Muslims from late Soviet discourse (there are similarities with nineteenth-century British Indian uses of the term as a blanket condemnation of a regime's opponents). In independent Uzbekistan, the accusation of Wahhabism situates the accused beyond the scope of the national tradition and insinuates unhealthy Saudi influence. It is thus a nativist gesture. But more is at stake. In the post–cold war world order, "antifundamentalism" provides a universal language that allows regimes—liberal democratic as much as authoritarian—to position themselves on the right side of the fence, on the side of reason, enlightenment, and secularism, and against fanaticism, obscurantism, and reaction. Central Asian regimes have used this language with great liberality. They are not simply cynically manipulating world public opinion, however, for it would be idle to deny that the fears embodied in this rhetoric do resonate among the public. Many in Uzbekistan are wary of what has happened in Afghanistan since the 1980s, and the urban intelligentsia in particular is sympathetic to Karimov's antifundamentalist posture.

Conclusion

It is not simply state repression that will guarantee that Islam remains apolitical in Central Asia. Islam, nation, and tradition coexist happily in Central Asia today, in 2004. A "return" to Islam today is widely seen as a way of reclaiming the national cultural patrimony and of decolonization, but little more. Islam is deeply intertwined with powerful national myths. For the same reason, unlike in much of the Middle East, there is little interest on university campuses for a return to "true Islam." An opinion survey carried out in 1993 found only 11 percent of respondents in Uzbekistan and Kazakhstan expressing a preference for "an Islamic state" as the best possible future for Central Asia, and most of those seemed to associate the Islamic state with "fairness, goodness and other traditional or cultural values related to Islam" (Lubin 1995, 62)[4]—in short, an idealized version of an authentic Central Asian past set against Soviet-era corruption, rather than an idealized future based on the sovereignty of God and the Islamization of life. Official repression notwithstanding, we have little evidence that the carriers of Islam seek to transform their religious authority into political power.

Indeed, the problem for carriers of Islam is the opposite: For the majority of the population, Islam continues to be synonymous with custom and tradition, but now custom and tradition belong to nations imagined as "objective" ethnic entities. Post-Soviet national identities are powerful and compelling to most citizens. Discourses of the nations are also tied to discourses of modernity and progress, which in Central Asia tend to overshadow the rhetorical field of Islam. Islam thus becomes, for most people in Central Asia, an aspect of their national heritage—a dearly important one, but not the defining one. Islam-as-national-heritage renders ritual observance less important. Nevertheless, as I hope to have shown, "religious minimalism" and the lack of knowledge of the textual sources of Islamic authority should not be taken to mean that Central Asians do not think of themselves as Muslims or that they are "only superficially Islamized." Rather, we have in Central Asia a different (spatially and temporally specific) way of being Muslim, the result of radical social and cultural change in a Muslim society of long standing.

Notes

1.   The academic study of Islam, a fairly circumscribed field, provided one form of access to religious texts. Soviet Orientalism usually shunned religious topics, leaving the study of Islam to experts in the fields of "scientific atheism" and "atheistic propaganda." Nevertheless, there were examples of believing Muslims working in Soviet academia and teaching Islam privately at home; see Fathi 1997, 36–37.

2.   We still know little about the way these networks operated, but for a preliminary account of the career of Sharaf Rashidov, see Vaisman 1995.

3.   As Muriel Atkin noted, the complaints of these officials were a constant in the late Soviet period (1989, 57–58).

4.   The survey was based on questionnaires filled out by 2,000 respondents in Uzbekistan and Kazakhstan. I find the size and the nature of the sample to be problematic, but I see little reason to doubt the validity of the statement being made here. See also Ilkhamov 2001.

References

Abduvakhitov, Abdujabbar A. 1994. "The Jadid Movement and Its Impact on Contemporary Central Asia." In *Central Asia: Its Strategic Importance and Future Prospects,* edited by Hafiz Malik, 65–75. New York: St. Martin's.

Adams, Laura L. 1999. "Celebrating Independence: Arts, Institutions, and Identity in Uzbekistan." PhD diss., University of California, Berkeley.

Arzybov, Konstantin. 2001. "Turkmen President's Prophet Motive." *Reporting on Central Asia,* no. 55. http://www.iwpr.net/index.pl?archive/rca/rca_200106_55_3_eng.txt.

Atkin, Muriel. 1989. *The Subtlest Battle: Islam in Soviet Tajikistan.* Philadelphia: Foreign Policy Research Institute.

———. 1994. "The Politics of Polarization in Tajikistan." In *Central Asia: Its Strategic Importance and Future Prospects,* edited by Hafiz Malik, 211–233. New York: St. Martin's.

Basilov, V. N. 1970. *Kul't sviatykh v Islame.* Moscow: Mysi'.

Behbudiy, Mahmud Xo'ja. 1913. "Omolimiz yo inki murodimiz." *Oyina,* December 7.

Bobojonov, Bakhtyar. 1998. "Le renouveau des communautés soufies dans l'Ouzbékistan." *Cahiers d'Asie centrale,* nos. 5–6: 285–311.

Bohr, Annette. 1998. "The Central Asian States as Nationalizing Regimes." In *Nation-Building in the Post-Soviet Borderlands: The Politics of National Identities,* edited by Graham Smith, Vivien Law, Andrew Wilson, Annette Bohr, and Edward Allworth. Cambridge: Cambridge University Press.

Bo'riev, O. 1992. *Murodbaxsh kunlar.* Tashkent: Fan.

Brubaker, Rogers. 1996. *Nationalism Reframed: Nationhood and the National Question in the New Europe.* Cambridge: Cambridge University Press.

Critchlow, James. 1991. *Nationalism in Uzbekistan: A Soviet Republic's Road to Sovereignty.* Boulder, CO: Westview.

DeWeese, Devin. 1994. *Islamization and Native Religion in the Golden Horde: Baba Tükles and Conversion to Islam in Historical and Epic Tradition.* University Park: Pennsylvania State University Press.

Dudoignon, Stéphane A. 1996. "Djadidisme, merasisme, islamisme," *Cahiers du monde russe* 37: 13–40.

———. 1997. "Political Parties and Forces in Tajikistan, 1989–1993." In *Tajikistan: The Trials of Independence,* edited by Mohammad-Reza Djalili, Frédéric Grare, and Shirin Akiner, 52–85. New York: St. Martin's.

Edgar, Adrienne L. 1999. "The Making of Soviet Turkmenistan, 1924–1938." PhD diss., University of California, Berkeley.

Fathi, Habiba. 1997. "Otines: The Unknown Women Clerics of Central Asian Islam." *Central Asian Survey* 16: 27–43.

———. 1998. "La pouvoir des otin, instructrices coraniques, dans l'Ouzbékistan indépendant." *Cahiers d'Asie centrale,* nos. 5–6: 313–333.

Frye, Richard. 1965. *Bukhara: The Medieval Achievement.* Norman: University of Oklahoma Press.

Gonzalez-Quijano, Yves. 1998. *Les gens du livre: Édition et champ intellectuel dans l'Égypte républicaine.* Paris: Éditions CNRS.

Hanaway, William, and Mumtaz Nasir. 1996. "Chapbook Publishing in Pakistan." In *Studies in Pakistani Popular Culture,* edited by William Hanaway and Wilma Heston, 343–437. Lahore: Sang-e-Meel.

Hefner, Robert W. 2000. *Civil Islam: Muslims and Democratization in Indonesia.* Princeton: Princeton University Press.

Human Rights Watch (HRW). 1998. "Crackdown in the Farghona Valley: Arbitrary Arrests and Religious Discrimination." http://www.hrw.org/hrw/reports98/uzbekistan.

———. 1999. *Human Rights Watch World Report 1999.* New York: Human Rights Watch.

———. 2001. "Memorandum to the U.S. Government Regarding Religious Persecution in Uzbekistan." August 10. http://www.hrw.org/backgrounder/eca/uzbek-aug/persecution.htm#P68_14813.

Ilkhamov, Alisher. 2001. "Impoverishment of the Masses in the Transition Period: Signs of an Emerging 'New Poor' Identity in Uzbekistan." *Central Asian Survey* 20: 33–54.

Kamp, Marianne R. 1998. "Unveiling Uzbek Women: Liberation, Representation, and Discourse, 1906–1929." PhD diss., University of Chicago.

Kaplan, Samuel. 1996. "Education and the Politics of National Culture in a Turkish Community, circa 1990." PhD diss., University of Chicago.

Karimov, Islom. 1998. *Uzbekistan on the Threshold of the Twenty-First Century: Challenges to Stability and Progress.* New York: St. Martin's.

Keller, Shoshana. 2001. *To Moscow, Not Mecca: The Soviet Campaigns against Islam in Central Asia, 1917–1941.* Westport, CT: Praeger.

Khalid, Adeeb. 1998. *The Politics of Muslim Cultural Reform: Jadidism in Central Asia.* Berkeley and Los Angeles: University of California Press.

———. 1999. "The Emergence of a Modern Central Asian Historical Consciousness." In *Historiography of Imperial Russia: The Profession and Writing of History in a Multinational State,* edited by Thomas Sanders, 433–453. Armonk, NY: M. E. Sharpe.

Koroteyeva, Victoria, and Ekaterina Makarova. 1998. "Money and Social Connections in the Soviet and Post-Soviet City." *Central Asian Survey* 17: 579–596.

Lubin, Nancy. 1995. "Islam and Ethnic Identity in Central Asia: A View from Below." In *Muslim Eurasia: Conflicting Legacies,* edited by Yaacov Ro'i, 53–71. London: Frank Cass.

Martin, Terry. 2001. *An Affirmative Action Empire: Nations and Nationalism in the Soviet Union, 1923–1939.* Ithaca, NY: Cornell University Press.

Massell, Gregory J. 1974. *The Surrogate Proletariat: Moslem Women and Revolutionary Strategies in Soviet Central Asia, 1919–1929.* Princeton: Princeton University Press.

Munis, Khorazmiy, and Muhammad Rizo Ogahiy. 1999. *Firdaws al-Iqbal: History of Khorezm.* Translated by Yuri Bregel. Leiden: Brill.

Nazimo, Aliy. 1994. *Qizlar tarbiyasi.* Translated by Teshaboy Ziyoev. Tashkent: Kamalak.

Northrop, Douglas T. 1999. "Uzbek Women and the Veil: Gender and Power in Soviet Central Asia." PhD diss., Stanford University.

Privratsky, Bruce G. 2001. *Muslim Turkistan: Kazak Religion and Collective Memory.* London: Curzon Press.

Roy, Olivier. 1997. *La nouvelle Asie centrale, ou La fabrication des nations.* Paris: Seuil.

Samarqandiy, Vasliy. 1995. *Imom A'zam tarixi.* Tashkent: Yozuvchi.

Schoeberlein-Engel, John. 1994. "Identity in Central Asia: Construction and Contention in the Conceptions of 'Özbek,' 'Tâjik,' 'Muslim,' 'Samarqandi,' and Other Groups." PhD diss., Harvard University.

Schubel, Vernon. 1999. "Post-Soviet Hagiography and the Reconstruction of the Naqshbandi Tradition in Contemporary Uzbekistan." In *Naqshbandis in Western and Central Asia: Change and Continuity,* edited by Elisabeth Özdalga, 73–87. London: Curzon Press.

Slezkine, Yuri. 1994. "The USSR as a Communal Apartment, or How a Socialist State Promoted Ethnic Particularism." *Slavic Review* 53: 414–452.

Starrett, Gregory. 1995. "The Political Economy of Religious Commodities in Cairo." *American Anthropologist* 97: 51–68.

————. 1998. *Putting Islam to Work: Education, Politics, and Religious Transformation in Egypt.* Berkeley and Los Angeles: University of California Press.

Subtelny, Maria Eva. 1989. "The Cult of Holy Places: Religious Practices among Soviet Muslims." *Middle East Journal* 43: 593–604.

Suny, Ronald Grigor. 1994. *The Revenge of the Past: Nationalism, Revolution, and the Collapse of the Soviet Union.* Stanford, CA: Stanford University Press.

Tokhtakhodjaeva, Marfua. 1995. *Between the Slogans of Communism and the Laws of Islam.* Translated by Sufian Aslam. Lahore: Shirkat Gah Women's Resource Centre.

Vaisman, Damien. 1995. "Regionalism and Clan Loyalty." In *Muslim Eurasia: Conflicting Legacies,* edited by Yaacov Ro'i, 105–123. London: Frank Cass.

Zürcher, Erik Jan. 1999. "The Vocabulary of Muslim Nationalism." *International Journal of the Sociology of Language,* no. 137: 81–92.

Chapter Six

Islam in China
Accommodation or Separatism?

D RU C. G LADNEY

China's Muslims are now facing their second millennium under Chinese rule. Many of the challenges they confront are the same ones they have faced for the last 1,400 years of continuous interaction with Chinese society, but many others are new, resulting from China's transformed and increasingly globalized society and, especially, from the watershed events of the September 11, 2001, terrorist attack and the subsequent "war on terrorism." Muslims in China live as minority communities amid a sea of people whom they see as largely pork-eating, polytheistic, secularistic, and "heathen" *(kafir)*. Nevertheless, many of their small and isolated communities have survived in inhospitable circumstances for over a millennium.

Though small in population percentage (about 2 percent in China, 1 percent in Japan, and less than 1 percent in Korea), the Muslim populations of East Asia are nevertheless numerically large in comparison with those of other Muslim states. In fact, there are more Muslims living in China today than there are in Malaysia, and more than in every Middle Eastern Muslim nation except Iran, Turkey, and Egypt. East Asia is also increasingly dependent on immigrants from Muslim-majority nations for energy and cheap labor, thus raising the importance of its Muslim diasporic communities for international and domestic relations. Japan has a rather small resident Muslim community, estimated to be less than 10,000; however, recent waves of Middle Eastern and South Asian migrant laborers to Japan's large industrial cities suggest that the total Muslim population in Japan could be nearing the million mark. Though these communities are made up of temporary residents, they have as strong an impact on Japan's rather insular society as the Turkish and Kurdish populations have on the Scandinavian heartlands (Turks and

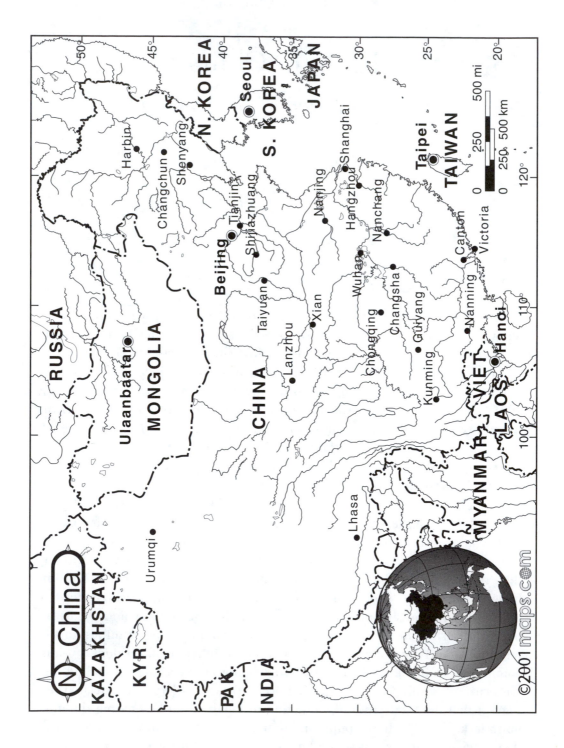

China

N

RUSSIA

KAZAKHSTAN

KYR.

PAK.

INDIA

Urumqi

MONGOLIA

Ulaanbaatar

Harbin

Changchun

Shenyang

N. KOREA

Seoul

S. KOREA

JAPAN

Beijing

Tianjin

Shijiazhuang

Taiyuan

Lanzhou

Xian

Nanjing

Hangzhou

Shanghai

Nanchang

Wuhan

Chongqing

Changsha

Guiyang

Kunming

CHINA

Lhasa

Canton

Victoria

Nanning

MYANMAR

VIET.

LAOS

Hanoi

Taipei

TAIWAN

500 mi

500 km

250

250

0

0

50°

45°

40°

85°

30°

25°

20°

120°

110°

100°

©2001 maps.com

Kurds now make up more than 10 percent of the population of Scandinavia). As Jonathan Lipman insightfully noted, these long-term Muslim communities have often been the "familiar strangers" found in small enclaves throughout Asia (1997, 2). And if Kosovo and Bosnia are to serve as lessons, failure to accommodate Muslim minorities can lead to national dismemberment and international intervention. Indeed, China's primary objection to NATO involvement in Kosovo was based on its fear that involvement there might encourage the aiding and abetting of separatists generally, a potential problem in light of the fact that independence groups in Xinjiang, Tibet, and even Taiwan remain a major Chinese concern.

This chapter will seek to examine Muslim-minority identity in Asia with specific reference to China, not only because that is where I have conducted most of my research, but also because, as the largest Muslim minority in East Asia, China's Muslims are clearly the most threatened in terms of self-preservation and Islamic identity. At the same time, some of the lessons gleaned from the study of the Chinese case might be useful for other Muslim communities in East Asia, and perhaps elsewhere in the world as well. Most relevant to this is the thesis that successful Muslim accommodation to minority status in Asia can be seen as evidence that Muslim groups can reconcile the dictates of Islam to the contexts of their host cultures. This goes against the opposite view that can be found in the writings of some analysts of Islam in China, such as Raphael Israeli and Michael Dillon, who argue that Islam in the region is almost unavoidably rebellious and that Muslims as minorities are inherently problematic to a non-Muslim state (Israeli 1978; Dillon 1997).

Islam in China

According to the reasonably accurate 1990 national census of China, the total Muslim population is 17.6 million, including Hui (8,602,978), Uyghur (7,214,431), Kazakh (1,111,718), Dongxiang (373,872), Kyrgyz (373,872), Salar (87,697), Tajik (33,538), Uzbek (14,502), Bonan (12,212), and Tatar (4,873). The Hui speak mainly Sino-Tibetan languages; Turkic-language speakers include the Uyghur, Kazakh, Kyrgyz, Uzbek, and Tatar; combined Turkic-Mongolian speakers include the Dongxiang, Salar, and Bonan, concentrated in Gansu's mountainous Hexi corridor; and the Tajik speak a variety of Indo-Persian dialects. It is important to note, however, that the Chinese census registered people by nationality, not religious affiliation, so the actual number of Muslims is still unknown, and all population figures are influenced by politics in their use and interpretation.

Archaeological discoveries of large collections of Islamic artifacts and epigraphy on the southeast coast suggest that the earliest Muslim communities in

China were descended from Arab, Persian, Central Asian, and Mongolian Muslim merchants, militia, and officials who settled first along China's southeast coast from the seventh through the tenth centuries. Later, larger migrations to the north from Central Asia under the Mongol-Yuan dynasty in the thirteenth and fourteenth centuries added to these Muslim populations by gradually intermarrying with the local Chinese populations and raising their children as Muslims. Practicing Sunni Hanafi Islam and residing in independent small communities clustered around a central mosque, these communities were characterized by relatively isolated, independent Islamic villages and urban enclaves who interacted via trading networks. However, these scattered Islamic settlements shared a recognition of belonging to the wider Islamic community *(umma)* that was connected by traveling Muslim teachers known locally as *ahung.*

Hui Muslims and Islamic Accommodation to Chinese Society

Islam in China has primarily been propagated over the last 1,300 years among the people now known as Hui, but many of the issues confronting them are relevant to the Turkic and Indo-European Muslims on China's inner Asian frontier. Though Hui speak a number of non-Chinese languages, most Hui are closer to Han Chinese than are other Muslim nationalities in terms of demographic proximity and cultural accommodation. The attempt to adapt many of their Muslim practices to the Han way of life has led to criticisms among some Muslim reformers. In the wake of the modern Islamic reform movements that have swept across China, a wide spectrum of Islamic belief and practice can now be found among the Hui Muslims in China.

The Hui have been labeled the "Chinese-speaking Muslims," "Chinese Muslims," and most recently, as "Sino-Muslims."[1] However, this terminology is misleading because by law, all Muslims living in China are "Chinese" by citizenship and because there are large Hui communities who primarily speak the non-Chinese languages dominant in the areas where they live. This is the case, for example, with the Tibetan, Mongolian, Thai, and Hainan Muslims of China, who are also classified by the state as Hui. These "Hui" Muslims speak Tibetan, Mongolian, and Thai as their first languages and learn Han Chinese in school, as the national language, along with the Arabic and Persian that some of them also learn at the mosque. Interestingly, since Tajik is not an official language in China, the schoolchildren among the Tajiks of Xinjiang (who speak a Darian branch language, distantly related to old Persian and quite different from the Tajik languages spoken in Tajikistan) go to schools where they are taught in either Turkic Uyghur or Han Chinese.

In the past, accommodation to the Han way of life was not as much of an issue for some Turkish and Indo-European Muslim groups as it was for the Hui, for the former were traditionally more isolated from the Han and their identities were not as threatened by extensive interaction. However, this has begun to change since the 1960s. As a result of the state-sponsored nationality-identification campaigns launched in recent decades, these various groups have begun to think of themselves as ethnic nationalities, as something more than just "Muslims." The Hui are unique among the fifty-five identified nationalities in China in that they are the only nationality for whom a religion (Islam) is the only unifying category of identity, even though many members of the Hui nationality may not actively practice Islam.

Hui Sufi Orders and Chinese Culture

Sufism began to make a substantial impact in China proper in the late seventeenth century, arriving mainly along the Central Asian trade routes with saintly *shaykhs*, both Chinese and foreign, who brought new teachings from the pilgrimage cities. These charismatic teachers and tradesmen established widespread networks and brotherhood associations, including most prominently the Naqshbandiyya, Qadiriyya, and Kubrawiyya. Unlike in the Middle Eastern or Central Asian Sufi orders, where one might belong to two or even three orders at once, the Hui belong to only one. Among the Hui, one is generally born into one's Sufi order *(menhuan)*, or one converts dramatically to another. In fact, this is the only instance of conversion I encountered among my sojourn among the Hui. I never met a Han who had converted to Islam in China without having been married to a Hui or adopted into a Hui family, though I heard of a few isolated instances. Joseph Fletcher records the conversion to Islam of twenty-eight Tibetan tribes and their "Living Buddha" by Ma Laichi in Xunhua, Qinghai, in the mid-eighteenth century (Trippner 1961, 154–155). After the 1784 Ma Mingxin uprising, the Qing government forbade non-Muslims from converting to Islam, which may have had some influence on the subsequent rarity of recorded Han conversions. This goes against the common assumption that Islam in China was spread through proselytization and conversion. Islamic preachers in China, including Ma Laichi, Ma Mingxin, Qi Jingyi, and Ma Qixi, spent most of their time trying to convert other Muslims. Islam in China, for the most part, has grown through birth and intermarriage.

The tensions and conflicts that led to the rise and divisions among various Sufi orders in China and subsequent non-Sufi reforms are complex and impossible to enumerate. An overview of major developments can, however, give evidence of the ongoing struggles that continue to make Islam meaningful to Hui Muslims. These tensions between Islamic ideals and social realities are often left unresolved. Their very dynamism derives from the questions they raise and the doubts they engender among people struggling with traditional meanings in the midst of changing social contexts. Questions of purity and legitimacy become paramount when the Hui are faced with radical internal socioeconomic and political change and are exposed to different interpretations of Islam from the outside Muslim world. These conflicts and reforms reflect an ongoing debate in China over Islamic orthodoxy, revealing an important disjunction between "scripturalist" or "mystical" interpretations.

In a similar fashion, the study of Southeast Asian Islam has often centered on the contradiction and compromise between the native culture of the indigenous Muslims and the *shari'a* of orthodox Islam, between the mystical and the scriptural, between the real and the ideal.[2] The supposed accommodation of orthodox Islamic tenets to local cultural practices has led scholars to dismiss or explain such compromise as syncretism, assimilation, and "sinification," as has been described among the Hui. An alternative approach, and one perhaps more in tune with the interests of the Hui themselves, sees this incongruence as the basis for ongoing dialectical tensions that have often led to reform movements and conflicts within Muslim communities (Eickelman 1976, 10–13). Following Max Weber (1978), one can see the wide variety of Islamic expression as reflecting processes of local world construction and programs for social conduct whereby a major religious tradition becomes meaningful to an indigenous society.

In the competition for scarce resources, these conflicts are also prompted by and expressed in economic concerns. For example, Fletcher notes that one of the criticisms of the Khufiyya order in China was that their recitation of an Islamic religious text entitled the *Ming Sha Le* took less time than the normal Qur'anic readings as performed by non-Sufi clergy, and therefore Khufiyya imams were cheaper to hire for ritual ceremonies. Fletcher suggests that this assisted their rise in popularity and contributed to the criticism they received from traditional religious leaders (Fletcher 1996, 21). Similarly, the Chinese Muslim reformists known as the *yihewani* criticized both traditional Muslims and Sufis for only performing rituals in believers' homes for profit, and condemned such practices altogether. They summarized their position on such matters in the oft-repeated axiom "If you recite, do not eat; if you eat, do not recite" *(Nian jing bu chi, chi bu nian jing)*. A 1958 document criticizing Ma Zhenwu, a Sufi *shaykh* of the Jahriyya order, contains the following revealing accusations:

> According to these representatives, Ma Chen-wu instituted many "A-mai-lis," or festival days to commemorate the dead ancestors to which the A-hungs must be invited to chant the scriptures and be treated with big feasts, thereby squeezing money out of the living for the dead. For example, he has kept a record of the days of birth and death of all the family members of his followers and has seen to

it that religious services be held on such days. These include "Grandmother's Day," "Wife's Day," "Aunt's Day," and others, sixty-five of such "A-mai-lis" in a year. On the average, one such "A-mai-li" is held every six or seven days, among which are seven occasions of big festival. . . . All the A-hungs of the Islamic mosques have been appointed by Ma Chen-wu. Through the appointment of A-hungs he has squeezed a big sum of money. . . . Ma has regularly, in the name of repairing the "kung-peis" [i.e., tombs], squeezed the Hui people for money. (Quoted in MacInnis 1972, 171–172)

Tendencies toward Acculturation and Purification

The tensions arising from the conflict between Chinese cultural practices and Islamic ideals have led to the rise and powerful appeal of Islamic movements among Hui Muslims. I explored one way of looking at this tension between cultural practice and Islamic ideals in an earlier work (Gladney 1996, 75).[3] In China, there were many attempts to reconcile Chinese culture with Islam, leading to a range of levels of integration. At one extreme are those who reject any integration of Islam with Chinese culture, advocating instead a return to an Arabized "pure" Islam. Conversely, at the other extreme, there are those traditionalist Chinese Muslim leaders who accept greater degrees of integration with traditional Chinese society. Ma Qixi, for example, stressed the complete compatibility of Chinese and Islamic culture, the importance of Chinese Islamic Confucian texts, the harmony of the two systems, and the reading of the Qur'an in Chinese.

In between, one finds various attempts at changing Chinese society to "fit" a Muslim world, through transformationist or militant Islam, as illustrated by the largely Naqshbandiyya-led nineteenth-century Hui uprisings. The Jahriyya order sought to implement an alternative vision of the world in their society, and this posed a threat to the Qing as well as to other Hui Muslims, earning them the label of "heterodox" *(xie jiao)* and leading to their persecution by the Chinese state. By contrast, other Hui reformers have attempted throughout history to make Islam "fit" Chinese society, such as Liu Zhi's monumental effort to demonstrate the Confucian morality of Islam. The alternative advocated by the Qadiriyya order in China represents an attempt to resolve this tension through ascetic withdrawal from the world. A *shaykh* of this order, Qi Jingyi, advocated an inner mystical journey in which the dualism of Islam and the Chinese world is resolved by grasping the oneness of Allah found inside every believer. These various approaches in Chinese Islam represent sociohistorical attempts to relate the world religion of Islam to local Chinese culture.

The hierarchical organization of the Sufi networks helped in the mobiliza-

A pagoda-shaped minaret atop a mosque in Linxia, a predominantly Muslim city in Gansu Province, People's Republic of China. (Bohemian Nomad Picturemakers/Corbis)

tion of large numbers of Hui during economic and political crises of the seventeenth through the nineteenth centuries, assisting widespread Muslim-led rebellions and resistance movements against late Ming and Qing imperial rule in Yunnan, Shaanxi, Gansu, and Xinjiang. The 1912 Nationalist Revolution allowed further autonomy in the regions of northwest China where Muslims were concentrated, and wide areas virtually came under the control of Muslim warlords. This situation gave rise to frequent intra-Muslim and Muslim-Han conflicts until the eventual Communist victory in China led to the reassertion of central state control. In the late nineteenth and early twentieth centuries, Wahhabi-inspired reform movements, known as the *yihewani*, rose to popularity under Nationalist and warlord sponsorship. They were noted for their critical stance toward traditionalist Islam, which they viewed as being overly acculturated to non-Muslim Chinese practices and to forms of popular Sufism such as veneration of saints and saints' tombs.

Beyond such internal Muslim critiques, the Chinese state has also launched its own criticisms of certain Sufi orders among the Hui. The stakes in such debates were often economic as well as ideological. For example, during the Land Reform campaigns of the 1950s, the state appropriated mosque and *waqf* (Islamic endowment) holdings from traditional Muslim religious institutions. These measures met with great resistance from the Sufi *menhuan*, which had accumulated a great deal due to their hierarchical centralized leadership.

Islam and Chinese Nationalism

In the twentieth century, many Muslims supported the earliest Communist call for economic equality, autonomy, freedom of religion, and recognized nationality status and were active in the early establishment of the People's Republic of China (PRC). However, many of them later became disenchanted by growing critiques of religious practice during several periods in the PRC beginning in 1957. During the Cultural Revolution (1966–1976), Muslims became the focus of both antireligious and anti-ethnic nationalist campaigns, leading to widespread persecutions, mosque closings, and at least one large massacre of 1,000 Hui following a 1975 uprising in Yunnan Province. Since Deng Xiaoping's post-1978 reforms, Muslims have sought to take advantage of liberalized economic and religious policies while keeping a watchful eye on the ever-swinging pendulum of Chinese radical politics. There are now more mosques open in China than there were prior to 1949, and Muslims travel freely on the *hajj* to Mecca and engage in cross-border trade with coreligionists in Central Asia, the Middle East, and, increasingly, Southeast Asia.

With the dramatic increase in the number of Muslims traveling back and forth to the Middle East came new waves of Islamic reformist thought, including criticism of local Muslim practices in China. Through similar channels, Chinese Muslims have also been exposed to various new, often politically radical, Islamic ideologies. These developments have fueled Islamic factional struggles that have continued to further divide China's Muslims. For example, in February 1994, four Naqshbandi Sufi leaders were sentenced to long-term imprisonment for their support of internal factional disputes in the southern Ningxia Region that had led to at least sixty deaths on both sides and that had required the intervention of China's People's Liberation Army. Throughout the summer and fall of 1993, bombs exploded in several towns in Xinjiang, indicating the growing demands of organizations pressing for an "independent Turkistan." In February 1997, a major uprising in Ili led to the deaths of at least thirteen Uyghur Muslims and the arrests of hundreds. It is clear that Hui and Kazakh Muslims are critical of these separatist actions among the Uyghur, but it is not yet clear how much support there is even among the Uyghur for the violent acts, especially for such dramatic moves as an attempt to assassinate a "collaborating" imam in Kashgar. Beijing has responded with increased military presence in the region, particularly in Kashgar and Urumqi, as well as with diplomatic efforts in the Central Asian states and with Turkey to discourage foreign support for separatist movements.

Increasing Muslim political activism on a national scale and rapid state responses to such developments indicate the growing importance Beijing attaches to Muslim-related issues. In 1986, Uyghurs in Xinjiang marched through the streets of Urumqi protesting against a wide range of issues, including the environmental degradation of the Zungharian plain, nuclear testing in the Taklimakan district, increased Han immigration to Xinjiang, and ethnic insults at Xinjiang University. Muslims throughout China protested the publication of a Chinese book, *Sexual Customs,* in May 1989 and a children's book in October 1993 that portrayed Muslims, particularly their restriction against pork, in a derogatory fashion. In each case, the government responded quickly, meeting most of the Muslims' demands, condemning the publications, arresting the authors, and closing down the printing houses.

These developments have influenced all Muslim nationalities in China today. However, they have found their most overtly political expressions among those Hui who are faced most directly with the task of accommodating new Islamic movements in the framework of Chinese culture. By comparison, the Uyghur, whose more recent integration into Chinese society was a result of Mongolian and Manchu expansion into Central Asia, have been forced to reach different degrees of social and political accommodations that have challenged their identity. The Uyghur as a people are perhaps the least integrated into Chinese society, whereas the Hui, due to several historical and social factors, are at the other end of the spectrum.

One way to examine this range of alternatives is to generalize about the

Muslim nationalities themselves. In this scheme, the Uyghur are much more resistant to accepting integration into Chinese society than are other Muslim groups. They are the only Muslim minority in China expressing strong desires for a separate state, which they refer to as Uyghuristan. However, it is not at all clear that all Uyghur desire such independence. At the other extreme, the Hui are arguably the most integrated of all the Muslim minorities into Chinese society and culture. This is both an advantage and a disadvantage: They often have greater access to power and resources within Chinese society, but at the same time they risk either the loss of their identity or the rejection of other Muslim groups in China as being too assimilated into Chinese society, to the detriment of Islam. In between there is a range of Muslim nationalities. Some, the Uzbeks, Kazakh, Kyrgyz, and Tajiks, are closer to the Uyghur in resisting Chinese culture and maintaining a distinct language and identity. Others, Dongxiang and Bonan, are much closer to the Hui in accommodation to Chinese culture. Much of this difference is due to historical interaction and locale and can also serve as a heuristic way of examining the challenges faced by each Muslim minority in their daily expression of identity and Islam in Chinese society. It must be clearly noted, however, that there are many exceptions to this overly generalized pattern. For example, there are some Uyghur, such as Communist Party officials and secularists, who are quite integrated into Chinese society, and at the same time, there are also some Hui, including some religious leaders and rebellious youths, who live their lives in strident resistance to Chinese culture.

Increased Muslim activism in China might be thought of as "nationalistic," but it is a nationalism that often transcends the boundaries of the contemporary nation-state, via mass communications, increased travel, and the Internet. Earlier Islamic movements in China were precipitated by China's opening to the outside world. No matter what conservative leaders in the government might wish, the politics of China's Muslims have reached a new stage of openness. If China wants to participate in an international political sphere of nation-states, this is unavoidable. With China's opening to the West, travel by Chinese to and from the Islamic heartlands has dramatically increased. In 1984, over 1,400 Muslims left China to go on the *hajj* to Mecca. This number increased to over 2,000 in 1987, representing a return to pre-1949 levels, and in the late 1990s, official *hajj* numbers regularly surpassed 6,000, with many others traveling in private capacities through third countries. Several Hui students are presently enrolled in Islamic and Arabic studies at the Al-Azhar University in Egypt, and many others seek Islamic training abroad.

Encouraged by the Chinese state, relations between Muslims in China and their coreligionists in the Middle East are becoming stronger and more frequent. This appears to be motivated partly by China's desire to establish trading partners for arms, commodities, and currency exchanges and partly by

China's traditional view of itself as a leader of the Third World. Delegations of foreign Muslims regularly travel to prominent Islamic sites in China, in a kind of state-sponsored religious tourism, and donations are encouraged. While the state hopes that private Islamic investment will assist economic development, the vast majority of grants by visiting foreign Muslims have been made for the rebuilding of mosques and Islamic schools and hospitals. As Hui in China are further exposed to Islamic internationalism and as they return from pilgrimages and periods of study abroad, traditional Hui identities are once again being reshaped and called into question, giving rise to new manifestations of Islam in China. Global Islam is thus localized into Hui Islam, finding its expression as a range of accommodations between Chineseness and Muslimness as defined in each local community.

Uyghurs, Muslims, and Chinese

In 1997, bombs exploded in a city park in Beijing on May 13 (killing one) and on two buses on March 7 (killing two), as well as on February 25 in the northwestern border city of Urumqi, the capital of Xinjiang Uyghur Autonomous Region (killing nine). In recent years, there have been over thirty other bombings, six of them in Tibet alone. Most of these are thought to have been related to demands by Muslim and Tibetan separatists. Eight members of the Uyghur Muslim minority were executed on May 29, 1997, for alleged bombings in northwest China, and hundreds were arrested on suspicion of taking part in ethnic riots and engaging in separatist activities. Though sporadically reported since the early 1980s, such incidents have been increasingly common since 1997 and are documented in a recent scathing report by Amnesty International (1999) on Chinese government policy in the region. An article in the *Wall Street Journal* of August 11, 1999 (Johnson 1999) reported the arrest of a well-known Uyghur businesswoman named Rebiya Kadir during a visit by the U.S. Congressional Research Service delegation to the region. The article indicates that China's random arrests have not diminished since the report and that China remains relatively unconcerned about Western criticism of such measures.

As we consider the interaction of Uyghur Muslims with Chinese society, we must examine three interrelated aspects of regional history, economy, and politics. First, Chinese histories notwithstanding, most Uyghur firmly believe that their ancestors were the indigenous people of the Tarim basin, which did not become known in Chinese as Xinjiang ("New Dominion") until the eighteenth century. Nevertheless, I have argued elsewhere for the constructed "ethnogenesis" of the Uyghur, arguing that the current understanding of the indigeneity of the present people classified as Uyghur by the Chinese state is a rather recent phenomenon related to Great Game rivalries, Sino-Soviet geopolitical maneuverings, and Chinese nation-building (Gladney 1990, 3). Although a collection of nomadic steppe peoples known as the "Uyghur" existed from before the eighth century, this identity was lost from the fifteenth through the twentieth centuries. In the historical record, we find the beginnings of the Uyghur Empire following the fall of the Turkish Khanate (552–744 C.E.), when Chinese historians first mention a people called the Hui-he or Hui-hu. At that time, the Uyghur were but a collection of nine nomadic tribes, who initially, in confederation with other Basmil and Karlukh nomads, defeated the Second Turkish Khanate and then dominated the federation under the leadership of Koli Beile in 742.

The Uyghur gradually became sedentary, and they defeated the Turkish Khanate precisely as trade with the unified Tang state (618–907) was becoming especially lucrative. During that time, sedentarization and interaction with the Chinese state was accompanied by socioreligious change: The traditional shamanistic Turkic-speaking Uyghur came increasingly under the influence of Persian Manichaeanism, Buddhism, and eventually, Nestorian Christianity. Extensive trade and military alliances along the old Silk Road with the Chinese state developed to such an extent that the Uyghur gradually adopted many Chinese cultural and even agricultural practices. Conquest of the Uyghur capital of Karabalghasun in Mongolia by the nomadic Kyrgyz in 840 led to further sedentarization and to the crystallization of Uyghur identity. At the time of this attack, the Uyghur received no assistance from the Tang Chinese state, who by then may have become intimidated by the wealthy Uyghur Empire and thus would not lament the breakup of this potential rival for power in the region. One group of Uyghur moved out to what is now Turpan. There, they took advantage of the unique socioecology of the glacier-fed oases surrounding the Taklimakan and were able to preserve their merchant and limited agrarian practices, gradually establishing Khocho, or Gaochang, the great Uyghur city-state that lasted for four centuries (850–1250).

From that time on, the people of Turpan-centered "Uyghuristan" who resisted Islamic conversion until the seventeenth century were the last to be known as "Uyghur." Muslims in that region, on the other hand, were referred to either by the name of their local oasis settlement or by the generic term "Turki." Thus, with the further spread of Islam in the region, the ethnonym "Uyghur" faded from the historical record. It was not until 1760 that the Manchu Qing dynasty exerted full and formal control over the region, establishing it as their "new dominions" (Xinjiang). This administration lasted for a century before it fell to the Yakub Beg rebellion (1864–1877) and expanding Russian influence.[4] The end of the Qing dynasty in 1912 and the rise of Great Game rivalries among China, Russia, and Great Britain saw the region torn by competing loyalties. The period was marked by two short-lived and drastically different attempts at independence: the proclamations of an "East Turkistan Republic" in Kashgar in 1933 and another in Yining in 1944 (Benson 1990). As Andrew Forbes has noted, these rebellions and attempts at self-rule did little to bridge competing political, religious, and regional differences among the Turkic people who became known as the Uyghur (Forbes 1986, 29). Furthermore, Justin Rudelson's (1997) research suggests that regional diversity persists along three, and perhaps four, macro-regions of Uyghuristan: the northwestern Zungharian plain, the southern Tarim basin, the southwest Pamir region, and possibly the eastern Kumul-Turpan-Hami corridor.

Uyghur Indigeneity and the Challenge to Chinese Sovereignty

The Chinese Nationalists, in a Soviet-influenced policy of nationality recognition, identified five nationalities *(minzu)* of China, with the Han in the majority. The "ethnogenesis" of the concept of "Uyghur" as a bona fide nationality and the recognition of the Uyghur as an official Chinese nationality *(minzu)* has contributed to today's widespread acceptance of the idea that there is continuity with the ancient Uyghur kingdom. The *minzu* policy was continued under the Communists, who eventually recognized fifty-six nationalities, with the Han occupying a 91 percent majority in 1990. The "peaceful liberation" of Xinjiang by the Chinese Communists in 1949, and its subsequent establishment as the Xinjiang Uyghur Autonomous Region on October 1, 1955, perpetuated the Nationalist policy of recognizing the Uyghur as a minority nationality under Chinese rule (Shahidi 1984). However, the designation of the Uyghur as a "nationality" masks tremendous regional and linguistic diversity. For it also includes groups, such as the Loplyk and Dolans, that have very little in common with the oasis-based Turkic Muslims who had come to be known as the Uyghur. At the same time, contemporary Uyghur separatists look back to the brief periods of independent self-rule under Yakub Beg and the East Turkistan Republics, in addition to the earlier glories of the Uyghur kingdoms in Turpan and Karabalghasan, as evidence of their rightful claims to the region.

Today, in 2004, a number of Uyghur separatist organizations exist, based mainly in foreign cities, including Istanbul, Ankara, Almaty, Munich, Amsterdam, Melbourne, and Washington, D.C. These groups may differ on their political goals and strategies for the region, but they all share a common vision of a unilinear Uyghur claim on the region that has been disrupted by Chinese and Soviet intervention. The achievement of independence by the former Soviet Central Asian republics in 1991 has done much to encourage these Uyghur organizations in their hopes for an independent "Turkistan," despite the fact that the new, mainly Muslim, Central Asian governments all signed

A Muslim Uyghur man at a tea house in Kashgar, Xinjiang Region, China. (Kevin Lee/Getty Images)

protocols with China in the spring of 1996 stating that they would not harbor or support separatist groups.

Within the region, though the Uyghur are often portrayed as united around separatist or Islamist causes, they continue to be internally divided by religious conflicts—in this case between competing Sufi and non-Sufi factions—territorial loyalties (whether they be based on oases or places of origin), linguistic discrepancies, alienation between commoners and elites, and competing political loyalties. These divided loyalties were evidenced by the attack in May 1996 on the imam of the Idgah Mosque in Kashgar by other Uyghurs and by the assassination of at least six Uyghur officials in September 2001.

It is also important to note that Islam was only one of several unifying markers for Uyghur identity, depending on whom they were cooperating with at the time. For example, to the Hui Muslim Chinese, the Uyghur distinguish themselves as the legitimate autochthonous minority, since both share a belief in Sunni Islam. In contrast to the nomadic Muslim peoples (Kazakh or Kyrgyz), Uyghur might stress their attachment to the land and oases of origin. In opposition to the Han Chinese, the Uyghur will generally emphasize their long history in the region. This contested understanding of history continues to influence much of the current debate over separatist and Chinese claims to the region. The multiple emphases in defining their identity have also served to mitigate the appeal that Islamic fundamentalist groups (often glossed as "Wahhabiyya" in the region), such as the Taliban in Afghanistan, have had among the Uyghur.

Alleged incursions by Taliban fighters through the Wakhan corridor into China where Xinjiang shares a narrow border with Afghanistan have led to the area being swamped with Chinese security forces carrying out large military exercises, beginning at least one month prior to the attacks of September 11, 2001. These military exercises suggested that there was growing government concern about these border areas much earlier than 9/11. Under U.S. and Chinese pressure, Pakistan returned one Uyghur activist to China, apprehended among hundreds of Taliban detainees, which follows a pattern of repatriations of suspected Uyghur separatists in Kazakhstan, Kyrgyzstan, and Uzbekistan. Amnesty International has claimed that Chinese government roundups of so-called terrorists and separatists have led to hurried public trials and immediate, summary executions of possibly thousands of locals. One Amnesty International estimate suggested that in a country known for its frequent executions, Xinjiang had the highest number, averaging 1.8 per week, most of them of Uyghur. The Chinese government, in 1998, launched a nationwide campaign against crime known as "Strike Hard"; it includes the call to erect a "great wall of steel" against separatists in Xinjiang. Troop movements to the area related to this campaign have reportedly been the largest since the suppression of the large Akto insurrection in April 1990.[5]

Ethnic Muslim Nationalism in an Age of Globalization

International campaigns for Uyghur rights and possible independence have become increasingly vocal and well organized, especially on the Internet. Repeated public appeals have been made to Abdulahat Abdurixit, the Uyghur People's Government chairman of Xinjiang in Urumqi. Notably, the elected chair of the Unrepresented Nations and People's Organization (UNPO) based in The Hague is a Uyghur, Erkin Alptekin. Alptekin's father was the separatist leader Isa Yusuf Alptekin, who is buried in Istanbul, where there is a park dedicated to his memory. There are at least twenty-five international organizations and Web sites working for the independence of "East Turkistan," supporting primarily an audience of approximately 1 million expatriate Uyghurs (yet few Uyghurs in Central Asia and China have access to these Internet sites). Since September 11, 2001, each of these organizations has disclaimed any support for violence or terrorism, pressing for a peaceful resolution of ongoing conflicts in the region. The growing influence of "cyber-separatism" and the international popularization of the Uyghur cause concerns Chinese authorities, who hope to convince the world that the Uyghurs do pose a real domestic and international terrorist threat.

While further restricting Islamic freedoms in the border regions, at the same time the Chinese state has become more keenly aware of the importance that foreign Muslim governments place on China's treatment of its Muslim minorities as a factor in China's lucrative trade and military agreements. The establishment of full diplomatic ties with Saudi Arabia in 1991 and increasing military and technical trade with Middle Eastern Muslim states enhances the economic and political salience of China's treatment of its internal Muslim minority population. The official protocols signed with China's Central Asian border nations, beginning in 1996 with the group known as the "Shanghai Five" (China, Russia, Kazakhstan, Kyrgyzstan, Tajikistan) and expanded in 2001 to include Uzbekistan, underlines China's growing role in the region and its concerns over transnational trade and security. The increased transnationalism of China's Muslims will be an important factor in their ethnic expression as well as in their practiced accommodation to Chinese culture and state authority.

Beyond these political pressures, Uyghur relations with the Chinese state also involve significant economic issues. Since 1991, China has been a net oil importer; it also has 20 million Muslims. Mishandling of its Muslim populations thus runs the risk of alienating trading partners in the Middle East. After an ethnic riot on February 5, 1997, in the northwestern Xinjiang city of Yining that left at least nine Uyghur Muslims dead and several hundred arrested, the Saudi Arabian official newspaper warned China about the "suffering of [its] Muslims whose human rights are violated." Turkey's defense minister, Turhan Tayan, officially condemned China's handling of the issue, and China responded by telling Turkey not to interfere in China's internal affairs. Muslim nations on China's borders, including Pakistan, Afghanistan, and the new Central Asian states, though officially unsupportive of Uyghur separatists, may be increasingly critical of harsh treatment extended to fellow Turkic or Muslim coreligionists in China.

Unrest in the Xinjiang Uyghur Autonomous Region may thus lead to a decline in outside oil investment and revenues, which are already operating at a loss. Recently, Exxon reported that its two wells came up dry in China's supposedly oil-rich Tarim basin of southern Xinjiang, with the entire region yielding only 3.15 million metric tons of crude oil, much less than China's overall output of 156 million tons. The World Bank loans over $3 billion a year to China, investing over $780.5 million in fifteen projects in the Xinjiang region alone, with some of that money allegedly going to the Xinjiang Production and Construction Corps (XPCC), which human rights activist Harry Wu has claimed employs prison labor. International companies and organizations, from the World Bank to Exxon, may not wish to subject their employees and investors to social and political upheavals. As a result of these criticisms, many World Bank and Asian Development Bank projects have been curtailed in recent years.

At the same time, however, China's trade with Central Asia is expanding at a rapid rate, with the opening of direct rail, air, and six overland links since 1991. Energy economist James P. Dorian has noted that Xinjiang's trade with Central Asia increased from $463 million in 1992 to $775 million in 1996. The end of 1992 saw an increase of 130 percent in cross-border trade, with Kazakhstan benefiting the most. China is now Kazakhstan's fifth-largest trade partner, with China-Kazakhstan trade alone totaling more than Turkey's trade with all of Central Asia (Dorian, Wigdortz, and Gladney 1997).

In addition, China is hoping to increase revenues from tourism to the region, marketing it as an important link on the ancient Silk Road. It has been a tremendous draw to foreign Muslim tourists, as well as to Japanese, Taiwanese, Southeast Asian, and domestic tourists. This rise in tourism has driven the establishment of five-star hotels throughout the region, including a Holiday Inn in Urumqi. These economic developments have brought dramatic changes to the region, as witnessed by the building of eighty new skyscrapers over the last ten years in Urumqi alone. However, it is clear that Uyghur separatism or Muslim complaints regarding Chinese policy will have important consequences for China's economic development of the region. Tourists and foreign businessmen will certainly avoid areas with ethnic strife and terrorist activities, and China will continue to use its economic leverage with its Central Asian neighbors and Russia to prevent such disruptions.

Since the 1990s, cross-border trade between Xinjiang and Central Asia has grown tremendously, especially due to the reopening in 1991 of the Eurasian Railroad, which links Urumqi and Alma-Ata with markets in China and eastern Europe. Overland travel between Xinjiang and Pakistan, Tajikistan, Kyrgyzstan, and Kazakhstan has also increased dramatically with the relaxation of travel restrictions based on Deng Xiaoping's prioritization of trade over security interests in the area. The government's policy of seeking to buy support by stimulating the local economy seems to be working at the present. Income levels in Xinjiang are often far higher than those across the border, yet increased Han migration to participate in the region's lucrative oil and mining industries continues to exacerbate local ethnic tensions. Muslim areas in northern and central China, however, continue to be left behind, since China's rapid economic growth is occurring unevenly, enriching the southern coastal areas far more than the interior.

China's relations with its bordering nations and with internal regions such as Xinjiang and Tibet have become increasingly important not only for the economic reasons discussed above but also for China's desire to participate in such international organizations as the World Trade Organization and the Asia-Pacific Economic Council. Though Tibet is no longer of any real strategic or substantial economic value to China, it is politically important to China's current leadership to indicate that they will not submit to foreign pressure and withdraw their iron hand from Tibet. Uyghurs have begun to work closely with Tibetans internationally to put political pressure on China in international forums. In Istanbul on April 7, 1997, I had the opportunity to interview Ahmet Türköz, vice director of the Eastern Turkestan Foundation, which works for an independent Uyghur homeland. Türköz noted that since 1981, meetings had been taking place between the Dalai Lama and Uyghur leaders, initiated by the deceased Uyghur nationalist Isa Yusuf Alptekin. These international forums cannot force China to change its policy, any more than can the annual debate in the United States over the renewal of China's most-favored-nation status. Nevertheless, they continue to influence China's ability to cooperate internationally. As a result, China has sought to respond rapidly, and often militarily, to domestic ethnic affairs that might have international implications.

Since 1997, China has been in the process of developing ways to govern the newly integrated territory of Hong Kong. Given Chinese visions of eventually reuniting with Taiwan, residents of Taiwan will be watching how China deals with this and other problems of national integration. During the Dalai Lama's March 1998 visit to Taiwan, he again renounced independence, calling for China to treat Tibet under the same "two systems, one country" policy as Hong Kong, yet the *People's Daily* continued to call him a "separatist." Taiwan will certainly be watching how well Hong Kong is integrated into China as a "special administrative region" with a truly separate system of government, as opposed to Tibet and Xinjiang, which, although so-called autonomous regions, have very little actual autonomy from decisionmakers in Beijing.

China's handling of ethnic and integrationist issues in Xinjiang and Hong Kong will have a direct bearing on any future possible reunification with Taiwan. Beyond the official minorities, China possesses tremendous ethnic, linguistic, and regional diversity. Intolerance toward difference in Xinjiang might be extended to limiting cultural pluralism in Guangdong, where at least fifteen dialects of Cantonese are spoken and folk religious practices remain strong. Memories of the repressions of the Cultural Revolution, when all forms of diversity, political or cultural, were severely curtailed, are still very much alive there, as elsewhere. If rising Chinese nationalism entails reducing ethnic and cultural difference, then anyone who is regarded as "other" in China will suffer, not just the Uyghurs.

China is not immune from the new tide of ethnic nationalism and "primordial politics" sweeping Europe, Africa, and Asia in the post–cold war period. Much of that movement is clearly a response to globalization in terms of localization: increasing nationalism arising from the organization of the world into nation-states. No longer content to sit on the sidelines, the nations within these states are playing a greater role in the public sphere, which Jürgen Habermas (1989) suggests is the defining characteristic of civil society in the modern nation-state. In most of these nationalist movements, religion, culture, and racialization play a privileged role in defining the boundaries of the nation. In China, as elsewhere, Islam will continue to play an important role in defining the nation, especially in countries where nationality is defined by a mix of religion and ethnicity.

Notes

1.   For the debate over the definition of Hui and reference to them as "Sino-Muslims," see Lipman 1997, xxiv.

2.   This distinction was most fully articulated in Roff 1985, 8–10.

3.   This interpretive scheme is influenced by H. Richard Niebuhr's *Christ and Culture* (1951).

4.   For the best treatment of the Yakub Beg rebellion, see Ho-dong 1986.

5.   This was the first major uprising in Xinjiang that took place in the Southern Tarim region near Baren Township, which initiated a series of unrelated and sporadic protests which took place in the Southern Tarim region near Baren Township.

References

Amnesty International. 1999. "Peoples Republic of China: Gross Violations of Human Rights in the Xinjiang Uighur Autonomous Region." London, April 1. http://web.amnesty.org/library/index/engASA170181999.

Benson, Linda. 1990. *The Ili Rebellion: The Moslem Challenge to Chinese Authority in Xinjiang, 1944–1949.* New York: M. E. Sharpe.

Dillon, Michael. 1997. *Hui Muslims in China.* London: Curzon Press.

Dorian, James P., Brett Wigdortz, and Dru Gladney. 1997. "Central Asia and Xinjiang, China: Emerging Energy, Economic, and Ethnic Relations." *Central Asian Survey* 16, no. 4: 461–486.

Eickelman, Dale F. 1976. *Moroccan Islam: Tradition and Society in a Pilgrimage Center.* Austin and London: University of Texas Press.

Fletcher, Joseph. 1996. *Studies on Chinese and Islamic Inner Asia.* Edited by Beatrice Manz. London: Variorum Press.

Forbes, Andrew D. W. 1986. *Warlords and Muslims in Chinese Central Asia.* Cambridge: Cambridge University Press.

Gladney, Dru C. 1990. "The Ethnogenesis of the Uighur." *Central Asian Studies* 9, no. 1: 1–28.

———. 1996. *Muslim Chinese: Ethnic Nationalism in the People's Republic.* Cambridge, MA: Harvard University Press.

Habermas, Jürgen. 1989. *The Structural Transformation of the Public Sphere.* Translated by Thomas Burger and Frederick Lawrence. Cambridge, MA: MIT Press.

Ho-dong, Kim. 1986. "The Muslim Rebellion of the Kashgar Emirate in Chinese Central Asia, 1864–1877." PhD diss., Harvard University.

Israeli, Raphael. 1978. *Muslims in China.* London: Curzon Press; Atlantic Highlands, NJ: Humanities Press.

Johnson, Ian. 1999. "China Arrests Noted Businesswoman in Crackdown in Muslim Region." *Wall Street Journal,* August 18.

Lipman, Jonathan. 1997. *Familiar Strangers: A History of Muslims in Northwest China.* Seattle: University of Washington Press.

MacInnis, Donald E. 1972. *Religious Policy and Practice in Communist China.* New York: Macmillan.

Niebuhr, H. Richard. 1951. *Christ and Culture.* New York: Harper and Row.

Roff, William. 1985. "Islam Obscured? Some Reflections on Studies of Islam and Society in Asia." *L'Islam en Indonesie* 1, no. 29: 8–10.

Rudelson, Justin Jon. 1997. *Oasis Identities: Uyghur Nationalism along China's Silk Road.* New York: Columbia University Press.

Shahidi, Burhan. 1984. *Fifty Years in Xinjiang* [Xinjiang Wushi Nian]. Urumqi, China: People's Press.

Trippner, Joseph. 1961. "Islamische Gruppe und Graberkult in Nordwest China." *Die Welt des Islams* 7: 142–171.

Weber, Max. 1978. *Economy and Society.* 2 Vols. Berkeley and Los Angeles: University of California Press.

Chapter Seven

Muslim Thought and Practice in Contemporary Indonesia

ANNA GADE AND R. MICHAEL FEENER

The vast majority of the world's Muslims today live in Asia, including the Indian subcontinent, Central Asia, and China. The Muslim population of Southeast Asia alone is roughly equal to that of all the Arabic-speaking countries combined. There are sizable Muslim minority populations in many Southeast Asian nations, including Thailand, Singapore, and the Philippines, and Brunei, Malaysia, and Indonesia have majority-Muslim populations. These countries have long been at the center of Asian maritime trade networks; for centuries, anyone traveling by boat from India or Africa to China passed through Southeast Asia. The global connection of systems of religion and culture to Indonesia in particular existed long before the present era of globalization. Since the coming of Islam to Southeast Asia, Islamic worldwide models for religious life have combined with distinctive local Indonesian patterns, supporting the development of vibrant regional Muslim cultures. Today, these cultures continually shape and are shaped by the changing conditions of life in contemporary Indonesia.

Nearly 90 percent of Indonesia's population, approximately 200 million people, identify themselves as Muslim, giving Indonesia the largest Muslim population of any country. Indonesia is made up of a vast archipelago that includes people of many languages and cultures. In part because of its position at the crossroads of extensive global networks, Indonesian religious systems, and especially Islam, are vitally cosmopolitan. Today, although patterns of contemporary Muslim revitalization in Indonesia are unique to Southeast Asia, they share key components of the renewal of Islamic thought and practice in other Muslim societies. These components include the textual foundations of the Qur'an and *hadith*, obligatory Muslim practices such as the *hajj*, and the

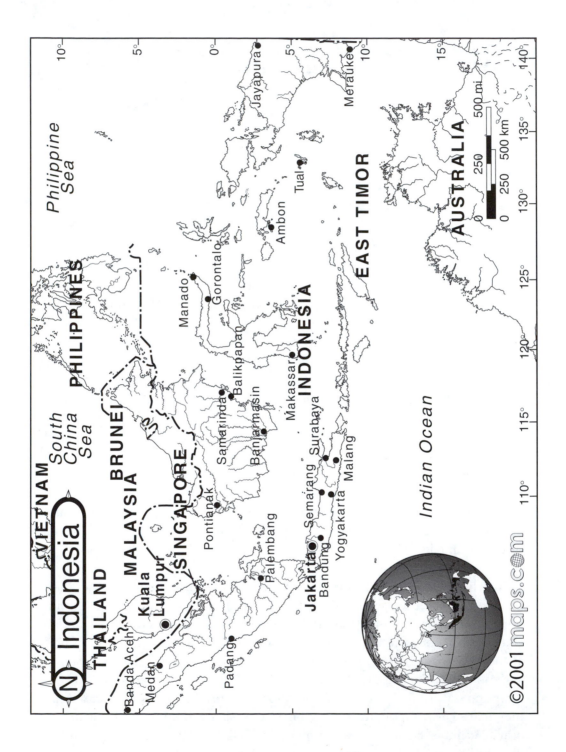

N Indonesia

Philippine Sea

THAILAND

VIETNAM

South China Sea

PHILIPPINES

MALAYSIA

BRUNEI

SINGAPORE

Banda Aceh
Medan
Kuala Lumpur

Pontianak
Padang
Palembang

Samarinda
Balikpapan
Banjarmasin

Manado
Gorontalo

Ambon
Tual

Makassar

INDONESIA

Jakarta
Bandung
Semarang
Surabaya
Yogyakarta
Malang

Jayapura

Merauke

EAST TIMOR

AUSTRALIA

Indian Ocean

0 250 500 mi
0 250 500 km

©2001 maps.com

flexible structures of Islamic thought, piety, and ethical and legal traditions. Muslims in contemporary Indonesia have also taken a leading role in finding new, Qur'an-based solutions to the challenges of the modern world faced by people of all faiths. Many Indonesian Muslims, like most religious people, want to apply the ideals of their faith to the realities of their lives and communities. Naturally, the specific ways these ideals are envisioned and implemented vary. Using the comparative terminology of Indonesianist Clifford Geertz (1968), some of the styles of religious thought and practice now developing in contemporary Islamic Southeast Asia, which have strong ties with the past, are now seen by Muslims in other regions of the world as models for a shared future in an increasingly interconnected world.

The Coming of Islam and Formative Institutions of Learning

Islam came to Indonesia through networks of world trade. There are records of small Muslim settlements in Indonesia dating to the first centuries of Islamic history. Significant numbers of local conversions to Islam, however, did not occur until the fourteenth century. By that time, Southeast Asia had already long been at the nexus of important seafaring networks that extended across the Indian Ocean, from East Africa and the Middle East to the coast of the Indian subcontinent and China (Reid 1988–1993). From 1300 to 1700, many societies in Indonesia integrated Islam into their most basic institutions and religious traditions, including educational, political, and ethical and legal systems.

Muslim students and teachers traveling between Southeast Asia and the Middle East supported these developments. Scholars traveled to study with renowned teachers in centers such as Mecca, Medina, Cairo, Damascus, the scholarly towns of Yemen, and elsewhere (Azra 1992). In addition, Muslim scholars from India and the Middle East found their way to various parts of the archipelago, where they evidently had no difficulties in attracting students. Some of these individuals spent years as itinerant teachers, moving from one port to the next. Others settled in Southeast Asia, where they married into prominent local families and thus gained further influence in local political and economic circles.

"*Pesantren*" or "*pondok pesantren*" is a Javanese term for a residential Muslim school. The term has come to be used generally to refer to traditional Muslim institutions of learning elsewhere in the archipelago, such as *daya* in Aceh and the *surau* in Minangkabau, both on Sumatra. Beginning with the memorization of the Qur'an and Arabic grammar, students were prepared to engage ideas, institutions, and individuals from all across the Muslim world. Although these institutions were often located in remote areas of the countryside, set apart from local structures of power and authority, they tended to maintain a globally cosmopolitan outlook because extensive networks connected them directly to similar institutions of Muslim learning around the archipelago and overseas.

Traditional settings for Islamic education emphasized and valued highly the personal bond between students and their teachers. Such ties could link rural scholars with colleagues who were hundreds, even thousands, of miles away. For instance, many of the leading families of religious scholars on Java and the nearby island of Madura were related through close webs of intermarriage (Bruinessen 1995). Students and teachers associated with these schools were also linked in complex scholarly networks that extended to the broader community of scholars in Mecca, Medina, and the maritime Muslim cities ringing the coastlines of the Indian Ocean. Since the earliest institutionalization of Islam in Indonesia, these connections based on textual and educational traditions have maintained the dynamic participation of Southeast Asian Muslims within the wider world of transregional Islamic thought and culture.

The Islamic subjects that Southeast Asian scholars originally studied with foreign teachers or acquired in far-off centers of learning were selectively adopted and adapted to local needs in Indonesia, creating a unique version of global Muslim traditions of education. Over time, a certain body of texts became widely circulated in Southeast Asia, disseminating ideas in the fields of legal studies, Arabic grammar, esoteric thought and practice, theology, and interpretation of the Qur'an. These writings—which came to be referred to as the "yellow books" *(kitab kuning)* because of the yellowed paper on which they were written—were the mainstay of the curriculum in the *pesantren* well into the twentieth century. Over the second half of the twentieth century, the kitab kuning have increasingly been displaced by other kinds of works more recently added to Islamic religious studies curricula in Indonesia (Bruinessen 1994). Since the primary language of international Muslim scholarship was Arabic, most subjects were taught in that language. However, over time, a number of these works were translated, interpreted, or otherwise brought into Malay and other local languages for those, such as beginning students, who were more comfortable working in Southeast Asian languages. Later, some authors—native Indonesians as well as immigrants to the archipelago—composed original works of Muslim learning in their languages, including Javanese, Sundanese, Buginese, Makassarese, and especially the transregional language, Malay, which is the basis for the national languages of both Indonesia and Malaysia today (Bahasa Indonesia and Bahasa Malaysia). These many Southeast Asian languages, like the languages all across the Islamic world, came to be written in the Arabic script, much as non-Romance European languages like English and Welsh are written in the "roman" alphabet.

Other, related patterns of the dissemination of power and ideas existed along with these systems and institutions for the transmission of traditional Muslim knowledge. The confluence of many modes of Islamic tradition can be seen in the work of the early writer and thinker Hamzah Fansuri, who lived circa the seventeenth century in Sumatra. His writings demonstrate the intellectual currents and disputes of his day, and their controversial nature mirrored debates all over the Muslim world at the time, especially in Mughal India. Hamzah's work was based on an impressive knowledge of the Qur'an, Arabic language and grammar, Persian expression (which some say he studied with Muslim communities in Thailand), and esoteric tradition, following a thinker known as Ibn Arabi (d. 1240). All these currents were a part of the global world of Islam in this period. Hamzah's writings, while a part of a cosmopolitan system, also represent the ways Islamic ideas were consciously adapted to local conditions in Southeast Asia. In his writings, for example, he incorporated regional geography and local, lived experience such as the China Sea, boats, and even the wax-resist process of dying the batik cloth for which the region is famous to this day. He once wrote, "How strange it is that the whale, having its habitat in the China Sea, looks for water on Mount Sinai, and hence its efforts are useless" (Hamzah Fansuri, "Poem XXXII," in Drewes and Brakel 1986, 141). Hamzah Fansuri, a Southeast Asian mystic, held that authentic and universal religious truths are discovered not just in far-off lands but also very close to home.

Hamzah's work also indicates that Sufism, or traditions of esoteric piety, is an essential basis to Muslim cultural history in Southeast Asia. As elsewhere, especially in Asia, Sufism has been foundational to the integration of Islam and local tradition. Sufi *tarekat,* social networks connected by common lineages, are in themselves global Islamic social and intellectual frameworks that are at the same time embedded in regional experience through the establishment of local lines of authority. Some of the Sufi orders, or *tarekat,* that were very influential in Indonesia actively focused on renewing and reforming the self and society, such as the Naqshbandiyya (Bruinessen 1992). For this reason, they provided local rulers with a potential basis for political authority and with ready-made social networks for resistance to the colonial interests that were the next global system to influence both Indonesia and the wider Islamic world.

European Colonialism and Muslim Reaction and Resistance

From the sixteenth century onward, a growing European presence in the archipelago, culminating in widespread colonial control, exerted new forces on the ongoing religious change in the region. Since at least the seventeenth century, first the Portuguese and then the Dutch had a profound impact on economics, politics, and social and religious developments in Indonesia. For example, the Portuguese actively promoted Roman Catholicism among the peoples they encountered, especially in the eastern parts of the archipelago. The Dutch tended to invest a different kind of effort into Protestant missionary activity, and as foreign colonizers, they were ultimately able to exert an enormous impact on the religious culture of the region. The Netherlands eventually became the imperialist ruler of the entire Indonesian archipelago, from Sumatra to western New Guinea, a regime that endured until World War II.

Dutch rule in the region did not stand unchallenged, however. From the seventeenth century until Indonesian independence in 1945, many Muslim leaders took up the struggle for autonomy from foreign rule. Although resistance movements during these 300 years arose out of local concerns and conditions, many shared important characteristics with Muslim anti-imperialist and anticolonial movements across the globe. These commonalities included appeals to many modes of authoritative Islamic traditions as powerful symbols and ideals of justice that could motivate political action.

Political and military struggles against the Dutch both inspired and were inspired by the continuing Islamization of social attitudes and practices in Southeast Asia. Muslim leaders of anticolonial movements drew on long-distance relationships with Muslims from other islands and even further away for support. For example, such transnational connections are very clear in the anti-Dutch activities in seventeenth-century Banten, West Java, led by an influential leader called Shaykh Yusuf. Yusuf was born in South Sulawesi and studied under some of the most prominent local Muslim scholars before traveling to continue his education in Banten; from there he moved on to Gujarat in India, Yemen, Mecca, and Syria. After returning to Southeast Asia from the Middle East, he taught in Banten until 1682, when the local prince rose against the authority of the sultan (his own father) with the backing of the Dutch East India Company.

At this time, Shaykh Yusuf took up a campaign of opposition against Dutch interests that he pursued for over a year, ending in his capture by the Dutch. He was imprisoned at Batavia (Jakarta) and then exiled to Sri Lanka, where he continued to advocate resistance against the Dutch through his correspondence with Muslim communities of the Indonesian archipelago. In 1693, Dutch authorities intercepted some of these communications, and as a result he was exiled to the Cape of Good Hope in Africa. Upon his arrival there, he became a founding figure of the vibrant Muslim community in South Africa.

Shaykh Yusuf is an example of a Muslim scholar and activist whose ideas and impact were global even though he was primarily engaged in local political and religious action. In many such historical cases, the ideas and concepts deployed in anticolonial movements resonated widely because they were common and natural responses to the colonial circumstances experienced across the Muslim world and also because of the salience of shared frameworks of Islamic ideas for Muslims.

In each epoch of the history of Islam, according to John Voll, there are people whom Muslims recognize as renewing *(tajdid)* Islamic ideals in their community or reforming *(islah)* their society in accord with these ideals (Voll 1983). Many of the renowned "renewers" in Islamic history have greatly affected the development of Islam in Indonesia in particular. For example, one such renewer was Abu Hamid al-Ghazzali (d. 1111), whose work combined key ideas from philosophy, theology, law, ethics, and esoteric thought in a way that has appealed to Muslims for almost a millennium. In the eighteenth century, many Southeast Asians took a renewed interest in this medieval scholar, finding in his scholarship helpful ideas for revitalizing Islamic thought and practice to suit conditions in a rapidly changing world. Likewise, in the twentieth century, a growing number of Indonesians turned to the work of Ibn Taymiyya (d. 1328) for inspiration for activities of renewal and reform. Ibn Taymiyya had been a member of a Sufi order, but more important, he was a legal scholar who strove in particular to counteract certain practices (like the veneration of "saints" at their tombs) that he was certain confused Muslims and distorted Islamic ideals.

Both al-Ghazzali and Ibn Taymiyya influenced many Indonesian renewers and reformers, as did more modern thinkers from the Middle East and elsewhere who also strove to reinvigorate Islam as a moral and political response to the challenges of new global conditions. The fact that some of the key models used by modern Indonesian movements are actually figures from the distant past of Islamic intellectual history should not be understood as implying that Muslims in modern Indonesia are several centuries behind the times in relation to the rest of the Muslim world. In fact, nothing could be further from the truth. Southeast Asia has in the past half century been on one of the leading edges of innovative Islamic thought. For the renewed attention to the work of certain medieval scholars in recent centuries in Indonesia and elsewhere has been part of broader trends in Islamic revival across the Muslim world. This attention is part of an ongoing process in which authoritative ideas gain new meanings in the continuing development of Islamic thought and practice in the contemporary world.

During the eighteenth century, the ongoing and deepening Islamization of the archipelago underwent developments that matched broader trends across the Muslim world as a whole. A surge of Islamic reform movements swept across the regions of the Muslim Middle East, Africa, and Asia. One example is the movement in Arabia led by Abd al-Wahhab (d. 1787), which ultimately became the authoritative orientation of Islam in Saudi Arabia. The Wahhabi phenomenon, however, is only one manifestation, and a somewhat atypical one at that, of broader trends in Islamic religious reform in the eighteenth century. Many of the other reform movements of that time combined a renewed emphasis on the study of *hadith* with a positive reevaluation of Sufi tradition in a more self-consciously "orthodox" and activist vein. This emphasis was often pursued through newly established or reformulated Sufi orders *(tarekat),* such as the Qadiriyya-Naqshbandiyya and the Sammaniyya. The latter in particular had an important impact on the development of Islam in Southeast Asia, especially through prominent adherents such as Abd al-Samad al-Palimbani.

Palembang, the home town of Abd al-Samad al-Palimbani, is a site on the island of Sumatra that was once at the center of Srivijaya, one of the most important and far-reaching pre-Islamic empires ever known in South Asia or Southeast Asia. In the eighteenth century, long after the coming of Islam, it was home to a number of prominent Muslim scholars and authors of Malay literature (Drewes 1977). Palembang emerged as a center of Islamic culture in the region in part because of a growing Arab community there and especially because it facilitated increased contact between South Sumatra and the Middle East. Scholars coming and going from Palembang brought with them Islamic reformist ideas from outside the region while also introducing new texts and translations that redirected and redefined local Islamic discourse. Such contact integrated even further local Southeast Asian Muslim cities and cultures into a more global Islamic civilization.

In general, increased contact between Indonesian Muslims and their coreligionists in the Middle East during the eighteenth century supported such transregional interaction. The career of Abd al-Samad himself exemplifies the dynamic connection between the two regions during this period. Abd Al-Samad left his Sumatran birthplace early in life to pursue studies of Islamic religious sciences in Arabia. He never returned to Southeast Asia, in fact, and he died of old age in Arabia after extended periods of study, teaching, and writing in Yemen and elsewhere on the Arabian peninsula. His students, however, carried his writings back to Southeast Asia, where they had a considerable impact on the evolving Islamic intellectual history of the region. In addition to works on the Sammaniyya order of Sufism and Malay adaptations of the work of Abu Hamid al-Ghazzali, Abd al-Samad is known for a series of tracts and letters urging Muslims of the Malay world to struggle against increasing European encroachment.

The eighteenth century saw a growing trend toward further mobilization, under the banner of Islam, against colonial interests. This mobilization was among the earliest of the major developments that transformed disparate and local Muslim responses in Southeast Asia into the more consolidated and consciously Islamic social and political movements in the modern period. These early movements took various forms, reflecting the particular local conditions in which they were situated. One example is the Java War of 1825–1830 in re-

Muslim students working on Arabic calligraphy in South Sulawesi, Indonesia. (R. Michael Feener)

sistance against the Dutch. The war was led by a Javanese prince, Diponogoro, who laid the political and symbolic foundation for his campaign during his younger days traveling between Islamic holy sites in Java (Carey 1992). By Diponogoro's time, devoting a stage of one's life to local pilgrimage and religious study had become standard practice for young Javanese aristocrats. Diponogoro, however, used his Javano-Muslim wanderings to contact Muslim teachers and students across a wide area and to communicate to them his ideas on the centrality of Islam to his struggle to purify Java and Javanese culture from the threat he saw posed by the Dutch.

Increasingly during the nineteenth century, resistance movements against Dutch colonialism inside and outside Java appealed to forms of Islam that claimed to express universally Islamic, rather than local or culturally specific, ideals. One well-known example of such a movement is the Padris, a West Sumatran revolt that lasted for most of the 1820s and 1830s (Dobbin 1983). It began with a group of Sumatran Muslim students returning home after studying in Arabia, which at the time had only recently been revolutionized by Abd al-Wahhab's movement. These returning *hajjis* brought with them a considerable amount of reformist orientation and energy, and they quickly convinced local *pesantren* and *tarekat* leaders to join their campaign to purify Islamic practice and establish Islamic law in their region of Sumatra. They appear at first to have been less directly concerned with colonial encroachment than with concerns over the purity and reform of Islamic religious lifestyles and practices. Their criticism of local custom and conflict with the established Muslim elites soon began to attract the attention of the Dutch, however, who were concerned with the region's lucrative coffee trade. Thus, this internal Islamic struggle about faith and practice, connected to events elsewhere in the Muslim world, grew into an anticolonial campaign. To this day, some of the leaders of the Padri movement are remembered as national heroes in Indonesia.

Islam and Rapid Change in the Modern Era

In the era leading up to the birth of modern Indonesia, there was a great expansion of the connections between Muslim Southeast Asia and the broader Islamic world, due to breakthroughs in technologies of transportation and communications. Later in the nineteenth century, contact between Arabic-speaking lands and the Malay world was further facilitated by the opening of the Suez Canal in 1869 and the replacement of sailing vessels with steamships. The early twentieth century saw a sharp increase in the amount of steamship traffic moving into the Indian Ocean, including more ships that could carry Muslim pilgrims between Southeast Asian ports and the holy cities of Arabia (Vredenbregt 1962). Aside from conveying many short-term visitors for *hajj* observances, these ships also carried Southeast Asian Muslims who stayed longer in the Middle East (Snouck 1931). In this period, more Muslim students from the archipelago could follow the footsteps of Shaykh Yusuf and Abd al-Samad to Arabia than were ever before conceivable.

These same developments also fostered a massive increase in the numbers of new immigrants to the archipelago, including a considerable number of Arabs from the Hadhramawt region along the coast of Yemen. Given that these rapid increases in the numbers of Indonesian *hajjis* and new Arab immigrants to the archipelago were made possible by technology introduced from Europe and by the policies of colonial population movements, it is ironic that they were ultimately the source of considerable concern and conflict for colonial powers in the region. For example, religious leaders from Yemen who claimed to be descended from the Prophet Muhammad himself were believed to have been important influences in the Aceh War. This conflict prevented Dutch power from achieving the subjugation of Sumatra for decades in the late nineteenth and early twentieth centuries. In this movement, not only did the local *ulama* (religious leaders) mobilize their *pesantren* and *tarekat* networks for struggle, but they also succeeded in presenting their cause as a distinctly Islamic one. Muslim leaders accomplished this both locally, such as by popularizing poems and songs on the virtues of *jihad,* and globally, by tapping into anticolonial discourses in the broader Muslim world.

The reconstructed image of a global Islamic opposition to European colonial rule was a powerful symbol that was meaningful for more than just those involved in the regional Muslim resistance movements in Indonesia. The idea was increasingly significant to the Dutch as well. The development of a Dutch "Orientalist" image of Islam, which came along with what Europe imagined Islam's role to be in the so-called Netherlands East Indies, also proceeded rapidly in the later nineteenth century. At that time, colonial officials in the archipelago, along with diplomatic staff at the new Dutch consulate in Jeddah, turned a new eye toward the activities of Islamic networks—especially those of Sufi *tarekat* like the Naqshbandiyya—that connected Muslim movements in Southeast Asia to broader, pan-Islamic ideologies (Laffan 2003).

The rapid expansion of such Sufi orders during the latter half of the nineteenth century followed and further enhanced preexisting Islamic networks in the archipelago. During this time, the *pesantren* experienced phenomenal growth and development. Although there had long been a tradition of Islamic education in the region, its appeal seemed to strengthen proportionately to intensifying Dutch colonial control. This may have been in part due to the fact that these institutions were thought to be free from European influence and also independent of the "official Islam" of the local ruling aristocracies, which were believed to have been co-opted by the European colonials. Such local political factors combined with patterns of a broader, global Islamic revival to produce key changes in the institutional character of Indonesian Islam. For example, Azyumardi Azra has written that between 1850 and 1900, the number of *pesantren* in Java alone grew from under 2,000 to nearly 15,000; the number of students trained in them increased from about 16,000 to over 220,000 (Azra 1997, 164). Muslim Indonesians in the latter part of the nineteenth century also witnessed a phenomenal growth in the production of Islamic religious texts in Arabic and Malay by Southeast Asian religious scholars. Many such texts used in the *pesantren* curriculum were originally produced in Arabia by Southeast Asians who spent many years in the Arabian peninsula, studying, living, marrying, and even dying there, like Al-Nawawi al-Banteni, Abd al-Ghani Bima, and Ahmad Patani.

In many ways, the nineteenth century might be seen as a golden age for the development of the Indonesian *pesantren* tradition and its associated traditions of Muslim texts and Islamic learning. The manuscript culture of the *pesantren,* the *kitab kuning* genre, and the Sufi *tarekat* had reached their apex by the end of this period. Over the course of the century that followed, however, major changes came upon this constellation of institutions. Against a backdrop of changing global conditions, including the ongoing challenges of religious community, diversity, and change, the promise of Indonesian nationhood and self-determination led to another reconfiguration of the ways that Indonesian Muslims imagined the ideals and traditions of Islamic learning and the development of Muslim religious life.

The Rise of Muslim Modernism in Southeast Asia

The world of Muslim Southeast Asia underwent tremendous social, economic, cultural, and intellectual changes at the turn of the twentieth century. A number of influences, although long in effect and coming from both Europe and the wider Muslim world, were becoming increasingly pronounced in Southeast Asia. These forces interacted with a complex array of local institutions to produce new expressions of Malay-Muslim culture. In particular, changes in Muslim education fostered the emergence of more-heterogeneous voices, which challenged, on new bases, the position of the established *ulama* as the authoritative interpreters of Islamic tradition. In Indonesia, a number of new figures emerged in this period who offered alternative perspectives within public discussion of religious and social issues, thus creating a new possible style of intellectual leadership for the community.

Criticizing what they viewed as the resigned and quietist behavior of some traditionalist *ulama,* a number of Muslim reformists called for scholars to take a more active role in the affairs of the society in which they lived. The new model of the activist Muslim scholar came to be a scholar whose institutional base was not the rural *pesantren* or Sufi *tarekat* but, rather, modern voluntary associations. These associations were of many types, covering a broad spectrum of social and ideological interests, ranging from literary and scientific clubs to labor and trade organizations, educational collectives, and religious movements. They created a new social space for personal action in the Muslim public sphere, providing an alternative to existing *tarekat* and *pesantren* circles.

One early example of such an organization was the Jami'yyat Khayr, which heavily emphasized education and print publication in order to promote its goals. This organization was founded at Batavia (now Jakarta) in 1911, and it recruited its teachers from Tunisia, Morocco, and Sudan. After the Jami'yyat Khayr, the most influential Indonesian voluntary association of the early twentieth century was the Sarekat Dagang Islamiyah (Islamic Commercial Union), also founded in Batavia, in 1909. Within a year, the organization's first branch opened at Bogor, near present-day Jakarta, and it subsequently expanded rapidly. In 1911, the group's central leadership encouraged the establishment of a branch for batik traders in Surakarta (Solo, a city in Central Java). The organization expanded and evolved into what was to become a nationwide political party, which shortened its name to Sarekat Islam (SI) in 1915 (Kahin 1952, 65–70).

The rise of organizations like SI, which were active in both the economic and political spheres, was paralleled in this period by the establishment of organizations with specifically religious concerns, such as the Islamic modernist organization Muhammadiyya, founded in 1912 by K. H. Ahmad Dahlan in Yogyakarta, Central Java. The Muhammadiyya movement spread rapidly to the Minangkabau region of West Sumatra and elsewhere. West Sumatra by that time was already home to a wide array of Muslim reformist institutions. Such institutions were "modernist," a term that in this period meant they had a new impetus for progressive reform that in many cases usually set itself against the idea of "tradition." For example, in West Sumatra, the Diniyah Putri School was a Muslim women's school and a "modernist" institution. Founded in 1915, it was first in the area to introduce a formal class system on a European model and a standard curriculum including nonreligious subjects. Its structure seems to have been influenced by its founder's experience of study in Egypt. It is an example of how many Muslim reformers in Asia and elsewhere in the colonial period turned to building educational institutions as a means to enact "modernizing" social change.

Over the years that followed, more local organizations began appearing in other areas of the archipelago. In response to the proliferation of modernist, reformist, and other types of organizations, more traditionally oriented *ulama* organized themselves into the Nahdlatul Ulama (NU). This important group, founded in 1926 by Kyai Haji Hasjim Asjari of Pesantren Jombang, located in East Java, also promoted the practical benefits of modern organizational models and attempted to adapt them to suit their goals (Barton and Fealy, 1996).

In the early twentieth century, especially as conditions under Dutch colonialism became harsher, many Muslims in the Indonesian archipelago were imagining how to organize for eventual autonomy from foreign European domination. They questioned what role Islam would play in a future national system. The organizations formed in this period would come to make up the basis for the Islamic political landscape of present-day Indonesia. Developing Muslim ideologies ranged across a wide spectrum, from the work of "secular" thinkers who considered religion to be a personal and private matter, to that of Islamists who felt that the ideals of Islamic law *(shari'a),* however understood, should be realized concretely and applied within actual constitutional or statutory systems.

In this period, direct Muslim opposition to foreign rule also assumed the form of voluntary associations, such as the Persatuan Ulama–Ulama Seluruh Aceh (PUSA), which was founded in 1939 by Mohammad Daud Beureu'eh. This organization eventually evolved into a full-blown separatist movement, developing alongside other Islamic separatist movements that were at that time underway elsewhere in the archipelago: in West Java, South Kalimantan, and South Sulawesi (Dijk 1981). These particular movements were known as Darul Islam, and each declared itself to be an Islamic state autonomous from any kind of secular, external authority or governance. Under pressure from various Muslim groups, the Dutch made a number of significant concessions to Islamic groups in 1940. These measures appear, however, not to have affected the widespread frustration and resentment of Muslims living under Dutch colonial rule or the emerging Indonesian nationalist resolve of Indonesia overall.

In the World War II period, a new imperialist power, Japan, transplanted the Dutch and took control of Indonesia as part of Japanese military expansion in Asia. The Muslim experience of the politics of Islam under Dutch rule seems to have facilitated the relatively open reception the Japanese received from some Muslim leaders when they arrived in the archipelago in the name of the Great East Asian Co-Prosperity Sphere. Under the Japanese occupation, Indonesian Islam underwent significant changes in structure and organization, mobilizing the Muslim population as never before (Benda 1958). As historian M. C. Ricklefs has pointed out, although both the Dutch and the Japanese wanted to control Indonesia for their own interests, they pursued this objective in very different ways, especially with respect to their policies on Islam. The Dutch were accustomed to imposing an "orderly quiet" on Muslim activities in their colonies, whereas the Japanese, strapped by wartime demands for energy and resources, chose to govern through mass mobilization (Ricklefs 1993, 201). Islamic groups that were strengthened by Japanese institutional support emerged from the war more powerful than they had ever been under the Dutch.

Following the surrender of the Japanese, Muslim groups that had acquired a more organized power base and more sophisticated political tactics played an important role in the early formation of the independent Republic of Indonesia. The most influential of these organizations for later Indonesian history was Masjumi, which was founded in 1943 to be an umbrella organization for various Indonesian Islamic groups under the Japanese occupation. This group had originally brought together Muslims of all orientations, ranging from traditionalists to modernists. Such organizations put in place the Islamic political movements of contemporary Indonesia while launching the political careers of some of its most important figures. The conversations that began in this time about how to realize ideals of Islam, law, the state, and society continue today in Indonesia, as national and global conditions continue to change.

Muslim Communities of Nation-Building in Contemporary Indonesia

Before the Japanese surrender, Indonesian Muslims had asserted the political will for self-rule in an independent Indonesia. Right after the war, Indonesians vigorously resisted Dutch attempts to regain political control over their country. At the same time, Muslims began to imagine the shape of a new Indonesian state, including sorting out how Islam would be configured into the national political picture. In June 1945, the nine members of Soekarno's Advisory Council came to a compromise on a draft for the Preamble to the Constitution, a document that came to be known as the Jakarta Charter (Piagam Djakarta). The issues relating to Islam are critical to the political landscape of Muslim Indonesia to this day (Anshari 1997).

In the disputes over the Jakarta Charter, the principal orientations to Islam and the state in Indonesia were delineated. The charter included the controversial pronouncement that the Republic was to be founded on a set of principles, known as *Pancasila*, the first of which was "the belief in God, with the obligations for adherents of Islam to practice Islamic law." The second clause in this phrase, referring to Islamic law *(shari'a)*, was later struck from the Preamble out of regard for Christian populations of the eastern archipelago. Some Indonesians saw this move as a testament to the triumph of nationalist over communitarian religious ideas, consistent with the nonsectarian political ideology of President Soekarno. Others in the Muslim community, however, viewed the decision as a compromise of their aspirations for an autonomous Muslim-majority nation as well as a betrayal of their own participation and sacrifice in the struggles that led to autonomy.

As Muslim resentment mounted over the wording of the final version of the Preamble, the nationalist government of the new Republic realized that certain compromises would have to be made with respect to the interests of organized Islamic religious and political groups who desired a more Islamicized state system. One of the most significant of these compromises was the establishment of the Indonesian Ministry of Religious Affairs in 1946. The ministry grew out of the Office for Religious Affairs that had been established under the Japanese occupation government. The movement for the continuation of this body, however, as well as its incorporation into the state structure of independent Indonesia, was at first rejected by the secular nationalists. Mounting pressure, however, convinced the government to grant a major concession to Muslim interests in the form of a national government ministry. Capitalizing on the one foothold that overtly Muslim interests had now been granted in the administration of the Republic, leaders of the ministry transformed it from a political concession to Islamic interests into an active agent for the mobilization and engagement of Muslims. In particular, it would come to play a key role in the advancement of formal and informal Muslim education and schooling nationwide.

President Soekarno was in office for two decades: from independence in the 1940s to the mid-1960s. In this period, the supporters of the Ministry of Religious Affairs faced a number of significant challenges and obstacles on the way toward realizing their objectives. Under Soekarno's administration during the 1950s and early 1960s, the interests of the military, leftists, those who were more Islamically oriented in politics, and others all hung in a delicate balance. A tense situation was further exacerbated by internal Muslim factional disputes, which had increased dramatically following a decision by the "traditionalist" Muslim organization, NU, to leave the Muslim political party, Masjumi following arguments over leadership positions in the Ministry of Religious Affairs in 1952. The appointment of a modernist to the head of the ministry was viewed by many within NU as a political setback in terms of potential influence over the official interpretation of Islam in schools, courts, and official publications. While Muslims contested such matters, other groups began to assert more power in Indonesian politics and society. The most notable of these was the Indonesian Communist Party (PKI), whose rise to prominence on the national stage eventually ended in a failed coup, a wave of tragic violence, and a rapid destabilization of Soekarno's hold on power.

The turbulent toppling of Soekarno's government in 1965 was followed, especially on the islands of Java and Bali, by the killing of tens of thousands of Indonesians. Suspected leftists, among others, were targeted. In the wake of this turmoil, a general named Suharto came to power as president and declared a "New Order" for Indonesian society. Especially after the horror of 1965, many committed Muslims turned away from direct mass mobilization politics under Suharto's New Order. In addition, in the early years of the New Order, the new government's drive to consolidate power resulted in a political disenfranchisement of some Muslim political parties and organizations. Outside the sphere of politics proper, however, significant changes in the Islamic character of Indonesian Muslim society were taking shape. Some of these changes were actually facilitated by the success of the New Order's developmental agenda and occurred despite official policies on Islam that were not always warmly received. Economic growth and the restructuring of the national educational system had produced a burgeoning new class of literate Indonesian Muslims who were keen on mainstream religious revitalization. Robert Hefner has documented that during the late 1970s and 1980s, the ranks of Indonesia's educated middle class expanded dramatically, and new Muslim print media flourished (Hefner 2000). In this period, Indonesia witnessed an Islamic resurgence that mirrored the "Islamic Awakening" in cultures elsewhere in the Muslim-majority world, such as Egypt. Although this development seems to have initially caught some of the New Order leadership off guard, by the end of the 1980s, an expanding Islamic revival had established itself centrally on the national scene, as evidenced by President Suharto's own well-publicized *hajj* pilgrimage earlier in the decade.

Indonesian Islamic "Renewalism"

Movements of renewal and reform take diverse forms in island Southeast Asia today, constituting part of a contemporary movement in religious revitalization that some consider a continual process of Islamization. The troubles of Islamic party politics in the decade before the fall of Soekarno in 1965 and during the subsequent rise of the New Order left many Muslims disillusioned with applying direct political means to social transformation. In the aftermath of the turbulence and trauma of the mid-1960s, many of them began to develop alternative ways to participate Islamically in the New Order's program of nation-building and national development. Something of a consensus eventually evolved among most Muslim groups that direct political action as it had been previously pursued by Islamic parties was no longer a feasible or desirable option under the New Order, and thus they envisioned new ways of participating in Muslim public leadership. For many, a positive solution for pursuing the Islamization of society while affirming difference and pluralism was found in a cultural rather than an ideological strategy. That is, rather than following the classically modernist or reformist program of advocating top-down social change through political parties, focus was shifted toward the Islamization of society more informally and by bottom-up means. The goal was to support Muslim individuals and groups and to embrace constructive Islamic values that would improve Indonesian social experience in both private and public Muslim life.

Studying the Qur'an at home in East Java, Indonesia. (R. Michael Feener)

Members of the growing and increasingly Islamicized Muslim middle class were among the major supporters of new Islamic social and cultural patterns. Members of this sector of society became a significant factor in the nation's political and sociocultural dynamics. Many of them were employed in education and in the government bureaucracy. Over the last three decades of the twentieth century, they contributed to the development of a broad movement for the renewal *(pembaharuan)* of Islamic education, law, doctrine, and practice in order to make them more inclusive and participatory for Muslims in contemporary Indonesia, as well as consistent with the ideal of supporting the diversity of Indonesia's Muslim and non-Muslim faith communities overall.

Some of the foundations of the *pembaharuan* movement were first formulated within the context of what is known as the Limited Group discussions, held from 1967 to 1971, during which a group of young Muslim intellectuals began to explore a wide range of ideas in a search for new ways in which Islam could be interpreted and implemented with greater relevance to conditions in contemporary Indonesia. During the 1970s, participants in these discussions and other younger activists made significant contributions toward the development of new currents of modernism and what has been referred to as a "new Islamic intellectualism" in Indonesia (Barton 1995).

The most prominent proponent of this movement is Nurcholish Madjid, who established the Paramadina foundation in Jakarta as a forum for the free and open discussion of issues connected with Islam and its role in Indonesian society. Underlying nearly every aspect of his thought is a sense of dynamism and ever-evolving adaptability of ultimate Islamic ideals that is based upon an historically contextualized conceptualization of *ijtihad*. In this case, the technical legal term *"ijtihad"* is best understood as meaning a generalized effort to apprehend the appropriate application of Islamic ideals to particular circumstances. In formulating vibrant and revitalized interpretations of Islam, supporters of Indonesia's emerging neomodernist movement developed a deep and nuanced appreciation of past-historical traditions of Muslim scholarship and the variety of methods used by *ulama* throughout history to answer the challenges of change.

More traditionally trained *ulama* in the period of the New Order tended to belong to the NU. They also developed new models and adapted those of others to suit their own vision and ideals. The NU is today the largest Muslim organization in Indonesia and possibly even in the entire world. Although its appeal to the *pesantren* tradition of Muslim scholarship has been a mainstay of the organization from its very inception, since the 1970s it has also developed in some very nontraditional ways. This change in character is due in part to its "modernized" organizational structure and in part to the influence of well-funded nongovernmental organizations, many of which have provided considerable financial support for projects involving the NU during the last decades of Suharto's New Order. It has thus opened itself up to allow some of its members to experiment with ideas on the cutting edge of Muslim legal religious and social thought in Indonesia.

Throughout the struggle for independence and during the first twenty years of the Republic, the NU was a loyal supporter of Soekarno, despite his overtures to socialists and communists. This pattern of cooperation was considerably altered, however, with the fall of Soekarno and the rise of the New Order. Throughout the 1970s, relations between the political wing of the NU and the New Order government were visibly strained over such issues as marriage law. However, after a period of protracted and increasingly bitter struggle, the organization formally accepted the state's 1984 "mandate of monoloyalty" to *Pancasila* as the official ideology of the Indonesian state. *Pancasila* is a five-part state doctrine affirming ideals of social equality, opportunity, and justice. Its first precept, "belief in one God," had been objected to by some committed Muslims because of its Islamically neutral formulation.

In the mid-1980s, members of NU cast its new stance toward the government as a "return" to the original design of the organization at the time of its founding in 1926. NU's relationship to the New Order government grew increasingly friendly during the 1980s; a significant amount of new subsidies were provided for *pesantren* education, especially during the 1990s. Some NU institutions, in turn, agreed to allow non-NU teachers to participate. Beyond this, there were also a number of more general compromises in which at least some of the more politically oriented figures within NU were willing to support government development programs, including those considered religiously controversial, such as family planning. In general, a shift in organizational orientation that accompanied the return was acknowledged in order to allow NU to redirect its energies, especially in the area of education, in more productive directions than those pursued in relation to the organization's previous political preoccupations.

Although NU has long been considered to represent adherents to a more traditionalist Islam, this characterization must be considerably qualified to describe its later configuration. The reorientation of the NU's primary focus away from party politics and toward religious and social activities also afforded a reascendancy of wider influence for the *ulama,* who had originally been the organization's core constituents. In addition, since NU's acceptance of *Pancasila* in 1984 as an ideological foundation, a spirit of open inquiry into religious questions grew within the younger ranks of the organization. The NU continues to emphasize the traditions of Muslim scholarship, especially the importance of following the jurisprudence of one of the established Sunni schools of law, and it has also in the New Order years and after effected a powerful transformation of mainstream Islam in a secular state.

These developments within the ranks of the NU involved a conscious reevaluation of the traditional corpus of Muslim scholarship with an eye to establishing its relevance to contemporary needs. The changes within the NU in the New Order years coincided with a renewed interest in the canon of established Muslim scholarship by thinkers outside the organization. It may be that these developments within the NU were actually facilitated by the development of a growing appreciation of the traditional corpus of Muslim scholarship by Indonesian neomodernists. Across a spectrum of Muslim thought in contemporary Indonesia, many progressive thinkers had come to recognize the shortcomings of "classical modernism" and were searching for ways to access universally Islamic sources of depth, authenticity, and authority in their approach to Islam in order to solve real social and religious problems. In thought and practice, many Indonesian Muslims were reaffirming models of revelation, especially the Qur'an, the primary orientation for what Mark Woodward (1996) has termed a "new paradigm" of positive social change in the modern world.

Scripturalist Reformism and the Call for *Ijtihad*

To this day, the mainstay of Muslim education in NU circles remains the *pesantren* tradition. Other Muslim organizations, as well as the Indonesian government, of course introduced some major structural, curricular, and institutional innovations into systems of schooling over the course of the twentieth century. Accompanying the programs of several Indonesian Muslim reformist movements in the twentieth century was a strong emphasis on reforming the institutions of Muslim education in order to better serve the needs of their members in a rapidly developing society. The impetus for educational reform, which began at the primary level, had by the middle part of the twentieth century extended to include innovations in higher education. This culminated in the establishment of a national system of university campuses known as State Institutes for Islamic Studies (IAIN) located throughout the archipelago.

One fundamental factor in all these modern educational developments was the rapidly expanding Muslim print culture of Indonesia and the wider Muslim world. In the early twentieth century, printed publications began to have an increasingly pronounced effect on the urban populations of the archipelago. Although there was some limited printing activity by Muslims in Southeast Asia prior to the turn of the twentieth century, large-scale printing enterprises, especially those producing periodicals and other materials, came several decades later. Before this time, the majority of Arabic-script books available in the region—other than rare and expensive manuscript copies—were imported from locations in the Middle East such as Mecca, Istanbul, and especially Cairo.

Over the twentieth century, the texts that continued to be produced overseas for the Southeast Asian market were increasingly supplemented by local publications. These included specialized religious tracts meant for Muslim scholars and also more popular forms of literature, such as novels and collections of short stories that conveyed ideas of Islamic reform. This genre appealed to a number of Malay-language authors who were associated with Islamic reform in the twentieth century, such as Sayyid Shaykh Abdul Hadi and Haji Abdul Malik Karim Amrullah, popularly known as Hamka. Hamka was one of the most prominent public figures in Indonesian Islam until his death in 1981. Under the influence of Hamka and others like him, a public discourse on Islam that extended well beyond the circles of classically trained scholars became an important dimension of modern Indonesian society.

Working in the milieu of newly reformed institutions of education, especially those sponsored by various new voluntary institutions, Southeast Asian Muslim writers evolved a distinctive orientation and new format for their works. In doing so, they established new approaches to authority in Indonesian Islam. One prominent example of such a writer was A. Hassan, a prolific and polemical author associated with an organization called Persatuan Islam (PERSIS). PERSIS was founded in 1923 in Bandung, a city in the western part of Java, as an organization to promote Islamic study and other activities. Under Hassan's influence in the 1930s, the flexible and ideologically mixed character for which the organization had previously been known was streamlined into an insistence on reformist principles and a more unified approach overall (Federspiel 2001).

PERSIS became known as an organization claiming strict allegiance to the text of the Qur'an and reliable *hadith,* and its members sharply criticized Muslims who accepted any other standards of religious authority. Hassan, who had formerly been a tire vulcanizer in Singapore, thus became a pioneer of a vigorous, "public *ijtihad*" in modern Southeast Asia and a prominent proponent of bringing the discussion of Islamic religious and legal issues outside the walls of traditionalist *pesantren* and into the expanding national print market. Not all of those reading Hassan's popular columns may have agreed with his stances on particular issues, but many were nonetheless attracted to the more general message of reform. In the contemporary period, there has also been widespread approval of claims that Muslims of any background can legitimately interpret tradition for themselves or their communities or exercise *ijtihad,* based on the authority of the sources rather than on classical or rigorous training in such traditional Islamic subjects as legal thought.

Despite differences of opinion, which add vitality to any religious or cultural tradition, there are many points on which modern Indonesians agree. Among these is the ideal of a shared project among Muslims to explore potential relationships between Islamic ideas and practices and other personal and community values. This exploration has taken place, in Indonesia and elsewhere, not only by talking about these possibilities in the abstract but also more directly by "re-Islamizing" actual religious practices in which, ideally, any Muslim can take part. In other words, continuing Islamization in the form of Islamic "resurgence" has been occurring in Indonesia not only through interpretation of canonical texts and foundational ideas but also through the reinvigoration of normative practices under new and changing conditions.

Revitalization of Contemporary Piety: Popular Education and Expression

In recent decades, there has been an energetic revitalization movement in Islamic thought and practice in Indonesia that embraces a deepening of Islamic commitment and social betterment. The Indonesian form of the global "Islamic Awakening" has been a powerful movement in Qur'anically based piety, but unlike other parts of the Muslim-majority world, it has tended not to include a politically radical vision in its mainstream expression. Instead, focus has generally been on the renewal and reform of society through positive personal engagement with such social and cultural activities as education, performance, and community projects. These programs are solidly based in the universal aspects of Islamic tradition (such as the Qur'an), they usually derive their structure from flexible associations, and finally, they use the vocabulary of contemporary international Islam, developing piety and practice in ways consistent with conditions of present-day Indonesia. Many of the aspects of mainstream Islamic revitalization, key to Indonesian movements especially—such as Qur'anic expression, aesthetics, and piety—are now being recognized internationally as models for "inviting" Muslims to participate more deeply in Islamic life in a way that is inclusive and that embraces Muslim diversity as a positive value in its own right.

Much of the reinvigorated Islamic activity in Indonesia enhances practices that have existed since the first Islamic times. In the contemporary period, established practices like recitation of the Qur'an and Islamic pilgrimage have been reinvigorated with a new awareness and attitude, and they connect local Indonesian systems to global communities in new ways. These practices may now be influenced by modern technologies (such as jet travel and broadcast media), yet in their basic religious aspects they also stay fundamentally the same as they have been for centuries, and they remain the same throughout the Muslim-majority and Muslim-minority worlds. In present-day Indonesia, they are the basis of a resurgence in Islamic activity because these practices are understood to be powerful agents for renewing and reforming society through the dedication of individuals who are deeply committed to Islamic values.

One example of reinvigorated Islamic practice is the *hajj*, or pilgrimage to the holy city of Mecca, which is obligatory for all Muslims once in a lifetime provided that certain conditions are met. When President Suharto performed his *hajj* in the 1980s, it was seen as a turning point in the state's approach to Islam. *Hajj* represents continuities and connections that stretch back to the original Islamic community of the Prophet Muhammad; today, Indonesians are represented in great proportion in the annual pilgrimage. Although Indonesia lies far from Mecca, each year more and more Indonesians make the effort to fulfill this foundational component of piety. Even those who remain at home focus much attention on those who have had the opportunity to travel to the Middle East that year. Indonesians embarking on *hajj* come into contact with other Muslims from all over the world, thus bringing to the shared, global dimensions of Islamic religiosity a distinctively Indonesian viewpoint. Contemporary Indonesian pilgrims, each with his or her own perspective, return from *hajj* to their local mosques and neighborhoods with an enriched sense of their participation in the worldwide Muslim community as well as of their own identity as Indonesian Muslims. In this way, a religious activity based on the practice of the Prophet Muhammad continues to reinvigorate public and personal religious experience in the present.

The ritual and practice-oriented aspects of Islam, especially those that are Qur'an related, have gained special focus in contemporary Indonesian revitalization projects. In these programs, social Islamization mirrors internal Islamization, which then is understood to reflect back out to the larger society.

This kind of Islamization effort comes under the rubric of *da'wa*, a term that means to "invite" people who share faith to deepen their own understanding and commitment to a way of life that is spiritually fulfilling and that offers the satisfying sense of participating in religious community. The term can have very different connotations in different parts of the contemporary Muslim world. In Indonesia, the idea of *da'wa* is often closely associated with Muslims learning more about Islam. These activities take place in new kinds of schools, through Islamic cultural performances, or by way of the "Islamic arts." For example, one practice that is increasing in popularity in contemporary Indonesia is the aesthetic and pious recitation and appreciation of religious texts. Most significantly, this includes practices that engage the Qur'an, such as Arabic calligraphy or reading the Qur'an out loud with great technical artistry. In Southeast Asia, many of these projects, based on Qur'anic systems, have an aesthetic component that is consistent with the emphasis on beauty in the Qur'an's own terms and in other Muslim traditions of piety, and this element is also recognized as a highly effective way to invite others to a more meaningful Muslim lifestyle and to the development of more supportive religious communities (Gade 2004).

The Islamic tradition of the recitation of the Qur'an, understood to be the actual speech of God, combined with the emphasis in contemporary Indonesia on participating in vibrant practices of Qur'anically oriented piety, shows that a religious text is a living document. The Qur'an not only relates a revelatory message, according to Muslims, but is also an ongoing experience of personal and collective engagement. The Qur'anic activities that have been so popular in Indonesia are an expression of a crucial dimension of Islamic practice, based on the "fundamental" experience of the revealed Qur'an; however, although certainly based in scripture, this energetic expression bears little resemblance to the stereotype of "fundamentalism" that many North Americans associate with religious resurgence among Muslims and other religious groups.

Reading the Qur'an is one of the most important ways Muslims express religious piety, along with the basic duties known as the Five Pillars of Islam (the testimony of faith, canonical prayer five times daily, fasting during the month of Ramadhan, pilgrimage to Mecca at least once in a lifetime, and legal almsgiving). Muslims recite some of the Qur'an from memory every time they perform canonical prayer, and the reading of the Qur'an aloud at other times has always been strongly encouraged. The Qur'an is understood by Muslims to have been revealed by God to the Prophet Muhammad by way of the oral recitation of the Angel Gabriel, and the word "Qur'an" itself is usually said to be a form of the Arabic word for "reading." The Prophet and his companions are believed to have transmitted the Qur'an orally to others even before its text was written down for the first time. Learning to read the Qur'an out loud—whether or not the reader can understand the Arabic words—is also the first and most basic kind of formal Islamic religious schooling. There are special guidelines Muslims follow when reciting the Qur'an, but there are no restrictions against making the "reading" a beautiful one. Verses in the Qur'an and statements attributed to the Prophet in fact encourage beautifying the recitation of the Qur'an so that it will deepen the faith of readers and listeners. Ideally, the development of technical artistry helps others feel a connection between religious ideas of revelation and their immediate experience.

Techniques for teaching the reading of the Qur'an have been developed in contemporary Indonesia as an activity that is especially appealing to young children. Indonesians have applied ideas about "making learning fun" to the Islamic tradition of teaching a child how to read the Qur'an. This has occurred particularly in new kinds of schools called "Qur'an kindergartens," which feature varied activities, such as singing in class songs that are also available as sound recordings. Learning to read the Qur'an has become so popular, in fact, that many older people are also returning to study how to read better. Some of the learning strategies are adaptations of centuries-old models and some are derived from other places in the contemporary Muslim world, such as Egypt, but overall, the learning environment is unmistakably Southeast Asian. Some of the most popular techniques for learning to read the Qur'an have been exported from Indonesia to other parts of the Muslim world because they are so effective.

Since the earliest times, according to tradition, the Qur'an has been preserved most authoritatively by generations of Muslims through memorization and recitation aloud, and only secondarily through the written text. In Islamic law, the memorization, or "preservation," of the Qur'an is an obligation placed on every community, and it is understood that a community will have met this obligation as long as there are always some people who carry the entire text in memory, repeating parts of it every day so that they do not forget. In Indonesia, this transmission is basic to the *pesantren* curriculum. When one is memorizing the text of the Qur'an, it is necessary to have a teacher present in order to make sure that no unintentional mistakes are being made and that the reading is correct overall. In Indonesia in the twentieth century, Qur'an memorizers usually came from families of other memorizers, male and female, supporting the discipline of repeating the text often. In earlier decades, many of these families had connections to the Arabic-speaking Middle East, perhaps with a father or a grandfather who had studied in Arabia, but today memorization has become more popular among college-aged men and women more generally. This is especially the case at colleges in Jakarta and other areas that have "Qur'an institutes," which emphasize not only traditional Qur'anic learning in fields like theology and law but also Qur'anic practices such as memorization and recitation.

Muslim girls practicing aerobics in the courtyard of their Muslim madrasa *in the Menteng area of Jakarta, Indonesia. (Sergio Dorantes/Corbis)*

Adding energy to the reinvigoration of traditional Qur'anic practices in contemporary Indonesia is a kind of competition in the reading, memorization, calligraphy, and comprehension of the Qur'an. This competition seems to have had its roots in Southeast Asia in the earliest period of Islam, but it is now spreading throughout Indonesia and even through the wider Islamic world as a form of *da'wa*. Many Indonesians see popular contests in the recitation of the Qur'an as a way to "invite" others to share in the moving experience of religious piety, whether or not they continue their study of Qur'anic reading beyond the beginning level. Contests for the recitation of the Qur'an have been held by many kinds of institutions and professional groups in Indonesia; every year, there is one very large national recitation competition that features a great parade with floats and performances in Islamic cultural arts as well as the competition in recitation, memorization, and calligraphy. Such contests are rarely seen as controversial, even among very conservative Muslims who might otherwise object to competing for prizes. This is because Indonesians promote the competitions' positive effects on Islamic communities and their role in encouraging young people, especially, to enjoy Qur'anic activities. Indonesian Muslims also recognize that contestants are coached to do their best in order to present a positive Qur'anic experience to everyone involved, according to Qur'anic values, and that they are not encouraged to compete simply in order to win.

The winners of these contests also look forward to the opportunity to participate in international competition in places such as Malaysia and Saudi Arabia. One contest champion who has been an international figure is Maria Ulfah, originally from Java, who has studied in Egypt and who visited the United States to perform in 1999. She is a scholar, educator, and performer who has a position at a flagship Qur'anic college in Jakarta (Rasmussen 2001). Some people in the United States were surprised that the leading Qur'anic reciter from Indonesia is a woman, but gender balance is characteristic of Southeast Asian Qur'anic performances. Men are allowed to study advanced recitation with the top female teachers as well as with male ones. Leading reciters, such as Maria Ulfah, also represent the international character of revitalized Qur'anic practice in Indonesia. They work with models of vocal performance from Egypt and develop them in a Southeast Asian style, and, in Ulfah's case, she then travels the world to give others the opportunity to realize the depth of Qur'anic piety and commitment in Indonesia.[1]

The promotion of Qur'an-centered practice has not been happening in contemporary Indonesia only in the form of contests. There is, for example, an exhibit at a national amusement park outside Jakarta, Indonesia's capital, called the House of the Qur'an (Baitul Quran), which first opened in 1996. This House features what is said to be the largest decorated text of the Qur'an in the world, exhibits of old religious manuscripts from Indonesia's Islamic past, and artistic interpretations of the Arabic of the Qur'an in modern calligraphy and illumination. These Qur'anic renderings use indigenous motifs inspired by Indonesian flowers and textiles. The roof of the building itself is topped by a model of a stand on which the Qur'an is placed during its recitation, and Muslim schoolchildren visit the exhibit often. Although this project was government supported, it also captures the energy of a movement that has been widely popular at the roots of contemporary Indonesian Muslim culture, especially among younger people.

Contemporary Islamic revitalization in the form of *da'wa* and performance in Indonesia has increasingly used mass media, such as radio and television broadcasting, sound recordings on cassettes and compact discs, and print media as tools of teaching and learning. Although this is the case throughout the Muslim world, in Indonesia, Islamic arts in particular are recognized as ideal vehicles for popular Islamic expression that can be disseminated through these media. One example of this is a danceable musical form known as *dangdut,* a favorite of young people. There has also been a flood of new literature about religious thought and practice and increased availability of recordings of the live performances of entertaining preachers, some of them very funny while also very pious. The impact of the Internet on Indonesian Islamic expression is starting to be felt at the beginning of the twenty-first century as well.

Da'wa in the form of Indonesian performing arts draws on both Islamic models and uniquely Southeast Asian aesthetic expression, combining them in a way that is both authentically Islamic and characteristically Indonesian. The Javanese performing arts of the gamelan (a gong orchestra) and the shadow puppet theater are well known. Although some have viewed aspects of these Javanese cultural practices as "un-Islamic," contemporary Muslim performers such as Emha Ainun Naguib, a Javanese poet, combine, for example, the Javanese gamelan with Arabic vocal performance and contemporary studio instruments to produce a unique kind of popular Muslim musical performance.

Another example of the combination of local and global traditions in Muslim aesthetic expression in Indonesia, this one from the visual arts, is the work of an artist from Aceh, A. D. Pirous. Pirous has used Qur'anic verses, indigenous Islamic expression such as the poetry of a Sumatran from an earlier era, Hamzah Fansuri, and his own unique vision to render a personal expression of a global Islam (George and Mamannoor, 2002). His work is informed by his own unique experiences as a citizen of Indonesia and also as a member of a specific local Muslim community, that of Aceh. Drawing on patterns shared by all Muslims, individual expressions of Qur'anic and Islamic piety among contemporary Indonesians affect others in the community and the nation, and in turn reflect back out to the rest of the Muslim world.

All of these changes in the spheres of personal piety and cultural Islamization in Indonesia are also part of a broader global phenomenon. The mainstream movement of Islamic religious revitalization in contemporary Indonesia, evidenced by remarkable creative production, draws not only on the Qur'an and basic Islamic principles but also on Southeast Asian values of aesthetics, inclusivism, and participation. At the same time, and despite the New Order's sustained efforts to separate a cultural religious revival from any political manifestations of this turn to Islam, a number of Indonesian Muslims appear to see such distinctions as artificial and foreign to their understanding and experience of Islamic religious renewal, and they support transformation in both areas. Intellectual and cultural Islamization in Indonesia progressed steadily through the last decades of Suharto's New Order, and this process prepared the way for a renewed emergence of Islam onto the national political stage in the final years of the twentieth century. Especially in the post-Suharto years, Indonesian Muslims have developed distinctive, Islamically grounded orientations to issues of justice, pluralism, and participation in pious and political life in ways consistent with other aspects of Muslim life in a diverse and globalizing world.

Global and Local Trends in Muslim Politics: Islam and the State after Suharto

In 1997, a financial crisis of staggering proportions in Southeast Asia prompted the International Monetary Fund (IMF) to press the Suharto government for a series of financial and administrative reforms. Severe economic hardship and frustration with the enforcement of the reforms served to exacerbate mounting opposition to the regime. This dissatisfaction had been building throughout the 1990s as the gap between rich and poor drastically widened. In addition, actions taken against potential political challengers like Megawati Sukarnoputri, the daughter of former president Soekarno, drew widespread negative attention and anger against the political mechanics of the regime.

Suharto's "election" to his seventh term in 1997 was no surprise, and the figures who were appointed to fill the cabinet were all too familiar to many. Within a year, street protests erupted in the capital, several of which turned into clashes with the police and military. Four students were shot and killed by government security forces at Tri Sakti University, and their deaths unleashed further protest and unrest in Jakarta. Amid clamorous calls for the president's resignation, groups of radical Islamists, some of whom had actually been quietly courted by the New Order government over the previous few years, took to the streets. This ignited religious and ethnically motivated violence against non-Muslims, particularly Indonesians of Chinese descent. President Suharto, who had led Indonesia since the events of 1965, stepped down in May 1998.

Accompanying a new openness in the post-Suharto era came the challenges of a pluralistic society, confronted by Indonesians of every religious orientation. A few have capitalized on opportunities to further particularistic or factionalist ideals. In the absence of constraints from the New Order government, the conditions of contemporary Indonesia have allowed for the emergence of a number of Islamist organizations (Dijk 2001). Immediately following a tragic bomb blast in Bali in 2002, however, some radical groups, such as the Lasykar Jihad, were officially disbanded, while others, such as the Jemaah Islamiah, came under increased intelligence scrutiny, legal prosecution, and media attention. Such extremist groups have, however, not been successful in influencing the mainstream of Indonesian Islamic thought, nor even the thought of that minority of Muslims within the mainstream who would like to see a more Islamicized legal system as a way to realize Islamic ideals in a pluralistic society.

With the end of the New Order, President Suharto delivered the presidency to his vice president, B. J. Habibie. Habibie, a German-educated technocrat and close compatriot of Suharto, had over the previous decade been named the head of a semigovernmental organization, the Indonesian Association of Muslim Intellectuals (ICMI). This organization took on the role of the prime vehicle for what has been termed the "greening" (Islamization) of the late New Order regime. ICMI, however, was also criticized by Muslim leaders outside of ICMI, who saw it as having been co-opted by the designs of New Order government interests. Critics of ICMI included some of the major figures in a call for "total reform" in the post–New Order era. These included Abdurrahman Wahid, who declined to join the organization, and Amien Rais, who had split from the group some years earlier. Between them, these two figures represented the country's two largest Muslim organizations, those of the traditionalists and the modernists, respectively.

Amien Rais, who earned his doctoral degree in the United States, led the Muhammadiyya Muslim modernist organization beginning in 1993. Rais was received as a Muslim advocate of social justice and at times garnered significant support in a political coalition with Megawati Sukarnoputri. Previous anti-Christian and anti-Chinese remarks and calls for the establishment of an Islamic state by Amien Rais, however, had caused considerable concern among his potential constituents, many Muslims among them. After the 1999 parliamentary session, some might have expected Amien Rais to become president, since he was at the forefront of the political opposition to Suharto at the end of the New Order. Similarly, many at that juncture would have predicted that the presidency would go straight to Megawati. Instead, however, it went to a third major player at the forefront of the broad-based movement for "*reformasi*," Abdurrahman Wahid.

Wahid is the grandson of the founder of the NU and had chaired that organization since 1984. He was educated in Javanese *pesantren* as well as in the Middle East. While there in the 1960s, he left the prestigious center of Islamic education in Egypt, al-Azhar University, in order to take up a more secular program of study at the University of Baghdad (Barton 2002). Ever since, Wahid has been a prominent public voice against what he has termed "Islamic formalism," which includes some calls to establish Islamic legal ideals as a "basis of the state," in favor of interpretations that take more extensive account of contextualized issues. In this vein, he has been known both as a strong advocate for the interpretation of Islam in Indonesia according to localized or indigenized models and as a supporter of the official ideology of the Indonesian state, *Pancasila*.

Since the end of the Suharto era, calls for the implementation of the *shari'a* have been increasingly pronounced in Indonesian public discussions. Wahid's positions were thus unpopular with some segments of the Muslim community on this point. Islamist groups that emphasized more legal-formalist approaches to Islam were especially quick to criticize Wahid's presidency. Such groups proclaim the ultimate solution to Indonesia's moral and social crises to be in the formal implementation of Islamic law. Some of these same groups had been encouraged and supported by the Indonesian government during the final years of Suharto's New Order. For example, in 2000, Islamist activists pressed the government for the implementation of a new economic system based on the *shari'a,* and in January 2002, the Internal Affairs minister, Hari Sabarno, seemed not to completely rule out the issue, stating in response only that any aspirations for the Islamization of Indonesian law must be pursued through the official political processes of the National Assembly (DPRD).

Leaders of the Dewan Dakwah Islam Indonesia (DDII) advanced an appeal not long after that, arguing that the national Constitution should be amended so that the "seven words" of the Jakarta Charter—"with the obligation of Muslims to uphold the *shari'a*"—would now be reinstituted. One can see significant political stakes animating these discussions of religious ideals. The DDII and allied Islamist groups argued that under their reading of Islamic law, a woman could not serve as head of state. Thus, according to them, the implementation of the *shari'a* would immediately have required the removal from office of President Megawati Sukarnoputri, who had become president following Wahid's resignation in July 2001. In this context, Megawati's own vice president, Hamzah Haz, who is himself openly sympathetic to the formalization of Islam's role in national politics, preferred, however, to speak about the possible implementation of the *shari'a* only on a provincial, rather than a national, level.

Even among the most pious and committed Muslims, however, in the post-Suharto era, most do not seem to be in favor of the implementation of a formalist conception of the *shari'a*. This includes much of the constituencies of the traditionalist NU, as well as the modernist Muhammadiyya, both of which formally stated their opposition to movements to reintroduce the famous "seven words" of the Jakarta Charter to the national Constitution in a special forum on religious issues held in the national assembly during February 2002. Overall, the range of contemporary perspectives on "Islamic law" shows its salience as a political symbol and reveals the diversity of views that Muslims have today in Indonesia on how to apply religious ideals to the realities of contemporary Indonesian life. Just as they have in the past, global, regional, local, and individual religious dynamics interact in contemporary Southeast Asian Islamic systems to create a considerable range of Muslim approaches to such basic human questions in the modern world as democracy, social justice, religious authority, and cultural change, as well as to issues of pluralism and diversity.

Indonesia's rich history of cultural cosmopolitanism contributes to the maintenance of deep and long-standing traditions of diversity. Some of the most important values for many Indonesian Muslims include an awareness of the pluralism of contemporary global experience and a recognition of the diversity within the Indonesian nation itself. Although the great majority of Indonesians are Muslims, there are considerable minority populations of other faiths, such as Protestant Christian and Roman Catholic communities in North Sulawesi, in North Sumatra, and in the eastern islands, Hindu communities in Bali, and Buddhist communities in many parts of the country, as well as a number of small-scale traditions that face the challenges of globalization and pressures to define themselves in terms of globalizing categories such as "religion."

Indonesian Islam itself is internally a very diverse phenomenon in its variations of Muslim orientations toward Islamic religious traditions in the contexts of local cultures. The challenges now faced by Muslims in Indonesia, and by Indonesians of all faiths, are in many ways the same as those faced by all of us, Muslims and non-Muslims, all over the world in our own local, national, and global contexts: How will we apply our own highest human ideals to a shared experience of the real circumstances of diversity, difference, and rapid social change?

Notes

1.   Recordings of Maria Ulfah reciting the Qur'an can be heard on the compact disc included in Sells 1999.

References

Anshari, H. E. S. 1997. *Piagam Jakarta, 22 Juni 1945: Sebuah Konsensus Nasional tentang Dasar Negara Republik Indonesia (1945–1949)*. Jakarta: Gema Insani Press.

Azra, Azyumardi. 1992. "The Transmission of Islamic Reformism to Indonesia: Networks of Middle Eastern and Malay-Indonesian 'Ulamâ' in the Seventeenth and Eighteenth Centuries." PhD diss., Columbia University.

———. 1997. "Education, Law, Mysticism: Constructing Social Realities." In *Islamic Civilization in the Malay World,* edited by Mohd Taib Osman, 141–195. Istanbul: IRCICA.

Barton, Greg. 1995. "Neo-Modernism: A Vital Synthesis of Traditionalist and Modernist Islamic Thought in Indonesia." *Studia Islamika* 2, no. 3: 1–75.

———. 2002. *Abdurrahman Wahid: Muslim Democrat, Indonesian President.* Honolulu: University of Hawai'i Press.

Barton, Greg, and Greg Fealy, eds. 1996. *Nahdlatul Ulama, Traditional Islam, and Modernity in Indonesia.* Clayton, Australia: Monash Asia Institute.

Benda, H. 1958. *The Crescent and the Rising Sun.* The Hague: W. van Hoeve.

Bruinessen, Martin van. 1992. *Tarekat Naqsybandiyah di Indonesia.* Bandung, Indonesia: Mizan.

———. 1994. "Pesantren and Kitab Kuning: Continuity and Change in a Tradition of Religious Learning." In *Texts from the Islands: Oral and Written Traditions of Indonesia and the Malay World,* edited by Wolfgang Marschall, 121–146. Berne: University of Berne Institute of Ethnology.

———. 1995. "Tarekat and Tarekat Teachers in Madurese Society." In *Across Madura Strait: The Dynamics of an Insular Society,* edited by K. van Dijk, H. de Jonge, and E. Touwen-Bouwsma, 91–118. Leiden: KITLV Press.

Carey, Peter. 1992. "Satria and Santri: Some Notes on the Relationship between Dipanagara's Kraton and Religious Supporters during the Java War (1825–30)." In *Dari Babad dan Hikayat sampai Sejarah Kritis: Kumpulan karangan dipersembahkan kepada Sartono Kartodirdjo,* 271–318. Yogyakarta: Gadjah Mada University Press.

Dijk, C. van. 1981. *Rebellion under the Banner of Islam: The Darul Islam in Indonesia.* The Hague: Martinus Nijhoff.

Dijk, Kees van. 2001. *A Country in Despair: Indonesia between 1997 and 2000.* Leiden: KITLV Press.

Dobbin, Christine. 1983. *Islamic Revivalism in a Changing Peasant Economy: Central Sumatra, 1784–1847.* London: Curzon Press.

Drewes, G. W. J. 1977. *Directions for Travellers on the Mystic Path: Zakariyya' al-Ansari's "Kitab Fath al-Rahman" and Its Indonesian Adaptations.* The Hague: Martinus Nijhoff.

Drewes, G. W. J., and L. F. Brakel, eds. 1986. *The Poems of Hamzah Fansuri.* The Hague: Martinus Nijhoff.

Eickelman, Dale, and Jon W. Andersen, eds. 1999. *New Media in the Muslim World: The Emerging Public Sphere.* Bloomington: Indiana University Press.

Federspiel, Howard M. 2001. *Islam and Ideology in the Emerging Indonesian State: The Persatuan Islam (PERSIS), 1923–1957.* Leiden: Brill.

Gade, Anna M. 2004. *Perfection Makes Practice: Learning, Emotion, and the Recited Qur'an in Indonesia.* Honolulu: University of Hawai'i Press.

Geertz, Clifford. 1968. *Islam Observed: Religious Development in Morocco and Indonesia.* New Haven: Yale University Press.

George, Kenneth M., and Mamannoor. 2002. A.D. *Pirous: Vision, Faith, and a Journey in Indonesian Art, 1955–2002.* Bandung, Indonesia: Yayasan Serambi Pirous.

Hefner, Robert W. 2000. *Civil Islam: Muslims and Democratization in Indonesia.* Princeton: Princeton University Press.

Kahin, George McTurnan. 1952. *Nationalism and Revolution in Indonesia.* Ithaca, NY: Cornell University Press.

Laffan, Michael F. 2003. *Islamic Nationhood and Colonial Indonesia: The Umma below the Winds.* London: Routledge.

Rasmussen, Anne. 2001. "The Qur'an in Indonesian Daily Life: The Public Project of Musical Oratory." *Ethnomusicology* 45, no. 1: 30–57.

Reid, Anthony. 1988–1993. *Southeast Asia in the Age of Commerce, 1450–1680.* 2 vols. New Haven: Yale University Press.

Ricklefs, M. C. 1993. *A History of Modern Indonesia, c. 1300 to the Present.* Bloomington: Indiana University Press.

Riddell, Peter G. 2001. *Islam in the Malay-Indonesian World: Transmission and Responses.* Honolulu: University of Hawai'i Press.

Sells, Michael. 1999. *Approaching the Qur'an: The Early Revelations.* Ashland, OR: White Cloud Press.

Snouck Hurgronje, C. 1931. *Mekka in the Latter Part of the 19th Century.* Leiden: Brill.

Voll, John. 1983. "Renewal and Reform in Islamic History." In *Voices of Resurgent Islam,* edited by John L. Esposito, 32–47. New York: Oxford University Press.

Vredenbregt, J. 1962. "The Hadjdj. Some of Its Features and Functions in Indonesia." *Bijdragen tot de Taal-, Land- en Volkenkunde* 118: 91–154.

Woodward, Mark R. 1996. *Toward a New Paradigm: Recent Developments in Indonesian Islamic Thought.* Tempe: Arizona State University Program for Southeast Asian Studies.

Chapter Eight

Religion, Language, and Nationalism
Harari Muslims in Christian Ethiopia

TIM CARMICHAEL

Ethiopia is often thought of as a Christian country, but at least a third and possibly half (or more) of its population is Muslim, and the history of Islam there traces back to the lifetime of the Prophet Muhammad. Regrettably, there is relatively little scholarship on Ethiopia's Islamic history, and the country's geographical vastness and ethnic diversity add to the challenges of making confident, meaningful generalizations about the subject. This chapter therefore concentrates primarily on the impact of state policies in Harar, the ancient Islamic capital of the Horn of Africa. The emphasis is on the twentieth century, when some of the country's rulers—who were Christian—tried to transform national administration along what they perceived to be modern lines. This approach helps shed light on the sometimes complementary and sometimes conflicting relationships among linguistic, ethnic, and religious identities as well as on their relevance to nationalist sentiments and unity. Investigating these complex relationships, which have changed over time and continue to change today, contributes to a better understanding of Ethiopia's contemporary Islamic revival, which has been moderate in comparison to that of other regions of the world but has nevertheless alarmed many non-Muslim Ethiopians and some foreign observers. In brief, historical context, ethnoreligious sentiments and relations, language use, economy, and government policies all affect the beliefs, practices, and political agendas of Ethiopian Muslims.

Historical Background

Outside of the Hijaz, in present-day Saudi Arabia, Ethiopia was probably the first region to which Islam spread. A few years after the Prophet Muhammad's

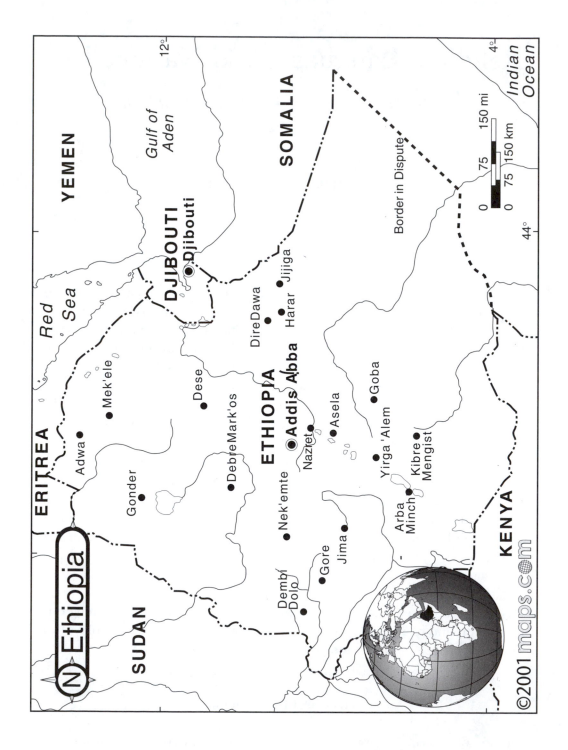

Ethiopia

N

SUDAN

ERITREA

YEMEN

Red Sea

Gulf of Aden

DJIBOUTI
● Djibouti

SOMALIA

Adwa ●
● Mek'ele

Gonder ●
● Debre Mark'os
● Dese

Dire Dawa ●
● Harar ● Jijiga

ETHIOPIA
◉ Addis Abba

● Goba

Dembi Dolo ●
● Gore
● Jima
● Nek'emte
● Nazret
● Asela
● Yirga 'Alem
Arba Minch ●
● Kibre Mengist

Border in Dispute

Indian Ocean

12°

4°

44°

0   75   150 mi
0   75   150 km

KENYA

©2001 maps.com

first revelations, members of the Quraysh tribe—fearing that their socioeconomic dominance in Mecca was threatened—began strongly to persecute the fledgling Islamic community. The Prophet ordered a number of his followers to seek refuge in Ethiopia, for he had heard its king was kind, just, and a protector of the weak. Long-established trade routes facilitated this important journey, whose participants included Ruqayyah, a daughter of the Prophet Muhammad, and Uthman, who later became the third caliph. Islamic tradition maintains that their reception by Ethiopia's Christian king was excellent and that they were protected and looked after until those who wanted to return to Mecca were able to do so. As a result of this episode, Muhammad is said to have declared, "Leave the Abyssinians alone, so long as they do not take the offensive." Many credit this *hadith* for explaining why Ethiopia was never subjected to external Islamic invasion despite its close proximity to Islam's geographical homeland.

Between the seventh and sixteenth centuries, the historical development of Islam in Ethiopia, as far as it is known, was restricted to certain states and principalities, the details of which are not important here. In contrast, the sixteenth century witnessed extensive conflicts, accounts of which have been passed down in both Christian and Muslim writings and oral traditions. By the early 1500s, competition for control of Ethiopia's profitable trade routes fostered antagonism between members of the Christian and Muslim ruling classes. Tensions came to a head when Imam Ahmad ibn Ibrahim, a religious leader who was probably Somali, was named *amir* of the eastern Islamic city of Harar. Known in Christian chronicles as Grañ (the "left-handed") and in Muslim accounts as al-Ghazi ("the conqueror"), he ignored the Muslim faction that favored peaceful relations conducive to unfettered trade with the Christians, and from the late 1520s to the early 1540s, he called for a *jihad* and launched a series of attacks against his Christian neighbors to the west. During these conflicts, an extreme aversion to Islam took root among Ethiopian Christians. Indeed, in the words of Haggai Erlich, "From that sixteenth century event until today the idea that Islam, once politically revitalized, could well unite to destroy their national existence, has been an integral and central part of Ethiopian consciousness" (1994, 31). After Imam Ahmad's death, the warfare gradually died out. Although enmity still existed between Muslims and Christians, both sides were exhausted and apparently more interested in trade than fighting. However, in the late sixteenth century the country again underwent a period of intense change, when a series of widespread and multitudinous population movements forever altered Ethiopia's demographics. Ethnic Oromo peoples expanded rapidly throughout the country, often incorporating those whom they conquered or who submitted peacefully, but also adopting local customs and religions, notably Christianity and Islam.

The period 1769–1855 is commonly known as the Zamana Mesafint, or Era of the Princes/Judges. It witnessed perennial political, religious, economic, and military conflict as politically powerless emperors were confined to their capitals and autonomous regional rulers jockeyed for dominance. Members of various ethno-linguistic groups succeeded in joining the most important political circles throughout the country, but in order to do so they needed to be—or to become—Orthodox Christians and to speak either Amharic or Tigrinya. Despite this multiethnic, politically flexible situation, in which culture and language were deemed more important to advancement than socioreligious or "racial/ethnic" origins, the larger picture was one of a fractured empire plagued by general devastation. Long-distance trade routes were disrupted or destroyed, local economies were ravaged, historical land tenure systems were undermined, and there was little if any incentive for investment in or improvement of the land.

Islam in a Christian Empire

The Zamana Mesafint came to a close in 1855, when a former frontier bandit who had married into an elite family subdued his rivals and was crowned as Emperor Tewodros. After theoretically restoring the unity of the Orthodox Church, which had split into several factions, Tewodros pursued myriad reforms for his country. Because his plans required increased taxation, they aroused the resentment and opposition of many Ethiopians, and he soon found himself constantly on the march to suppress revolts. He was succeeded by Yohannes IV, who also strove to reunite Ethiopia. Fervently Christian, and responding to the radicalization of the clergy that Tewodros's controversial reforms had caused, Yohannes made religion a cornerstone of his conceptualization of the state, and he succeeded in mobilizing his people to resist territorial incursions by Islamic Egypt and Sudan. However, his strict doctrinal stance alienated many of his fellow Christians, and his brutal persecutions and forced conversions of Muslims generated profound and lasting hostility among that sector of the populace, too.

Despite these two emperors' ardent commitment to Christianity, the nineteenth century also witnessed the spread of Islam in parts of Ethiopia, most notably among various Oromo groups. Hussein Ahmed, the foremost historian of Islam in Ethiopia, has argued persuasively that Ethiopians converted to Islam in areas that benefited from profitable trade. As Muslim merchants amassed capital from commerce in hides, skins, slaves, gold, and coffee, they funded clerics who established mosques and schools, led prayer services, wrote texts, and sometimes adopted positions of local political leadership (Hussein 2001). This argument is important, since it adds human depth to the common though vague explanation that "Islam spread with trade." It should be kept in mind, however, that Islam's success was greatest outside the central highlands. The highlands historically were home to Ethiopia's dominant (and Orthodox Christian) political culture, which later formed the basis for the modern Ethiopian state. Indeed, it might be argued that noting this regional and religious distinction is essential to understanding subsequent Ethiopian history.

The next emperor, Menilek II, oversaw the genesis of Ethiopia's attempt to transform from an unstable and quasi-feudal empire into a modern state. Previously, as the regional king of a southern province, Menilek had come to appreciate the riches of the lands to the west, south, and east of his own area, and by conquering them he was able to increase the size of his state and to enrich his economic base. In the late nineteenth century, Menilek took advantage of British, Italian, and French rivalries in the Red Sea region to acquire large numbers of modern arms. In addition to helping him enlarge his realms and eventually attain the emperorship, this weaponry was put to use at the historic Battle of Adwa in 1896, when an Ethiopian army crushed an Italian invasion and secured Ethiopia's continued independence during a period when much of the non-Western world was falling under European economic and political subjugation.

Menilek followed up his military success with a careful foreign policy that secured his country's boundaries, earned Ethiopia international respect, and allowed him to pursue his plans for building his nation. Among other moves, Menilek founded a new capital, created new administrative, legal, and taxation structures, and began to establish telegram and telephone services throughout the countryside. In short, he generally strengthened the central government's control over the loosely integrated region called Ethiopia. Such measures, however, require capital, which Menilek obtained by revising land tenure systems and conquering new regions, including those inhabited by Muslim populations. Important among the latter was the ancient Islamic city-state of Harar.

Probably founded around the year 1000, Harar had long been the Islamic capital of northeast Africa, and during the sixteenth century, it served as Imam Ahmad's home base during his *jihad* against the Christians. After the conclusion of those wars, Harar, like other regions in Ethiopia, witnessed the immigration of increasing numbers of Oromo pastoralists and farmers, whose language, like Somali, belongs to the Cushitic family. Yet the town itself largely remained the preserve of the Harari people, who were Muslim and spoke a Semitic language related both to Arabic, the language of Islam, and to Amharic, generally perceived in Ethiopia as a "Christian" language. By the 1820s or 1830s, the Harari and the Oromo had come to enjoy a mutually dependent relationship. As the nineteenth century wore on, however, Harari power vis-à-vis the Oromo lessened considerably, and by 1875 the Oromo held the upper hand. In that year, the town was conquered by Egyptian forces trying to carve out a sub-Saharan African empire.

During their occupation, the Egyptians implemented an extensive series of infrastructural, health, administrative, and religious reforms. The Harari were restored to dominance over the Oromo, and Harar's urban, Islamic culture was emphasized as an ideal throughout the larger region. Because of fiscal and political problems in Cairo, the Egyptians withdrew in 1885. However, their encouragement of an Islamic revival of sorts continued to inspire the Harari. After taking over leadership of the town, Amir Abdullahi, a Harari, attempted to spread Islam among the rural Oromo, and he strictly enforced Islamic laws in the town, efforts that earned him an honored position in Harari historical recollections.

Despite Harar's recently restored independence, its strategic geographical location made it a tempting target for others. Situated between the central Ethiopian province ruled by Menilek and trading ports along the Red Sea and the Gulf of Aden, it promised secure trade access to a more regular and less expensive supply of modern weapons and other coveted foreign goods. Thus, although subduing Ethiopia's Islamic stronghold must have been symbolically appealing, Menilek's decision to take the town was probably made primarily with economic and political considerations in mind. Nonetheless, at the Battle of C'alanqo on January 6, 1887, his Christian armies defeated a combined Muslim force of Harari, Oromo, and others. The Horn of Africa's historical Islamic capital has, ever since, been ruled by dominantly Christian governments based in Addis Ababa in central Ethiopia.

Over the course of history, relations between Muslims and Christians in Ethiopia were not always warm. In the regions where Muslim traders and craftsmen had lived and traveled for centuries, there tended to be separate Muslim towns or neighborhoods. In fact, Emperor Yohannes I (1667–1682) "convened a council that ordered Muslims to live separately from Christians in villages and town quarters of their own." When Christians met Muslims, "they greeted Muslims with the left hand—a sign of contempt—and called them, pejoratively, *naggade* (merchant), or *eslam*." Similarly, "Christian Ethiopians would not eat with them, drink from cups they had used (unless purified by a man of religion), or eat meat slaughtered by Muslims" (Kapteijns 2000, 230–231). The pattern was repeated in late nineteenth- and early twentieth-century Harar, where Christian soldiers and settlers initially lived outside the town's 200-year-old protective wall, thus maintaining spatial and social separation. Further reflecting these social tensions, the red earth of Harari homes was said to symbolize the blood spilled at C'alanqo; Christianity was belittled by calling a certain butterfly *Amhara kitab* ("Amhara book," or Bible) because "the cryptic and nonsensical markings on the wings were said to be like Amharic writing, and the opening and closing, and flitting about, were intrinsic to the image also." Moreover, Harari who married Christians were socially rejected, Harari women began to dress more modestly, Islam's prohibition on drinking alcohol was increasingly respected, and some people rejected coffee, claiming it was a Christian beverage (Waldron 1980, 252–254).

Although such issues may have been noted by Menilek's administration in Harar, more practical concerns of ruling the province were of primary importance: The area was enormous, its population was diverse, and state resources were limited. Thus, the conquerors implemented a system of indirect rule. Instead of destroying Harar's historical governing structures, the Ethiopians retained them but subsumed them under the newly created Governor's Office. In the process of trying to establish its own political position, the Governor's Office became a coordinating body that attempted to control and regulate the functioning of various pre-conquest structures of authority. In that context, Harari men with a command of Amharic and a willingness to work with the Christian conquerors found opportunities for considerable upward mobility. There were nevertheless probably only limited opportunities for working with the state, even if there were more than a few Harari who were able or willing to do so.

Harari acceptance of Ethiopian rule was not encouraged by the disorder that ravaged Ethiopia during World War I. In addition to economic problems, political infighting plagued the empire. Before his death, Emperor Menilek had named his grandson Lej Iyasu as his successor. A headstrong youth and the son of a Muslim provincial ruler who had been forced to convert to Christianity in the late nineteenth century, Iyasu lacked respect for the old nobility, forged good relations with prominent Muslims, allegedly enjoyed sexual relations with any woman (married or not) he fancied, and otherwise offended the conservative and Christian ruling class. His policies, his actions, and his vision of an ethnically and religiously integrated ruling elite increased the hostility of his political opponents. In the face of European fears of Ottoman (that is, Islamic) influences on Muslim colonial subjects in Africa and Asia after the outbreak of World War I, Iyasu's relations with Germany, rumors of his conversion to Islam, his preoccupation with the Ogaden region (inhabited by Muslim Somalis resisting British and Italian intrusions), and his communications with the Somali anticolonialist leadership ensured that Britain, France, and Italy would oppose him as well.

Because of his sympathy toward Islam and his frequent visits to Harar, Iyasu was popular in the town and in the Somali lands east of it. But that does not mean he was able to improve life for the town's inhabitants. The British consul, Dodds, reported in early 1916 that "[l]awlessness, unrest and discontent [were] the order of the day throughout the Province. The courts [had] never been so busy . . . every chief, every soldier, every trader [was] tired of the condition of the country. From their point of view trade [had] diminished, prices [had] increased, revenue [had] decreased, and there [was] no security" (Dodds to Wilfred Thesiger, February 14, 1916, United Kingdom, Foreign Office). He also commented that he received daily complaints "of murder, assault, false imprisonment, blackmail and interference," and that the *majlis* (tribunal) that investigated them was "no more than a farce." Finally, the British observer noted that many Harari were imprisoned for expressing their loyalty to Lej Iyasu, that trade stagnated, and that violence within the town increased (ibid., November 5 and November 9, 1916).

Encouraged by the anti-German and anti-Ottoman Europeans resident in Addis Ababa, and supported by the Orthodox Church, Ethiopia's outraged ruling elite finally made its move against Iyasu, toppling him from power in the autumn of 1916. As part of the coup, Christian forces in Harar hunted down and slaughtered several hundred of Iyasu's Muslim Somali allies, an event that came to be known as Somali Black Monday. Events such as this one did nothing to soothe Muslim reservations about living under Christian rule, and tales about rivulets of blood running down the streets after the murders still circulate today.

By that point, nearly thirty years after the town's conquest, it was clear to many Harari that there was little hope for substantive political change. At the same time, they saw their community sinking lower and lower in the hierarchy of ethnic prestige of which they had formerly been the top, and Christian settlers took advantage of the community's increasing impoverishment to buy properties and houses within the old walled town, formerly the preserve of Muslims. Alarmed by and seeking to stem this development, a group of prominent Harari founded an organization known as Firmach (literally "signatures," meaning the group was composed of those who signed a covenant) in the early 1920s. The group's aim was to bolster Harari unity and stamp out economically damaging practices, such as the common custom of pawning houses and property at exorbitant interest rates to Christian money lenders in order to pay for lavish funeral ceremonies whose costs were clearly beyond the ability of the debtors to repay. One Firmach member was reported as taking to funerals a small whip, which he used to dissuade attendees from tearing perfectly good clothing while engaging in traditional mourning ceremonies. While railing against such practices, whose long-term effects threatened Harari prosperity, Firmach also advanced a program of positive proposals designed to strengthen the community and eliminate its need to depend on others. One of the major projects the organization implemented was the establishment of a privately funded Islamic school, which was to teach the Arabic language and Islamic religious studies as well as more "modern" subjects such as foreign languages, mathematics, and science.

Harar under Haile Selassie

Firmach had begun to meet with some success by 1930, when Ras Tafari Makonnen, the son of Harar's first Christian governor, was crowned emperor of Ethiopia, adopting the regnal name Haile Selassie I. The event is often lauded as the grandest of its kind in Ethiopian history. The capital city, Addis Ababa, underwent extensive remodeling, including the paving of roads, the relocation of slums and their inhabitants, and the installation of electricity in selected areas. Preparations and the excitement of anticipation extended throughout the empire, including Harar, which celebrated the event for nearly a full week. At Shawa Gate, one of the entrances to the city, officials pitched a tent and displayed a large picture of the emperor. A band played music while priests watched military troops march by the tent making war boasts and other ceremonial offerings to the image.[1]

After this military parade in the country's Islamic capital, a Christian official in the Governor's Office gave a speech on behalf of the nobility, recollecting biblical history and the legendary foundations of the Ethiopian state. He thanked Haile Selassie for making arrangements with Egypt so that Ethiopians could be named as subpatriarchs of the Orthodox Church, even if the patriarch himself remained an Egyptian appointed by Cairo. Following the speech, at least according to the official newspaper account, the Muslims sitting on top of the city wall observing the events proceeded to clap and ululate. This opening oration was followed by six days of communal feasting.

The coronation thus marked an occasion for the state to use pomp to display power, for consumption in both the capital and the provinces. Since Christian servants were served before Muslim notables, the celebrations in Harar also afford a noteworthy insight into social hierarchies based on religion, social status, and occupation, matters that the celebrations reified publicly and at state expense. Finally, the state-sponsored newspaper coverage enabled speeches to be published and circulated elsewhere in the country. They praised the "enlightened prince" and his modernization efforts, as well as his efforts to avoid "fanaticism" and to bring Christians and Muslims together in Ethiopia (see Hajji Abdulla Shariff and the Harari Muslim Brothers 1923 E.C./1930; Yelma Mängäsha 1923 E.C./1930; others in *Berhanenna Sälam* 1923 E.C./1930).

Nevertheless, the state continued to favor Christians over Muslims in government jobs, and although prosperity increased for some Harari, resentment stemming from their limited opportunities grew as well. Many Harari and other Ethiopian Muslims thus welcomed Italy's conquest of the country in 1935–1936. The ensuing five years of occupation were, overall, a good period for Ethiopia's Muslims. Owing to Italian interests in its predominantly Islamic colonies elsewhere, Benito Mussolini sought to show that he was a friend of Islam, and his Italian administration encouraged the religion in Ethiopia. Its favoritism was especially apparent in Harar, where the five years after 1936 witnessed considerable development of the city's infrastructure and appearance. Despite the fact that some Harari lands were confiscated for various projects, material life un-

Outside the Grand Mosque in Addis Ababa. (Ricki Rosen/CORBIS SABA)

doubtedly improved under the Italians for Harar's Muslims, who also experienced a revival of Islamic practice. In the wake of Menilek's conquest, some Harari had begun to switch from agriculture to trade, first serving as assistants to Greek, Armenian, Arab, and Indian traders and later running their own shops. This shift increased markedly under Italian tutelage, and the improved economic prosperity affected Harari society in a variety of ways. Greater funding for Islamic education set them apart from Christians and their generally less-learned Muslim neighbors in the rural countryside. The distinctive *gey ganafi* pants, an attractive fashion unique to Harari women, were redesigned to display larger amounts of expensive imported cloth. Travel outside the city became easier and more affordable. Perhaps most significantly, class distinctions within the Harari community became more pronounced and visible.

World War II forced the Italians to give up Ethiopia in 1941. After Emperor Haile Selassie was restored to power, he continued his own policies of modernization. One of the minor projects involved in this process was widening the main street in Harar. The episode allegedly resulted in the destruction of Harari personal property and of such Islamic holy sites as mosques and saints' shrines—acts that further alienated the Harari (Waldron 1980, 255). The social and political tensions in the town and region later culminated in the central defining event of twentieth-century Harari history: an affair and movement known today as Kulub or Hanolato.

Having returned to Ethiopia in 1941, Haile Selassie's overriding concern was to reestablish his sovereign control and to undermine British efforts to restrict his authority in what he regarded as his country and what the British regarded as occupied enemy territory and treated like a colony. He was especially preoccupied with regaining recognition of Ethiopia's rights over the northern province of Eritrea and the southeastern province of Ogaden. Because those two regions were largely inhabited by Muslims, he was intent on countering any "Islamic" opposition that might generate negative publicity for Ethiopia in the Middle Eastern and Western presses. In that context, the Muslim Harari found themselves disadvantaged in seeking employment, especially within government administration or the military. Similarly, they encountered official resistance to their attempts to assemble publicly, pursue Islamic education, and speak Arabic at sociopolitical functions.

Harari whom I interviewed in the 1990s were unanimous in believing that Harari notables and King Menilek had signed an agreement, after the 1887 Battle of C'alanqo, guaranteeing the Harari various rights, including limited self-autonomy and complete religious freedom, in return for which Harari would pay an annual tribute to the Christian king. In the late 1940s, it was belief in the existence of such a document that inspired dissatisfied Harari to agitate for the long-since-undermined rights they believed had been granted. However, by 1948, Kulub, the political movement formed by Harari in alliance with an Islamic, Somali nationalist organization, had been brutally crushed, large amounts of Harari property and wealth had been confiscated, and hundreds of Harari men had been imprisoned.

From a historical perspective, one highly significant result of these events was that the previously powerful cognitive hold of Harar town on the Harari people was broken. Until then, the vast majority of Harari were born and died in the town, even though during their lifetimes they may have traveled outside it for trade or other purposes. Illustrating the close tie between geography and identity here is the fact that in the Harari language, the city is called *gey* (the city), its inhabitants are *gey usu'* (the people of the city), the culture *gey ada* (customs of the city), and the language itself *gey sinan* (tongue or language of the city). And hinting at the close tie between geography and religion is the fact that an Arabic name for the city is Madinat al-Awliya, or the City of Saints. Indeed, there are hundreds of saints' shrines in Harar, some of which are even today the sites of regular Sufi ceremonies. It is thus significant that only in the wake of Kulub did Harari persons begin to leave their urban homeland *permanently*. It was only after 1948 that relatively large numbers of Harari established permanent residence and distinct communities in other Ethiopian urban centers such as Jijjiga, Dire Dawa, Addis Ababa, and Jimma and in regions further abroad such as Egypt, Sudan, and Saudi Arabia. In their diaspora, the Harari tended to seek out other Muslim regions or groups.

Educational Politics in Modernizing Ethiopia

Sometime after 1948, in another reflection of the intense socio-cultural stresses of the period, the Harari began attending government-sponsored schools in relatively large numbers. Most Harari had previously avoided these institutions owing to their Christian orientation. These educational dynamics were especially important because educational success in Ethiopia was predicated on fluency in Amharic—speakers with an accent often faced social ridicule and professional glass ceilings—and because local languages (which most Ethiopian Muslims spoke) were generally looked down upon by members of the ruling class and expanding state bureaucracy. Even after Harari students began enrolling, they encountered difficulties because of the anti-Muslim hostility of some of their government-appointed Ethiopian and Indian teachers and because of the high level of Harari distrust of the Christian government. Nevertheless, some were inspired by those few whom the Harari author Mahdi Shumburo has dubbed the "scholarship guys": Harari boys who had been offered scholarships to continue their education at the Tafari Makonnen School in Addis Ababa. The fact that such assistance was available shows that the Ethiopian government was not anti-Islamic per se. And over time, the scholarship guys demonstrated to the rest of the Harari community that achieving success in government schools did not necessarily mean betrayal or abandonment of Harari values. In encouraging younger students to stick with their education, they undermined some of the general Harari resistance to modern government-sponsored education (Mahdi 1998, 37–47).

In the 1950s, the most important modern educational institution for advanced Ethiopian students of any faith was the national college, founded in 1952 by French-Canadian Jesuits. Although the campus was no oasis of free speech, for many of the students it provided the first forum in which they experienced sustained, relatively open contact with members of other ethnic groups (Balsvik 1985, 73). As a result, young Harari collegians met other Ethiopians from around the country, and for the first time, they came to learn about others' political and social views. Although the Harari students did not always agree with their fellows, they did come to see the validity of other viewpoints, and they

> discovered that their claim to a "monopoly" of state persecution was evaporating before their own eyes, and they came to realize that the practice of persecution by the system was rather pervasive. Gradually they found themselves in the unenviable dual role of trying to convince their people to listen more open-mindedly to what the other side had to say, while simultaneously attempting to explain to their non-Harari schoolmates and friends that the grievances of their people against the government were real, and that it would be a gross mistake to ignore them. It was not an easy task. (Mahdi 1998, 46)

In addition to impressing the rest of the community with their continued adherence to Harari customs, the students who returned to Harar were granted "educationally commensurate positions," though ones outside of politically sensitive sectors. Furthermore, other Harari, for the first time, found themselves accepted in the Ethiopian military, and a few eventually attained high rank (Mahdi 1998, 47–48). However, despite the success of some members of this generation in gaining entry into national structures, not everything changed for the majority of Harari.

The basis of the economy for the Harari who did not pursue advanced formal education was basically twofold. For the majority, rent paid by Oromo sharecroppers and tenant farmers made up the most important part of their income; for the better-off class, trade and shop-keeping boosted family incomes, sometimes considerably. However, continued government fear and distrust of Islam led to periodic harassment of Muslims; Ethiopians who did not possess a good command of Amharic were sometimes disparaged, especially as its importance as the national language increased; and the failure of the government to appoint a governor from among the Harari themselves or any other Muslim peoples generated further resentment. The Harari who could afford to leave Harar did so increasingly, and those who could not had to adjust to the new sociopolitical and economic situation. For example, many Harari claim that it was during the 1950s that increasing numbers of Harari women began working outside the home for the first time, owing to the need to supplement their families' incomes.

Harari Society

Harari have historically been Muslim, and most Harari (in Harar, at least) have also been and still are polyglots, speaking *gey sinan* and any number of other languages, including Amharic, Arabic, Argobba, English, French, Italian, Oromo, and Somali. Beginning at least in 1887, however, Harari discourse began highlighting group differences, usually in terms of religion (for example, versus the Christian Amhara) but also sometimes in terms of the perceived sophistication, or lack thereof, of the manners or culture of members of other ethnic groups who had converted to Islam (for example, versus the Muslim Oromo) (Waldron 1974, 268, 270–271; 1980, 251–252).

Concisely, Harari society is built on and organized around three social institutions. They are *afocha*, "community organizations," whose primary responsibilities are at weddings and funerals; *ahli*, "family networks"; and *mariññet*, which are organized friendship groups. A Harari's involvement in *afocha*, *ahli*, and *mariññet* activities ties him or her into an extensive and overlapping series of alliances that stretch across and throughout the city, like a spiderweb, and eventually tie all the Harari together. These organized relationships provide the means for keeping abreast of current events in the town, for enforcing established norms of behavior (particularly through the threat and force of gossip), and for maintaining a sense of common identity. In order to be considered Harari, one must participate in all three of these social institutions. Naturally, in order to participate in *afocha, ahli,* and *mariññet,* one must be Muslim and one must speak *gey sinan.* Therefore, religion and language are as integral to Harari culture and group identity as social behavior is. This point cannot be stressed enough. In fact, the American anthropologist Sidney Waldron has noted that Harari who converted to Christianity were referred to as if they were dead (Waldron 1980, 252).

Waldron argues that one means by which the numerically small Harari were able to maintain a distinct ethnic identity over the centuries while surrounded by much larger social groups (that is, the Oromo and the Somali) and to succeed so visibly in trade was to restrict knowledge of the Harari language to their own community (Waldron 1974, 267, 286–287, 289; 1984, 314). As some Harari began to build large amounts of personal wealth, in comparison to other peoples, the Harari language—though never dominant or hegemonic and never displacing or replacing another language—may well have come to occupy a position of relatively high prestige locally. And in fact, an understanding of Harari was indeed for the most part limited to persons born and raised within the walls of the old town, whether Harari or not, and, presumably, to some of the children born to one or two Harari parents residing elsewhere in the country or world.

Waldron focuses on the Harari resident in Harar town, but he points out that in 1977, there were more Harari living in the nation's capital, Addis Ababa, than in Harar itself (Waldron 1979, 401). Unfortunately, nowhere in his published work is this important fact deeply pondered, especially in terms of its implications for what Harari ethnicity is or how it is (or was) changing. Instead, Waldron's earlier research focus on the town itself seems to have obscured the elements that actually do or may constitute a Harari group identity transcending a shared, inhabited space. This point is raised here because although his approach illuminates many important issues, it also elides, for the recent past, the dynamic and historically changing relationships between ethnicity, language, and religion, as well as how they all articulate with nationalist sentiments. These ideas will be elaborated below.

In addition, the initial permanent exodus of Harari from Harar in the wake of the 1948 upheavals forever altered Harari demographics. These demographics were further skewed during the years that followed Ethiopia's 1974 Marxist-Leninist coup, when the military overthrew Haile Selassie, the 225th monarch of Ethiopia's Solomonic dynasty. The new government, which became known as the Derg, proceeded to usher in a period of state terror. Tens of thousands of Ethiopians were forced against their wills to relocate to other parts of the country, military conscription was implemented, and tens of thousands were assassinated by state military and police forces. In order to claim the corpses of the victims, family members had to pay for each bullet that had been fired to kill their loved one. Although many Muslims were initially happy to see a change in government, the Derg's brutality soon disillusioned them. Therefore, huge numbers of young Harari fled not only their hometown but also their country, seeking new and better lives abroad. The national and global dispersal of Harari people over the last half century and the present-day Ethiopian government's political emphasis on ethnicity as an administrative category add layers of complexity to any attempt to understand the effects of contemporary policies on group identity among Ethiopians, including the Muslim Harari.

Islamic Revivalism in the 1990s

It is important to situate recent events in Harar within larger national processes, one of which is Islamic revivalism. Unfortunately, Islamic revivalism in Ethiopia has been little researched, even though Ethiopian magazines, newsletters, Internet sites, and even scholarship have averred that it will help split the country. Hussein Ahmed is one of the few scholars to study the phenomenon seriously. He found that Ethiopian Muslims' historical grievances against Christian-dominated governments began to wane in the early 1990s, when Islam made considerable gains in various spheres of Ethiopian life (Hussein 1994). Hussein also argued, based on his reading of books, newspapers, magazines, and pamphlets published by Islamic presses in Ethiopia, that throughout the 1990s Islam in Ethiopia was not fundamentalist but, rather, resurgent. That is, rather than espousing a return to strict literal interpretations of the Qur'an and *sunna* as the basis of life, Ethiopian Muslims derived inspiration from Islamic movements in other countries and sought to reinvigorate Ethiopian Islamic practice along lines they deemed more "religiously correct." Toward this end, Ethiopians went to study in the Middle East, established new schools and organizations, and hosted conferences (Hussein 1998, 106–107).

My own research in Harar and in travels throughout the country support Hussein's conclusions to the effect that although there may be scattered Ethiopian Muslims who could be classified as fundamentalist, they are few and far between. Though, like in other countries, their public visibility in terms of press coverage may be quite high, they actually command little respect from the vast majority of Ethiopian Muslims, and in Harar, where they are referred to as *akrari* (fanatical, extremist) or Wahhabi, they are actually looked down upon by most people, including fellow Muslims. Thus, it is important to keep in mind that Islamic resurgence or revivalism is not necessarily the same thing as Islamic fundamentalism.

Like religious movements elsewhere, Ethiopia's Islamic revivalism should be studied within the context of political change and with an eye to the present government's emphasis on ethnicity as the primary focus of political organization. In this view, Hussein's convincing argument that the recent blossoming of Islamic publications in Ethiopia reflects Islamic revivalism as opposed to Islamic fundamentalism is salient. The distinction is important because over the last decade many Ethiopians, including many Muslims, have feared the rise of Islamic fundamentalism.

"Luqtat al-Tarikhiyya" [Gleanings of History]

As an example of one sort of document that circulated in Ethiopia's Muslim communities in the 1990s, I include as an appendix to this chapter a translation of a text that I first encountered at a friend's house in Harar and later saw at other residences there.[2] It was circulated in Arabic as a six-page computer printout entitled "Luqtat al-Tarikhiyya" (Gleanings of History), and it consists of a treatment of the history of Christian-Muslim relations in Ethiopia and of the two religions' impact on the country. This informally disseminated text was of interest to members of the Harari Muslim community, and an examination of it can highlight issues that became politically important during the 1990s, including the politicization of Islam outside a religiously fundamentalist framework.

Reading Muslim History in Contemporary Harar

Fully unpacking the text of the "Luqtat al-Tarikhiyya," explaining its correct claims and exposing those that are misleading, exaggerated, or simply wrong, is far beyond the space available here and is not really necessary for our purposes. Pursuit of the ever-elusive "Truth" about the past is one thing, but more important than "Truth," in terms of shaping popular attitudes and social consciousness—which determine how people act, interact, and vote, among other things—are the ideas espoused by perceived authorities, whether they be political, religious, or military leaders; public intellectuals; or popular documents such as "Luqtat al-Tarikhiyya." Therefore, rather than analyzing degrees of historical accuracy, identifying larger themes and ideas in authorities' discourse is arguably more relevant to understanding the prevailing social currents that affect the daily lives of Muslims in contemporary Harar and the decisions they make in social interactions and political spheres.

The "Gleanings of History" are generally hostile to Ethiopian Orthodox Christianity, clearly identifying it with military conquest and feudalist oppression. Conversely, Islam is portrayed as a liberating force, as well as threatening to the Christian "conquerors." Only after Islam posed a danger to the church did the rulers begin to lighten up on their "enslaved" subjects. Yet despite the alleged mutual hatred between Muslims and Christians, Muslims were not always persecuted. This leniency is related to the fact that the headquarters of Ethiopia's Orthodox Church were located in Egypt, where Christians were a minority. By linking the fates of Egypt's Christians, ruled by Muslims, to Ethiopia's Muslims, ruled by Christians, a sort of détente was achieved.

The text also contains a fair amount of detailed information about Harar and its "freedom-fighting sons." The tenor of those sections is that the city has long been a major Islamic center and that the Harari hold Islam near and dear to their hearts. Only when the Christian King Menilek II conquered Harar, aided by modern firearms provided by European countries, did Harari fortunes change. The bitter memories of that event are still symbolized in wedding customs today.

That not all of Ethiopia's Muslims are the same is acknowledged in the section on the Afar, whose Islamic learning and customs do not seem to meet the author's approval. However, the text argues that Arab immigration from the Gulf, Sudan, and North Africa was crucial to the spread and strengthening of Islam in Ethiopia. Implied here is that Ethiopia's indigenous Muslims welcomed external support to improve their local positions vis-à-vis the Christian rulers and that thus they were happy and willing to receive and assist fellow Muslims from other countries. While admitting to "mutual aversion" between Christians and Muslims, the document seems to blame the problem on Christian fanaticism. Departing from the text's dominant tone, however, the suggestion that Muslims are also guilty of fanaticism and thus somehow responsible for the tensions stands out.

It is important to note that this text was written in Arabic, which many Ethiopians have learned to speak from either religious study or participation in trade networks. However, the ability to *read* the language, let alone have access to texts such as this one, is not so common. Therefore, it is worth asking what impact the content of this and other texts might have had on Ethiopian Muslims' thinking about history and religious relations. In short, in the mid-1990s, this text and others were read individually by those who could do so, were read aloud in various social situations to others who could not, and were translated orally for those unable to understand Arabic. The fact that Arabic is the language of Islam lends it considerable cachet in many Muslims' eyes. That is, texts written in Arabic are judged to be authoritative in ways that they might not be if they were written in other languages. Moreover, accounts published abroad are appreciated because they demonstrate that other Muslims know

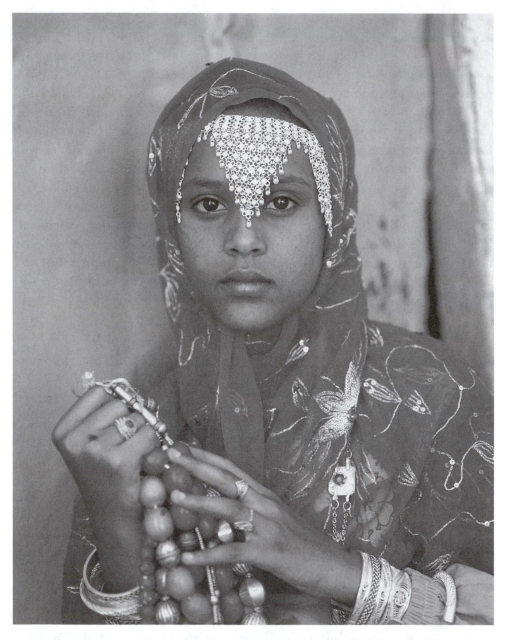

Young Muslim girl wearing traditional dress in Harar, Ethiopia. (Rob Howard/Corbis)

about Ethiopia's Muslims and deem them important enough to write about. This perceived international support bolsters Muslims' confidence and inspires them to be more outspoken about their political views and desires.

These points bring us to the issue of the relationships among religion, language, and ethnic identity, which were major topics in discussions about national and local political policies in 1990s Ethiopia. Language, of course, is centrally important to human identity anywhere. However, the ways the promotion of a certain language or languages can affect conceptions about nationality, ethnicity, regionalism, or localism and even about religion are considerably influenced by the social and political conditions of particular contexts.

Contemporary Ethiopian Language Policy

After decades of civil war in Ethiopia, a military coalition toppled the former Marxist-Leninist regime. Since 1991, for the first time in Ethiopian history, political decentralization based on so-called ethnic regionalization—rather than centralization built on national uniformity—has become a key pillar of central government ideology. A salient influence behind the shift was the realization that past opposition regarded the major political language, Amharic, as symbolic of ethnic (Amhara) and religious (Orthodox Christianity) domination. Seeking to pacify past discontent and minimize present opposition, the new ruling elite—dominated by (Christian) speakers of the Tigrinya language—has aimed to reduce the appearance of central control and thereby undermine the validity of religious or linguistic/ethnic condemnations. Since "language" and "ethnicity" are generally synonymous in today's Ethiopia, language policy is central to the new official ideology.

For many of Ethiopia's peoples, past resentments centered on what was perceived as a policy of "Amharicization," a process of ethno-homogenization that in practical terms was inseparable from "Christianization." While Amharic, though widely perceived among non-Christian Ethiopians as a "Christian language," is still employed as the dominant national language in government and education, the new constitution empowers the nine regional governments to conduct official business in the language(s) they choose and legalizes and encourages the development of and instruction in all the country's more than seventy languages. Although the policy is often interpreted as part of a larger divide-and-rule strategy, it has radically challenged dominant views about the fabric of national society. By responding to the long-ignored grievances of politically marginalized groups, present Ethiopian government language policy—and its inherent opposition to linguistic (or ethnic or religious) homogeneity or hegemony—seems to have satisfied some of the major concerns of many social groups. For by vesting those local interests in a new conception of national integrity, the policy seems to have helped foster the transethnic and transreligious national political stability that was apparent as of mid-1998, when my fieldwork in Harar concluded.

In Harar, the long-term importance and relevance of Amharic, as a national language, came to be increasingly appreciated after the Harari language gained the official recognition that many speakers had long felt it deserves. In brief, present Ethiopian national policies, of which language policy is an integral part, seem to have fostered a number of unappreciated or generally ignored social developments, including greater respect for social differences and, if not the mechanisms to overcome social tensions based on group or religious identity, then at least the desire and willingness to do so. The changes of language policy have also served to foster an increased political awareness and participation, as well as the cultivation of a new, more inclusive (and therefore more widely acceptable) sense of Ethiopian nationalism—notably one that is not predicated on an Orthodox Christian identification.

Harar's regional constitution follows the national one in not declaring an official language. Though far too often glossed over in politicized debates, the distinction between official and working languages is significant. Indeed, if Amharic had been declared the official language of the federal government, it is possible that the paths the opposition has taken would have been quite different, assuming as they would the continued dominance of a highland, Semitic, and Christian government ideology. Similarly, had Harari and Oromo been named official languages in the Harari state, the de facto official status of Amharic—a status derived from practical necessities as much as anything else—would have caused many problems. A result of denying Amharic official de jure status and instead formally recognizing local languages is that the Harari no longer feel that Amharic, the "Christian language," is being imposed upon them, and since they now enjoy the freedom to employ their own language in public and official settings, they do not resent Amharic as much as they have in the past. Consequently, they claim to no longer view school instruction in or the government's use of Amharic as a tool of Christianization.

Laws upholding equality among all of Ethiopia's peoples (for example, Article 25 of the national constitution), however, are interpreted differently by different people in Harar. Some individuals feel that respect of their personal rights means that their language(s) must be spoken to them at all times. Such views led to increased social tensions over the late twentieth century, when some members of different groups refused to speak other languages. Reasons offered by Hararis that I have spoken with to explain why multilingual people might want to speak only their mother tongue included (1) not being fully comfortable speaking other languages or being afraid of making mistakes in them, and (2) being too politically "fanatical" (akrari). Owing to a generally heightened ethno-linguistic awareness and to wishes that different languages be respected, in some casual encounters between non-Amhara persons—regardless of religion—it is easier simply to use Amharic, despite its ethnic or Christian associations, rather than get into a squabble over whose own language should prevail. The point may be that politically charged personal interactions between individuals of different ethnic backgrounds will contribute to the continued and future importance of Amharic in the region, if not elsewhere in the country.

I heard one story about a Harari whom others classified as being unnecessarily "fanatic." He was one of the occasional court litigants who are known to speak Amharic yet who, because of their anti-Amhara, anti-Amharic, or anti-Christian views, claim that they do not and therefore that they need to be assigned a translator. In this humorous incident, after claiming not to know Amharic and demanding a translator, the Harari man interrupted proceedings in order to correct the court official's translation, sending all present into peals of laughter. Abdurahim Ahmed, the president of Harar's Supreme Court in 1998, explained that since language issues were still very much in flux, judges had been lenient in such cases and did not charge such persons with contempt of court (interview with the author, June 19, 1998).

As part of Ethiopia's ethno-linguistic revival, Harari authorities have been working to standardize a writing system for Harari, a language that in the past has been written in the Arabic, Ethiopic, and Latin alphabets. In the early 1990s, when Harar had been established as a region separate from Oromiya (the regional state of the Oromo people) but before local elections were held, the interim government decided temporarily to adopt the Latin script. After elections in 1994, a special committee was formed to study the issue. Around 1996, according to Abdurahman Mohammed Korram of the Harari National Council, the Harari regional government decided on the Ethiopic syllabary (interviews with the author, June 16, 1998 and August 5, 1998). It is likely that the choice was made as much on political grounds as any other. In Harar, there was considerable opposition to the Oromo, the majority population in the area whose own separate region engulfs Harar (or, more specifically, there was opposition to the Oromo Liberation Front; see below). When the Harari made their decision, the Oromo, of whom most in and around Harar are Muslim, had already abandoned the Ethiopic syllabary in favor of the Latin alphabet. Therefore, to judge from the sociopolitical situation of the time and from the fact that Harari had been written in Latin for a couple of years before the switch back to Ethiopic, it is likely that what influenced the choice of the syllabary was the opportunity for the Muslim Harari to ally themselves more closely with the secular/Christian government in Addis Ababa and thereby distance themselves further from the dominantly Muslim Oromo around Harar. This switch from Latin characters back to Ethiopic was no small thing. Previous expenditures had included the production of educational materials in the Latin alphabet; under the revised system, the materials must be redone yet again.

In some cases, then, ethnicity appears to have been judged to be more important than religion in defining communal identities. Indeed, my conversations with non-Oromo (for example, Harari, Amhara, Somali, and Gurage) residents of Harar revealed that one factor tying them together was a shared fear of the Oromo Liberation Front (OLF), an armed organization active around Harar and widely viewed by non-Oromo as dangerous and threatening. In this context, diverse people living together shed other differences for the sake of what was perceived as a greater need: restricting OLF influence and preventing the Harari People's National Regional State from being swallowed up by the much larger Oromiya region that surrounds it. It is important to note this point because, while many Oromo are Muslim, the OLF does not avow a particularly religious line, emphasizing instead the ethno-linguistic one.

How have views of or feelings about either religion or Ethiopian nationalism been affected by the drive to encourage local (or ethnic) identities? The answer is complex, but looking at language policy and its implementation sheds some light on the issue. Ethiopia's most recent language policy has afforded the Harari the opportunity to develop their language and to publish in it, as well as to organize conferences and symposiums aimed at exploring their group identity. It has also fostered increased political awareness among the community generally. In the process, the relatively small number of Harari have realized that despite their new freedoms and relative self-autonomy, they have a vested interest in the new national system and, despite political differences, in maintaining good relations with their much more populous Oromo and Somali neighbors, both of whom are almost entirely Muslim.

Literature, Education, and Language Attitudes

Critics of the government's language policy argue that with every region teaching in its own language, there will be nothing to tie the country together as a nation. In Harar, instructing children in local languages lasts only until the sixth grade. During those years, students also study Amharic and English as regular subjects. Beginning in sixth grade, local languages are dropped and all work is conducted in the latter two tongues. Many Harari whom I have spoken with think this arrangement is a good thing. They explain that a child who starts school learning in his or her own language gets comfortable with being in school and gains confidence in the lessons. They are nevertheless quick to add that if instruction in local languages were to last through high school, then Ethiopia would certainly split up into ethnic regions. The present system, therefore, seems to the Harari with whom I spoke to be an acceptable compromise that both satisfies groups who in the past resented the imposition of Amharic and at the same time highlights the necessity for a (de facto) national language to unite the country. And for the present, owing to historical reasons, there is no more logical choice than Amharic.

Ethiopia's new language policy has also led to the publication of a growing number of books and pamphlets in Harari. They include some fiction, but the bulk of the literature is related to culture, history, and language studies, including dictionaries. This literature holds the potential to affect Harari Islamic group identity in many ways. First, by demonstrating by its very existence that Harari is a language worth writing in, it may cause Harari persons—particularly young people—to see their mother tongue in a new light. Second, in its focus on culture and history, it draws on the past to instill pride in Harari readers, something that can contribute to improved group cohesion. Third, in making a corpus of literature available, it will assist Harari who have moved away or were born elsewhere—such as in Addis Ababa or abroad in any number of countries—to maintain their grasp on Harari, and it will make it easier for them to transmit that knowledge to their children, should they so desire. And fourth, it will help standardize the language more than has occurred previously, thus reducing the chances of different versions (or "dialects") of Harari developing in different parts of Ethiopia or throughout the world. Of course, since the Harari are a Muslim people, their literature and culture is replete with Islamic references. Thus, the development of this literature reifies their self-identification not only as Harari but also, implicitly, as Muslims.

In addition, Harari who enjoy reading for pleasure were happy and enthusiastic when discussing this new literature, and a few of them wondered aloud if other ethnic groups around the country were producing similar work on their cultures and histories. Not only were these people curious, they expressed an interest in reading about the other groups too, including the non-Muslim ones. Here, it seems obvious that such comments may reflect a search for political allies as much as an honest desire to learn more about other Ethiopians. But in the process, they underscored the continued importance of Amharic as a national language when they expressed their hope that other groups writing about their own histories and cultures would translate those books into Amharic so that Harari and others could read them as well. Some Harari express similar attitudes about music, for linguistic freedom and the encouragement to resurrect suppressed histories and cultures has generated new music from all around the country, and these new traditions are widely appreciated and enjoyed across the barriers of language, culture, religion, and distance. These developments mark a stark departure from the previous attitude among the Harari and others that Amharic and other cultural impositions were tools of Christianization rather than something that unites all Ethiopians at the national level.

Paralleling the early stages of the development of a new Harari literature has been an increase in official efforts to promote education about Harari history and culture. For example, a daily, half-hour Harari-language radio program is broadcast daily throughout the country. The topics it covers range from conversations or interviews, to editorials and cultural-historical lectures that discuss readings from classical Harari poems and other literature, to recent historical and anthropological studies written in Harari and other languages. I knew many people who scheduled their daily routines so they could listen to these programs, which were often the subject of conversation around town afterward.

Language and Ethnicity in the Muslim Cultural Politics of Harar

Sometimes the Harari ethnic revival accompanied moves to forge and to improve interregional (and interethnic) relations. In the fall of 1997, the Five Neighboring Regions (Harar, Oromiya, Somali, Afar, and Dire Dawa), all of whose populations are dominantly Muslim, jointly hosted a cultural festival in Harar. From the event, a magazine devoted to history and culture in the five regions was published. All the articles about Oromo topics were written in Oromo, but with the exception of one short piece in Somali, some Harari poetry, and an article on Harar in English, the rest of the magazine was in Amharic or provided Amharic translations.

Harari politicians and members of the regional Bureau of Culture and Sports with whom I spoke offered two explanations. The first is the obvious one: that it makes sense to use Amharic, despite past resentment of it, since it is the one major language the five regions and their peoples hold in common. The second was that when certain other regions did not submit material for inclusion, the Harari organizers had to pen something about the other regions and they chose to do so in Amharic, the more widely shared language. Perhaps most significant, however, is that the five regions have formed an administrative council that meets every three months. Representatives at these council meetings discuss their contiguous territories and the advantages of shared policies on education, economy (including the considerable contraband trade), culture, sports, and so on (interview with Abdurahman Mohammed Korram, August 5, 1998). By forming a regional bloc, they also hope to increase the power of their (common, and arguably Islamic) voice in the Council of the Federation, the second chamber of parliament in Addis Ababa. The potential fruits of a close cooperation at home are perhaps best illustrated by an Amharic-language cartoon that appeared on the last page of the festival magazine. It shows a tree with five branches, with roundish objects that look like fruit dangling from each, and each branch named: Dire Dawa, Oromiya, Harar, Afar, and Somali. At the base of the tree is a man watering it out of a container labeled "The Cooperative Congress of the Five Neighboring Regions" (*Yä5tu Tägorabach Keleloch* 1990 E.C./1997, 48).

A few months later, this regional cooperation was emphasized again, at a meeting to mark the 111th anniversary of the Battle of C'alanqo, when Harar lost its independence. The meeting was held in a large public lecture hall that was decorated with toilet paper, balloons, and banners; representatives from each of the five neighboring regions spoke, reciting poetry and making speeches in Harari, Oromo, Somali, and Amharic. The common theme was the long-term peaceful coexistence and shared historical experience of oppression under Christian Ethiopian colonialism. Undoubtedly, there is an underlying current of political expediency to this discourse, but it is a notable phenomenon considering the normal emphasis on ethno-linguistic difference among government critics, as well as many ordinary Ethiopians' past resentment of Amharic as a public, official language.

More narrowly, other events focus on only certain ethnic groups. For example, in late June 1998, the Harari National Council, the city's dominant political party, and the policy-making branch of the Harari People's National Regional Government hosted the Harari History, Culture, and Language Symposium. Presenters included local Harari, both independent individuals and members of the regional administration, and scholars invited from Addis Ababa. Also, Abdullahi Ali Shariff, a resident of Harar who had worked exceptionally hard to establish a private museum that was more impressive than many similar government institutions, set up a selective but extensive display of his considerable collection. This symposium led to a number of interesting discussions about the relationship between regional people and the central government, discussions in which religion was often a theme. For example, the Federal Ministry of Culture, based in Addis Ababa, had earlier come to Harar to take photographs of churches, mosques, clothing styles, and various historical materials relating to *all* groups in the area. After returning to the capital to develop their film, however, the federal authorities only sent back pictures of the churches, claiming that all the others had failed to turn out properly. In Harar, this incident was interpreted as just another example of continued domination of the central government agencies in Addis Ababa, despite new and generally welcomed policies since 1991, by Christians who in practice are hostile to Islam.

Muslim Cultural Celebrations in Harar

Greater political autonomy and increased attention to and respect for all Ethiopian languages have inspired many Ethiopians to reconsider various aspects of their religious, ethnic, and other identities. In Harar, as elsewhere, Islamic revivalism and ethno-linguistic resurgence have tended to parallel one another. At the same time, other cultural practices also encourage and reinforce these processes. Although weddings, funerals, and public observances of religious holidays may not be recent innovations, the larger political-economic context in which they now occur lends them new meanings and significance for the construction of Harari identity. Beyond these historical practices, other, more "modern" events and institutions, such as conferences and radio broadcasts, promote certain images and ideas for public consumption. These issues are worth considering because they provide windows into examining how the privileging of local identities affects national identities and loyalties.

Weddings, funerals, and social gatherings have long been important in tying the Harari community together. They bring members of different *afocha*, *ahli*, and *mariññet* together and thereby create the conditions in which social norms may be emphasized and social deviance discouraged. Since 1948, when the Harari began to disperse permanently, some weddings and funerals have also brought Harari from other cities, regions, or countries back to the home city, thus emphasizing a broader Harari identity that is not restricted by geographical residence, even if it is centered on one place. While gender segregation is not strictly enforced at these events, men and women usually sit separately, though they do wander in and out of each other's spaces. At weddings I attended, men spoke about local and national politics, world events, local news, national and international business opportunities, and history, as well as about such lighter topics as recent gossip, jokes, and sex.

In general, during Ramadhan as well as at other times, there are a wide range of religious practices in Harar. In some places, Sufi devotional poems *(dhikr)* are chanted while wooden clappers and drums keep the beat and listeners dance with each other. Other gatherings are quieter, marked by recitations from the Qur'an and the reading of religious poetry, such as "Mustafa," a supplication to the Prophet Muhammad whose particular linguistic blend of classical Harari and Arabic is probably several hundred years old. All of these practices are ostensibly Islamic, though the degree to which they are so is open to debate and is definitely not a topic on which there is widespread consensus. In sum, the variety of Harari Islamic practices, hinted at here through a brief description of some holiday observances, testifies to the plurality of Islamic beliefs and standards that obtain in Harar.

Islamic holidays are other occasions that bring the Harari community together, but by including other Muslim peoples, such as Oromos and Somalis, they also emphasize a broader religious identity that transcends ethno-linguistic divisions. At the same time, religious celebrations are diverse in practice and subject to different interpretations. For example, in some regions of the Islamic world, the month of fasting, Ramadhan, is followed by an optional extra week of fasting, for which there are varied explanations. Some say that since women are forbidden for health reasons to fast during menstruation, it provides the chance to make up for that lost Ramadhan time. Others suggest that elderly folk, among others, choose to fast in hopes of gaining extra blessings from God. Regardless the motivations, since the early 1990s, there has been increasing Harari observance of the post-Ramadhan fast.

Historically, I was told, mostly old people and women would fast and devote extra time to study and prayer during the additional week of fasting. A number of testimonies also indicated that increasing numbers of young Harari today fast as well, because when they do so their parents permit them to go out at night to eat and visit friends, which gives them the opportunity to have fun and meet members of the opposite sex.[3] One friend, about forty years old, told me he was fasting that year for the first time because his wife had decided to do so and he did not feel right about her fasting without him.

The observation of the post-Ramadhan fast is marked by celebrations throughout Harar, which takes on a festival-like atmosphere, and since the 1990s the celebrations have become a tourist event for non-Muslim Ethiopians from the capital and elsewhere. During the final days, there are big celebrations, larger in some places than those signaling the end of Ramadhan. The general atmosphere is merry, and there are *dhikr* ceremonies throughout town. One, near the Erer Gate of the town wall, takes place during the last three nights of the week. It is held in a room and led by a *shaykh,* accompanied by numerous people with wooden hand clappers and several drummers. At the sessions I attended, prayer songs—in Harari and Arabic—were led by various persons, and both men and women (many of whom were young teenagers) danced, most with infectious enthusiasm. Some women had their heads covered, and almost all jumped up and down, smiling broadly, clapping and singing loudly with the prayer leader. Most adults were chewing *qat,* a leaf that produces narcotic-like effects and is often used in conjunction with religious study and other activities.[4] Notably, the attendees included not only Muslims but also Christians, two of whom flanked the *shaykh.*

Harari Identity and Ethiopian Nationalism in Harar

Social scientists have often found that social or political conflict exposes underlying issues and emotions that are otherwise difficult to discern. On May 6, 1998, a border dispute erupted into war between Ethiopia and Eritrea, both of whose central governments are dominated by Tigrinya-speaking Christians. In the immediate wake of the conflict, however, a broad base of support rallied in Ethiopia around the central government. Surely, many observers thought, smoldering resentment against Eritrea, which had attained its independence from Ethiopia in 1993, contributed to this support, as did more recent anger at Eritrea's having rejected the birr, Ethiopia's currency, so that it could print its own money.[5] But the two sides failed to reach a peaceful settlement, and my conversations with Harari and other Ethiopians revealed much deeper emotions and an underlying sense of satisfaction with the present national system.[6]

They explained that during Haile Selassie's reign and that of the subsequent military dictatorship, being Ethiopian meant not being permitted to enjoy an ethnic identity, or rather, being permitted only an Ethiopian nationalist one. This Ethiopian nationalist identity was then made up of speaking Amharic and prioritizing the development and well-being of the country as a whole rather than just one's own area. It meant seeing history in terms of the entire nation and in terms of interpretations dominated by the center, a viewpoint that incorporated the periphery only as it played a positive role in centrist policies. Although lip service was paid to other religions, being Ethiopian also inherently meant being associated with an Orthodox Christian identity, even though much of the country was Muslim and other religions were practiced too.

According to many Harari and other Muslims in eastern Ethiopia, being Ethiopian today means different things. Primarily, it means having the legal freedom to acknowledge, to be proud of, and to develop local cultures and languages. It means being able to give ethnic identities priority over the national one and being able to write one's own history with one's own interpretation, or, as it is commonly or popularly put, to write the "truth." It means being able to reject the old, standard, nationalist history claim that only positive influences radiate from the center. Even more important, being Ethiopian today means having the freedom to practice religions other than Orthodox Christianity, including Islam. When I pushed Harari, Somali, and other people on these points, I was told that in the new Ethiopia, the group identity that is prioritized is an ethno-linguistic one. People associate this shift with freedom and with making up for past oppression.[7] As such, many Muslims in Ethiopia today appreciate the present central government, which implements and continues to support these policies.

Concluding Remarks

Ethiopia's new political system has opened further possibilities for the country's diverse peoples, including large numbers of Muslims who had been sidelined by governments in the past. As a result, the Muslims of Harar have become more willing to accept and support the Christian-dominated national government. Their political awareness and involvement is considerable, and though they have embarked upon a quest to recapture and build up their community's ethnic and religious pride, they also readily emphasize that they are nevertheless also "Ethiopian."

Government policies have succeeded for the most part in subsuming religious difference or religious revivalism to that of ethno-linguistic identity. History, however, indicates that religion is an enduring sociopolitical force and, among its many functions, it may be invoked to express discontent with factors that on the surface have nothing to do with faith per se. Thus, as evangelical Christian and Muslim missionaries increase their activities and as an avowedly democratic government attempts to create a new political culture in which language rights are formally recognized, the relationships between ethno-linguistic identities and the propaganda of religious leaders and ruling officials will remain areas of ongoing debates in the continuing redefinition of Muslim identities in Ethiopia.

Appendix: Translation of "Luqtat al-Tarikhiyya" [Gleanings of History]

According to historical knowledge, Christianity in Ethiopia found its first home in the north, in southern Eritrea, where the ancient kingdom of Axum was located. And the history of the spread of Christianity in the geographical region that comprises Ethiopia today is the history of the military expansion of the Semitic peoples called Amhara, who live near southern Eritrea and take Gondar as their historical capital. Some studies favor the view that the Amhara are Semites who emigrated from southern Arabia, and we see the similarities between Amharic pronunciation and that of the Maharat, who are Arabs still living in southern Arabia between Oman and southern Yemen. And it is worth mentioning that the alphabet in which the Amharic language (it is the official language of Ethiopia) is written is the same alphabet that the Sabeans and the Himyars used and that is called in writing "the *masnad*." This race [the Amhara] still retains Semitic features.

The southern spread of the Amhara is distinguished by its military nature: The tribes living in the south submitted at sword point. The agricultural lands were completely distributed among the conquerors, as feudal landlords, and the original inhabitants became only slaves there. The big change in economic activity for some inhabitants in the conquered regions was from whatever activity they originally pursued to agriculture, which the conquerors forced them to adopt as their profession. Some regions remained safe from these changes, which brought slavery with them.

This association between Christianity, military conquest, and feudalism made the church the largest possessor of agricultural lands in Ethiopia until the occurrence of the last revolution and its confiscation of church lands.

The conversion of the conquered regions to the Christian religion did not lead to any substantial changes in their inhabitants' social or economic positions within the harsh feudal system that the Christian conquerors brought with them. Thus, it was the appearance of Islam and its expansion into most regions of Ethiopia that caused big changes in social relations. Islamic ideology is magnanimous, and its conceptualization of brotherhood under God formed the escape from the slavery that the conquerors had imposed on the remaining Ethiopian tribes. Thus, it [Islam] spread quickly.

By the time the Islamic dynasties, like the Harari emirate and the Yifat emirates and others, were along the frontiers of Ethiopia, they composed a serious danger to the domination of the conquerors and the Orthodox, Coptic Christian Church. Due to the church's and the Amhara government's increased need for the inhabitants of the conquered regions in their agonizing, long military struggle against the Muslims, they loosened slightly the grip of the slavery system.

Then the conquests of the great warrior, Imam al-Ghazi Ahmad bin Ibrahim al-Aa'sir, famous as Ahmad Grañ, led to the wide spread of the Islamic religion until it covered nearly all of Ethiopia. That was the Islamic expansion, which the church could not withdraw from nor eradicate, despite the weakness and the destruction which affected the Islamic dynasties. Because of this long history of Christian-Muslim struggle in Ethiopia, there were real divisions, and mutual hatred between the followers of the two primary religions in Abyssinia, and they are Coptic (Orthodox) Christianity and Islam. The Christians did not continue killing the Muslims after military and political weakness still affected them [the Muslims], and in spite of their subjugation to the grip of Christian government. This is related mainly to the Ethiopian Coptic Church following the Egyptian Coptic Church, which continued to appoint Egyptians to be the head of the Ethiopian Coptic Church until recently, when the Ethiopian church became independent from its Egyptian mother during the last reign of the Ethiopian King Haile Selassie in the fifties of this century. Therefore it is possible to say that there were relations there of some sort, tying the safety and freedom of religious worship of the Ethiopian Muslims to the security and peace of mind of Egyptian Christians. And these relations have strong historical evidence.

Thus, because of that and regardless of the consequences of the military struggles between the followers of the two religions, Islam neither gained nor lost [territory] in that country. Rather, its followers continued to increase rapidly, being strong and weak in turn, as a result of the struggles and their outcomes. Only, the spread of Islam was never stopped.

Islam certainly found important support and strengthened its position in Eritrea when Arab tribes coming from Sudan with the Islamic tide settled there. From among these tribes, the largest in number was the Beni

Amir. These Arab tribes played a very important role in the Arabization of a big part of Eritrea and the spread of Islam and the Arabic language south into Ethiopia.

Thus, the spread of Islam in most of the province of Wallo [in the northeast] is explained by the dual influence of the Muslim Arab tribes in the north and the influence of Harar, which is located immediately to the south of that province. The province of Wallo is considered today one of the most important Islamic strongholds in the country. Although the majority of the inhabitants of that province are Muslim and others, they are Amhara.

Harar and its freedom-fighting sons had the biggest role and largest participation when Harar was still the flashing, glittering origin of the deeply rooted belief that spread the light of Islam to the corners of the country until it was possible to say that there was not a son of a Yemeni or Arab immigrant in Ethiopia, let alone the Muslim sons of Ethiopia's inhabitants, who had not acquired Qur'anic and Arabic learning at the hand of one of the sons of Harar. And Harar embodied the full glories in her traditions, including Islamic documents and culture in the Arabic language, and Islamic folklore and dress. And why not? For Harar gave birth to the great fighter Imam al-Ghazi Ahmad bin Ibrahim. Harar was able to carry on this historical role during Islam's history in Ethiopia, enjoying geographical advantages, deeply controlling Muslim territories and peoples represented in all the Afar and Somali tribes. Harar was a prosperous independent emirate ruling the east coast of the Horn of Africa and its deserts until the Egyptians ruled it between the year 1875 and the year 1885. That is the date of the downfall of the Egyptian administration at the hands of the British, who sent a British administration to Harar when the Egyptian administration left.

The Harari rebelled against this invading authority, as usual being proud and rejecting any government that was not Muslim. And they reestablished their emirate again.

In the year 1887, the Ethiopian Emperor Menilek II dared, with the support of imperialist Britain and Italy, to invade Harar with a tremendous army including forty leaders of the rank of *dajjazmach* [a high level military title], with 4,000 fighters being led by each of them, while the Harari troops did not exceed 30,000 fighters. The two groups met in the area called C'alanqo, where there were 300 *hafiz* [memorizers of] *al-Qur'an* in the Muslim army to remind their brothers that "Allah hath purchased of the Believers their persons and their goods; for theirs (in return) is the Garden (of Paradise)" [Qur'an 9:111][8] and that "[i]f any do turn his back to them on such a day . . .he draws on himself the wrath of Allah and his abode is Hell" [Qur'an 8:16].[9] And Menilek's forces, well-armed with firearms provided to them by the Europeans, encircled the Muslim forces. And on that day there were martyred 30,000 from Harar's sons and the Kottu tribes who fought with them. Among those individuals were 300 *hafiz al-Qur'an* and 700 newly married youth from Harar's sons.

And the remembrance of these 700 wedded martyrs became part of the Harari wedding customs until today, when every Harari groom is given fabric that is called *"satti baqla"* in Harari, which means "seven hundred." It is a rectangular cloth from white woven cotton, suitable for covering [that is, clothing] or for a turban, ornamented with a red stripe along the edges symbolizing the martyrs' murders. When he presents it, the gift giver, who usually is the paternal uncle of the woman's father, whispers in the ear of the groom: "So that you do not forget."

The Afar and Somali to the south of their brothers, the people of Harar, participated in the wars that Imam al-Ghazi Ahmad bin Ibrahim led, and in the battles that preceded and followed them. The Afar are distinguished by their violence and harshness and pride, and after the fall of Harar after the battle of C'alanqo, they certainly continued to enjoy their independence and their haughtiness and a great Islamic zeal, owing to which no unbeliever dared to set foot on Afar soil. The Afar continued under the government of their sultans who persisted in carrying out *shari'a* punishments. The last of these sultans is the Sultan Ali Murah, who currently resides in Jeddah in the kingdom of Saudi Arabia, after having led tenacious struggles in the defense of his people's independence and the Islamic religion.

In spite of all this Islamic zeal that the Afar enjoyed, illiteracy spread widely among them, until ignorance of the Islamic *shari'a* among the rank and file became a reason for the persistence of traditional customs, which Islam rejects, among them. And this is one of the results of ignorance and lack of religious education.

The spread of Islam and the Arabic language acquired an additional momentum at the beginning of the current century as the result of the large immigration of Yemenis and some of the sons of the Hijaz and Najd to Ethiopia. This immigration led to the biggest spread of the Arabic language among many of the inhabitants of that country. It did not take long before the Arab immigrants were joined by Arabs arriving from Libya with the Italian forces who invaded Abyssinia in the thirties of this Christian century.

The relations between these Arabs and the inhabitants of the country developed through marriage and through their trading activities, which they extended to all corners of Ethiopia, along with their retention of their customs, their culture, and their profound devotion to the performance of their Islamic religious rituals. All of this had its effect on the spread of the Islamic religion and the increase in its followers. The biggest example of that Arab immigrant influence was on the city of Dire Dawa, which is the third-largest Ethiopian city and located in the province of Harar, where Arabic gained ascendancy over all the languages and dialects, including Harari and Amharic, because of the density of existence of Arabic, which caused the Arabization of other languages.

And to the Arabs who immigrated to them, the Abyssinian Muslims sincerely showed all kindness, and their respect was the greatest, and they gave to them their daughters to marry, and enabled them to farm lands. They accorded them love and honor and dignity that exceeds description. And all that regard and generosity is a link in the relationship that binds Arabs through the merciful Prophet Mustafa [that is, Muhammad], may the prayers of God, and peace, be upon him. And the brotherhood in God was so beautiful and respectful that most of the immigrants forgot their people and their nations, and they got used to the country and its people and were reassured by the abundant life, the love, and the exquisite hospitality that encircled them. Most of these Arabs were from simple rural areas and left their country in search of sustenance. They kept to their religion and its culture, like religious zeal, good repute, haughtiness over vile things, and adherence to religious rituals. They brought up their women and children like that, or, say they exerted their greatest effort in that direction. And they were deserving of the honor, the welcoming and the open-armed reception with which they were met.

It is worth mentioning that Islam spread widely among the pastoral tribes that remained away from the influence and authority of the feudal Orthodox Church, where the imposition of the serfdom system on the inhabitants was associated with the order to convert to Christianity. Indicative of that were the pastoral Arsi tribes, who live in the province of Arsi, southwest of the province of Harar, who converted to Islam, while the Darasa and Guji tribes in the province of Sidamo [in the south] remained difficult for Christianity, which makes them a good target for Islamic missionary work.

Religion occupies a broad and very important part in the Orthodox person's life. This is apparent from the large number of priests and monks [and from] the increase in symbols, rites, rituals, and religious events devoted to the saints, to the extent that no day in the year was lacking them. For these link the Christian to his church through strong ties, which are strengthened by the traditional separation from other Christian sects and from Islam, which is the issue that creates a state of religious fanaticism that, fortunately, did not reverse the loyalty of the Muslims to previous conditions mentioned above. Therefore, even if the Orthodox person left his faith, he always remained a goal difficult to obtain in the face of Muslim missionaries, despite the existence of individual cases that are not statistically significant. This mutual aversion restricted interaction between the followers of the two religions. Behavioral appearances strengthened this aversion, such as the Muslim refusal to eat meat slaughtered by Christians, in spite of the Qur'anic text declaring it permissible, and similarly, the refusal to ever marry Christian women. Like the fanatical Christian washes many times or gets rid of utensils that the Muslim touched, hatred and similar things are fanatical behavior.

Notes

For the funding that made research for this chapter possible, thanks and appreciation are due to the Social Science Research Council International Predissertation Fellowship, Fulbright-Hays, and the Wenner-Gren Foundation for Anthropological Research.

1.   This paragraph and the following are based on Anonymous 1930.
2.   Its pagination runs 6–13, but I never saw any other pages from the larger document of which this is clearly one part. I would like to thank Malik Balla for checking my translation against the original Arabic version.
3.   In fact, this practice can be traced back much further, though under a different guise. In the mid-1950s, elderly Harari reminiscing about the then largely defunct *mugads* (that is, formal groups of young boys and girls) described similar activities, especially during the Arafa feast (Duri 1955, 15).
4.   Legal in Ethiopia, as well as Great Britain and other countries in Europe, *qat* is illegal in Saudi Arabia, other strictly Islamic nations, and the United States. In Harar, it is chewed weekly by a majority of adult men and many adult women.
5.   The basic unit of currency was provocatively named the nakfa, the name of a battlefield where Eritrean forces won a major victory over Ethiopian forces in 1988.
6.   Somali support was influenced by fears that instability in southern Somalia would spread into eastern Ethiopia, and Harari support was influenced by the fear of Oromo domination.
7.   There is, sadly, a horrific exception. It was clear to me that feelings in Harar and Jijjiga toward Eritrea and Eritreans varied widely from those dominant in Addis Ababa. Because the two eastern cities were largely insulated from the conflict and because of the constant bombardment of government propaganda and the despicable deportations of Eritreans and Ethiopians of Eritrean descent, people there supported the Ethiopian cause but expressed concern for their Eritrean "brothers and sisters." In Addis Ababa, nationalist fervor and anti-Eritrean hostility had been stirred up to a far greater degree, and in many cases, the deportees (as well as "mixed" Eritrean-

Tigrean individuals and families) were taken advantage of in morally reprehensible ways.

8.   A theme of this chapter is how to deal with enemies who have broken agreements with Muslims.—Trans.

9.   Muslim tradition holds this text to have been revealed not long after the Battle of Badr. Among its topics is the notion that even in the face of overwhelming odds, God will grant victory to those fighting for his cause.—Trans.

References

Abbink, Jon. 1998. "An Historical-Anthropological Approach to Islam in Ethiopia: Issues of Identity and Politics." *Journal of African Cultural Studies* 11, no. 2: 109–124.

Anonymous. 1923 E.C./1930. "BäHarar Kätäma: SiläQädamawi Haile Sellassie Negusä Nägäst yäZäwd Bä'al" [On the Celebrations in Harar of Haile Selassie I's Coronation as Emperor]. In *Berhanenna Sälam* [Light and Peace], 2 Tahsas (December 11).

Balsvik, Randi Ronning. 1985. *Haile Sellassie's Students: The Intellectual and Social Background to Revolution, 1952–1977*. East Lansing: Michigan State University African Studies Center.

Berhanenna Sälam [Light and Peace]. 1923 E.C./1930. 2 Tahsas (December 11).

Duri Mohammed. 1955. "The Mugads of Harar." *University College of Addis Ababa Ethnological Society Bulletin* 4: 15–19.

Erlich, Haggai. 1994. *Ethiopia and the Middle East*. Boulder, CO: Lynne Rienner Publishers.

Hajji Abdulla Shariff and the Harari Muslim Brothers. 1923 E.C./1930. "YäZäwd Bä'al Diskur" [Discourse on the Coronation]. In *Berhanenna Sälam* [Light and Peace], 2 Tahsas (December 11).

Hussein Ahmed. 1994. "Islam and Islamic Discourse in Ethiopia (1973–1993)." In *New Trends in Ethiopian Studies: Papers of the 12th International Conference of Ethiopian Studies*, edited by Harold G. Marcus, vol. 1, 775–801. Lawrenceville, NJ: Red Sea Press.

———. 1998. "Islamic Literature and Religious Revival in Ethiopia (1991–1994)." *Islam et sociétés au sud du Sahara*, 12: 89–108.

———. 2001. *Islam in Nineteenth-Century Wallo, Ethiopia: Revival, Reform, and Reaction*. Leiden: Brill.

Kapteijns, Lidwien. 2000. "Ethiopia and the Horn of Africa." In *The History of Islam in Africa*, edited by Nehemia Levtzion and Randall L. Pouwels, 227–250. Athens: Ohio University Press.

Mahdi M. Shumburo. 1998. "A Background Account to the Hannolatto Movement in Harar, and Reminiscences of Its Aftermath (circa 1945–1960)." Unpublished manuscript.

Tibebe Eshete. 1998. "A Reassessment of Lij Iyasu's Political Career, with Particular Emphasis upon His Fall." In *Personality and Political Culture in Modern Africa*, edited by Melvin Page, Stephanie Beswick, Tim Carmichael, and Jay Spaulding, 163–179. Boston: Boston University African Studies Center.

United Kingdom. Foreign Office. 371, 39, 2854.

Waldron, Sidney. 1974. "Social Organization and Social Control in the Walled City of Harar, Ethiopia." PhD diss., Columbia University.

———. 1979. "Harar: The Muslim City in Ethiopia." In *Proceedings of the Fifth International Conference of Ethiopian Studies,* edited by Robert L. Hess, 239–257. Chicago: Office of Publications Services, University of Illinois at Chicago Circle.

———. 1980. "A Farewell to Bab Haji: City Symbolism and Harari Identity, 1877–1977." In *Working Papers on Society and History in Imperial Ethiopia: The Southern Periphery from the 1880's to 1974,* edited by D. L. Donham and Wendy James, 247–270. Cambridge, England: African Studies Centre.

———. 1984. "The Political Economy of Harari-Oromo Relationships, 1559–1874." *Northeast African Studies* 6, nos. 1–2: 23–39.

Yä5tu Tägorabach Keleloch: YäBahel Féstival, Leyyu Etem [The Five Neighboring Zones: Cultural Festival; Special Edition]. 1990 E.C./1997. Harar: Harari Bureau of Culture and Sports, 17 Mäskäräm (September 27).

Yelma Mängäsha. 1923 E.C./1930. "Diskur" [Discourse]. In *Berhanenna Sälam* [Light and Peace], 2 Tahsas (December 11).

Chapter Nine

Race, Ideology, and Islam in Contemporary South Africa

ABDULKADER TAYOB

According to the South African census of 1996, Muslims in South Africa number only 553,717. At a mere 1.36 percent, they constitute a tiny proportion of the South African population. And yet the presence of Islam, particularly in the major cities and urban areas, is unmistakable. Muslims regularly make themselves heard in the media, the politics, and the streets of Cape Town, Durban, and Johannesburg. The call to prayer sounds from hundreds of mosques scattered throughout the country, and Muslims figure prominently as members of cabinet, parliament, and other governmental structures in post-apartheid South Africa. Although Muslims do not make up a large percentage of the population, their history is vitally important for understanding how Islam has shaped people's responses to a racially divided society constructed by colonialism and apartheid.

This chapter begins with an interpretation of the history of Muslims in South Africa focusing on their origins and their development over the past 350 years. First, the history of Islamic institutions and practices are placed in the context of slavery, colonialism, and apartheid. The discussion then turns to the impact of democracy and globalization on established institutions and patterns of thought and social behavior in Muslim society. Here I will provide an overview of some key challenges presented to Muslims and their responses, and I will argue that South African Muslims have seized upon democracy and globalization as opportunities for growth and dynamic change.

Islam Taking Root

Muslims came to South Africa mainly from Asia and to a lesser extent from other parts of Africa. The Asian component dominates the landscape and will

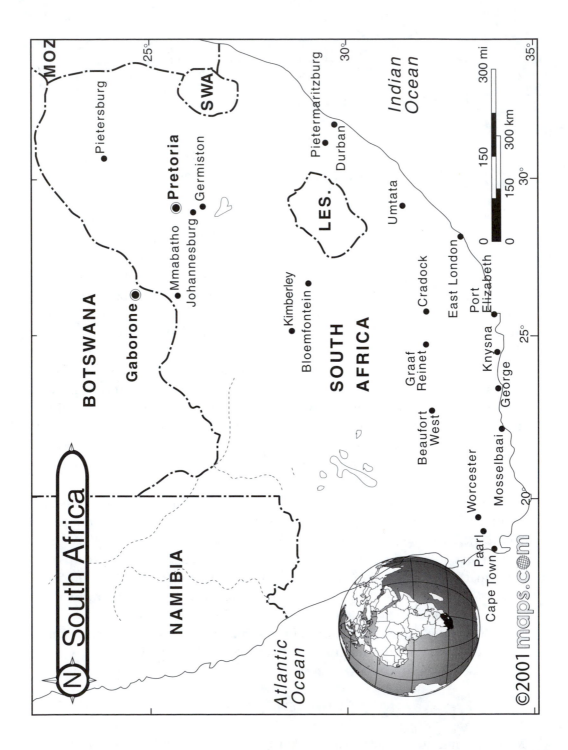

South Africa

N

BOTSWANA

NAMIBIA

SOUTH
AFRICA

MOZ

SWA

LES.

Atlantic
Ocean

Indian
Ocean

Pietersburg

• Mmabatho
Pretoria
Johannesburg •
• Germiston

Gaborone

Pietermaritzburg
• Durban

Umtata

Kimberley •
Bloemfontein •

Cradock •
East London
Port
Elizabeth

Graaf
Reinet •
Knysna •
George •

Beaufort
West •
Mosselbaai •
Worcester •
Paarl •
Cape Town •

25°

30°

35°

30°

25°

20°

300 mi

300 km

150

150

0

0

©2001 maps.com

be the key focus of this chapter. The first group of Muslims arrived in 1658, soon after the first Dutch settlement at the Cape of Good Hope. They were followed by a large number of Asian and African Muslim slaves owned by the Dutch East India Company. In addition to these Muslims, the Dutch also exiled a number of Muslim political prisoners from the Indonesian archipelago to the Cape. Among them were a number of prominent religious figures who had opposed various Dutch economic and political operations in the Netherlands Indies (present-day Indonesia). The best-known of the exiles was Shaykh Yusuf, a notable mystic teacher, who engaged in a campaign against Dutch incursions into the sultanate of Banten in West Java. Shaykh Yusuf's deportation to the Cape in 1694 has been marked as the first significant date in the history of Islam in South Africa. The local Dutch governors treated the political prisoners with respect but complained about the drain on resources that their maintenance entailed. Meanwhile, freedom of religious expression was severely curtailed, and conditions of slavery did not provide much opportunity for the establishment and development of Muslim religious life during this period.

Some degree of religious freedom was granted a hundred years later when the British occupied the Cape in 1795. At that time, another Muslim political exile from the Netherlands Indies, Abdullah Kadi Abdus Salaam, affectionately known as Tuan Guru, took advantage of this new atmosphere. After thirteen years of exile on Robben Island, just off the coast at Cape Town, he established a religious school and an organized congregation of Muslims at the Cape. His Awwal Mosque was founded at the turn of the nineteenth century, and as the Muslim community in Cape Town grew, the mosque attracted converts from the local slave and freed black populations. The Awwal Mosque was also home to an elementary religious school that played an important role in the foundation of the Muslim community. The Awwal Mosque and school marked the first stage of Islamic institutionalization in South Africa, and by 1820 it reported 491 "Free Black scholars and slaves" as members of the community (United Kingdom, Parliament 1968–1971).

Although Muslims were first brought to South Africa under the aegis of European imperialism, the establishment of Islam generated patterns of religious life in the Cape that extended beyond the interests of colonialism. Quite apart from governmental needs, Islamic practices in the Cape inscribed patterns of community life that created a unique sense of being Muslim. For example, the Awwal Mosque, with its prominent leader and popular school, served the social and religious needs of the emerging Muslim community. Attending to the needs of a slave society, the imam provided an anchor and a source of stability for members of his congregation in a sometimes-hostile environment. The services he provided included giving infants Islamic names on their seventh day, educating them in the basics of Islam, conducting Islamic marriages, and providing for dignified Muslim burials. Always there at the rites of passage, the

A mosque in Bo-Kaap, the traditionally "Malay" Muslim quarter of Cape Town, South Africa. (R. Michael Feener)

imams provided a sense of meaning to many of those at the margins of Cape society. His presence at a wide range of periodic and occasional community events ensured the development and maintenance of a community spirit sorely lacking for the underclass in colonial society. As one modern scholar has expressed it, "the impressive network of social, educational, and religious institutions created by the early Muslims at the Cape attracted many individuals in an economically or socially marginal position" (Shell 1984, 37).

The success of the Awwal Mosque was followed by the development of similar mosques and congregations throughout the Cape in the nineteenth century. As the Muslim population grew and when slavery was eventually abolished, new imams established more mosques to serve the needs of growing congregations. The imams of these mosques were mainly taught and trained in Cape Town, but there were also some international contacts with Mecca and various parts of the Ottoman Empire. A few imams had managed to go on pilgrimage to Mecca in the first half of the nineteenth century, but after the Suez Canal was built in 1869, many more were able to make the trip thanks to the increased availability of steamship transport in the Indian Ocean. Some of the same modern means that brought South African Muslims to the Middle East also brought Middle Eastern Muslims to South Africa. One of the most prominent early examples was Abu Bakr Effendi, who in 1863 was sent by the Ottoman Empire to teach Islam and resolve local disputes among Muslims in South Africa. Increasing global contact produced a vibrant society in which religious practices enriched and sustained a dynamic community under the shadow of an authoritarian and often-hostile political authority.

Another prominent group of Muslims in South Africa originated not from the Netherlands Indies but from the British colonies of the Indian Subcontinent. Most of these Muslim immigrants arrived under circumstances quite different from those of the earlier generations of Muslim political exiles at the Cape. When the British colonized the eastern coast of the country, they needed cheap labor to work on farms and in other industries. Having had success with Indian labor in other colonies, the British decided to bring in indentured laborers from South Asia to South Africa, beginning in 1860. A small number of South Asians came on their own accord, not as indentured labor but as free persons willing to take advantage of trading opportunities. In spite of the tough economic conditions of indentured labor and hostile European officials, some Indians managed to diversify their economic pursuits and exploit new opportunities in the growing diamond and gold fields further inland. But racial prejudice against Indians did not take long to surface, and first the British colony of Natal and later the Boer republics passed successive laws that restricted ownership of land, free movement, and educational opportunities.

The growing South Asian population of South Africa included Hindus as well as Muslims, and Muslims themselves were divided along class lines be-

South African Muslim men performing holiday prayers at the Gray Street Mosque in Durban. (Gideon Mendel/CORBIS)

tween, on the one hand, hawkers and traders who supported the building of mosques and, on the other, indentured workers whose religious life was governed by annual festivals imported from India. Among these festivals is the first month of the Islamic calendar, Muharram, in which the martyrdom of the grandson of the Prophet Muhammad is commemorated. This has been a very popular occasion for Muslims in South Africa to mark their identity. With the arrival of Soofie Saheb in 1895, such popular religious practices among Indian Muslims of indentured origins were promoted, and they have since become part of local Muslim religious life (Vahed 2001, 311, 319). However, the class lines demarcated between Muslims associated with mosques and communities oriented toward more popular festival observances have persisted among the South Asian population of South Africa to this day.

Like their counterparts in the Cape, Muslims in Natal and the province of Transvaal established mosques and schools to support their religious activities. The first mosque at Durban was founded in 1884, and that of Pretoria, the capital of the Boer South African Republic, was established in 1887. It was South Asian Muslim traders who founded these mosques, after duly obtaining permission from the colonial authorities. During the late nineteenth century, certain areas in Durban were set aside for Indian occupation, while the Boer republics instituted ever-more-draconian legislation limiting Indian participation in the community. For example, the Orange Free State completely prohibited Indian residence within its territory, and the Zuid Afrikaanse Republiek placed severe limitations on land ownership by nonwhites. Both racial prejudice and discriminatory laws in these areas favored the development of a nonreligious elite in Indian Muslim communities. In response to these measures, Indian Muslim traders devised innovative ways to pursue their economic interests, and the mosques they founded followed similar patterns. Thus, for example, almost all mosques in the South African Republic were officially owned by government officials (Tayob 1999b, 65). Indian leaders persuaded individual white officials to take ownership on behalf of the Muslims. In this precarious situation, prominent businessmen in the Muslim community became extremely influential and powerful. Having established significant and vital relationships with demanding and often-fickle officials, the traders became the undisputed patrons of religious life within the Muslim communities. These Muslim communities thus came to be led not by specially trained religious leaders but, rather, by members of the local Muslim commercial establishment.

Muslims of African origin constitute a much smaller group in South Africa, but their presence can be traced over a long period of time as well. African slaves are mentioned among the Muslims associated with the early mosques at the Cape, and records indicate a number of African Muslims were also in the British army at the turn of the nineteenth century. Moreover, a significant number of African Muslims from northern Mozambique were settled in Natal, also as indentured laborers, in the second half of the nineteenth century. They had been rescued by the British from slave vessels off the east coast of Africa. Consisting of both Muslims and Christians, they settled in Durban, and came to be known as the Zanzibaris. The Muslims among them were later joined by a small trickle of Malawian Muslims and Zulu converts. They maintained contact with the eastern coast of Africa, and their practices, beliefs, and traditions reflect this. Mustapha Osman was one of the first teachers to come from the Comoros in the 1880s. In South Africa, he taught the Qur'an and became a respected imam. In the twentieth century, a growing number of indigenous people have converted to Islam throughout South Africa, and mosques have been established in many black African communities. However, considerable tension exists between them and some other Muslim groups over issues related to race and culture.

The Racialization of South African Society

Three distinct features have characterized the history of Muslims in South Africa over the course of the twentieth century. First, following the racialized identities of the country as a whole, Muslim identities were themselves racialized. Second, religious attitudes and religious authority mimicked both the racial demands of the society and the authoritarianism of the state. And third, a new approach to Islam as a counter-hegemonic discourse was nurtured within the contexts of rapidly increasing modernization and racial conflict.

In earlier sections of this chapter, I sketched some of the different contexts in which various Muslim communities developed in South Africa. These histories of location and settlement shaped Muslim responses and left an indelible mark on their institutions as well as on their social and political attitudes. In the twentieth century, certain patterns of community life were reinforced and others were newly created.

With the discovery of mineral deposits in the Boer republics, the British sought to gain access and control of this wealth. After two wars, the territories were finally combined in 1910 under the leadership of a united white group. Mining and related industrialization was developed under a regime of white dominance. On the broader political stage, the disparate regions of British colonies and Boer republics were brought together under the Union of South Africa in 1910. This unification was offset by an opposite process of fragmentation among the South African population. It was within this context that an Afrikaner apartheid ideology developed that urged its adherents to exploit their presumed racial purity to take political control over the country. In this way, the racialization of society that had begun much earlier in South African history was increased, and it ultimately became rigidly institutionalized in the political system of the country. English-speaking people of European descent were grateful for this authoritarianism as long as the mines and factories were provided with cheap labor. Afrikaner ideology increasingly racialized nearly all aspects of South African society. It systematically and institutionally relegated the subjugated classes into separated racial groups that could be easily dominated. The promulgation of an official apartheid ideology beginning in 1948 was the ultimate outcome of this process. The political and economic context of the twentieth century—one strong state, and many racial groups generated and controlled by racial ideologues—provides the background for understanding Muslim communities in South Africa today.

Muslim Communities and Racial Identities

As we have seen, the first group of Muslims to arrive in the country came from different parts of Asia and Africa. The Muslim artilleries established to defend the Cape in the service of the Dutch were called "Javanese Artilleries" and were under the guidance of a Javanese Muslim chaplain. But in 1824, when a colonial commission inquired into the condition and treatment of indigenous inhabitants, Achmat van Bengalen, a prominent imam at the Awwal Mosque, said he was "of Malay extraction," and his associate Muding was also referred to as a Malay "priest." The term "Malay" thus appears to have come to be used generally to denote Muslims originating from any part of the Indonesian archipelago.[1]

In the twentieth century, "Malay" was used as a distinct racial category promoted by Afrikaner ideologues in their creation of a radically racialized partition of society under their dominion. At first, the Malays were actively courted by early Afrikaner nationalists for their votes in the Cape province. This enterprise was followed by an extensive program, under the direction of the well-known Afrikaner poet I. D. du Plessis, to institutionalize a distinctly "Malay" culture in South Africa. He founded the Cape Malay Choir Board in 1937, of which he was life-president, with a view to creating and preserving Cape Malay culture (Davids 1985, 9–10). Other cultural associations followed suit, and eventually the term "Malay" came to designate a distinct racial identity accepted by a large number of Muslims in the Cape. Not all Muslims designated Coloured became officially Malay, but the Malay identity was used to designate a presumed racially designated group of Muslims in the Cape. One of the most striking things about these developments was that the Afrikaner promoter of Malay culture was later to become the secretary of coloured affairs, and the apartheid state accepted Malay as a separate group under the broad rubric of Coloureds. Thus, with the support of the state, "Malayness" became entrenched as a term denoting Muslims in the Cape as the racialization of Muslim identity reflected broader trends in the racialization of the society as a whole.

Like the Malay Muslims of the Cape, Indian Muslims in other provinces were also racialized in the context of South African political history. The construction of a Muslim Indian subject was more subtle but equally evident in South Africa, as Muslims were divided into different ethnic and linguistic groups. Such group identity was clear right from the beginning, and it continues to dominate social and religious relations. Language and customs from specific subregions of South Asia dominated religious and cultural practices in various Muslim communities. In some well-known mosques in South Africa, discussions on issues facing the community were reached under a system whereby a mosque board would establish proportional representation from among the mosque's constituent ethnic groups. The first mosques in Durban and Pretoria were built by members of specific ethnic groups, but they then developed constitutions that ensured the representations of other Muslim populations living in the area (Tayob 1995, 61–62). Many other mosques followed this practice in an effort to provide equal representation. This arrangement of representation indicated a tendency toward acknowledging a common Indian Muslim identity, even as it entrenched and institutionalized differences among Muslims. The Indian Muslim identity has lived with the contradictions of this unity and diversity ever since.

Beyond the confines of the Muslim community, a nonconfessional, multi-ethnic Indian identity in South Africa had been constructed more successfully in the political struggle against unfair discrimination and the threat of mass deportation to India. Under white rule, freedom of movement was severely curtailed, and Indian land ownership was restricted to certain areas in Natal. The Natal Indian Congress and many other trade associations petitioned the authorities to reduce the effects of such discriminatory laws. The laws were not always directed at Indians as a whole. Rather, there were distinctions made between Indian-born and colonial-born, and some Muslims represented themselves as "Arab," as opposed to others who were Free Indians. Indians also petitioned the British authorities as British subjects (Tayob 1995, 59). Nevertheless, the political struggle led by Mohandas Gandhi and the Indian congresses spoke on behalf of a single Indian subject, which was eventually reflected by apartheid ideologues who regarded Indians as a single group. The divisions among Indians were numerous, but the fiction of a single overriding racial identity suited the needs of a state apparatus determined to see South African society as consisting of distinct racial units. The "Indian" subject in South Africa was thus constructed around a complex combination of religious, ethnic, and class differences. Muslims, by and large, accepted these increasingly institutionalized definitions of difference.

The Beginnings of Islamic Revival

For Muslims in South Africa, the twentieth century witnessed significant developments toward a consolidation of normative Islamic practice. Within the various racial groups just mentioned, Muslims established organizations to promote normative Islamic behavior and beliefs. They were not always successful in ensuring a uniform Islamic creed and code of conduct, but their attempts contributed to a renewed conceptualization of Islamic models and expectations. The first group of Muslim religious leaders to organize themselves into modern institutional structures were those in the Transvaal (1922), followed by the Cape Moslem Judicial Council in 1945 and later by those in Natal (1952). The leaders in the Transvaal followed the lead of their counterparts in India, where a group named Jamiat-i Ulama-i Hind promoted Islamic values on a personal, religious level. Similar issues also formed the agenda of the Jamiatul Ulama Transvaal (http://www.islamsa.org.za/), which was formed "to give religious guidance to the Muslim community and invited inquiries from the public concerning the *Shari'ah*" (Naude 1982, 27). Apart from leading prayers in the mosque, the Jamiat in the Transvaal established a network of religious schools and issued regular religio-legal opinions (*fatwas*) in response to questions and queries from members of the community. Through these programs, the organization was successful in raising new awareness of issues relating to various aspects of Islamic thought and practice. In addition, on a corporate rather than an individual level, it represented the body of scholars and imams who served the congregations in the region. The Jamiat Ulama Natal (http://www.jamiat.org.za/) and the Muslim Judicial Councils in Natal and Cape Town performed similar functions in their respective regions. However, despite this progress in the religious sphere, the religious authorities associated with these groups continued to accept the construction of the racialized Muslim subject as an essential aspect of South African politics.

Beyond the borders of the country, however, these Muslim organizations established and maintained active contacts with international Islamic bodies, especially with institutions where South African religious scholars themselves had studied. For instance, many members of the Jamiat in the Transvaal and Natal were from the networks of the Deoband or Bareilly schools in India. These groups differed in either promoting popular Sufi practices (Bareilly) or rejecting them as innovations (Deoband), and the two trends reflected the class origins of different groups of Indian Muslims in the nineteenth century. On the other hand, many Muslim Judicial Council members had studied in Arab countries, especially in Mecca, Medina, and Cairo. Upon returning to South Africa, they continued and expanded upon patterns of interaction with the Arab world that had begun in the nineteenth century. The best-known example of such contact was the so-called Transvaal *fatwa*, a published juridical opinion by the famous Egyptian Muslim modernist Muhammad Abduh, issued in response to a question posed by a South African correspondent (Adams 1968).

Abduh was asked whether it was permissible for Muslims to consume meat slaughtered by Christians and Jews, to wear European hats, and to perform worship behind a leader of a different school of Muslim jurisprudence. Following his modernist interpretation of Islamic law, Abduh answered yes to all these questions, and this marked a significant point in the development of modernist Islamic thought in South Africa. The *fatwa* advocated a more integrative approach between Muslims from diverse schools of thought, but it also anticipated later discussions about relations between Muslims and non-Muslims. However, most of the religious leadership in South Africa at the time followed not this trend but the more religiously traditional approaches emanating from the Muslim world. Nevertheless, Abduh's comments demonstrate the global connection of ideas and people between South Africa and the wider Muslim world. This trend continued throughout the twentieth century even under apartheid, when officials selectively granted permission and opportunities for such contacts and correspondence. Sometimes, at least, this "liberality" was due to the fact that some apartheid officials, otherwise very hostile to Islam, opportunistically promoted such religious contact and adherence to counter a perceived communist, atheistic assault against the "Christian" values of apartheid.

Irrespective of conservative or modernist slant, the introduction of new Islamic reformist ideas from the Arab world and the Indian Subcontinent led to a greater awareness of text-based definitions of Islamic orthodoxy as opposed to more popular religious practices. As a result, in the modern period, Islam in South African society has witnessed an increasing degree of devotion to such religious obligations as daily prayers, fasting, and regular pilgrimage. The associated increase in the number of South African mosques and South African pilgrims to Mecca cannot be ignored. Since the 1980s, about 5,000 individuals go on pilgrimage annually. At home, worshipers attend daily prayers at mosques, and overflowing crowds at Friday prayers can bring traffic in some Muslim neighborhoods to a standstill. This increase in public displays of piety has led to a public presence for Islam in contemporary South Africa that is remarkably palpable in spite of the small percentage of Muslims in the population. However, while these practices were overtly based on the *shari'a*, they at times also continue to reflect the racialized social contexts of apartheid. Thus, for example, new mosques were built specifically for the respective ethnic populations of both Indian and Coloured/Malay group areas. Different religious schools were established in these racial ghettoes as well. All places of worship, including mosques, were granted recognition by the state through the special allocation of sites for religious development in the racially segregated areas. In the overwhelming number of cases, the communities accepted these conditions. Thus, the greater degree of devotion and adherence to religion was inextricable from the racial categories under the apartheid state.

These aspects of Islamic social life in South Africa in the twentieth century presented growing and sustained challenges to religious leaders and scholars. The growth of modern education produced a new Muslim elite whose members had not been educated in traditional Islamic religious institutions and who could challenge the traditional authority of the *ulama* in society.

Over the course of the twentieth century, Islam in South Africa took on two distinctive features: First, its political character was closely tied to the question of race and racism, and second, it was deeply involved in debates over issues relating to the contestation of religious authority and the rise of Islamic modernism. The first feature has been most evident in the Cape; Muslim teachers and students in Cape Town came to reject the racial construction of the Malay identity. The Malay racial identity had been constructed to suit the political ideology of apartheid, and the Muslim Teachers Association regarded it with contempt. In response to I. D. du Plessis's book on the Malays, the association argued that "the book propagates Islam as a Malay religion whereas Islam is a universal religion and has only one law for all Muslims throughout the world" (quoted in Jeppie 1987, 80). Increasingly frequent statements of such sentiments prodded the Muslim Judicial Council and other cultural bodies to reject the "Cape Malay" identity for the Muslim community. Malayism, they argued, had been constructed as a way of being Muslim in the service of apartheid. The Muslim Teachers Association was successful in mobilizing Muslims to reject this construct, and as it did so, it injected elements of an antiapartheid discourse in the midst of Muslim religious life. In 1961, Muslims came together to declare apartheid an abhorrence to Islamic values. As the emerging leader of this movement, the charismatic Cape Muslim leader Imam Haron stood up against apartheid until he was killed in police custody in 1969. However, other movements for such mobilization followed until the fall of the apartheid regime.

The second major feature of this period, that of Muslim modernism, was more pronounced in the Transvaal and Natal among Indian Muslims. In contrast with the Muslim Teachers Association in the Cape, the Natal Muslim Council in the 1940s supported women's rights, the integration of secular and religious education, and a generally more modern outlook on Islamic life. At one of its conferences, for example, the Natal Muslim Council expressed its desire to found a religious institution that would train people to "lecture on Islamic subjects" who were "qualified in religion, modern technique and modern education" (Tayob 1995, 94). These were merely aspirations at this stage, but they expressed the frustrations of a growing body of individuals with the attitudes and approaches of traditional religious leaders. In contrast to the founders of the Natal Muslim Council, who were businessmen, professionals, and students at secular institutions, the Muslim religious leaders knew little English and were seen as being out of touch with the demands of life in a modern urban city such as Durban. The proliferation of Muslim youth organizations represented a generation gap within Islamic communities between religious leaders and professionals, between those who were raised in India and those who were socialized in South Africa, and between modernity and tradition. In addition to an antiapartheid ethos, then, this paradigm shift in Islamic thinking was characterized by more general aspirations to become modern, socially relevant, and respectable.

The Cape Youth associated with Imam Haron and the Natal Muslim Council was among the number of religious organizations that proliferated in the country during the second half of the twentieth century. Like their individual religious leaders, such organizations developed links with international organizations, such as the Muslim Brotherhood of Egypt and the Jama'at-i Islami in India. The first phase of such developments emerged in South Africa during the 1950s with organizations such as the Arabic Study Circle, the Islamic Propagation Centre, and the Women's Cultural Group. As the tide of Islamic revival increased in the 1970s, the groups proliferated in South Africa and developed alongside nationwide organizations such as the Muslim Students Association, the Muslim Youth Movement, the Qiblah Mass Movements, and the Call of Islam. Exceptions notwithstanding, the organizations in the Cape tended to develop socially and politically activist approaches, whereas those in the Transvaal and Natal were generally happy to present an Islamic message that was modern, rational, and vaguely more "relevant" to South Africa.

Muslims against Apartheid

A number of these youth groups mobilized Muslim students and masses against apartheid in the 1980s, and three prominent individuals emerged as leaders in the Islamic antiapartheid movement. Achmat Cassiem had been an outspoken activist against apartheid since his school days. But when the Islamic Revolution in Iran overthrew the shah in 1979, he formed the Qiblah Mass Movement to bring about a similar Islamic revolution in South Africa. He has remained a consistent protagonist of a mass-based struggle against oppression, first against apartheid and then, as we will see, against the new democratic regime. Ebrahim Moosa and Farid Esack, like many other South African Muslim scholars of their generation, traveled to India and Pakistan to gain a "traditional" Islamic education. On their return, neither joined the leadership organizations of the *ulama*. Instead, inspired by the student movements in the Cape and activist movements in the Indian Subcontinent, they joined the Muslim Youth Movement.

After playing a very active role in giving the Muslim Youth Movement a more overtly political slant, Farid Esack broke away when he felt that the organization was too slow in committing its resources and energies against apartheid. He has since campaigned, organizationally and intellectually, to articulate an Islamic message against oppression. As a scholar, his numerous writings justified a South African Muslim commitment to the country and particularly to the plight of the downtrodden in South Africa. Esack argues that Qiblah was overly influenced by Iranian revolutionary ideas, while the Muslim Youth Movement leaned too much toward Egyptian and Pakistani Islamist trends. Instead of either of these approaches, he championed a nationalist agenda against the foreign inspiration of the other groups (Esack 1988b). On a broader religious level, his doctoral dissertation on reading the Qur'an in the struggle against apartheid has been cited as a turning point in modern Muslim hermeneutics. Esack, following the approach of Christian liberation theology, argued that a religious text should be authentically read in struggle. Using this approach, he has called for a reconsideration of Islamic symbols and values that reject democracy and human rights (Esack 1988a, 1997).

Ebrahim Moosa, on the other hand, stayed with the Muslim Youth Movement and steered it in a similar direction. Along with the imam of the Claremont Main Road Mosque, Abdul Rashied Omar, Moosa committed the Youth

Movement to contextualized interpretations of Islam. While Esack has been provocative and challenging in the reading of the Qur'an, Moosa has matched this with an incisive and critical reading of the Islamic legal and theological traditions. Following in the footsteps of the Fazlur Rahman of Pakistan, Moosa has argued for a rethinking of the ethical and legal framework of Islam. In the context of apartheid, this implied that questions of interreligious affairs, conversion, gender, labor, and capitalism could be approached from a rereading of Islamic source texts and traditions. These broader religio-political debates became the hallmark of the Muslim Youth Movement's discussions and mobilization of youth against apartheid. In each case, Moosa argued that traditional formulations were context bound and ought to be revised in favor of more just, egalitarian interpretations (Moosa 1989, 1991, 1996b). Cassiem, Esack, and Moosa can be credited, from different vantage points, with ensuring that Islamic discourses stood side by side with other critical condemnations of apartheid. Nevertheless, it was always very clear that organizational and ideological differences among them would persist beyond apartheid.

Although Cassiem, Esack, and Moosa had numerous supporters, the Islamic rhetoric against apartheid was not unequivocal. The biggest fear dominating the Muslim community, and even some of the youth, was that the anti-apartheid movement was too big and the Islamic organizations and individuals too few to have a representational presence in the national movement. The Islamic identity of these organizations, it was argued, was in danger of becoming lost in the general antiapartheid movement. Those expressing such sentiments argued that the Islamic discourse against apartheid was excessively engaged with other non-Muslim groups (Tayob 1990). There were also suspicions of the secularist and socialist orientation of the South African liberation struggle, which lacked respect for religion in general and for Islam in particular. Much of this suspicion was nurtured by the apartheid government itself, but the feeling nonetheless coincided closely with the tendencies among those Muslim groups that adhered to a radical religious exclusivism that regarded Islam as the sole path to God.

In general, then, twentieth-century youth organizations were identifiable by two prominent features. First, although some wanted a dynamic, modern Islamic message, they feared the dilution of Islamic identity in the process. And second, these organizations were not able to completely unseat the racial construction of the Muslim subject in South Africa. Islamic religious practices, confined to racial groups, had become more visible as the apartheid state increased its hold on the society, and resistance was confined to the margins of Muslim community life. Racialized identities for Muslims in the country persisted. The normative teachings of the religious scholars, comfortably located in such racial ghettoes, were more successful in bringing about the proliferation of mosques, religious schools, and popular adherence than they were in creating programs of social transformation. Others rejected the racialized Malay and Indian identities in favor of a unifying Islamic identity. Those struggling for liberation against racism demanded that all Muslims shed their racial identities and embrace the fight against apartheid. To a greater or lesser extent, they located their vision within the broader struggle against the injustices resulting from the racialization of South African society. But they also strove to project a dynamic Islamic message that reflected the concerns and demands of a modern society. Often, the two features competed for dominance.

Postapartheid South Africa: Islam and Democracy

When negotiations began in 1990 between the white minority regime and the African National Congress, Muslims almost immediately began to discuss their future in relation to these political and social changes. A National Muslim Conference was held in the same year to discuss how Muslims should respond to the negotiations. There was no specific consensus at the conference, but the meeting marked a transition in the Muslim community as the country changed course from repression to democracy. The transition to a more open society and democracy opened the floodgates to a wide variety of views and ideologies in South Africa, and the Muslims were no exception. The increased level of freedom of religion and freedom of expression led to intense debate among the many groups and individuals representing Islam in the country. Using one of the most important pieces of legislation affecting Muslims as a religious group, this section explores some of the ways in which the South African state and its Muslim constituents have related to each other during the postapartheid period. This will be pursued by way of a discussion of issues related to the implementation of pluralistic models of personal law in a constitutional democracy. The particular legislation that will be discussed here relates to the official recognition of Muslim marriages that came before the legislature at the turn of the twenty-first century. It represents a significant change in understandings of the role and function of Islam and Islamic law in the democratic government of postapartheid South Africa. First, however, some more general remarks are required to situate these developments.

The South African constitution is unequivocal about freedom of religion and about recognizing the rights of religious communities in the society. Even though some limited forms of religious freedom were granted to minority religions under apartheid, life was characterized by suspicion toward non-Christian religions. Numerous obstacles were placed in their way, and Christian National Education was the philosophy of the nation's educational institutions. The postapartheid constitution of South Africa removed the privileged status of Christianity and granted equal recognition to all religions. The Bill of

Rights in the constitution declares that "everyone has the right to freedom of conscience, religion, thought, belief and opinion" (Article 15.1) and "persons belonging to a cultural, religious, or linguistic community may not be denied the right, with other members of that community to enjoy their culture, practice their religion and use their languages" (Article 31.1). Through these provisions, the new constitution reversed more than 300 years of institutional privileging of Christianity in South Africa.

Since 1994, Muslims have begun to enjoy some tangible benefits of this recognition and acceptance. Muslim leaders have been recognized by the state and have often been invited to open important state functions, such as presidential inaugurations. The relationship between the state and Muslim religious leadership has improved steadily since the end of apartheid. National television has provided proportional time for Muslim programming, and when radio wavelengths were made available for community radio stations, a number of communities in South Africa applied for and received licenses to broadcast Islamic programs. Muslim community radio stations in Cape Town, Johannesburg, and Durban have become extremely popular. Two such stations share a frequency in Cape Town, where Radio 786 (http://www.radio786.co.za) represents the views of Achmat Cassiem, and the Voice of the Cape, that of the Moslem Judicial Council. The Voice of the Cape in Johannesburg represents the Muslim Youth Movement and is the most progressive Islamic voice in South African radio. In contrast, The Islamic Voice, from the outskirts of Johannesburg, presents the most traditional face of Islam. In 1998, a small group of Muslims complained that this particular radio station was violating its license agreement by refusing to allow women announcers (Haffajee 1998). Also from the same township, Channel Islam (http://www.channelislam.com) broadcasts an Islamic message via satellite to a large part of Africa and Asia. Radio al Ansaar continues the tradition of guarded modernism and political conservatism of its predecessors in Durban.

The opening of South Africa's borders has seen an increasing number of Muslim immigrants from Asia and other parts of Africa. Somali refugees, Senagalese traders, and Pakistani store assistants have joined the mosaic of Muslim community life in South Africa. This new surge in Muslim immigration has been complemented by a greater contact with the global village through pilgrimage, travel, telecommunications, and media. As a result, Muslims in South Africa are increasingly exposed in myriad ways to the flow of goods, ideas, and images called globalization. These global contacts have added more nuances to Islamic religious and cultural life in South Africa than was possible during apartheid. In these contexts, the legislation on Muslim personal matters promises to have an impact on how Muslims see themselves in relation to a secular state, and a democracy.

The recognition of Islam by the constitution has translated into a number of unexpected outcomes for the Muslim community. While freedom of religion has ensured the place of Islam in an open society, freedom of expression has provided a space for debate and argument among Muslims, one that could not have been imagined before. Islamic debates during apartheid did not directly engage the state in a constructive manner. Apartheid was condemned while compromises were made with officials, but the relationship between Muslims, and in particular Islamic law, and the state was never an issue. Moreover, debates about Islam were significantly curtailed by the authoritative structures of earlier Muslim religious organizations. But the divergent discourses that were born under the struggle against apartheid were given freedom in democratic South Africa. The radio stations provide a strong indicator of this freedom in a most general sense. The state recognition of Muslim personal law illustrates the implications of this freedom for the ways Muslims read the constitution, think about the state, and extend the limits of how they relate to a democratic dispensation. Thus the legislative proposals on the recognition of Muslim marriages offers an opportunity to examine some of the most significant issues related to the development of Islam in contemporary South Africa.

The most dramatic provision for Islam in the constitution has been the recognition of Muslim marriages *or* a complete system of Muslim personal law. Article 15.3 of Freedom of Religion, Belief, and Opinion includes such a provision:

(a) This section does not prevent legislation recognizing
    (i) marriages concluded under any tradition, or a system of religious, personal or family law; *or* [my emphasis]
    (i) *systems* [my emphasis] of personal law and family law under any tradition, or adhered to by persons professing a particular religion.
(b) Recognition in terms of paragraph (a) must be consistent with this section and the other provisions of the Constitution.

In 1994, the government appointed a Muslim Personal Law Board to propose a *system* of Islamic law as provided by Article 15.3.a.ii. The board's members represented both the religious leadership and the youth organizations that were active against apartheid. The board collapsed in April 1995 when its members could not reach agreement (Moosa 1996b, 139). Recognizing the importance of the issue, the South African Law Commission appointed a project committee under the chair of Justice M. S. Navsa of the Supreme Court of Appeal. The committee appears to be enjoying greater success than the Muslim Personal Law Board. At the end of 2001, after numerous consultations and workshops, it produced for public discussion a proposed bill for recognizing Muslim marriages. The process leading to this proposed bill provides an opportunity for understanding how Muslims have responded not only to legal reform but to religious freedom, freedom of expression, and their role in a democratic state.

The Muslim Personal Law Board set about to discuss the system "of personal law and family law" allowed by the constitution. The members reached agreement on the desirability of the state's recognition of Islamic personal law. This agreement is significant because the implementation of Muslim personal law is only a small part of the Islamic legal code. The present Muslim personal law is a product of the nineteenth century, a fact that has not been lost on critics who argue that all of Islamic law should be applied. The Muslim Personal Law Board, though, agreed that Muslim personal law should be applied to Muslims in South Africa.

However, the board split into two camps over the substantive content of the law. Women's interest groups and progressive Islamic organizations insisted that the particular article in question should be read in its entirety. For them, the crux of the matter rested on the fact that the system of Islamic law implemented in the new South African state should be consistent with the "other provisions of the Constitution." Thus, they argue that the system of Muslim personal law in South Africa should be interpreted with this condition in mind. Most important, they contend that this condition should ensure an interpretation of Islamic law that would not disadvantage women. The leading and most articulate spokesperson for this new interpretation of Muslim personal law has been Ebrahim Moosa. In both academic and newspaper articles, he has argued that many traditional provisions associated with the *shari'a* should be regarded as human rulings that were produced by earlier generations of male scholars whose interpretations need no longer be held as valid (Moosa 1991, 1996a). Making a distinction between a divine and idealized *shari'a* and humanly constructed *fiqh,* Moosa argued that the latter could be reconstructed in terms of the constitution. Moosa taught and inspired students and activists to revisit traditional issues in Islamic law. Reflecting this approach, Najma Moosa, a member of the new project committee, concurred: "Muslims can only give practical legal effect to the Constitution if due recognition is given to a *reformed* [my emphasis] MPL [Muslim personal law] and its implementation" (Moosa 1998, 201). With Ebrahim Moosa in the lead, a strong and principled voice thus emerged for a significant reformulation of Islamic law.

Nevertheless, his view was not acceptable to all the members of the Muslim Personal Law Board. Before looking at the key counterarguments, however, it would be important to note that the innovative definitions and interpretations were facing not only traditionalist rejections. The landmark case of *Rylands v. Edross* in 1996 had raised the issue of the interpretation of Islamic law in court. The judgment revealed the impact of the new constitution, then still an interim constitution, on the recognition of Islamic mores in South African society. The case involved a woman who demanded a fair share in the conjugal estate at the time of divorce. The marriage had been conducted only according to Islamic rites and without state recognition. The judge appealed to the interim constitution in turning against a long-standing legal tradition that considered Muslim marriages potentially polygamous and thus against the dominant social norms of society. Since the constitution recognized the pluralist nature of South African society, the judge felt comfortable in extending legal recognition to Muslim marriages:

> Can it be said, since the coming into operation of the new Constitution, that a contract concluded by parties which arises from a marriage relationship entered into by them in accordance with the rites of their religion and which in fact is monogamous is "contrary to the accepted customs and usages which are regarded as morally binding upon *all* members of our society" or is "fundamentally opposed to our principles and institutions"? I think not. (*Rylands v. Edross* 1996, 708)

The judge in this case was referring to a precedent involving an Islamic marriage that was heard in 1983 in South Africa (*Ismail v. Ismail* 1983 [1] SA 1006 [A]). In that case, the court refused to recognize a Muslim marriage on the grounds that it was "potentially polygamous" and thus "void on grounds of public policy." In doing so, the judge noted the change brought about to the values of public policy by the Bill of Rights in the new constitution.

But he then had to consider the issue of how to interpret this particular ruling of Islamic law with regard to property acquired during an Islamic marriage. The contentious issue raised in the case was whether or not the wife was entitled to an equitable share of the property accumulated by the husband during the marriage. Two competing interpretations were presented to him. The first, led by Ebrahim Moosa on behalf of the plaintiff (the wife), argued that a Malaysian precedent had been established that property acquired during marriage should be equitably shared. The Malaysian case was based on a synthesis of Islamic law and local custom *(adat)*. Such coexistence of Islamic law and local custom is not unusual in Islamic communities, but only in Malaysia was such a synthesis officially recognized by courts of law. Moosa argued that such an approach ought to be followed in South Africa as well.

On the other hand, Alie Moosagie, the expert witness on behalf of the defendant (the husband), presented the opposing viewpoint that such a condition of matrimonial property was not implied in Islamic law. He asserted that Islamic law should be applied irrespective of any contextual application and interpretation, and he did not present a counterargument to the contextual application espoused by Moosa. The judge picked up this nuance and insisted on a relevant South African custom. Since the Malaysian case depended on a particular customary practice, the judge insisted on finding a similar practice in the Western Cape. In the absence of such a custom, conceded by both Moosa and Moosagie, the application was turned down:

> In view of the fact that no other Islamic country, on Dr Moosa's own evidence, adopts this approach, I cannot see on what basis I can regard the Malaysian rules as being part of the provisions of Islamic personal law incorporated by the parties into their contract unless a custom similar to the Malay *adat* relating to *harta sepencarian* prevails among the Islamic community, to which the parties belong, in the Western Cape. (*Rylands v. Edross* 1996)

Thus, from the judge's point of view, the recognition of Islamic law in South African courts would have to reflect the norms and values of the local South African Muslim community. The learned judge was not prepared to simply reinterpret Islamic law in terms of the Bill of Rights. The recognition of Islamic law in the constitution bound the judges to the norms and practices of South African society. As the case opened the debate to a contextual interpretation, the existing context of South Africa had to be reflected in any novel interpretation. Thus, in the absence of actual legislation, a reformed approach to Islamic law did not stand much chance of success. The judgment was a landmark case in that it extended a constitutional recognition to Muslim marriages as such. However, it also indicated that innovative interpretations of Islamic law were bound to face challenges from certain sectors of South African society. This is a crucial point that has proved very important in subsequent proposed legislation.

The majority of the Muslim Personal Law Board members rejected the new interpretations offered by Moosa and his supporters. They raised two important objections to the new interpretations. First, some Muslims felt that a parallel legal system for Muslims should be tolerated. And second, it was felt that Muslim personal law should not be subservient to the Bill of Rights of the national constitution. The judge was correct in assuming that most Muslims believed that Muslim personal law, as a part of the *shari'a,* was divine and thus not susceptible to change and interpretation, particularly with regard to issues clearly stated in the Qur'an and the *sunna* of the Prophet. In response to the charge that the "system" be subject to the Bill of Rights in general, some of the proponents suggested that a system of legal pluralism be adopted by the South African constitution. Abdul-Karriem Toffar, a Muslim religious scholar from Cape Town, rejected a secular constitution that made provision for an Islamic juridical system, arguing that "it is ludicrous to suppose that our family and personal law will function properly according to Shari'ah in the present set-up" (Toffar A.H. 1422/2001, 18). Citing the model of Singapore, he called for a completely separate judicial system for Muslims under a regime that does not impose its secularism on Muslims:

> This is practical, guaranteed, just and fair minority rights in action and avoids the application of the abuse and cruelty of the democracy of numbers—a seemingly inherited phenomenon in virtually all democracies. One may wonder why the aforementioned system [of Singapore] is not considered seriously. Instead, systems of a secular imposed value and administrative system appear to receive apparent favour. (Toffar A.H. 1422/2001, 19)

This appeal to legal pluralism was a popular option because it seemed to indicate that Islamic law would not be forced to adapt and change. For different reasons, Ebrahim Moosa supported such a notion against a uniform, authoritarian legal code, but not one ranged against civil liberties and the inherent equality between men and women (Moosa 1996b, 150). The idea of a parallel legal system appeared attractive, but it neatly avoided the conflict between human rights and Islamic law that had already been raised in public discourse (Cachalia 1991, 48). Legal pluralism remained an idealized option, but the calls for a new interpretation of Islamic law from a human rights perspective marked the difference between the views of Toffar and Moosa.

Without calling for a separate parallel system of Muslim Personal law as Toffar did, other Muslims have also appealed to the Limitation of Rights within the constitution: "the rights in the Bill of Rights may be limited only in terms of law or general application to the extent that the limitation is reasonable and justifiable in an open and democratic society based on human dignity, equality and freedom" (Article 36.1). Those who advocated a system of law directly taken from the books of *fiqh* for the South African legislature argued that the limitation clause should apply to Muslim personal law. The interim constitution may have given the impression that customary or religious laws pertaining to personal matters would not be subject to a Bill of Rights, and Toffar believed that the absence of a specific clause such as 15.3.b cited above should guide the interpretation of Muslim personal law in the interim constitution. This particular model was followed in Zimbabwe, where personal laws originating from customary practices were exempt from equality provisions in the rest of the constitution. According to Najma Moosa, such a presumption was plausible but unacceptable in the interim constitution (Moosa 1998, 202). To clear any such presumption, the final South African constitution specified the limits of Muslim personal law by introducing the limitation clause under Article 15.

While Ebrahim Moosa and others argued that elements of Muslim personal law would have to take into consideration the principles of the constitution, and accordingly revised, neotraditionalist religious scholars generally resisted such reinterpretation under any circumstances. The Muslim Personal Law Board collapsed in the face of this irreconcilable difference in outlook. The new committee entrusted with formulating a solution faced a difficult task.

From the perspective of many progressive organizations, the committee was mainly composed of individuals who supported more-traditionalist interpretations of Islam. From the point of view of religious leaders, the committee appeared certain to produce a bill that conformed to the constitution. Thus, it seemed that the committee was bound to disappoint both. And yet the committee eventually produced a document that appears consistent with the constitution, agreeable to at least some members of the conservative religious bodies, and responsive to the concerns of women's groups. The proposed act, therefore, demands an explanation of how the project committee was able to arrive at such a compromise between radical reform and tradition. The committee's approach seems to indicate a unique stance toward the constitution and towards the general problem of the nonrecognition of Muslim marriages.

By releasing a piece of legislation entitled "Islamic Marriages and Related Affairs," the project committee apparently gave up the attempt to propose "legislation recognising systems of personal or family law" (Article 15.3.a.ii), as the earlier Muslim Personal Law Board had done. Such an approach had opened up ideological differences that could not easily be settled. They were reflections of global Islamic debates, for which there were no immediate resolutions on the horizon in South Africa or elsewhere. Instead, the committee opted to develop the first provision for "legislation recognising marriages concluded under any tradition" (Article 15.3.a.i). There is a subtle difference between the two, and the constitution has an important disjunction ("or") between the two clauses. The earlier attempt of the Muslim Personal Law Board was bogged down in the development of a comprehensive *system* of personal law. According to Najma Moosa, also a member of the committee, nothing short of a complete code would have been acceptable: "MPL should be codified into a separate code of law which would form part of the statutory law of the South African legal system," and the best solution lay "in codifying Islamic law and enacting a comprehensive bill or 'uniform Muslim code'" (Moosa 1998, 201, n. 36).

By rejecting this approach, the new committee came to directly address the critical problem of Muslim marriages in South Africa, a source of a great many social problems. Muslim marriages conducted by imams in the mosques were not recognized until the promulgation of the constitution. Even in the new dispensation, however, effective court decisions were hamstrung in the absence of legislation. In the apartheid days, as pointed out above, Muslim marriages were considered "potentially polygamous" and hence repugnant to the Western cultural norms adopted by South African courts (Moosa 1996b). By choosing to abandon or sidestep the ideological debate in favor of the actual needs of the society, the proposed bill suggested a unique approach. The approach of the committee confirmed an important democratic principle of working from concerns and issues that directly affected people. The ideological and theological debates tended to obscure the issues of recognition that the constitution sought to address in the first place. By directly addressing the source of the grievances in South Africa at grassroots level, the project committee made a significant breakthrough in this matter.

A few examples from the proposed legislation illustrate the interface between human rights and social mores in the new South Africa. One of the significant issues affecting customary marriages concerns the appropriate marriageable age, particularly for girls, and this is true of Islamic marriages as well. The legislation proposes consent on the part of both spouses as well as a mandated minimum marriageable age of eighteen. However, in view of the fact that Islamic law does not specifically prohibit marriage under that age, the legislation allows for the possibility of appealing to the minister of justice for permission to marry younger. It even goes further by making it possible for marriages conducted between minors to be declared valid after the fact. The guiding principle seems to be a reasonable age (eighteen), but with sufficient possibilities for allowing minors to marry under certain conditions. And most important, the implication of such a provision is that marriage between minors could immediately follow. A similar reasoning seems to be at work in the case of registering marriages. Again, it is not absolutely essential according to Islamic law to formally register a marriage in any particular institution. The proposed act thus insists that all marriages should be registered, but it allows for the possibility of recognizing all Muslim marriages whether they are registered or not.

A connected issue arose in the early debates within the Muslim community concerning the issue of polygyny. The initial proposed legislation did not completely outlaw polygyny; rather, it insisted that permission for a husband to contract a second marriage can only be given by the courts. Such permission could be granted if the following three conditions were met:

1. The husband has sufficient financial means;
2. There is no reason to believe, if permission is granted, that the husband shall not act equitably toward his wives;
3. There will be no prejudice toward existing wives.

Each of these conditions is regarded as being implied in Qur'anic verses pertaining to this issue. Moreover, they are the kind of conditions that Muslims in South Africa would customarily expect to be fulfilled before a polygynous marriage would be acceptable under existing social norms. However, traditionally such conditions are rarely given the kind of scrutiny that some thought the legislation was bringing into effect. The proposed legislation also adds a further feature by insisting that in the event of such a second marriage within an existing marriage, the financial impact of an additional spouse must immediately be assessed on the existing marriage. Under these stipulations, failure to obtain permission for a second marriage is subject to a fine of 50,000 rands.

The project committee's approach to these issues indicates a breakthrough in the broader debates over Islam and democracy. The earlier Muslim Personal Law Board did not simply break down on conflicting readings of the constitution, for their differing readings of the constitution were signs of some deeper misgivings relating to the place of Muslims and Islam in a secular democracy. This tendency was most evident in Toffar's approach (discussed above). While Muslims were enjoying the fruits of an open society and taking advantage thereof, they were also exposed to a wide variety of modern interpretations of Islam that regarded democracy as anathema. The dominant tendency in that discourse rejected democracy as a man-made system that potentially or actually violated the terms of the *shari'a*.

These ideological challenges initially seemed intractable, as powerful Muslim groups on the streets of Cape Town and allied voices in the media openly advocated a rejection of democracy and the South African constitution in the name of Islam. With Muslims constituting less than 2 percent of the population, others in the community saw the talk of an Islamic state as totally inappropriate. But as participants in a global arena where Islamic ideas were shared, some Muslims who held such notions received support among some sectors of the Muslim community in South Africa (Esack 1988b; Tayob 1999a).

PAGAD and Politics

In this context, the rise of one organization in particular has dominated the perceptions on Islam and democracy in South Africa in recent years. Since 1996, the People against Gangsterism and Drugs (PAGAD) movement has emerged as a powerful pressure group in the country. Even though PAGAD is not a political movement in the strictest sense of the term, its ultimate motivation seems to be the vision of a religious or "theocratic" Islamic state. It was ostensibly founded to rid the Cape of the scourge of gangsters and drugs. Eventually, it is believed, PAGAD was infiltrated by Qiblah operatives hoping to lead an Islamist campaign against the new democratic order of South Africa (Rossouw 1996). A leader and one of PAGAD's principal speakers at rallies and marches has been Achmat Cassiem, who felt that the promised Islamic revolution of the 1980s had not yet advanced in his own country. Drawing parallels between apartheid and the democratic state in its treatment of PAGAD supporters, Cassiem legitimized violence against the new government. According to a leading journalist, Cassiem and the militant PAGAD members have no regard for democracy and its values: "Underpinning this is a conviction that the current government is as illegitimate as the past one [that is, the apartheid

A march against violence on the Cape Flats, Cape Town, South Africa, August 21, 2001.
(Cape Argus *newspaper, courtesy of Abdulkader Tayob*)

state]. In Cassiem's political philosophy, no secular state can be legitimate" (Gevisser 1996). According to some observers, PAGAD's interpretation of Islam is essentially and inherently fundamentalist, and the underlying motive of Muslim support and sympathy for PAGAD seems to confirm this Islamist rejection of the democratic order (Mattes 1996; Rossouw 1996).

PAGAD's mobilization of Muslims in Cape Town led to open clashes between its paramilitary "G-Force" and criminal gangs. PAGAD accused the police of involvement with the drug lords and with protecting their territories, and it has not hesitated to turn its anger against the state as well. Responsibility for a series of bomb blasts has been laid at the organization's door, and some of its leading members have been convicted for other instances of public violence. Although PAGAD pleads its innocence on all counts, its rhetoric and slogans have confirmed its radical Islamist orientation. More important, its approach to the state has reinforced the perception that those whom they would regard as "true" and devout Muslims cannot reconcile democratic values with their faith.

Many Muslims' attitudes toward PAGAD have changed over the past few years. Earlier unconditional support has turned to cautious support and sympathy only for its goals of eradicating illegal drugs and gangs from the streets of Cape Town. Doubts about PAGAD's motives grew as its members were arrested and as its spokespersons revealed their political motives in the campaign. But PAGAD also generated an intense conflict between the organization and Muslim leaders. Most Muslim religious leaders and intellectuals have argued that the organization does not express the views of Islam or of Muslims on religious and political matters. The Muslim responses to PAGAD, particularly in the Western Cape, have been quite significant in the eventual marginalization of the movement, for many religious leaders, who initially spoke at PAGAD rallies, slowly withdrew their support.

On the other hand, a number of Muslim intellectuals have been outspokenly critical of PAGAD's threat to the new democratic state. As critics of PAGAD's approach, they also accused the government of ignoring the roots of the Islamic rage in the colored townships of Cape Town. Farid Esack has been one of the most vociferous in his condemnation of PAGAD and its attacks on the state. As an appointed member of the Commission of Gender Equality from 1996 to 2001, Esack has been alarmed at PAGAD's attacks on the state, and in response he has defended South African democratic institutions in numerous newspaper columns and scholarly articles. Feeling the effects of its shrinking support among the Muslim community, PAGAD launched a series of attacks on leaders of the Muslim Judicial Council and key intellectuals. Ebrahim Moosa's house was attacked with a pipe bomb in 1998, and a number of religious leaders were abused and attacked. The debate between PAGAD, on the one hand, and the religious scholars and intellectuals, on the other, slowly drove a wedge between PAGAD and the majority of South African Muslims. The reaction to PAGAD's militant Islamism from both religious leaders and intellectuals has given rise to a powerful prodemocratic voice within South African Islam.

The legislation concerning the recognition of Muslim marriages can be viewed as a counter trend to PAGAD's antidemocratic discourse. The proposed legislation on Muslim personal law has the potential to change perceptions about democracy within the Muslim community, especially by reassuring Muslims, who have been hesitant, as a religious group, to endorse the democratic regime. Keeping in mind the progressive legal developments toward democratic reform, even the PAGAD phenomenon might be seen as a blessing in disguise. For although there has been much media coverage of PAGAD and Islamic fundamentalism, the state has chosen to follow an open legal process in bringing criminal cases related to the group's activities to trial. This approach has minimized the potential appeal of a radical Islamist approach in contemporary South Africa. In contrast to the political and ideological debates surrounding PAGAD's activities, the legislative process against the group's supporters and the legislative proposals on Muslim personal law have the potential to set deeper roots for human rights values in Muslim homes. The proposed legislation has recognized Muslim marriages and addressed issues of equity and justice in everyday practices on multiple levels. These vital discussions of rights and obligations between the state and Muslim interests have the potential for showing human rights and democracy at work with religious ideals in a pluralistic society. Without being too optimistic about the legal system, it can be said that the proposed legislation is a significant landmark for Muslims and democracy in South Africa. Thus, PAGAD and its committed supporters should be regarded as only one voice in the South African Muslim debate, and its undertones against democracy as a minority view within the country.

Conclusion

The history of Islam in South Africa is a fascinating story of ways religious values in the contexts of slavery, freedom, colonialism, apartheid, and now democracy have shaped aspects of contemporary Muslim life. The Muslim community in South Africa is small, but its experiences present a story of resilience and creativeness in the face of tremendous odds. Over the course of its history, institutions were established, organizations formed, global contacts cultivated, and ideologies imported. The nineteenth century may be regarded as the period of institutionalization, while the twentieth century witnessed diverse developments in responses to apartheid and democracy. The earlier racialization of the Muslims was countered by a greater degree of awareness of and adherence to Islamic practices as the foundations of communal identity. The South African Muslim community has also produced a space and context for critical debates and innovative developments in its encounters with the ongoing processes of modernization. Their experiences as a Muslim-minority community living in a secular democracy has thrown the community into global debates about Islam and democracy. It may be too premature to judge, but there are signs that the experience of Islam in South Africa may have much to offer for the future development of Muslims in secular democracies that are not inherently hostile to religion. The recognition of Muslim personal law in the country has gone through some difficult times, but I have argued that the experiences of South African Muslims with the constitution may offer some valuable insights on human rights and religious values in the contemporary world.

Notes

1.   For more on Achmat van Bengalen and the history of the "Malay" Muslim community at the Cape, see Davids 1980.

References

Adams, C. 1968. "Muhammad 'Abduh and Transvaal Fatwa." In *The Macdonald Presentation Volume,* edited by W. G. Shellabear, 13–29. Freeport, NY: Books for Libraries Press (Princeton University Press).

Cachalia, F. 1991. *The Future of Muslim Family in South Africa*. With a foreword by Albie Sachs. University of the Witwatersrand, Occasional Paper 12. Johannesburg: Centre for Applied Legal Studies, University of the Witwatersrand Press.

Davids, Achmat. 1980. *The Mosques of Bo-Kaap: A Social History of Islam at the Cape*. Cape Town: South African Institute of Arabic and Islamic Research.

———. 1985. *From Complacency to Activism: The Changing Political Mood of the Cape Muslims from 1940–1945*. Cape Town: Centre for African Studies Workshop.

Esack, F. 1988a. *The Struggle*. Cape Town: Call of Islam.

———. 1988b. "Three Islamic Strands in the South African Struggle for Justice." *Third World Quarterly* 10 (April 2): 473–498.

———. 1997. *Qur'an, Liberation, and Pluralism: An Islamic Perspective of Interreligious Solidarity against Oppression*. Oxford: Oneworld.

Gevisser, M. 1996. "The Imam of the Flats." *Mail and Guardian*, August 16–22.

Haffajee, F. 1998. "Gender War Becomes a Radio Jihad." *Weekly Mail and Guardian*, January 16. http://web.sn.apc.org/wmail/issues/980116/NEWS10.html.

Jeppie, M. S. 1987. "Historical Process and the Constitution of Subjects: I. D. du Plessis and There-Invention of the 'Malay.'" PhD diss., University of Cape Town.

Mattes, R. B. 1996. "PAGAD: Collective Action against Crime." Paper presented at the Research Colloquium: South African Political Studies Association Conference, Hunter's Rest, Rustenburg, October 10–11.

Moosa, E. 1989. "Muslim Conservatism in South Africa." *Journal of Theology for Southern Africa*, December: 69, 73–81.

———. 1991. "Religion and Human Rights: Taking Rights Religiously." Paper presented at the Contribution of South African Religions to the Coming South Africa Conference, Pietermaritzburg, University of Natal, September 15–17.

———. 1996a. "Government Failure Led to Rise of Pagad." *Cape Times*, August 19.

———. 1996b. "Prospects of Muslim Law in South Africa: A History and Recent Developments." In *Yearbook of Islamic and Middle Eastern Law*, edited by E. Cotran and C. Mallat, vol. 3, 130–155. London: Kluwer Law International.

Moosa, N. 1998. "The Interim and Final Constitutions and Muslim Personal Law— Implications for South African Muslim Women." *Stellenbosch Law Review Regtydskrif* 9, no. 2: 196–206.

Naude, J. A. 1982. "The 'Ulama' in South Africa with Special Reference to the Transvaal 'Ulama.'" *Journal for Islamic Studies* 2: 23–39.

Rossouw, R. 1996. "Holy Warriors behind Pagad." *Mail and Guardian*, August 16–22.

Rylands v. Edross. 1996. (2) SA 690 (C). 1997, 691–719. Cape Provincial Division.

Shell, R. C. 1984. "Rites and Rebellion: Islamic Conversion at the Cape, 1808 to 1915." *Studies in the History of Cape Town* 5: 1–46.

Tayob, A. I. 1990. "Muslims' Discourse on Alliance against Apartheid." *Journal for the Study of Religion* 3, no. 2: 31–47.

———. 1995. *Islamic Resurgence in South Africa: The Muslim Youth Movement*. Cape Town: UCT Press.

———. 1999a. "The Function of Islam in the South African Political Process: Defining a Community in a Nation." In *Religion and Politics in South Africa: From Apartheid to Democracy*, edited by A. Tayob and W. Weisse, 15–27. Munich: Waxmann.

————. 1999b. *Islam in South Africa: Mosques, Imams, and Sermons.* Gainesville: University of South Florida Press.

Toffar, A. K. A.H. 1422/2001. "The Qur'anic Constitution and Its Expression in Law— A Legal Dilemma in a Non-Muslim State." *Occasional Journal of ICOSA* 2: 1–20.

United Kingdom. Parliament. 1968–1971. Papers relative to the condition and treatment of the native inhabitants of the Cape of Good Hope. Colbrooke and Bigge Commission Report of 1825. In *British Parliamentary Papers; Colonies: Africa,* v. 20; xxxxix (50) and (252), 207–210. Irish University Press Series. Shannon: Irish University Press.

Vahed, G. H. 2001. "Mosques, Mawlanas, and Muharram: Indian Islam in Colonial Natal, 1860–1910." *Journal of Religion in Africa* 31, no. 3: 305–335.

Chapter Ten

Peril and Possibility

Muslim Life in the United States

E D W A R D   E.   C U R T I S   IV

Immediately after the September 11, 2001, tragedies in New York, Washington, and Pennsylvania, U.S. Muslim leaders rushed to condemn the attacks and to help the victims. Muslim academics and religious leaders argued that the wanton violence was un-Islamic, that it violated the fundamental principles of Islam and the hundreds-of-years-old traditions of *shari'a* (Islamic law). In addition to issuing statements of condemnation and sympathy, Muslim organizations like the Islamic Society of North America (ISNA) and the Council on American-Islamic Relations (CAIR) helped organize blood drives and relief funds on behalf of the victims. At the same time, Muslim leaders appealed for calm, expressing their fears that U.S. Muslims might themselves be the victims of anti-Muslim backlash and hate crimes.

Unfortunately, their fears were realized. In the days following the events of 9/11, several Muslims, or those who just "looked like" Muslims, were attacked. On September 15, 2001, Hassan Waqir, a Dallas convenience store owner, was gunned down. On the same day, Balbir Sodhi, a Sikh man who was apparently mistaken for a Muslim, was killed at his place of work in Mesa, Arizona, and Adel Karas, an Arab Christian, was murdered in his import shop in San Gabriel, California. Others who may have been the victims of hate crimes following 9/11 included Ali al-Mansoop, Ali W. Ali, Abdullah Mohammed, Surjit Singh Samra, Abdo Ali Ahmed, and Vasudev Patel. There were other forms of anti-Muslim violence, as well, including physical assaults, bomb and arson attacks, and attacks on mosques across the country.

Over the next several months, some prominent evangelical Christian leaders added to what was already a challenging environment for Muslims in the United States, expressing views that alarmed many in the Muslim community.

The Reverend Jerry Vines, a former Southern Baptist Convention president, called the Prophet Muhammad a "demon-possessed pedophile." The Reverend Pat Robertson, the popular television host of the *700 Club*, declared Islam to be a religion of war, arguing that "the Qur'an makes it very clear, if you see an infidel, you are to kill him." And Franklin Graham, the son of the Reverend Billy Graham, called Islam "evil and wicked."

At the same time, many non-Muslim Americans, including other Christian leaders, disowned such views. President George W. Bush visited a mosque in downtown Washington, D.C., where he declared,

> The face of terror is not the true faith of Islam. That's not what Islam is all about. Islam is peace. These terrorists don't represent peace. They represent evil and war. When we think of Islam we think of a faith that brings comfort to a billion people around the world. Billions of people find comfort and solace and peace. And that's made brothers and sisters out of every race—out of every race. (Bush 2001)

In addition to such statements of support, a large number of Americans, of all faiths and of no faith at all, visited a mosque for the first time, supported interfaith dialogues, and reached out to Muslim neighbors. In San Antonio, Texas, dozens of people lined up to eat at a Persian restaurant that had been attacked; the owners temporarily installed plywood in place of their broken glass windows and proudly displayed over a dozen U.S. flags. In Toledo, Ohio, 2,000 people joined hands with Chereffe Kadri, the female president of the Islamic Center, and prayed around the mosque, whose stain-glass windows had been damaged by gunfire. And these are just illustrative examples of many acts of kindness and concern.

After 9/11, then, Muslims in the United States faced not only unprecedented challenges but also unprecedented opportunities. Many more non-Muslim Americans began to understand what U.S. Muslims had always known—that their presence in the United States is defined simultaneously by possibility and peril. As religious and often racial minorities in the United States, Muslims have known the horrible face of U.S. xenophobia, racism, sexism, and now, "Islamophobia." Many, especially African American Muslims, have also suffered from a lack of economic and educational opportunities. But Muslims in the United States have also managed to respond creatively to these challenges, building their own sense of community and forging ties with many outside the Muslim community. They have established political and self-help organizations, constructed their own places of worship, operated their own schools, and committed themselves to a wide array of vibrant Islamic religious practices.

Because this chapter is written in a time of peril and possibility, it is informed by a desire to contribute to understanding and dialogue rather than to

Muslims leaving the Islamic Center in Washington, D.C. (Catherine Karnow/Corbis)

despair and fear. The chapter begins with an analysis of the historical roots of anti-Muslim prejudice. It then offers a historical overview of Muslim diversity in the United States, focusing on both indigenous and immigrant Muslim communities. It concludes with an examination of contemporary Muslim life, exploring such key issues as Muslims and the state, contests over Muslim identity, and gender and Islam.

Anti-Muslim Prejudice in the United States

From colonial times to the middle of the 1900s, many Americans were alternately allured and repulsed by images of the Muslim Orient, which was often associated with political despotism, sexual excess, and cultural backwardness. A surprising number of U.S. literary works and genres discussed various elements of Islamic history and culture. For example, Washington Irving, the famous author of "Rip Van Winkle" and "The Legend of Sleepy Hollow," wrote a book about Muslim Spain called *The Alhambra* (1832) and a biography of the Prophet Muhammad (1850). During the 1800s, as a number of American male elites journeyed to the Christian Holy Land in Palestine, they also recorded their impressions of Middle Eastern Muslims in popular travelogues. For some, the chance to travel to the Middle East became an opportunity to affirm their male identities; they fantasized about and even imagined themselves as Turkish sultans who dominated exotic Oriental women at will. By the 1920s, the exotic Muslim Orient would also serve as an imaginative space for American women's sexual fantasy, as well. One of the most popular movies of that decade was *The Sheik* (1921), starring the olive-skinned and sensual Rudolf Valentino, a movie star who was particularly popular among the liberated "new women" of that era.

Islam also provided material for the symbolic and ritual acts of U.S. fraternal organizations. In the late 1800s, thousands of white and later African American males joined the Shriners, a fraternal organization that traced its imagined lineage to the "Grand Shaykh" of Mecca and to Sufism, the mystical branch of Islam. These Shriners, who are famous today both for driving small cars in the nation's street parades and for supporting a number of charities, donned Turkish fezzes and used a number of Islamic symbols in their lodge rites.

Some Christian Americans, however, saw Islam as a misguided religious tradition, a Christian heresy, and even a sign of the anti-Christ. In so doing, Americans reproduced centuries-old stereotypes of Islam that had emerged in Christian Europe at the time of the Crusades. The Prophet Muhammad was the object of much of this prejudice, which continued into late medieval and modern times. For example, Dante, the great Italian author of *The Divine Com-*

edy, placed Muhammad in the ninth circle of hell, where he was punished by being split from his anus to his chin in perpetuity. While such violent images of the Prophet did not always consume the U.S. Christian imagination, Muhammad was nevertheless considered to be violent and oversexed and was seen as spiritually a charlatan. At various points in the 1800s, images of Islam and its false prophet became important to those Christians who expected the imminent return of Christ. In fact, the demise of Ottoman Turkish power in the last half of the century was seen by some as a sign of the Second Coming of Christ.

What is striking about all these U.S. images of Islam is that they were often imaginary encounters between Muslims and non-Muslims. With few exceptions, real human contact between Muslims and non-Muslims in the United States was quite rare. In 1893, however, the World Parliament of Religions invited a Muslim to represent Islam at its Chicago, Illinois, assembly. Their choice was Mohammed Alexander Russell Webb, a Euro-American convert to the faith, but the decision to reach out to non-Christians expressed at least an interest in interacting with persons of other faiths. At the same time, the underlying and sometimes publicly voiced interest in world religions was, for some, the result of a missionary impulse to convert others to Christianity.

After World War II, the relationships between the U.S. government and key Muslim nations would increasingly be defined by political, economic, and military conflict. During the cold war between the United States and the Soviet Union, the U.S. government generally opposed political regimes that refused to side with the United States in its conflict with the U.S.S.R., even if the country only wanted to remain neutral. Moreover, the United States was implicated in the overthrow of several Third World governments, including, for example, that of Prime Minister Mohammad Mosaddeq of Iran in 1953. In addition, the United States generally sided with Israel in its conflicts with its Arab neighbors, contributing to anti-American feeling in many Muslim countries.

Increasingly, many Americans came to see Muslims and Islam as a potential enemy, despite the fact that the religion of Islam seemed to have little to do with the root causes of various conflicts. For example, in 1973 and 1974, the Organization of Petroleum Exporting Countries (OPEC), a global oil cartel led by Arab nations, refused to export oil to the United States because of U.S. military support for Israel during the 1973 Arab-Israeli War. As Americans waited for hours to fill up their gas tanks or simply stopped driving their cars altogether, many became more and more resentful of the "oil sheiks" who had turned off the gas spigots. Political cartoonists depicted these sheiks, as some artists had portrayed Jewish bankers decades before, as ugly, hooked-nosed, miserly men who conspired to rule the world. Then, in 1979, revolutionaries led by Ayatollah Ruhollah Khomeini overthrew the government of the U.S.-backed shah of Iran and held dozens of Americans hostage for over a year. After unsuccessful negotiations and a failed rescue attempt, many Americans felt frustrated and even enraged by the country's seeming inability to bring home its citizens. Walter Cronkite, who was known as the most trusted news anchor in the United States, would end the *CBS Evening News* each night by reminding his audience of how many days the hostages had been held in captivity.

Though the hostages were freed just as President Ronald Reagan was being inaugurated in 1981, Americans would once again receive bad news from the Middle East the next year. In 1982, President Reagan intervened in the Lebanese civil war, sending U.S. naval ships and Marines to Beirut. When the Marines' barracks were bombed, hundreds of U.S. soldiers died. For some Americans, it brought back painful memories not only of the hostage crisis in Iran but also of the U.S. loss in the Vietnam War. This time, however, it was not Southeast Asians but Middle Eastern Muslims who were seen as the enemy. Such feelings would only increase in the 1991 Gulf War against Iraqi president Saddam Hussein, a former U.S. ally who had invaded the kingdom of Kuwait.

These less-than-peaceful and harmonious international relations helped breathe life into the old European Christian stereotype of Islam as violent and irrational. The conflicts also fueled the imaginations of some scholars, who feared that the menace of communism, a failed political project by the 1990s, would be replaced by an "Islamic threat." Famously, Samuel P. Huntington predicted a "clash of civilizations" between the West and an alliance of Islamic and East Asian cultures. Others, like Steven Emerson, focused on the enemy at home, attempting to portray various U.S. Muslims as potential terrorists. This type of alarmism only increased after 9/11 and may have helped produce the environment in which retributive violence and hate crimes against Muslims occurred.

A History of U.S. Muslim Diversity

Although negative images of Islam have had an impact on Muslims, they reflect little about the day-to-day realities of Muslim life either in the United States or abroad. Muslims in the United States are and always have been an incredibly diverse group. In a community of 2 million to 8 million U.S. Muslims—estimates vary greatly—there is no one dominant organization, race or ethnicity, or school of thought. While African Americans are often thought to make up the largest ethnic-racial group of Muslims in the United States, those who trace their roots to South Asia (especially India and Pakistan) may be just as numerous. Various studies estimate that 25–40 percent of all Muslims in the United States are black Americans. South Asians may account for up to 30 percent. The third largest ethnic-racial group is probably Arab Americans, those who trace their lineage to Arabic-speaking countries in the Middle East and North Africa. They may represent another 25 percent of the community. Ultimately, however, numerical estimates such as these have limited value in understanding the various guises of Muslim American life. In telling the story of Muslims in the United States, one cannot afford to exclude the voices of the comparatively smaller numbers of Iranian Americans, Bosnians, Turks, Afghanis, West Africans, Latinos, whites, and others who are members of the Muslim community.

U.S. Muslims are diverse not only in race or ethnicity but also in class, gender, sexual orientation, linguistic group, national origin, and religious practice. Muslims in the United States adhere to a wide a variety of Sunni, Shi'ite, and Sufi religious practices. In addition, some Muslims practice forms of Islam that many Muslims in other parts of the world would not recognize as "Islamic," including, for example, Minister Louis Farrakhan's Nation of Islam. Muslims also use a wide variety of sacred spaces for their religious practices. The mosque, while vitally important, is not always the center of communal religious practices. Other sites include the home, the Sufi lodge, inner-city streets, schools, and even nightclubs (for Muslim rappers, for example).

Muslim religious diversity cannot be explained merely by pointing out doctrinal differences; it requires knowledge of the history of Muslim communities in America—a history that is as old as the New World itself. Most of the Muslims who first came to the Americas were West African slaves. Although it is difficult to estimate the number of slaves who were Muslim, some scholars believe as many as 10–20 percent of all slaves brought to the Americas practiced some form of Islam. It makes sense that at least some slaves would have been Muslims, since the number of Muslim converts in West Africa grew rapidly during the time of the slave trade. Some of these Muslims were urbane and literate merchants, travelers, and *marabouts*, or mystics. Some had memorized the Arabic Qur'an by heart. In the Americas, these persons maintained their Arabic literacy by reading Arabic New Testaments given to them by Christian missionaries and by purchasing expensive supplies of paper to practice their writing. Among Muslims from the Yoruba region of West Africa in Bahia, Brazil, Arabic was used as a secret language in planning revolts during the first half of the 1800s.

How many black Muslims continued to practice Islam in British North America and the United States, however, is difficult to know. In general, historians have uncovered more evidence of Muslim practices in places where slaves lived in isolated or predominately black areas, or where there were more first- or second-generation African Americans. For example, in the 1900s, oral historians collected tales of several Muslims who continued to practice some form of Islam on the islands off of the Georgia coast. Sahih Bilali of Saint Simons Island, for example, was known to have fasted. Bilali Mohamed of Sapelo Island used a Muslim prayer rug and wore a fez. And the names of Gullah children sometimes showed Muslim influence. In the 1830s, Omar ibn

Sayyid, a North Carolinian slave originally from Futa Toro on the Senegal River, penned his autobiography in Arabic. Though he claimed to have been a baptized Christian for some years, he included a dedication in the work not only to God but also to the Prophet Muhammad. Whether he was hiding his true Muslim identity or had combined his Islam with his Christianity is unknown. But it does indicate the continued influence of Islam on his consciousness well after his conversion to Christianity.

On the whole, however, there is little direct evidence in North America for the large-scale practice of Islam among slaves. While some slaves may have brought their Islamic religion with them to North America, the meaning and function of their Islamic religious practices may have changed once they landed on American soil. The use of amulets, for example, certainly continued, but most who valued these charms probably did not think of them as "Islamic" objects. Muslims probably refashioned their religious traditions into new African American religious traditions. These traditions did not lead to the perpetuation of a self-consciously defined Muslim identity. Indeed, no major scholar of Islam in the United States has been able to make a direct historical link between the practice of Islam among African Americans today and the Islamic practice of their ancestors.

By the end of the Civil War, then, there seems to have been few practicing Muslims in the United States. In the 1880s, however, a large number of Muslims once again came to U.S. shores. From that decade until World War I, hundreds of thousands of persons from the Ottoman Empire came to the Americas. Many who came to the United States were Arabs from what is today Syria and Lebanon. Most were Christian, but a sizable number were Muslim. These Arabs, like others who immigrated to the United States during what Mark Twain called the Gilded Age, sought economic opportunity, often hoping to make a small fortune and return home. Many began humbly as peddlers, selling wares and Arabic foodstuffs along railroads and rivers. Others were unskilled laborers. In Quincy, Massachusetts, some were dockworkers. And in the plains states, such as in South Dakota, they became dry goods salesmen. By 1907, some immigrants were working in Henry Ford's automobile factory in Highland Park, Michigan, and in 1916, Ford's sociological department counted 555 Arab men as employees. This link to the burgeoning automobile industry in Michigan established an immigration pattern that continues to this day; in fact, by some estimates, one of the largest Arab American communities in the United States is in Dearborn, Michigan.

As more and more of these immigrants decided to stay in the United States, they began to establish institutions to further their religious life. One of the oldest continually operating mosques in the United States, the "Mother Mosque," was established in Cedar Rapids, Iowa. In 1919, Lebanese immigrant Muhammad Karoub helped construct one of the first mosques in the Detroit area. His brother, Husain, reportedly served as imam, or prayer leader. In 1920, hundreds of Turkish Muslims from the Balkans and Anatolia established a Detroit chapter of the Red Crescent, the Muslim equivalent of the Red Cross, and purchased grave plots so that they could bury the community's departed in accordance with Islamic law. Bektashi Muslims from Albania and Turkish *mevlavi*s, the so-called whirling dervishes, also continued to practice their particular forms of Sufism in the Motor City. And the Detroit area was home to some Shi'ite Muslims, as well.

During this period, Muslim missionaries also began to appear in the United States. One of the most successful was Muhammad Sadiq, a member of the Ahmadiyya. The Ahmadiyya were established in the late 1800s in the Indian Punjab, where followers of a man named Ghulam Ahmad proclaimed him to be a *mujaddid* (renewer of religion), the Christian Messiah, and the Islamic Mahdi (a divinely guided figure who appears at the end-time). While many other Muslims considered the followers of Ahmad heretics, they pressed ahead with their claims, becoming one of the most successful Muslim missionary groups to non-Muslims in modern times. Known for mass distributing English translations of the Qur'an, the Ahmadiyya established a center in Chicago, Illinois. Traveling around the country, head missionary Muhammad Sadiq praised Islam as a religion of peace and reason. He also targeted African Americans for conversion, promising that Islam offered them equality and freedom. He argued that Arabic was the original language of black people and said Islam had been their religion, stolen from them during slavery. This message attracted hundreds, perhaps thousands, of African Americans to the movement. And the Ahmadiyya seemed to practice the equality that they preached. In 1920s St. Louis, Missouri, for example, African American P. Nathaniel Johnson, who became Shaikh Ahmad Din, led a local Ahmadiyya group that included immigrant Muslims, blacks, and whites.

Some African Americans who joined the Ahmadiyya were almost certainly migrants from the U.S. South. During the years between World War I and World War II, over a million and a half blacks moved from rural areas in the South to cities in the North. Those who came as part of this Great Migration, as U.S. historians have dubbed it, lived near and sometimes worked with Muslim immigrants from the Middle East. As the conversion of African Americans to Ahmadiyya Islam shows, these black American migrants were now part of a dynamic cultural environment where the ideas and culture of Asian immigrants were beginning to have an impact on the formation of African American religious culture, and vice versa.

African American Muslims, however, were not simply borrowing ideas from Asian immigrants. They were also creating their own forms of Islam. The first to do so was Timothy Drew (1886–1929), a native of North Carolina who had traveled to New Jersey and later to Chicago as part of the Great Migration.

While living in Chicago in the 1920s, Drew established the Moorish Science Temple, the first indigenous African American group to claim that blacks were both biologically and historically Muslims. Producing a complicated historical genealogy based on scriptures in the Hebrew Bible, Drew argued that black people were racially linked to Asiatic peoples, whose natural religion was Islam. He took the title of Noble Drew Ali and became known as a prophet. Refusing to call himself "Negro," "black," or "colored," Noble Drew insisted that black Americans were members of the Moorish nation from Africa. His "Holy Koran of the Moorish Science Temple" (1927), a document entirely different from the Qur'an revealed to the Prophet Muhammad of Arabia, preached the importance of moral behavior, industrious work habits, and social solidarity and promised that the secrets of Moorish Science would bring earthly and divine salvation to persons of African descent. Many of the Islamic symbols that Drew adopted, including his fez and his title "Noble," came not from the Islamic culture of immigrants but from the black Shriners. In fact, the Moorish Science Temple was probably more a child of black fraternal organizations and African American popular culture than it was of Old World Islam.

And yet the Moorish Science Temple is central to an understanding of the development of Islam in the United States, since it was the first indigenous African American organization to propagate the idea that black people were, by nature, Muslims. It was an idea that Elijah Muhammad and his Nation of Islam would spread around the country. The Nation of Islam, the best-known African American Muslim organization in the history of the United States, began around 1930 in the Detroit area, where W. D. Fard, a mysterious peddler probably of Turkish or Iranian origins, promoted the idea that Islam was the original religion of the "Blackman." One of his followers was Elijah Poole, a black migrant from Georgia. By 1934, Fard had disappeared, apparently leaving Poole in charge. Poole, who became known as Elijah Muhammad, believed Fard to be God, or Allah, in person; he thought himself his messenger.

The Honorable Elijah Muhammad, as he was addressed by his followers, taught that blacks must seek economic and political independence from white America, return to their original religion of Islam, and abandon immoral "slave behaviors" such as eating pork, drinking liquor, and fornicating. In addition to a message of black nationalism and strict moral discipline, Elijah Muhammad offered his followers an apocalyptic myth that explained black suffering and promised black redemption. Called "Yacub's history," the myth taught that blacks were the original people of earth, living a glorious existence until a mad scientist named Yacub betrayed them by genetically engineering a white man. The white man was violent by nature and eventually overpowered and enslaved the black man, who had weakened himself by abandoning the true religion of Islam. But God would not leave his chosen people helpless. Appearing in the person of W. D. Fard, he commissioned the messenger to mentally resurrect the "so-called Negro" and prepare him for the end of the world, when God would destroy whites and restore the black Islamic nation to its original place of glory.

These teachings came to the nation's attention during the civil rights era, when black middle-class leaders such as the Reverend Martin Luther King Jr. argued that the Nation of Islam and other "black nationalist" groups were the product of poor race relations and inequality. In 1959, Mike Wallace of CBS News made similar arguments in a television documentary about the Nation of Islam entitled *The Hate That Hate Produced*. In addition to introducing the Nation of Islam to the United States, this program featured much footage of the attractive, articulate, and righteously angry Malcolm X (1925–1965), who was one of Elijah Muhammad's most effective organizers and representatives.

Because many scholars of African American Islam have focused their research on the Nation of Islam, much less is known about the thousands of African Americans who converted to and practiced other forms of Islam, including Sunni Islam, as early as the 1930s. Groups like the First Cleveland Mosque, guided by an African American Muslim convert named Wali Akram (d. 1994), often focused their attention on the Five Pillars of Islam and on the Qur'an. Other examples of early black Muslim communities include the Adenu Allahe Universal Arabic Association in Buffalo, New York, and Jabul Arabiyya, a Muslim communal farm also located in New York State. Their presence shows that the practice of Islam in the African American community was characterized by religious diversity from the time of its inception, and further, it suggests that the very diversity of Islamic communities may have been one factor in Islam's continuing growth among black Americans.

At the same time that more and more African Americans were coming to identify themselves as Muslims, the number of Muslims in the United States also rose due to another wave of immigration from the Islamic world. After World War II, many of the former European colonies in Asia and Africa declared their independence from the European powers. In the wake of these political revolutions, persons who had been aligned with the occupying powers or who were seen as opponents of the new regimes were often dispossessed. In the case of Israel, which declared its independence in 1948, many Palestinian Arabs lost their homes and livelihoods, and some sought refuge in the United States. After the 1952 revolution in Egypt, Egyptians who lost favor with the regime of Gamal Abdel Nasser also fled. These immigrants joined other Arab Muslim Americans who were, by this time, starting to organize on a national scale. In 1952, Muslim Americans formed the Federation of Islamic Associations in the United States and Canada, a network of more than twenty mosques in North America.

During the 1950s, students from the newly independent states in Africa and Asia also started to attend U.S. universities in large numbers. In many instances, they criticized what they saw as the assimilation of immigrant Muslims into U.S. culture. Many of these students were also influenced by the rise of Islam as a vehicle of social and political protest against the often-oppressive socialist and nationalist regimes of the "old country." In 1963, some of these students formed the Muslim Students Association at the University of Illinois, Champaign-Urbana. Among the founders were representatives of Egypt's Muslim Brotherhood, a politico-religious organization that opposed the Nasser regime by calling for an abandonment of Arab socialism in favor of an Islamically oriented political system.

Also during this time, Saudi Arabia began to fund Islamic missionary efforts in both Muslim and non-Muslim nations around the world. Attempting to soften derogatory images of Islam abroad and to support its own claims to leadership of the Muslim community, the Saudi government engaged in a number of different missionary activities. For example, in 1963 it established the University of Medina, which offered Muslim religious authorities and missionaries a Wahhabi interpretation of Islam—a particularly conservative version of Sunni Islam. It also established the World Muslim League, which brought together Muslim leaders from around the world to discuss Islamic religion and contemporary politics. In addition, the Saudis funded institutions and Islamic centers in the United States, helped distribute literature about Islam, and even sought to train some Americans as Muslim missionaries. As a result, most Americans even today are far more familiar with the Wahhabi version of Islam than with other interpretations.

Perhaps the most famous student of the Saudi-financed missionary activity was Malcolm X, who left Elijah Muhammad's Nation of Islam in 1964. During Malcolm's famous pilgrimage to Mecca (hajj) that year, he renounced Elijah Muhammad's teachings, rejecting the claim that all white people were blue-eyed devils. And he shared the news that he had felt spiritual kinship with some fellow Muslims on the hajj who happened to be white. What is often less noted about his trip was that he also became an official guest of the Saudi government. In fact, he developed several relationships with Muslims who were at the center of the missionary activity funded by the Saudi government. Later that same year, he was invited back to Mecca to be trained as a Muslim missionary by the World Muslim League. In the last year of his life, he proudly proclaimed his religious identity as an "orthodox" Muslim.

It is important to note, however, that his political agenda did not always parallel that of his sponsors. By financing various missionary efforts, the Saudi government did not only hope to spread the truth of Islam to faraway lands; they also hoped to rally Muslim support in their cold war with Egypt, whose revolutionary socialism and nationalism threatened to spread throughout the Arabian peninsula. Legitimating their regime by touting its explicitly Islamic identity, the Saudis at least implicitly criticized any sort of communal affiliation, whether political or racial, that was not based on Islam. Malcolm X, however, refused to accept the call of his Muslim brothers to abandon the fight for black liberation, saying he felt his first duty was to help persons of African descent achieve full equality. Some Muslims, like Said Ramadan of the Geneva Islamic Centre, encouraged Malcolm to abandon this focus on black liberation and instead champion the spread of Islam as a solution to the race problem in the United States.

The conflict between Malcolm X and those aligned with Saudi interests is important, since it reveals the centrality of transnational encounters and exchanges in the making of U.S. Islam. From the beginning of modern U.S. Islamic history, indigenous forms of Islam have developed partly in response to the encounter between immigrant Muslims and African Americans. As the story of Malcolm X shows, moreover, what was happening a world away could have an impact on the practice of Islam in the United States. In addition, Malcolm X's story shows how the domestic struggle for black liberation was a key factor in the formation of racially segregated Muslim communities in the United States. Like Malcolm X, many other African American Muslims insisted on a version of Islamic practice that made room for or responded to the fight for freedom and equality, and they felt that only by uniting with other black Muslims could they achieve their goals.

For some African Americans, one strategy to achieve liberation was to separate themselves from mainstream white and black society, forming vanguards that strictly followed the precepts of *shari'a*. In the early 1960s, for example, a predominately African American group of believers broke away from the State Street Mosque in Brooklyn to form their own Ya-Sinn Mosque. Others focused on more active community involvement and on building a multiethnic Islam. In the late 1960s, Sheik Tawfiq, an African American from Florida, founded the Mosque of the Islamic Brotherhood in Harlem, New York. Stressing the call of Islamic universalism, African Americans, Hispanics, and others prayed together, established housing and education programs, and ran small businesses.

In this pivotal decade of U.S. history, a serious rift also began to develop between working-class and middle-class Muslims. This divide took on distinctly ethnic and racial characteristics. In 1965, President Lyndon B. Johnson signed a new immigration bill that reversed the 1924 law severely restricting nonwhite immigration to the United States. As a result, thousands of persons from Latin America, Asia, and Africa began to arrive on U.S. shores. Between 1965 and 1990, over 800,000 persons came from South Asia alone. Some of the South Asian Muslim immigrants were successful doctors, engineers, and academicians. Although they eventually joined Arab and other Muslims in forming new Muslim communities, these middle-class Muslims did not often mix with predominately working-class African American Muslims. Even today, most mosques in the United States are predominately African American or Asian American (including Arabs, Iranians, and South Asians). Some academics argue that these divisions are partly the result of Asian American prejudices against blacks—prejudices adopted from white America.

By the 1970s, Muslims in the United States practiced so many forms of Islamic religion that it became difficult to track all of them. For example, looking only at Shi'i Muslims (or Shi'ites, as they are generally called in U.S. popular culture), who constitute 10–15 percent of all Muslims worldwide: Immigration from the Afro-Asian landmass after 1965 resulted in the growth of several distinct subgroups just within this Muslim minority population. Shi'ite Muslims trace their origins to a historical disagreement over the leadership of the Islamic community. Generally emphasizing the right of the family of the Prophet Muhammad to lead Muslims, many Shi'ites believe that Ali, the son-in-law and cousin of the Prophet Muhammad, was the Prophet's rightful heir. Many also see the death of the Prophet's grandson, Husayn (d. 680), at the battle of Karbala as a tragic turning point in Islamic history. After this point, many Shi'ites acknowledged other descendants from the *ahl al-bayt* (the family of the prophets) as their Imams, the rightful leaders of the Islamic community. The largest group is the Twelvers (or Ithna'asharis), who generally believe that the twelfth of these Imams went into hiding in 873 but remains on earth and still secretly guides his followers. It is also believed that this Imam will reappear at the end of the world to rule with peace and justice. Most Twelvers live in Iran, Iraq, Lebanon, and Pakistan, but theoretically speaking, U.S. Twelvers can be from anywhere. After the Iranian Revolution in 1979, the number of African American Twelver converts began to increase noticeably.

Another major Shi'ite group with a strong presence in the United States is the Seveners, or Isma'ilis. The Isma'ilis trace their origins to a disagreement over the successor to the sixth Imam in 765. The Isma'ilis, however, are themselves divided into several subgroups. Among them are the Nizaris, followers of the Aga Khan, whom they recognize as the living Imam. These Muslims, who live in various places around the world, often call their mosques *jama'atkhana*s and de-emphasize various aspects of Sunni Islamic ritual. The current Aga Khan, Prince Karim Shah, receives monetary donations from his followers and in turn is the patron of a number of public institutions, including health clinics and schools often known for academic excellence. Thousands of Nizaris, who trace their roots to East Africa and South Asia, came to the United States in the 1970s as refugees; today, many are successful academics and businesspersons.

Sufism in the United States also grew during this period. Though Sufis had been a part of the U.S. Muslim scene at least since Turks and Albanians immigrated to the United States, a larger number began to immigrate after 1965. In addition, a number of white Americans began to turn to Sufism as a religious path. Some of those who claimed to be Sufis did not label themselves Muslims. Others, however, sought to follow Sufi ideas in tandem with such foundational Islamic practices of piety as the daily prayers and fasting during Ramadhan. By the beginning of the twenty-first century, U.S. Sufism was a cross-class and multi-ethnic phenomenon. Americans followed Sufi masters who had come from various parts of the globe. Some Sufi masters created their own organizations, as Pir Inayat Khan, founder of Sufi Order in the West, had done earlier in the twentieth century. Others came as representatives of more traditional orders, including the Tijaniyya, Naqshbandiyya, Qadiriyya, Bektashis, Shadhiliyya, and the Ishraqiyya. These groups catered to the variety of tastes in the United States, and their memberships often reflected and sometimes reified the social divisions of U.S. Muslim communities. For example, the Tijaniyya, a West African order central to Senegalese society, appealed especially to African American Muslims, whom one could find at a Sufi lodge in Brooklyn, New York, engaged in types of *dhikr,* Sufi rituals of "remembrance," practiced by their African brothers and sisters across the Atlantic.

Another dramatic shift in U.S. Islam occurred in 1975, when Wallace D. Muhammad (b. 1933) assumed the leadership of the Nation of Islam after the death of his father, Elijah Muhammad. Although the number of African American Sunni Muslims had been increasing throughout the 1960s, Wallace D. Muhammad's "Second Resurrection" of the Nation of Islam led to a sudden realignment of thousands of black Muslims with Sunni Islamic tradition. Shortly after his ascension, he began to dismantle the racialist version of Islam that his father had worked so long to construct. He reinterpreted and ultimately rejected the teachings that W. D. Fard had been God in the flesh and that white people were devils. Instead, he encouraged followers to practice the daily prayers, to make the *hajj* to Mecca, and to fast during Ramadhan (rather than at Yuletide, as his father had instructed). He renamed the organization, calling it first the World Community of al-Islam in the West and eventually the American Muslim Mission. And he even introduced U.S. flags into the movement's temples and established a U.S. patriotism day. Finally, he decentralized authority in the movement, empowering local communities to chart their own course or, as some might put it, to fend for themselves.

Not all his followers agreed with such dramatic changes, however. The most prominent was Minister Louis Farrakhan (b. 1933), the former national spokesman for Elijah Muhammad. In the late 1970s, Farrakhan publicly stated his disagreements with the new leader and reconstituted a version of the old Nation of Islam. Farrakhan positioned himself as the true heir to Elijah Muhammad and eventually purchased Elijah Muhammad's old mansion and other former Nation of Islam properties. Farrakhan continues to lead this community today, although he has at least partially reconciled with Wallace Muhammad and has incorporated more Sunni traditions into his new Nation of Islam. Even more, Farrakhan, who has been strongly linked to anti-Semitism in the past, has become a spokesperson for interfaith dialogue, interracial harmony, and social justice.

Contemporary U.S. Muslim Life

During the recent past, especially after September 11, 2001, many non-Muslim Americans have become far more aware of their Muslim neighbors. Interfaith dialogues, governmental surveillance, civil rights activism, and unprecedented press coverage have acted as magnifying and sometimes distorting lenses through which various public faces of Islam have emerged. In order to understand these public guises of Muslim identity, one must pay close attention to the overlapping contexts and multiple sites in which these identities have been constructed and contested. One obvious site for scholarly examination is the "public square," where the relationship between Muslimness and Americanness is constantly debated.

In the past, some Muslims have questioned whether they should fully participate in U.S. public life. Before 1975, for example, members of the Nation of Islam refused to call themselves "Americans," formed all-black Muslim businesses and schools, and were willing to go to jail to avoid serving in the U.S. military, as did Elijah Muhammad in World War II and as did his son, Wallace, after the Korean War. Some Muslim immigrants in the 1960s and 1970s shared this ambivalence about active engagement with the state. They saw the United States as immoral and un-Islamic. Their current-day heirs, a marked minority among Muslims in the United States, hold similar views, questioning the extent to which Muslims should interact with non-Muslims and in what contexts, generally avoiding participation in elections, and discouraging their children from serving in the military. For example, the Tablighi Jama'at, a relatively nonpolitical organization with South Asian roots, fears that integration into popular U.S. Muslim culture will threaten Muslim piety and identity. The Hizb Tahrir (Liberation Party) sees the United States as *dar al-kufr* (the abode of disbelief) and advocates the restoration of unified political leadership in all of the historically Islamic lands.

But the overwhelming majority of Muslims support involvement in political and public affairs, and they are an incredibly diverse group. Some proudly and publicly proclaim their patriotism, and celebrate the United States as a land of freedom and opportunity where they can spread the message of Islam. Like Americans as a whole, however, those who advocate participation in U.S. public life disagree about the most basic social, economic, and cultural issues. They are Democrats, Republicans, and Independents, although most black Muslims, like other African Americans, tend to vote Democratic. How Muslims

Elijah Muhammad, Black Muslim leader, speaking to his followers at the Chicago Coliseum in 1971. (Bettmann/CORBIS)

vote on various issues depends on who they are—their race, gender, age, religious views, sexual orientation, national origin, class, and more. Some are social conservatives who, like some orthodox Jews and evangelical Christians, advocate "family values," oppose gay rights, and want to ban abortion. Others are far more concerned with poverty at home and abroad, a lack of equal opportunity, and the state of public schools. Most have at least some views in common, especially regarding certain aspects of U.S. foreign policy. For example, most U.S. Muslims tend to support the establishment of a Palestinian state and question U.S. policy toward Israel and toward the Middle East more generally.

For the past two decades, most national Muslim organizations have attempted to organize Muslims into viable interest groups that exert greater influence upon U.S. political life. For instance, ISNA, the largest national Muslim organization, educates Muslim voters about relevant political issues and encourages intra-Muslim dialogue on such matters. At the same time, ISNA, which was born out of the Muslim Students Association in 1982, provides many other public forums for Muslim community development; organizations operating under the ISNA umbrella include the Muslim Students Association, the Islamic Medical Association, the American Muslim Engineers and Scientists, and the American Muslim Social Scientists. ISNA also distributes a popular magazine called *Islamic Horizons* and holds a well-attended annual convention, whose location changes from year to year. Its national headquarters are in Plainfield, Indiana.

Other Muslim political organizations are far more narrowly focused on political activism and lobbying in Washington, D.C. Among them is the Council on American-Islamic Relations, founded in 1994. CAIR often leads the fight against anti-Muslim prejudice in the United States; its representatives, for example, regularly appear on rather cantankerous "shock-talk" shows, where they are generally hit with a barrage of questions equating U.S. Muslims to terrorists. CAIR also lobbies government officials on such foreign policy issues as the "war on terror" and the Israeli-Palestinian conflict, and it represents the civil rights of U.S. Muslims. Some of the organization's critics, in an effort to delegitimize it, have called it "radical," although such claims have not stopped many moderate Muslims from supporting its efforts.

Many of these national Muslim organizations tend to divide along lines of race and ethnicity. ISNA and CAIR, for example, are generally led and patronized by immigrant Muslims. African American Muslims, on the other hand, tend to follow the leadership of W. D. Muhammad, Louis Farrakhan, Jamil Al-Amin, or other African American Muslim leaders. Muhammad's group, now called the American Society of Muslims, and Farrakhan's Nation of Islam are the best-organized African American Muslim associations. Muhammad publishes the *Muslim Journal*, a newspaper dedicated to covering international, national, and local issues of concern to black Muslims. Similarly, Farrakhan is responsible for the *Final Call*, a newspaper that is distributed in part by a network of usually young, bow-tied men hawking the paper on the streets of urban black America. Both Muhammad and Farrakhan draw thousands, from long distances, to see them speak during their public appearances. In addition, both men have engaged in interfaith dialogue: Farrakhan at the Million Family March and Muhammad with Jews and especially Roman Catholics associated with the Focolare movement for unity and solidarity.

The racial divide among national Muslim leaders reflects deeper racial divisions among U.S. Muslims at the grassroots level. Most Muslims believe that God does not discriminate and that Islam is a religion applicable to all, regardless of race or any other social identifier. Most Muslims uphold values of racial equality and reject racism. But the realities of Muslim life in the United States do not always correspond to these ideals. African American Muslims, like other African Americans in the United States, often face racial prejudice and discrimination from nonblack coreligionists. In response to U.S. racism more generally, African Americans have built their own mosques and schools. Black Muslims also tend to marry other African Americans, as well. Some African American Muslims, such as DePaul University professor Aminah Mc-Cloud, have argued that immigrant attitudes toward blacks can be condescending, especially in assuming a lack of Islamic knowledge or legitimacy among African Americans. Some African American Muslims strongly defend the need for separate black Muslim institutions, arguing that black autonomy and pride are necessary in the fight for black liberation. They often advocate ethnic and racial particularity by arguing that the Qur'an itself sanctions such activity (49:13).

Contemporary Muslim communities, however, are divided not merely by race but by language, ethnicity, class, and religious orientation as well. Sometimes, groups of Urdu, Persian, or Arabic speakers establish cultural centers where they can speak with each other in their first languages and celebrate their particular linguistic and ethnic cultures. Other Muslim communities, especially the Islamic Center of Southern California, offer different models of communal formation, working to create an explicitly interethnic, interracial community of believers that relies on English as a common language.

On the whole, however, mosques tend to be racialized (that is, divided by race). The racial divide does not exist so much between different immigrant groups as it does between immigrant and indigenous Muslims, who are by and large black. In the case of immigrants, there are several examples of South Asians and Arabs joining together to sustain Islamic centers throughout the country. Moreover, one might find a smattering of Iranians, Bosnians, West Africans, African Americans, Turks, whites, Latinos, and others at these centers, especially for Friday prayers or major celebrations like *id al-adha*, which comes at the end of the *hajj* season. One recent survey, however, found much less interethnic mixing at historically African American mosques. It should be stressed that there is no easy explanation for this segregation and that those who might blame African American Muslims for "self-segregation" are probably blaming the victim. The racialized nature of the U.S. mosque reflects larger trends in U.S. religion and in Christian churches in particular; it is often said that Sunday morning church is the most segregated hour in America.

The mosque, then, is another key public site where U.S. Muslim identities are negotiated and constructed. Well over 1,200 mosques are now located in U.S. inner cities, towns, and suburbs; the buildings themselves express a wide variety of architectural styles, and include converted city storefronts, grand Middle Eastern–style structures, and small houses. Like some U.S. churches, synagogues, and other religious centers, mosques often house schools and recreational areas, in addition to the *masjid* (place of prostration, that is, prayer) proper. At times, the imam (prayer leader) of the mosque also acts as its administrative and spiritual leader, especially in many African American mosques. In these contexts, the imam performs duties similar to those of a minister, priest, or rabbi. In other mosques, however, imams are relegated to the role of teaching about Islam, delivering the Friday sermon, and leading the Friday prayers. An elected president or chairperson often acts as the leader of these mosques. These persons generally maintain employment outside the

mosque, and in the case of predominately immigrant mosques, they are generally professionals of one sort or another. Many community leaders, whether
imams or committee members, work on a volunteer basis, receiving little or no
compensation for their services. Moreover, while many of them have attended
at least some college and may have even completed postgraduate degrees, less
than half of U.S. mosque leaders have received any type of formal Islamic studies education.

Debates over who should lead the mosque reflect a much larger question
about what kind of Muslim identity is being created in these social spaces. In
the past, some mosques have sponsored some of the same sorts of activities
that some Roman Catholic parishes have. In the Toledo Islamic Center of the
1960s, for example, mosque members played bingo, performed the popular
Arab line dance called the *dabka,* and even enjoyed a beer or two together—
one reminder of how easy it is to overgeneralize about Muslims. Some scholars
attribute such behavior to "Americanization." Indeed, this particular use of
space at the mosque in addition to its operation as a "voluntary organization"
does seem to reflect larger trends in U.S. religion and culture. But the idea
that a Muslim could pray and fast—and drink and dance—is not distinctively
American. Such "impious" practices largely went unchallenged until the religious revival of the 1970s, especially when Saudi-trained imams began to serve
as leaders of various immigrant Muslim communities. Today, although one
should not expect to find any beer kegs at mosque functions, the pendulum of
mosque leadership has swung again. Local communities tend more and more
to reject Muslim missionaries who do not provide interpretations of Islam relevant to their lives as U.S. Muslims.

In addition to the mosque itself, Islamic schools, often connected to a
mosque, serve as places where Muslim children and adults construct their
Muslim identities. Most mosques feature some kind of weekend religious education programming, especially on Sundays. As of 2004, there are also two U.S.
Islamic colleges, one Shi'ite and one Sunni, that provide advanced training in
Islamic studies. Perhaps more significantly, over 200 full-time primary and secondary Muslim schools now operate across the United States. Approximately a
quarter of these are Clara Muhammad Schools, associated with African American Muslim leader W. D. Muhammad. Originally connected to Elijah Muhammad's Nation of Islam, these schools offer the usual secular subject matter,
such as math and reading, in addition to Qur'anic studies and Islamic history.
Clara Muhammad Schools are generally located in the inner city and provide
an educational alternative to Muslim and non-Muslim African American parents concerned about the state of their public schools.

The quality of these and other Muslim schools varies considerably, as do
their approaches to issues of morality and piety. Some Muslim schools, for example, encourage responsible interaction among boys and girls both in class

and during social activities; others maintain strict gender segregation. Muslim parents and children, of all ethnic backgrounds, actively debate whether Muslim children should attend separate schools. Many parents worry about dating, drugs, and the consumerist culture in U.S. public schools. Others worry that sending their kids to Islamic schools will make it more challenging for them to interact with non-Muslims and to develop a successful career. Some Muslim students also argue that their presence as a Muslim witness is important in U.S. public schools.

As important as mosques and schools are, however, they are not the only public sites where Muslims interact with one another. In fact, many scholars believe that as few as 10 percent of U.S. Muslims attend Friday prayers or Sunday school on a regular basis. In the 1990s, the Internet has emerged as a site where Muslims also meet, chat, and debate what it means to be a Muslim. "Cyber Islam" can be fruitfully analyzed as its own kind of religious expression, in which Muslims on the privileged side of the digital divide can issue their own legal interpretations of Islam and challenge the authority of centuries-old traditions of *fiqh* (Islamic jurisprudence). Like other Muslims around the world, some U.S. Muslims have bypassed the *shari'a* and looked directly to the Qur'an and *hadith* in order to craft their approach to the Islamic life. One need not be an *alim* (a traditionally trained Muslim religious scholar) or hold a prestigious position at an Islamic university to publish one's opinions; one only needs access to the World Wide Web. The Internet has also become a place where young Muslims, like other single people in the United States, look for potential mates. And it provides space for online Muslim support groups, like Al-Fatiha, an organization created by and for gay, lesbian, bisexual, and transgendered Muslims.

On the Internet, in national conferences, in mosques and schools, and in each other's homes, Muslims meet to discuss the critical questions of Muslim life in the United States. Of all the questions debated, however, none is more hotly contested than the issue of gender and Islam, a subject of great interest to non-Muslim Americans, as well. In fact, the intra-Muslim debate about gender is shaped partly by the assumption among many non-Muslim Americans that "traditional Islam" oppresses women. The ultimate symbol of that oppression for many is the practice of veiling, which is taken by some to be inherently discriminatory. On television and in movies in the United States, one seldom gets to hear a veiled woman speak. Instead, one is treated to a silent image of the covered woman, and this image is often intended as evidence of oppression. Some feminists call this practice "double objectification." That is, not only do women in Islamic societies, as in most other societies, face gender prejudice, but they are also silenced by their representation in U.S. society. Many Americans have never actually met a woman who wears a veil or heard them speak about why they wear such a garment.

However, very few U.S. Muslim women say that Islam is inherently oppressive of women. To the contrary, many U.S. Muslim women see Islam as a liberating force. But they disagree over what it means to be a liberated Muslim woman. For example, the popular South Asian American youth writer Asma Gull Hassan admits that there is much sexism in the Muslim world, but she blames what she identifies as patriarchal culture rather Islamic religion for this phenomenon. Hassan, who advocates the waging of "gender jihad," praises the United States as a world full of social, economic, and political opportunity for Muslim women. She also believes that the United States provides Muslims a chance to return to the pure Islam of the Qur'an, which she sees as democratic, capitalist, and feminist. She does not normally wear a *hijab* (head scarf) and argues that it is modesty of the heart that matters most. In fact, she says, the promotion of the *hijab* is part of a conservative Muslim political agenda. According to her reading of the Qur'an, for both men and women, it is only necessary to cover oneself in modest clothing when praying.

Qur'anic scholar Amina Wadud, an African American convert, also sees the Qur'an as a liberating document. Like Hassan, she argues that many Muslim communities are patriarchal, and she reports that many Muslims have rejected her scholarship as un-Islamic, Westernized, and feminist. Lest one think of the Islamic world as a sexist monolith, however, it is important to note that Wadud's most famous work, *Qur'an and Woman* (1999) was first published in Malaysia, a Muslim country. Wadud argues that the Qur'an depicts men and women as equal, different, and complementary, and she stresses that the Qur'an does not prescribe set gender roles for either. There is no gender hierarchy in the Qur'an, she argues, and women need not always be homemakers, mothers, and wives.

Other U.S. Muslim women, however, embrace the notion of differing social roles and find Islam liberating precisely because, according to them, it values their roles as wives and mothers. In addition, some women also support the notion of polygyny, and there are a few instances of extralegal polygamous marriages, especially among African American Muslims. Some women involved in such relationships have reported that they enjoy the sense of extended kinship and community that these arrangements engender; they say their co-wives are like sisters. Others complain that their husbands do not treat all their wives equally, as commanded in the Qur'an. It should be stressed that polygyny is rare, perhaps extremely rare, and that the overwhelming majority of married Muslims are monogamous.

Although discussions about "exotica" like the veil and polygamy threaten to monopolize non-Muslim public discourse on gender and Islam, U.S. Muslim women themselves are concerned about a much broader array of issues. For example, Muslim women often debate the question of what their roles should be as Muslim community leaders. For the most part, in U.S. mosques, women are prohibited from becoming imams. Some women see this as a sexist tradition that should be challenged. Others, however, emphasize the importance of alternate participation in the community. Ingrid Mattson, vice president of the Islamic Society of North America, has argued that although women do not qualify for the position of imam, there is no other position theoretically prohibited to women in the Muslim community.

For example, some Muslim women, including Mattson, stress the need for gender equality on mosque executive committees and boards, and women's participation in these bodies continues to increase. Some women have served as chairperson or mosque president. In Toledo, Ohio, for example, Chereffe Kadri helped lead the Islamic Center of Greater Toledo through difficult times after September 11, 2001. Some U.S. Muslim women also note that there are few impediments to female leadership in Sufi Islam. Gwendolyn Zoharah Simmons, an African American Sufi, argues that U.S. Muslims should look to traditions like Sufism to see a less hierarchical model for gender relations in Islam. Laleh Bakhtiar, another American Sufi, also notes the central message of gender equality in Sufism and notes the success of U.S. women as leaders in the Naqshbandi order. Still others argue that women must help the community more squarely face issues like domestic abuse and equal opportunity in employment and education.

There is, however, no easy way to present a summary of Muslim women's lives in the United States. Like Muslims more generally, Muslim women in the United States lead a life full of peril and possibility. They live under the authority of a government that, in practice, singles out Muslims for government surveillance while also promising to protect their human rights. Every day, Muslim women, like Muslim men, face suspicion from the general public. Just having a Muslim name or wearing a *hijab* immediately puts them at risk. They might be denied a seat on an airplane; they might face employment discrimination; and they might be the subject of stares, fear, and hostility. Muslim women of color, like men of color, may experience further discrimination because of their race. And as women, they know gender discrimination—the kind that comes from within the Muslim community as well as that which comes from without. At the same time, Muslim women often laud the ideals, if not always the practice, of the United States. The United States has a kind of religious freedom difficult to find elsewhere. It is a rich country that offers some degree of economic opportunity to many. And some say that living in such an ethnically and religiously diverse country gives them the chance to forge an Islam that is pluralistic, interracial, and socially just.

Whether such an Islam emerges in the United States depends not only on the actions of Muslims themselves but also on the larger contexts in which they attempt such a venture. In the past, the shapes and contours of U.S. Islam have often reflected the influence of larger trends in U.S. race and ethnic relations,

306 ISLAM IN WORLD CULTURES

economic life, and foreign policy, among other factors. The future of Islam in America, in other words, is likely to be shaped by U.S. responses to its Muslim citizens. Its future may be determined by the answer to this question: Will Muslims face more peril or more possibility?

References

Anway, Carol L. 1995. *Daughters of Another Path: Experiences of American Women Choosing Islam.* Lee's Summit, MO: Yawna Publications.

Austin, Allan D. 1997. *African Muslims in Antebellum America: Transatlantic Stories and Spiritual Struggles.* New York: Routledge.

Barboza, Steven. 1993. *American Jihad: Islam after Malcolm X.* New York: Doubleday.

Bush, George W. 2001. "Islam Is Peace." http://www.whitehouse.gov/news/releases/2001/09/20010917-11.html.

Curtis, Edward E., IV. 2002. *Islam in Black America: Identity, Liberation, and Difference in African-American Islamic Thought.* Albany: State University of New York Press.

Dannin, Robert. 2002. *Black Pilgrimage to Islam.* New York: Oxford University Press.

DeCaro, Louis A., Jr. 1996. *On the Side of My People: A Religious Life of Malcolm X.* New York: New York University Press.

Diouf, Sylviane A. 1998. *Servants of Allah: African Muslims Enslaved in the Americas.* New York: New York University Press.

Gardell, Mattias. 1996. *In the Name of Elijah Muhammad: Louis Farrakhan and the Final Call.* Durham, NC: Duke University Press.

Haddad, Yvonne Y., and John L. Esposito, eds. 2000. *Muslims on the Americanization Path?* New York: Oxford University Press.

Haddad, Yvonne Y., and Jane I. Smith, eds. 1993. *Mission to America: Five Islamic Sectarian Communities in North America.* Gainesville: University Press of Florida.

———, eds. 1994. *Muslim Communities in North America.* Albany: State University of New York Press.

Hasan, Asma Gull. 2000. *American Muslims: The New Generation.* New York: Continuum.

Lawrence, Bruce B. 2002. *New Faiths, Old Fears: Muslims and Other Asian Immigrants in American Religious Life.* New York: Columbia University Press.

Leonard, Karen Isaksen. 2003. *Muslims in the United States: The State of Research.* New York: Russell Sage.

Malcolm X and Alex Haley. 1973. *The Autobiography of Malcolm X.* New York: Ballantine Books.

McAlister, Melani. 2001. *Epic Encounters: Culture, Media, and U.S. Interests in the Middle East, 1945–2000.* Berkeley and Los Angeles: University of California Press.

McCloud, Aminah Beverly. 1995. *African American Islam.* New York: Routledge.

Nance, Susan. "Mystery of the Moorish Science Temple: Southern Blacks and American Alternate Spirituality in the 1920s." *Religion and American Culture* 12, no. 2: 123–166.

Said, Edward W. 1997. *Covering Islam: How the Media and the Experts Determine How We See the Rest of the World.* New York: Vintage Books.

Smith, Jane I. 1999. *Islam in America*. New York: Columbia University Press.

Turner, Richard Brent. 1997. *Islam in the African-American Experience*. Bloomington: Indiana University Press.

Wadud, Amina. 1999. *Qur'an and Woman: Rereading the Sacred Text from a Woman's Perspective*. New York: Oxford University Press.

Webb, Gisela, ed. 2000. *Windows of Faith: Muslim Women Scholar-Activists in North America*. Syracuse, NY: Syracuse University Press.

Chapter Eleven

Suggestions for Further Reading and Internet Resources

This chapter contains annotated bibliographies designed to facilitate further reading in the subjects discussed in this volume. The resources for each chapter are broken down into three subsections: primary sources available in English, secondary sources, and Internet resources. However, due to the diversity of Muslim societies covered, there is unavoidably some unevenness in the number and type of sources available in English.

1. Islam: Historical Introduction and Overview

Primary Sources Available in English

Al-Qur'an

There are many different translations of the Qur'an available in English, each with its own strengths and weaknesses. Several, including the translation by N. J. Dawood (*The Koran,* Penguin Books), are published in editions that also include the original Arabic text in parallel columns. There are also a number of Web sites offering searchable versions of different translations of the Qur'an, which can be helpful for comparing different renderings and interpretations of the text. However, the best introduction to the Qur'an available in English today is Michael Sells's volume, *Approaching the Qur'an.*

Esposito, John L. 1983. *Voices of Resurgent Islam.* New York: Oxford University Press.
Esposito, John L., and John J. Donohue. 1982. *Islam in Transition: Muslim Perspectives.* New York: Oxford University Press.

Both of these volumes contain English translations of writings by twentieth-century Muslim reformist authors from the Middle East and South Asia. In *Voices of Resurgent Islam,* the primary source texts are complemented by a series of essays that help to situate these writings in relation to the broader contexts of Islamic resurgence in the modern world.

Ibn Ishaq. 1997. *The Life of Muhammad: A Translation of Ibn Ishaq's "Sirat Rasul Allah."* Translated by A. Guillaume. Karachi: Oxford University Press.

This is a translation of one of the major traditional Muslim biographies of the Prophet. It is a rich resource for materials on Islam's early period, including the text of the Constitution of Medina, discussed in the introduction to this volume.

Kurzman, Charles, ed. 1998. *Liberal Islam: A Sourcebook.* New York: Oxford University Press.
———, ed. 2002. *Modernist Islam, 1840–1940: A Sourcebook.* New York: Oxford University Press.

These two readers are valuable resources for the study of Islam in the modern world. Each contains translations of dozens of short excerpts not only from the Arabic lands of the Middle East but from many other societies as well.

Renard, John, ed. 1998. *Windows on the House of Islam: Muslim Sources on Spirituality and Religious Life.* Berkeley and Los Angeles: University of California Press.

This anthology provides a great selection of texts from all across the Muslim world, covering the medieval as well as the modern periods.

Safi, Omid, ed. 2003. *Progressive Muslims on Justice, Gender, and Pluralism.* Oxford: Oneworld.

This volume contains essays by Muslim scholars dealing with some of today's most complex and pressing social issues, including essays by some of the writers quoted and referred to in the introduction to this volume, such as Ahmet Karamustafa and Khaled Abou El Fadl.

Sells, Michael. 1999. *Approaching the Qur'an: The Early Revelations.* Ashland, OR: White Cloud Press.

This book is the best introduction to the text of the Qur'an. Its fine translations of some of the shorter chapters of the Qur'an are complemented by an introduction, essays, and a CD containing recordings of several different styles of Qur'anic recitation by Muslims from around the world.

Williams, John. 1994. *The Word of Islam.* Austin: University of Texas Press.

This reader presents a good selection of English translations from classical Islamic texts in Arabic, including some from minority Muslim communities such as the Ibadis and Ismai'lis.

Secondary Sources

Cook, Michael. 2000. *The Koran: A Very Short Introduction.* New York: Oxford University Press.

This small handbook provides a useful introduction to the history of the Qur'anic text as well as to the practices of reading and interpreting the Qur'an in Muslim history.

Endress, Gerhard. 2002. *Islam: An Historical Introduction.* Translated by C. Hillenbrand. New York: Columbia University Press.

This volume provides a concise introduction to the history of Islam, focusing on the periods before 1900. It also includes an essay on the history of Islamic studies in the West as well as useful appendices on Muslim names and titles and on the lunar calendar and a time line of Muslim history.

Esposito, John L., and John O. Voll. 2001. *Makers of Contemporary Islam.* New York: Oxford University Press.

The chapters in this volume present introductions to the life and thought of a number of major figures in contemporary Islam, including Maryam Jameelah, Abdol Karim Soroush, Anwar Ibrahim, and Abdurrahman Wahid.

Fakhry, Majid. 1983. *A History of Islamic Philosophy.* 2nd ed. New York: Columbia University Press.

This helpful work provides an overview of and introduction to the history of Islamic philosophy.

Hodgson, Marshall G. S. 1974. *The Venture of Islam: Conscience and History in a World Civilization.* Vol. 1, *The Classical Age of Islam.* Chicago: University of Chicago Press.

An unfinished masterpiece of modern Islamic studies, this work is a rich and self-reflective examination of Muslim history from the origins of Islam to the modern period. Its introductory essay on the study of Islam by Western scholars is a great place to start reading in this field.

Johansen, Baber. 1999. *Contingency in a Sacred Law: Legal and Ethical Norms in the Muslim Fiqh.* Leiden: Brill.

Although this collection is mostly made up of rather technical studies for specialists, the first chapter, "The Muslim *Fiqh* as Sacred Law," provides a very good introduction to the basic workings of Islamic law.

Knysh, Alexander D. 2000. *Islamic Mysticism: A Short History.* Leiden: Brill.

This helpful handbook provides an overview of and introduction to Sufism, or Islamic mysticism, including discussions of Sufi doctrine and poetry and of the history of organized Sufi orders *(tariqa)*.

Makdisi, George. 1981. *The Rise of Colleges: Institutions of Learning in Islam and the West.* Edinburgh: Edinburgh University Press.

This classic study of the history of the medieval Muslim *madrasa*s examines both its intellectual and its institutional aspects. The book also presents an argument linking these developments to the cultural history of the West.

Nagel, Tilman. 2000. *The History of Islamic Theology.* Translated by Thomas Thornton. Princeton: Markus Wiener.

This translation from a German text provides an introduction and overview of the history of *kalam,* or Islamic theology.

Qureshi, Emran, and Michael A. Sells, eds. 2003. *The New Crusades: Constructing the Muslim Enemy.* New York: Columbia University Press.

This volume contains a remarkable selection of essays critically examining the Clash of Civilizations theory and its impact in contemporary societies.

Radtke, Bernd, and F. de Jonge, eds. 1999. *Islamic Mysticism Contested: Thirteen Centuries of Controversies and Polemics.* Leiden: Brill.

This massive collection of studies contains essays by specialists from around the world on the history of Sufism in Muslim societies ranging from medieval Turkmenistan to the modern Balkans.

Voll, John O. 1994. *Islam: Continuity and Change in the Modern World.* 2nd ed. Syracuse: Syracuse University Press.

This volume is the best monograph history of the development of various movements for Islamic revival and reform from the eighteenth through the twentieth centuries.

Internet Resources

There is an immense amount of material on the Web on Islam and Muslim societies. The trick is not finding information but, rather, selecting the materials that will be helpful. One should also always be sensitive to the various perspectives and biases behind different sites, in order to be able to put in context the information one finds.

There are several sites that provide access to primary texts, and there are a number of good gateways providing annotated links to a wide variety of resources. At http://www.usc.edu/dept/MSA/reference/searchquran.html, you can search the Qur'an in English, choosing from the texts of three alternate English translations: those of Mohammed Marmaduke Pickthall, Yusuf Ali, and M. H. Shakir. At http://www.usc.edu/dept/MSA/fundamentals/ hadithsunnah/, you can also search English translations of some of the major Muslim *hadith* collections.

Beyond these sites for the Qur'an and *hadith,* the Internet Islamic History Sourcebook, at http://www.fordham.edu/halsall/islam/islamsbook.html, contains links to a wealth of primary source documents in English translation. These include readings in the fields of Islamic law, theology, mysticism, and history, as well as the works of a number of modern Muslim writers. The Web site of Professor Alan Godlas at the University of Georgia (http://www.uga.edu/islam/) is an invaluable resource for Islamic studies. There one can find links and archives for a whole range of topics relating to the study of Islam and Muslim societies, including the events of September 11, 2001, and Islam, Muslim women and women's rights, and Islamic history, as well as images, population figures, and maps for various countries of the Muslim world. For an excellent review of current scholarship on nearly every part of the contemporary Muslim world, download the newsletter of the Institute for the Study of Islam in the Modern World under the publications section of their Web site, http://www.isim.nl/.

Over the past few years, PBS has produced a number of films that can be helpful guides to the study of Islam. *Frontline*'s show "Muslims" is a very good introduction to some of the major issues facing communities and to the diversity of Muslim opinions on them around the world. The Web site for this program, http://www.pbs.org/wgbh/pages/frontline/shows/muslims/, contains links and resources including video clips of interviews with "ordinary Muslims" living in New York, Nigeria, and elsewhere around the world. The PBS program *Islam: Empire of Faith* offers more background information on earlier periods of Islamic history, especially the Ottoman Empire. Its Web site, http://www.pbs.org/empires/islam/index.html, includes an interactive time line of Islamic history. One can also take a "virtual *hajj*" on the Web site for PBS's *Muhammad* at http://www.pbs.org/muhammad/index.shtml.

2. Islam after Empire: Turkey and the Arab Middle East

Primary Sources Available in English

Al-Banna, Hasan. 1978. *Five Tracts of Hasan al-Banna (1906–1949).* Translated by Charles Wendell. Berkeley and Los Angeles: University of California Press.
    This collection contains translations of texts produced by Hasan al-Banna, the founder of the Egyptian Muslim Brotherhood.

Kurzman, Charles, ed. 1998. *Liberal Islam: A Sourcebook.* New York: Oxford University Press.

———, ed. 2002. *Modernist Islam, 1840–1940: A Sourcebook.* New York: Oxford University Press.

In each of these volumes, Kurzman provides dozens of short, annotated translations of essays by Muslim writers reflecting on tradition and change in the modern world. Both include a number of selections from Middle Eastern Muslim writers relevant to the developments discussed in Chapter 2.

Qutb, Sayyid. 1991. *Milestones.* Burr Ridge, IN: American Trust Publications.

The author of this work is one of the leading voices of the Egyptian Islamic Brotherhood. *Milestones* (cited in Chapter 2 as *Signposts along the Road*) has been one of the most influential texts of modern Islamic fundamentalism.

Shahrur, Muhammad. 2000. *Proposal for an Islamic Covenant.* Translated by Dale F. Eickelman and Ismail S. Abu Shehadeh. http://www.islam21.net/pages/charter/may-1.htm.

This provocative text by an important Syrian Muslim author was written in response to a request from the International Forum for Islamic Dialogue to develop a plan of action for the twenty-first century.

Secondary Studies

Berkes, Niyazi. 1998. *The Development of Secularism in Turkey.* New York: Routledge.

This reprint of Berkes's classic work (originally published in 1964) is an in-depth examination of the various factors that contributed to the ascendancy of secularism in Turkey. It traces these developments from the eighteenth century through the *tanzimat* reforms and the establishment of the modern nation-state under Kemal Atatürk.

Doumato, Eleanor. 1999. *Getting God's Ear: Women, Islam, and Healing in Saudi Arabia and the Gulf.* New York: Columbia University Press.

Using historical and ethnographic data, Doumato explores women's religious practices in one of the most conservative Islamic countries in the world. Her work illustrates the differences between public and private religious life, as well as the gulf that sometimes exists between men's and women's religious interests and practices. Islam, far from being monolithic, differs not only from one country to another but even within the boundaries of the household.

Eickelman, Dale F., and Jon Anderson, eds. 2003. *New Media in the Muslim World: The Emerging Public Sphere.* 2nd ed. Bloomington: Indiana University Press.
Eickelman, Dale F., and James Piscatori. 1998. *Muslim Politics.* Princeton: Princeton University Press.

In each of these books, Eickelman and his colleagues place modern developments in the Muslim world in comparative perspective, showing how contemporary Middle Eastern societies adopt new methods—both electronic technologies and sociopolitical techniques. Drawing parallels between Muslim and Western experiences, these volumes de-sensationalize the media events we have grown used to.

Hourani, Albert. 1983. *Arabic Thought in the Liberal Age, 1798–1939.* Oxford: Oxford University Press.

This classic work examines the influence of European liberal philosophy—that is, the idea that encouraging individual freedom should be the highest goal of political systems—on the development of modern political and religious thought in the Middle East. It is particularly valuable for tracing the influence of European ideas in the development of Islamic modernism.

Keddie, Nikki, ed. 1968. *An Islamic Response to Imperialism: Political and Religious Writings of Sayyid Jamal ad-Din "al-Afghani."* Berkeley and Los Angeles: University of California Press.

Keddie summarizes the life and work of this important precursor both to moderate Muslim thought and to the anti-imperialist movements of the twentieth century. The book contains translations of a number of Jamal al-Din's own writings, including writings on Islam, science, and technology.

Mitchell, Richard P. 1969. *The Society of the Muslim Brothers.* Oxford: Oxford University Press.

This detailed history of Hasan al-Banna's organization is still the best description of the origin and activities of the Middle East's first modern Islamic political movement. Focusing on practical issues of inspiring, mobilizing, and organizing people, Mitchell shows how al-Banna revolutionized the way Islamic ideas could be spread by modern means.

Internet Resources

The Middle East Web Portal, found at http://www.albawaba.com, is a gateway for news and information on the Arab countries of the Middle East and North Africa. For materials produced at traditional Islamic institutions in the region, al-Azhar University's Arabic home page, http://www.alazhar.org, has a mirror site in English. A selection of sermons from Mecca and Medina is available at http://www.alminbar.com/default.asp. This site designates itself primarily as a resource for Muslim preachers and prayer leaders, but browsing through its sermons can be instructive on the kinds of topics and the tone of their discussions that are popular among some circles of contemporary Muslims.

Other Muslim organizations of more explicitly political orientations, such as the Islamic Salvation Front of Algeria (http://www.ccfis.org), also have significant Web presences. Web sites for such Islamist radical organizations as Hizbullah (Lebanon) and Hamas (Palestine), not to mention legitimate news organizations such as the English-language site of al-Jazeera, the satellite news network based in Qatar, are sophisticated, eye-catching, and more elaborate than those for most mainline Muslim institutions or movements. But they are regularly hacked, blocked, and otherwise disrupted by governments, individual hackers, and others, so links to them often do not work. In addition, changes in U.S. laws, law enforcement, and popular mood since 2001 mean that access or reference to these sites can sometimes be perceived as sinister or supportive of their aims and methods.

Alongside these more conservative materials, there are plenty of resources online for the study of Islamic modernism and liberalism. A great gateway for these materials can be found at http://www.unc.edu/~kurzman/LiberalIslam Links.htm. There is also a site dedicated to Muslims who are lesbian, gay, bisexual, transgender, or intersex at http://www.al-fatiha.net. Modern Muslim mystical groups are also represented in cyberspace at sites such as that dedicated to Turkish teacher Sayyid Nursi, at http://www.bediuzzaman.org/.

3. Shi'ite Islam in Contemporary Iran: From Islamic Revolution to Moderating Reform

Primary Sources Available in English

Khomeini, Ayatollah Ruhollah. *Islamic Government* [**Hokumat-e Islami**]. Translated by Hamid Algar. http://khomeini.hypermart.net/hukumat/right.html.

This is an English translation of Khomeini's Persian text, which argued for the establishment of a modern government guided by clerics. He applies the premodern Shi'ite idea of the guardianship of the jurist *(velayat-e faqih)* to solving contemporary problems of authority and power.

Nasr, S. H., H. Dabashi, and S. V. R. Nasr, eds. 1989. *Expectation of the Millennium: Shi'ism in History.* Albany: State University of New York Press.

This volume contains the most complete compilation of primary texts on Shi'ite political thought from both the premodern and the modern periods up to the Revolution. The book is divided into sections on politics, history, and minorities, and a preface introduces each section.

Shariati, Ali. 1980. *Marxism and Other Western Fallacies: An Islamic Critique.* Translated by R. Campbell. Berkeley, CA: Mizan Press.

This book is a collection of lectures and writings by Shariati, the major ideologue of the Iranian Revolution. It is an excellent example of his thought, showing how he employed modern Western philosophical notions in remaking traditional Shi'ite thinking into a type of political ideology.

Soroush, Abdol Karim. 2000. *Reason, Freedom, and Democracy in Islam: Essential Writings of 'Abdolkarim Soroush.* Translated, edited, and with a critical introduction by Mahmoud Sadri and Ahmad Sadri. New York: Oxford University Press.

This is currently the most complete English compilation of Abdol Karim Soroush's works. It is necessary reading for any understanding of his reformist thought.

Tabataba'i, Allamah Sayyid Muhammad Husayn. 1977. *Shi'ite Islam.* Translated from the Persian, edited, and with an introduction and notes by Seyyed Hossein Nasr. 2nd ed. Albany: State University of New York Press.

This book is a felicitous summary of key notions of Shi'ite belief and practice, written by one of the greatest authorities in this tradition. Although this book does not discuss the politics that led to the Revolution, it does offer, from a practitioner's perspective, a sense of what it means to be Twelver Shi'ite. This is a beautiful indigenous complement to Heinz Halm's more scholarly and contemporary presentation.

Secondary Sources

Arjomand, Said Amir. 1984. *The Shadow of God and the Hidden Imam: Religion, Political Order, and Societal Change in Shi'ite Iran from the Beginning to 1890.* Chicago: University of Chicago Press.

———. 2000. *The Turban for the Crown: The Islamic Revolution in Iran.* Bridgewater, NJ: Replica Books. Originally Oxford University Press, 1988.

These two works are classics of sociological exposition on the role and meaning of clergy in Iran from their appearance in the sixteenth century until the establishment of the Islamic Republic of Iran.

Ayoub, Mahmoud. 1978. *Redemptive Suffering in Islam: A Study of the Devotional*

Aspects of Ashura in Twelver Shi'ism. The Hague: Mouton.

The most complete pre-Revolution account of Twelver interpretations of the martyrdom of Husayn, from both textual and anthropological sources, this work also contains discussions of the meanings of the various acts that occur during the Ashura celebrations.

Chelkowski, Peter, ed. 1979. *Ta'ziyeh: Ritual and Drama in Iran.* New York: New York University Press.

This work, written before the Iranian Revolution, is the most complete discussion of the staging and performance of Ashura plays on Husayn's martyrdom, based upon both textual and anthropological data.

Esposito, John L., and R. K. Ramazani, eds. 2001. *Iran at the Crossroads.* New York: Palgrave.

This multidisciplinary collection of essays on the current situation of Iran covers topics including current reform movements, the changing role of women, the economy, and the history and state of U.S.-Iranian relations. It is currently the most complete interdisciplinary summary of developments in contemporary Iran.

Fischer, Michael M. J. 1980. *Iran: From Religious Dispute to Revolution.* Cambridge, MA: Harvard University Press.

This groundbreaking study of the social life and role of the clergy just before the Revolution offers impressive descriptions of life of the *madrasa*s, the rise of Qom as an important political center of clerical learning, colorful descriptions of Shi'ite rituals, and discussions of how these ideas and rituals were politically transformed to bring about the Revolution.

Halm, Heinz. 1999. *Shi'a Islam: From Religion to Revolution.* Translated from the German by Allison Brown. Princeton: Markus Wiener Publishers.

This work is the most complete and easiest to read introduction to the basics of Shi'ite doctrine and history.

Jahanbakhsh, Forough. 2001. *Islam, Democracy, and Religious Modernism in Iran (1953–2000): From Bazargan to Soroush.* Leiden: Brill.

Jahanbakhsh presents an in-depth analysis of central Shi'ite thinking on the compatibility between democracy and Islamic law.

Loeffler, Reinhold. 1998. *Islam in Practice: Religious Beliefs in a Persian Village.* Albany: State University of New York Press.

This anthropological account, based on twenty-five years of research, portrays the diversity of Islamic beliefs and practices in a peasant village in Iran.

Each chapter is structured as a question-and-answer interview devoted to a single person and is prefaced with a basic anthropological description of that person's life.

Mir-Hosseini, Ziba. 1999. *Islam and Gender: The Religious Debate in Contemporary Iran.* Princeton: Princeton University Press.

   This book is the most complete account of the debates raging over the meaning and social rights and abilities of women in Iran today. The author uses both copious anthropological fieldwork data and textual sources to support her analyses.

Mottahedeh, Roy. 1985. *The Mantle of the Prophet: Religion and Politics in Iran.* New York: Pantheon Books.

   This work, now a classic text on the rise of Shi'ite clerics in the modern period, is written in the form of a biographical novel about a fictitious clerical student in Qom. All the important thinkers and events of the modern period are mentioned in this beautifully written and very informative text.

Yaghmaian, Behzad. 2002. *Social Change in Iran: An Eyewitness Account of Dissent, Defiance, and New Movements for Rights.* Albany: State University of New York Press.

   In readable and poignant prose, Yaghmaian offers the most complete account of the growing current of social movements for government reform. He employs interviews, personal ethnographic experience, television, newspapers, magazines, and official government documents to paint a compelling picture of the tremendous groundswell of opposition to the current regime.

Internet Resources

The government of the Islamic Republic of Iran maintains a number of English-language Web sites. For example, news and information on culture, tourism, foreign policy, and consular affairs can be found at http://www.salamiran.org. Information in English on the Iranian president can be found at http://www.president.ir. Beyond these official government materials, there are also a number of independent Iranian Muslim Web sites accessible in English. For example, a site containing lectures and academic papers of Abdol Karim Soroush can be found at http://www.seraj.org. There are also less-academic sites, such as the "cyber tea house" of Mashhad (at http://www.farsinet.com/mashhad/), which contains images of this city as well as information on pilgrimages there and other cultural interests.

4. Debating Orthodoxy, Contesting Tradition: Islam in Contemporary South Asia

Primary Sources Available in English

Asad, Muhammad. 2000. *The Road to Mecca.* Louisville, KY: Fons Vitae.

This is the autobiography of Leopold Weiss, one of the highest-profile Western converts to Islam in the twentieth century. During one phase of his remarkable life, he spent time in Pakistan involved in political and diplomatic affairs.

Iqbal, Allama Muhammad. [1934] 1982. *The Reconstruction of Religious Thought in Islam.* Lahore: Ashraf Press.

This is the most widely read English prose work by the poet and philosopher Muhammad Iqbal. Through the latter half of the twentieth century, it was read by Muslims in South Asia and beyond and appreciated for its modern reappraisal of the place of *ijtihad* in the development of Islamic thought.

Jameelah, Maryam. 1976. *Islam and Western Society: A Refutation of the Modern Way of Life.* Lahore: Muhammad Yusuf Khan.

This popular polemical tract was written by an American woman convert to Islam who has spent most of her active life in Pakistan, where she came to be associated with Mawlana Mawdudi's Jama'at-i Islami.

Mawdudi, Sayyid Abu'l A'la. [1940] 1970. *Towards Understanding Islam.* Translated and edited by K'urshid Ahmad. Lahore: Idara Tarjuman-ul-Qur'an.

This is one of the most popular tracts written by the founder of the Jama'at-i Islami. Along with Sayyid Qutb of the Egyptian Muslim Brotherhood, Mawdudi has been one of the most influential voices in the development of Islamic fundamentalism in the modern world.

Metcalf, Barbara Daly, trans. 1992. *Perfecting Women: Maulana Ashraf 'Ali Thanawi's "Bihishti Zewar."* Berkeley and Los Angeles: University of California Press.

Metcalf's introduction to this work does an excellent job of framing discussions of this translation of one of the most popular works by the Deobandi *alim,* Maulana Ashraf Ali Thanawi.

Secondary Studies

Ernst, Carl W., and Bruce B. Lawrence. 2002. *Sufi Martyrs of Love: The Chishti Order in South Asia and Beyond.* New York: Palgrave Macmillan.

This is a comprehensive survey of one of South Asia's oldest and most dynamic Sufi orders. Drawing on a rich archive of textual and ethnographic material, the authors examine Sufi thought and ritual practice against the backdrop of social and political change.

Masud, Khalid, ed. 2001. *Travelers in Faith: Studies of the Tablighi Jama'at as a Transnational Islamic Movement for Faith Renewal.* Leiden: Brill.

This edited volume contains essays from twelve prominent scholars that explore the Tablighi Jama'at as a global Islamic missionary movement. The contributors examine the organization's history, ideology, and practices in South Asia, Africa, Europe, and North America.

Nasr, Seyyed Vali Reza. 1995. *Mawdudi and the Making of Islamic Revivalism.* New York: Oxford University Press.

This book is a study of the life, teachings, and enduring legacy of one of the most prominent Islamist ideologues of the twentieth century. It explores Mawdudi's revivalist teachings on Islamic scripture, faith and practice, and politics.

———. 2001. *Islamic Leviathan: Islam and the Making of State Power.* Oxford: Oxford University Press.

This monograph is a comparative study of the politics of Islamization in two postcolonial Muslim states: Pakistan and Malaysia. The author charts how political leaders in both countries have attempted to appropriate Islamic symbols and Islamist ideology to legitimize and solidify state power.

Rashid, Ahmed. 2000. *Taliban: Islam, Oil, and the New Great Game in Central Asia.* London: Tauris.

Written by a prominent Pakistani journalist, this book offers the most comprehensive analysis available on the history of the Taliban movement. Written before September 11, 2001, it provides information and insight on the tragic history of Afghanistan and the rise of Islamic militancy in South and Central Asia.

Zaman, Muhammad Qasim. 2002. *The Ulama in Contemporary Islam: Custodians of Change.* Princeton: Princeton University Press.

This book examines the complex and creative responses of Islamic religious scholars to the challenges of modernity. Focusing on the debates over Islamic authority and authenticity in numerous contemporary Muslim societies, the author explores the diverse roles of the contemporary *ulama* as religious thinkers, social commentators, and political activists.

Internet Resources

English-language Internet resources are plentiful for those interested in further exploring various aspects of Islam in contemporary South Asia. A number of major Muslim organizations active in the region have their own official English-language Web pages, including the Dar al-Ulum *madrasa* at Deoband (http://www.darululoom-deoband.com/english/index.htm), the Jama'at-i Islami (http://www.jamaat.org), and the Tablighi Jama'at (http://www.almadinah .org). Material related to the life and work of Muhammad Iqbal can be found at the home page of the Iqbal Academy of Pakistan, http://www.allamaiqbal .com, and the Chishti Sabiri Sufi order discussed in Chapter 4 runs an online bookstore at http://www.moonovermedina.com.

5. Islam in Contemporary Central Asia

Primary Sources Available in English

Aini, Sadriddin. 1998. *The Sands of the Oxus: Boyhood Reminiscences of Sadriddin Aini.* Translated by Rachel Lehr and John Perry. Costa Mesa, CA: Mazda Publishers.

This is one of the very few twentieth-century writings by a Central Asian Muslim to be translated into English. Aini grew up in rural Bukhara in the Russian imperial period. These reminiscences were written after the Russian Revolution, and they remain the greatest work of modern Central Asian autobiography. The translated volume contains only the first fourth of the original Tajik-language text.

Kurzman, Charles, ed. 2002. *Modernist Islam, 1840–1940: A Sourcebook.* New York: Oxford University Press.

This anthology includes excerpts from some of the writings of Central Asian Muslims associated with the Jadid movement.

Secondary Studies

DeWeese, Devin. 1994. *Islamization and Native Religion in the Golden Horde: Baba Tükles and Conversion to Islam in Historical and Epic Tradition.* University Park: Pennsylvania State University Press.

This is the best religious history of the region in the premodern period. Its sheer length may be a challenge for more casual readers, but it is richly rewarding and quite unparalleled in its scope and conceptual sophistication.

Keller, Shoshana. 2001. *To Moscow, Not Mecca: The Soviet Campaigns against Islam in Central Asia, 1917–1941.* Westport, CT: Praeger.

This recent monograph studies the early Soviet campaigns against Islam in Central Asia.

Khalid, Adeeb. 1998. *The Politics of Muslim Cultural Reform: Jadidism in Central Asia.* Berkeley and Los Angeles: University of California Press.

This is a study of the development of Muslim modernism in Central Asia during the Russian imperial period.

Levin, Theodore. 1997. *The Hundred Thousand Fools of God: Musical Travels in Central Asia (and Queens, New York).* Bloomington: Indiana University Press.

Although this book does not deal directly with Islam, it is an astute account of cultural transformations in the Soviet period and their post-Soviet aftermath. It is written with verve and humor, and as a bonus, it comes with a CD of Uzbek music.

Privratsky, Bruce. 2001. *Muslim Turkistan: Kazak Religion and Collective Memory.* London: Curzon Press.

It was practically impossible for foreigners to do fieldwork in the Soviet Union, and the first non-Soviet ethnographic accounts of Central Asia have just begun to appear in print. This account of contemporary Kazakh attitudes toward Islam is an excellent beginning.

Rashid, Ahmed. 2002. *Jihad: The Rise of Militant Islam in Central Asia.* New Haven: Yale University Press.

This account of contemporary Islamist militancy in Central Asia features some good reportage, but it suffers from a lack of historical perspective and is riddled with factual errors.

Ro'i, Yaacov. 2000. *Islam in the Soviet Union: From the Second World War to Gorbachev.* New York: Columbia University Press.

This work is a ponderous account of Soviet bureaucratic policies toward Islam in the post–World War II period.

Roy, Olivier. 2000. *The New Central Asia: The Creation of Nations.* London: Tauris.

There still does not exist an adequate account of twentieth-century Central Asian history in English, but this is the closest thing to one.

Internet Resources

There are several excellent English-language Web sites devoted to Central Asia or prominently featuring Central Asian material. Perhaps the best portal into contemporary scholarship on the region is the Central Eurasian Studies World Wide site Resources for the Study of Central Eurasia (http://cesww.fas.harvard .edu). For a general introduction to the region and its culture, see the delightful Silk Road Seattle site maintained by the University of Washington at http://depts.washington.edu/uwch/silkroad/exhibit/index.shtml. News from the region can be followed at a number of sites. The Eurasia Net Web site (http://www.eurasianet.org), supported by the Open Society Institute of the Soros Foundation, is the preeminent portal for current affairs in the region. The London-based Institute for War and Peace Reporting (http://www .iwpr.net) provides weekly news analysis. Human Rights Watch has maintained an office in Tashkent since the early 1990s and maintains a Web page on Central Asia (http://www.hrw.org/campaigns/cenasia/index.shtml), where issues of religious freedom are prominently featured.

6. Islam in China: Accommodation or Separatism?

Secondary Studies

Fletcher, Joseph. 1996. *Studies on Chinese and Islamic Inner Asia.* Edited by Beatrice Manz. London: Variorum Press.
   This collection of essays is still the leading reference work for scholars interested in connections among the Islamic societies in the Middle East, across Eurasia, and in China.

Forbes, Andrew D. W. 1986. *Warlords and Muslims in Chinese Central Asia.* Cambridge: Cambridge University Press.
   This is the best overview available in English of the internecine politics dividing China's Muslims, as well as a good introduction to the region now known as Xinjiang during the first half of the last century, before the Muslims of Xinjiang were finally and fully incorporated into the Chinese state.

Gladney, Dru C. 1996. *Muslim Chinese: Ethnic Nationalism in the People's Republic.* 2nd ed. Cambridge, MA: Harvard University Press.
   This work is the leading ethnographic study of China's Muslim nationalities, with four case studies of Muslim communities across China.

Israeli, Raphael. 1978. ***Muslims in China.*** London: Curzon Press; Atlantic Highlands, NJ: Humanities Press.

This early study examines the history of Islam in China as one of alienation and rebellion. Unfortunately, the work suffers from a biased view of Islamic accommodation to non-Muslim rule, but nevertheless it contains invaluable material on Chinese imperial rule over Muslim regions.

Lipman, Jonathan. 1997. ***Familiar Strangers: A History of Muslims in Northwest China.*** Seattle: University of Washington Press.

This book is a very readable and useful overview of the history of Islam in China, with a focus on the Republican nationalist period and last half of the Qing Empire (eighteenth to early nineteenth centuries).

Rudelson, Justin Jon. 1997. ***Oasis Identities: Uyghur Nationalism along China's Silk Road.*** New York: Columbia University Press.

This is the best available ethnographic study of Uyghurs in Xinjiang. It is based on fieldwork conducted in the mid-1990s and is geographically focused on the Turpan region.

Internet Resources

Photographs of northwest China and its Muslim populations and the text of lectures dealing with other aspects of Islam in China can be found at www.hawaii.edu/dru.

Information relating to Uyghuristan/East Turkistan, including maps, are available at www.ccs.uky.edu/~rakhim/et.html. As mentioned in Chapter 6, many of the transnational organizations advocating Uyghur autonomy from China have active Web sites. The home page of the East Turkistan (Uyghuristan) National Congress appears in English at www.eastturkistan.com/html/main.html. The East Turkestan information center—whose banner proclaims that it supports "Freedom, Independence and Democracy for East Turkistan!"—can be found at www.uygur.org/. As do many other sites of this kind, this one has mirror sites available in a number of languages, ranging from Arabic and Turkish to German and Chinese. The Web site of the Uyghur American Association (UAA) is www.uyghuramerican.org/.

7. Muslim Thought and Practice in Contemporary Indonesia

Primary Sources Available in English

Kurzman, Charles, ed. 1998. *Liberal Islam: A Sourcebook.* New York: Oxford University Press.

————, ed. 2002. *Modernist Islam, 1840–1940: A Sourcebook.* New York: Oxford University Press.

These two readers are great resources for the study of Islam in the modern world. Both contain translations of Indonesian texts, including pieces by Mohamad Natsir, Ahmad Hassan, and Nurcholish Madjid.

Renard, John, ed. 1998. *Windows on the House of Islam: Muslim Sources on Spirituality and Religious Life.* Berkeley and Los Angeles: University of California Press.

Among the short texts translated in this anthology are pieces from a number of modern Indonesian Muslim authors, including Nurcholish Madjid and Hamka.

Rodgers, Susan. 1995. *Telling History, Telling Lives: Autobiography and Historical Imagination in Modern Indonesia.* Berkeley and Los Angeles: University of California Press.

This anthropological study of two modern Indonesian memoirs includes an English translation of Muhamad Radjab's *Village Childhood.* Radjab grew up as a Muslim in the Minangkabau region of West Sumatra, and this work conveys aspects of the dramatic changes that the Muslim society there was experiencing in the early twentieth century.

Secondary Studies

Barton, Greg. 2002. *Abdurrahman Wahid: Muslim Democrat, Indonesian President.* Honolulu: University of Hawai'i Press.

This authorized biography of the Muslim leader Abdurrahman Wahid, affectionately referred to by his followers as Gus Dur, traces his experiences from his youth spent in the traditional Muslim milieu of Javanese *pesantren,* through his student days in Cairo and Baghdad and his rise to national prominence as head of the Nahdlatul Ulama organization, to his eventual presidency of the Republic of Indonesia.

Beatty, Andrew. 1999. *Varieties of Javanese Religion: An Anthropological Account.* Cambridge: Cambridge University Press.

This is an ethnographic study of a Muslim society in eastern Java that was heavily affected by the events of 1965. It addresses issues of religious identity and "Javanism," as well as interaction with and conversion to Hindu religious systems.

Bowen, John R. 1993. *Muslims through Discourse: Religion and Ritual in Gayo Society.* Princeton: Princeton University Press.

————. 2003. *Islam, Law, and Equality in Indonesia: An Anthropology of Public Reasoning.* Cambridge: Cambridge University Press.

Both of these works are excellent anthropological studies of the ways Islam is constructed and interpreted between local and broader contexts in the Gayo region of Sumatra. They are also sophisticated essays that go beyond this local focus to frame approaches that can be useful for the study of Islam in other societies as well.

Dijk, Kees van. 2001. *A Country in Despair: Indonesia between 1997 and 2000.* Leiden: KITLV Press.

This work chronicles the dramatic changes that took place in Indonesian society after the Asian financial crisis and through the fall of Suharto's New Order. It devotes considerable attention to developments within various sectors of the Indonesian Muslim community.

Gade, Anna M. 2004. *Perfection Makes Practice: Learning, Emotion, and the Recited Qur'an in Indonesia.* Honolulu: University of Hawai'i Press.

This is a study of widespread contemporary Islamic revitalization in Indonesia in the 1990s. It focuses on the promotion and popularity of practices relating to the recitation of the Qur'an, including reading, memorization, and competition.

George, Kenneth M., and Mamannoor. 2002. A.D. *Pirous: Vision, Faith, and a Journey in Indonesian Art, 1955–2002.* Bandung, Indonesia: Yayasan Serambi Pirous.

This portrait of the life and work of a Muslim artist from Aceh, Sumatra, vividly illustrates how his painting and calligraphy relate to half a century of contemporary experience in Indonesia with respect to politics, Islam, and local, national, and global systems of aesthetics.

Hefner, Robert W. 2000. *Civil Islam: Muslims and Democratization in Indonesia.* Princeton: Princeton University Press.

This historically informed anthropological study of the development of Islamic politics has already achieved the status of a classic for its analysis of important aspects of Indonesia's late twentieth-century Islamic revival, including Muslim debates on issues of pluralism and democracy in modern Indonesia.

Laffan, Michael F. 2003. *Islamic Nationhood and Colonial Indonesia: The Umma below the Winds.* London: Routledge.

This is a superb study of the influences of international Islam and Dutch colonial institutions on religious and political developments in the Indonesian archipelago during the modern period.

Ricklefs, M. C. 1981. *A History of Modern Indonesia, c. 1300 to the Present.* Bloomington: Indiana University Press.

This is a richly researched and readable introduction to the history of the Indonesian archipelago in the period since the arrival of Islam.

Riddell, Peter G. 2001. *Islam in the Malay-Indonesian World: Transmission and Responses.* Honolulu: University of Hawai'i Press.

This volume presents aspects of the religious thought of several major Muslim authors of Southeast Asia from the seventeenth through the twentieth centuries, with a special emphasis on works of Qur'anic interpretation.

Woodward, Mark R., ed. 1996. *Toward a New Paradigm: Recent Developments in Indonesian Islamic Thought.* Tempe: Arizona State University Program for Southeast Asian Studies.

This interesting collection of essays by both Indonesian and Western scholars covers a number of topics of contemporary importance to Indonesian Muslims, ranging from *hajj* tourism to Islamic banking.

Internet Resources

For a general gateway to resources for the study of contemporary Indonesia, visit Antara Kita, the Web site of the Indonesian Studies Committee, Association for Asian Studies (http://www.antarakita.net/index.html). The Dutch Royal Institute of Linguistics and Anthropology (KITLV) also has an English-language Web site (http://www.kitlv.nl/) full of useful materials from Indonesian studies, including a daily report of Indonesian current events and a searchable database. Another valuable resource for material of this kind can be found in the searchable archives of the Apa Kabar database at http://www.library.ohiou.edu/indopubs/. An informative report on Islam in Indonesia, from a public affairs conference cosponsored by the United States–Indonesia Society (USINDO) and the Asia Foundation can be found at http://www.usindo.org/Briefs/Islam%20in%20Indonesia.htm. An archive of scholarly articles on Indonesian Islam, culture, and politics, can be found at http://www.indopubs.com/inco.html. For a selection of writings in English by liberal Indonesian Muslims, visit http://islamlib.com/english.html.

8. Religion, Language, and Nationalism: Harari Muslims in Christian Ethiopia

Primary Sources Available in English

Leslau, Wolf, ed. 1965. *Ethiopians Speak: Studies in Cultural Background.* Vol. 1, *Harari.* Berkeley and Los Angeles: University of California Press.

This volume contains English translations of original documents written on Harari culture by Harari students in the United States.

"Luqtat al-Tarikhiyya" [Gleanings of History]

Because of the lack of easily available English-language primary sources on Ethiopian Islam, a translation of this Arabic text that recently circulated Harar is included in Chapter 8 of this volume. It is a short document that relates contemporary conceptions of Harari culture and history.

Secondary Sources

Bahru Zewde. 2002. *A History of Modern Ethiopia, 1855–1991.* London: James Currey.

This is one of the two best general histories of Ethiopia (see Harold Marcus, below), although it is limited to the modern period.

Braukämper, Ulrich. 1997. **"Islamic Principalities in Southeast Ethiopia between the Thirteenth and Sixteenth Centuries."** *Ethiopianist Notes* 1, no. 1: 17–56, and no. 2: 1–44.

These articles usefully supplement J. Spencer Trimingham's monograph (see below), however they assume prior knowledge of Ethiopian history and can be hard for beginners to follow. Owing to the limitations of available written sources, Braukämper also utilizes linguistics, stone inscriptions, archaeology, and oral traditions.

Caulk, R. A. 1977. **"Harär Town and Its Neighbors in the Nineteenth Century."** *Journal of African History* 18, no. 3: 369–386.

This is essentially an account of Harari-Oromo relations from the mid-eighteenth century to 1887. Caulk explores the ties between urban Harari and the predominantly pastoral Oromo. Depending on the Oromo for their livelihood, the Harari sought to convert them to Islam so as to be better able to control them.

Davis, Asa J. 1963–1964. **"The Sixteenth Century Jihad in Ethiopia and the Impact on Its Culture."** *Journal of the Historical Society of Nigeria* 2, no. 4: 567–595; 3, no. 1: 113–128.
    This two-part article argues that the *jihad* was initially "merely a continuation of perennial conflicts" whose purpose was primarily political. Davis explores the influences of Yemeni *Zaydis* on the jihad, as well as the conflicts' effects on Muslim groups.

Erlich, Haggai. 1994. *Ethiopia and the Middle East.* Boulder, CO: Lynne Rienner Publishers.
    This is an excellent study of historical relations and attitudes between Ethiopia and the Middle East over a period of 1500 years.

Hussein Ahmed. 2001. *Islam in Nineteenth-Century Wallo, Ethiopia: Revival, Reform, and Reaction.* Leiden: Brill.
    This text is primarily a regional history of southern and southeastern Wallo province, but Hussein engages larger questions such as the Islamization of Ethiopia, the relationships between local Muslim leaders and national Christian dynasts, and some of the ways in which politics, ethnicity, and religion have interacted.

Marcus, Harold G. 2002. *A History of Ethiopia.* Berkeley and Los Angeles: University of California Press.
    This book is the most readable general history of the country and is probably the best place to start a research project, but it is not as critically analytical as Bahru Zewde's (see above).

Taddesse Tamrat. 1972. *Church and State in Ethiopia: 1270–1527.* Oxford: Clarendon Press.
    Based largely on court chronicles and hagiographies, this is a major text in Ethiopian historiography. Seeking to trace the long-term and continuous development of the Ethiopian state, it also contains useful information on Islam.

Trimingham, J. Spencer. 1952. *Islam in Ethiopia.* London: Oxford University Press.
    The first and last major overview of Ethiopian Islamic history, this book is a classic. Written by a Christian missionary and now more than fifty years old, it has its biases and faults. However, it remains extremely useful and is a must read for those interested in the topic.

Wagner, Ewald. 1998. **"Harari Texts—A Literary Analysis."** In *Collectanea Aethiopica,* edited by Siegbart Uhlig and Bairu Tafla, 203–215. Stuttgart: Franz Steiner Verlag Wiesbaden GMBH.

This article analyzes Harari literary texts, situating them in broader Ethiopian and Islamic settings. The use of Harari enhances comprehensibility and the use of Arabic places works "on a higher literary level." Wagner concludes that Harari literature shares more with the Islamic/Arabic cultural world than the highland Ethiopian one.

Waldron, Sidney. 1974. **"Social Organization and Social Control in the Walled City of Harar, Ethiopia."** PhD diss., Columbia University.

This first of three dissertations that have been written on Harar town, this work is the starting place for anyone who wants to understand Harari society, culture, and history.

Internet Sources

Most of the Web sites on either Ethiopian history or Ethiopian Islam are so politicized, inaccurate, or both that none should be recommended. Nonetheless, the best one available for Harar is probably http://www.iharar.com. Some photographs of a Harari wedding may be seen at http://www.zawaj.com/weddingways/harar.html, although even there a couple of the captions are incorrect. A few somewhat useful links for religion in Ethiopia can be found at http://www.ou.edu/mideast/country/ethiopia.htm.

9. Race, Ideology, and Islam in Contemporary South Africa

Primary Sources Available in English

Adams, C. 1968. **"Muhammad 'Abduh and Transvaal Fatwa."** In *The Macdonald Presentation Volume,* edited by W. G. Shellabear, 13–29. Freeport, NY: Books for Libraries Press (Princeton University Press).

This short piece is an in-depth treatment of the brief Arabic text written by the Egyptian Islamic modernist Muhammad Abduh in response to legal questions posed to him by South African Muslims.

Esack, F. 1997. *Qur'an, Liberation, and Pluralism: An Islamic Perspective of Interreligious Solidarity against Oppression.* Oxford: Oneworld.

This seminal book on the Qur'an, situated in the antiapartheid struggle of the Muslim Youth Movement, departs from that specific context to formulate a more general approach to the Qur'an, an approach informed by concerns for social justice.

Safi, Omid, ed. 2003. *Progressive Muslims on Justice, Gender, and Pluralism*. Oxford: Oneworld.

This volume contains essays by Muslim scholars dealing with some of today's most complex and pressing social issues. Included among them are contributions from some of the writers referred to in Chapter 9 of this volume, such as Ebrahim Moosa and Farid Esack.

Secondary Studies

Chidester, D. 1992. *Religions of South Africa*. London: Routledge.

This book is an excellent overview of religions in South Africa and of the particular meaning of Islam in that context.

Davids, A. 1980. *The Mosques of Bo-Kaap: A Social History of Islam at the Cape*. Cape Town: South Africa Institute of Arabic and Islamic Research.

This richly detailed history of mosques in Cape Town chronicles the development of the Muslim community there in the contexts of slavery and colonialism in the nineteenth century.

Davids, A., and Y. da Costa, eds. 1994. *Pages from Cape Muslim History*. Pietermaritzburg, South Africa: Shuter and Shooter.

This collection covers various aspects of more than 300 years of Muslim history in the Cape. It includes several interesting articles on important founding figures of the community and on some of the distinctive cultural practices associated with traditional Muslim life in this part of South Africa.

Tayob, A. I. 1995. *Islamic Resurgence in South Africa: The Muslim Youth Movement*. Cape Town: UCT Press.

This work traces the history and development of modern approaches to Islam among young, activist Muslims in the Cape during the late twentieth century.

———. 1999. *Islam in South Africa: Mosques, Imams, and Sermons*. Gainesville: University of South Florida Press.

This work compares two different mosque traditions in South Africa, including analyses of their histories, politics, and respective interpretations of Islam.

Internet Resources

A basic resource for useful information and statistics on South Africa, as well as a time line of twentieth-century South African history, is provided by the BBC at http://news.bbc.co.uk/1/hi/world/africa/country_profiles/1071886.stm. Directories and links to a large number of South African Muslim mosques, organizations, and businesses can be found at http://www.muslims.co.za/. One group, Positive Muslims of South Africa, focuses on providing support for victims of HIV/AIDS and can be found on the Web at http://www.ifh.org .uk/positive_muslims.html. A number of the South African Muslim organizations that are discussed in this chapter also have home pages, including the Jamiatul Ulama Transvaal (http://www.islamsa.org.za/) and the Jamiat Ulama Natal (http://www.jamiat.org.za/). Access to South African Muslim broadcast media is also available online through Radio 786 (www.radio786.co.za) and Channel Islam (http://www.channelislam.com).

10. Peril and Possibility: Muslim Life in the United States

Primary Sources Available in English

Hasan, Asma Gull. 2000. *American Muslims: The New Generation.* New York: Continuum.

In this book, a young South Asian American woman tackles anti-Muslim prejudice, discusses her views on American Muslim women, and presents a self-consciously American view of Islam.

Malcolm X and Alex Haley. 1973. *The Autobiography of Malcolm X.* New York: Ballantine Books.

This classic of American literature describes the protagonist's religious and political transformations as a convicted felon, Nation of Islam leader, and Meccan pilgrim.

Safi, Omid, ed. 2003. *Progressive Muslims on Justice, Gender, and Pluralism.* Oxford: Oneworld.

The editor's introduction to this collection and many of its chapters are written by Muslim scholars active in the United States. They address a range of critical topics facing Muslims in the contemporary world, including those of identity politics and religious pluralism.

Wadud, Amina. 1999. *Qur'an and Woman: Rereading the Sacred Text from a Woman's Perspective.* New York: Oxford University Press.

This book, first published in Malaysia, has generated much discussion among Muslims around the world. Wadud uses both classical and modern modes of textual criticism to render an egalitarian view of Islam and gender.

Secondary Sources

Anway, Carol L. 1995. *Daughters of Another Path: Experiences of American Women Choosing Islam.* Lee's Summit, MO: Yawna Publications.
This book provides fascinating accounts of the experiences of over fifty American female converts to Islam.

Barboza, Steven. 1993. *American Jihad: Islam after Malcolm X.* New York: Doubleday.
This is an especially good resource for the classroom, featuring interviews with a wide array of American Muslims gathered and edited by an African American convert to Islam.

Curtis, Edward E., IV. 2002. *Islam in Black America: Identity, Liberation, and Difference in African-American Islamic Thought.* Albany: State University of New York Press.
This study examines the tension between particularistic and universalistic interpretations of Islam through an intellectual history of five major figures, including Edward W. Blyden, Noble Drew Ali, Elijah Muhammad, Malcolm X, and W. D. Muhammad.

Dannin, Robert. 2002. *Black Pilgrimage to Islam.* New York: Oxford University Press.
This important work offers rich ethnographies of African American Muslim life, focusing particularly on black Sunni Muslims and addressing issues of gender, class, and Muslim identity.

DeCaro, Louis A., Jr. 1996. *On the Side of My People: A Religious Life of Malcolm X.* New York: New York University Press.
This work is the most comprehensively researched study of Malcolm X's spiritual life and religious development.

Gardell, Mattias. 1996. *In the Name of Elijah Muhammad: Louis Farrakhan and the Final Call.* Durham, NC: Duke University Press.
This work contains both historical and theological examinations of the controversial minister Louis Farrakhan and his Nation of Islam.

Haddad, Yvonne Y., and John L. Esposito, eds. 2000. *Muslims on the Americanization Path?* New York: Oxford University Press.

This stimulating volume includes essays on Islamic law, women, and continuing debates about American Muslim identity.

Haddad, Yvonne Y., and Jane I. Smith, eds. 1993. *Mission to America: Five Islamic Sectarian Communities in North America.* Gainesville: University Press of Florida.

This volume presents useful overviews of five Muslim groups in the United States, including the Druze, the Moorish Science Temple, the Ansaru Allah, the Ahmadiyya, and the United Submitters International.

————, eds. 1994. *Muslim Communities in North America.* Albany: State University of New York Press.

This volume is still the most comprehensive collection of case studies on local Muslim communities in North America. It includes research on both indigenous and immigrant Muslim groups.

Lawrence, Bruce B. 2002. *New Faiths, Old Fears: Muslims and Other Asian Immigrants in American Religious Life.* New York: Columbia University Press.

Based on Lawrence's American Lectures on the History of Religions, this volume charts the importance of racialized class in the formation of American Muslim communities and offers new directions for analyzing U.S. religious pluralism.

Leonard, Karen Isaksen. 2003. *Muslims in the United States: The State of Research.* New York: Russell Sage.

A necessary volume for all scholars and teachers of Islam in the United States, this book offers the most comprehensive review of scholarly literature on American Muslims ever produced. It can also be used as a college-level overview of the history and life of Muslims in the United States.

McAlister, Melani. 2001. *Epic Encounters: Culture, Media, and U.S. Interests in the Middle East, 1945–2000.* Berkeley and Los Angeles: University of California Press.

Discussing such wide-ranging sources as popular movies, national security documents, and museum exhibits, McAlister shows the importance of the Middle East and Islam to U.S. politics and life, and in turn, she analyzes U.S. views and policies toward the Middle East.

McCloud, Aminah Beverly. 1995. *African American Islam.* New York: Routledge.

This pioneering overview of various African American Muslim groups addresses issues pertaining to black Muslim women and African American Muslim families.

Said, Edward W. 1997. *Covering Islam: How the Media and the Experts Determine How We See the Rest of the World.* New York: Vintage Books.

This provocative study examines the ways U.S. media and popular film images of Islam are shaped by dominant economic and political interests.

Webb, Gisela, ed. 2000. *Windows of Faith: Muslim Women Scholar-Activists in North America.* Syracuse, NY: Syracuse University Press.

This collection of essays offers discussions of Muslim women and the Qur'an, law, literature, and Islamic activism.

Internet Resources

Project MAPS (http://www.projectmaps.com) is overseen by the Center for Muslim-Christian Understanding at Georgetown University. The project sponsors large-scale studies of Muslims in the United States.

The Council for American-Islamic Relations (http://www.cair-net.org) is a Washington, D.C.–based political activism group that lobbies on behalf of Muslims and sponsors research on the American Muslim community.

The Islamic Society of North America (http://www.isna.net), the largest Muslim organization in the United States, publishes *Islamic Horizons* and holds a popular annual convention.

The Islamic Circle of North America (http://www.icna.com) is a national organization focused on the political and religious development of the Muslim community in North America.

Azizah (http://www.azizahmagazine.com) is a magazine "for the contemporary Muslim women" published in Atlanta, Georgia.

Al-Fatiha (http://www.al-fatiha.net) offers on-line support for gay, lesbian, bisexual, and transgendered Muslims.

Louis Farrakhan's Nation of Islam site (http://www.noi.org) offers information about the movement, the leader's speeches, and links to the *Final Call* newspaper.

Wallace D. Muhammad (now W. D. Mohammed) can be heard on New Africa Radio (http://newafricaradio.com), which also contains links to the American Society of Muslims and its official newspaper, the *Muslim Journal.*

Chapter Twelve

Key Terms

The heading for each entry in this section includes, in parentheses, the numbers of the chapters in which the term is used or discussed. Many of the terms listed are originally from Arabic, but they have also been integrated into the other languages of various Muslim societies. The entries are listed in the transliterated forms that are used in the various chapters of this volume, and their definitions reflect some of the variations in their meanings in the different times and places covered in this text. The boldface words in the texts of these definitions themselves have entries in this chapter.

Afocha (8)
Community organizations in Harar, Ethiopia. Their primary function is to plan and organize weddings and funerals. After the first year of married life, an individual is invited to join an *afocha* by a friend, relative, or neighbor already in the group. Members come from different **ahli** and **mariññet,** as well as from different neighborhoods, social classes, and occupations, so *afocha* provide yet another social institution that encourages Harari solidarity.

Agha Khan (10)
See **Isma'ilis**

Ahl al-sunna wa'l-jama'a (1, 4)
An Arabic term meaning "people of the way [of the Prophet] and the community." It has historically been used to denote the majority of Muslims—popularly referred to as **Sunnis**—as opposed to **Shi'ite** Muslims. However, in the modern period, the term has also come to be used within Sunni communities in polemics over religious authority to define Muslim tradition.

Ahli (8)
A term used to refer to extended family relationships in Harar, Ethiopia. Posi-

tion within one's *ahli* can establish an individual's connections to dozens of households throughout the town and further abroad.

Ahmadiyya (10)

A group established in the late nineteenth century in the Punjab region of India by Ghulam Ahmad, who proclaimed himself to be a "renewer" of religion, the Christian messiah, and the Islamic **Mahdi.** In most majority Muslim societies, the Ahmadiyya tend to be regarded as heretical. However, because of their active missionary programs and emphasis on distributing English translations of the **Qur'an,** they have sometimes had more success in spreading their message in some majority non-Muslim societies, including the United States, than have other Muslim groups.

Ahung (6)

Traditional Muslim teachers in China. Often these were itinerant scholars who moved from one Muslim settlement to another, rarely staying in one place for longer than a few years. The word is derived from the Persian *akhund,* which was used in Iran to refer to members of the **Ithna'ashari** Shi'ite clergy.

Akbariyya (1)

Followers of the Sufi teachings of Ibn Arabi (d. 1240), who is sometimes referred to as the Shaykh al-Akbar, or "the Greatest Master."

Alim (10)

A traditionally trained Muslim religious scholar. The word *alim* is the singular form of *ulama.*

Allah

The Arabic word for "God," in the sense of the monotheistic deity worshipped by Jews and Christians as well as Muslims.

Amhara/Amharic (8)

The people, most of whom are Orthodox Christians, generally regarded as the historic rulers of Ethiopia. Their Semitic language, Amharic, is spoken by about 30 million people and is the national language of Ethiopia. Its earliest written sources are fourteenth-century songs from the Ethiopian imperial court.

Amir (8)

Arabic political or military title generally meaning "commander," "prince," or "chief."

Apartheid (9)

The system of institutionalized racial segregation promulgated under white rule in South Africa until the early 1990s. The term is originally from the Afrikaans language.

Asbab al-nuzul (1)

Arabic term meaning "the occasions of revelation." It refers to the traditional method of textual analysis used to interpret the particular circumstances in which various Qur'anic verses are believed to have been revealed to Muhammad. Muslim scholars in both the medieval and modern periods have looked to the *asbab al-nuzul* in formulating various models for contextualized interpretations of the **Qur'an.**

Ashura (3)

The tenth day of the month of Muharram in the Islamic lunar calendar. For **Sunnis** it is a holy day, observed by an optional fast and other ritual practices that vary according to the cultural contexts of different Muslim societies. For **Shi'ites,** Ashura commemorates the martyrdom of the third **Imam,** Husayn, at Karbala in 680 C.E. In modern Iran, this day is observed with ritualized street processions and *taziyeh,* or ritual passion plays reenacting the events of his martyrdom. The name is from the Arabic term for "the tenth."

Awliya Allah (4)

Arabic for "friends of God." This term is used in a number of Muslim countries to refer to revered **Sufi** masters, both living and dead. In the modern Chishti Sabiri order, discussed in Chapter 4, the *awliya* are invested with a charismatic authority forged through self-discipline and experiential knowledge.

Ayatollah (3)

A title for high-ranking **Shi'ite** clerics in Iran. During the twentieth century, the term came to be used to distinguish rank among the growing population of Shi'ite *mujtahids,* or authorities on Islamic law. In earlier times, this title was accorded to various individuals through informal consensus among both clerics and their followers. Since the Islamic Revolution of 1979, however, the government now reserves the sole right to officially determine those allowed to bear this title. The Arabic term literally translates as "sign of God."

Al-Azhar University (2, 6)

The Muslim educational institution founded at Cairo by the **Isma'ili** Fatimid dynasty in the tenth century. Often considered the world's oldest college, al-Azhar has since the thirteenth century come to be recognized as one of the leading centers of Sunni Islamic learning. In the modern period, it has also been the center of a number of influential developments, including the Islamic modernism promoted by Muhammad Abduh (d. 1905).

Bahasa Indonesia (7)
The official language of the modern nation-state of Indonesia. It is based upon Malay, which in earlier centuries served the populations of the archipelago as a lingua franca of trade and Muslim learning.

Bareilly (9)
See **Barelwis**

Barelwis (4)
A modern Muslim movement founded by the scholar and Qadiri **Sufi** master Ahmad Riza Khan Barelwi (1856–1921). Its membership was composed mostly of South Asian *ulama* who followed the **Hanafi** school of *fiqh,* emphasized the importance of the way of the prophet and defended the role of the *awliya Allah* as patrons and intercessors. The Barelwis blamed both British colonial rule and reformist Muslims for the decline of the community and sought to preserve intact the foundations of Islamic identity rooted in local cultural practices. Identifying themselves as the *ahl al-sunna wa'l-jama'a,* the Barelwis championed themselves as the true heirs to the legacy of the Prophet Muhammad.

Batin (4)
The "interior," or esoteric—as opposed to the "outward," or exoteric *(zahir)*—dimension of Muslim piety. The Chishti Sabiri order discussed in Chapter 4 see **Sufism** as a means by which one can find a balance between these two dimensions.

Byzantine Empire (1)
A Greek Orthodox Christian state that ruled much of the area to the north of the Arabian peninsula during the lifetime of Muhammad. Within a few decades of Muhammad's death, the Byzantine Empire had lost much of its territory around the eastern Mediterranean, and it continued to shrink until its capital, Constantinople (present Istanbul), fell to the Ottoman Turks in 1453.

Caliph (1, 8)
Title given to the leaders of the Muslim community who succeeded the Prophet after his death in 632. The English term "caliph" is derived from the Arabic *khalifa,* "successor."

Cape Malay (9)
The Muslim populations of the Cape region of South Africa, so-called because many of the first Muslims settled there had been transported from the Malay-Indonesian archipelago by the Dutch in the seventeenth century. In the twentieth century, white, Protestant, Afrikaner ideologues used "Malay" as a distinct racial category in their radically racialized partition of society.

Constitution of Medina (1)

An Arabic document preserved in an early biography of Muhammad. It purports to record the original agreement signed between various segments of the population of the oasis town of Yathrib (later Medina) in accepting the leadership of Muhammad over their community.

Cushitic (8)

One of six branches of the Afro-Asiatic language family, which also includes the Berber, Egyptian, Chadic, Omotic, and Semitic branches. The most widely spoken Cushitic languages are **Oromo** and Somali, both of which are today written in the Latin alphabet with extra characters.

Dargah (4)

The sometimes-elaborate shrine complexes that some South Asians visit in search of spiritual power and the alleviation of worldly troubles. As centers of sacred geography and fonts for public social welfare, these regional shrines still thrive as pilgrimage sites and symbols of local Muslim culture and identity.

Da'wa (1, 2, 4, 7)

The call to Islam in the form of preaching and internal Muslim proselytizing. These calls for Muslims to deepen their faith are formulated and pursued in a wide diversity of forms in modern cultural settings ranging from Southern California to Southeast Asia. The Arabic term *da'wa* literally translates as "call" or "summons."

Deoband (4, 9)

Commonly used term for the influential Dar al-Ulum *madrasa* in the small town of Deoband, northeast of Delhi, India. Established in 1867, Deoband became a major center for the active reassertion of **Sunni** orthodoxy and a locus for conservative opposition to the growing spread of Western thought and institutions. The founders of Deoband accepted some elements of **Sufi** tradition, but they rejected ritual practices that were not specifically sanctioned by a literal reading of the **Qur'an** and the *hadith,* including such popular rituals as listening to music *(sama)* and pilgrimages to the shrines of Sufi saints. The Deoband *madrasa* also coupled a Western-style university format (with faculty, formal exams, and fund-raising) with a traditional Islamic curriculum. Its leadership was deeply distrustful of Western influences and sought to revitalize Muslim society through the revival of what it considered to be traditional values. The Deobandi *ulama* are often actively engaged in public discourses on religion and society through the dissemination of legal opinions *(fatwas)* and polemical pamphlets.

Dhikr (4, 8)

A range of **Sufi** devotional practices centered on the ritualized recitation of prayers, pious formulas, and the Arabic names of God. Its specific ritual components can vary considerably across different cultural contexts and among the different teachings of various Sufi **tariqas.** The Arabic term *dhikr* means "remembrance [of God]."

Dhu'l-Hijja (1)
See **Islamic Lunar Calendar**

Fatwa (2, 4, 9)

A judicial opinion issued by a qualified scholar *(mufti)* in response to a specific question by a given petitioner. The term *fatwa* comes from the technical vocabulary of Islamic religious scholarship. In traditional Muslim societies, *fatwa*s were regarded as nonbinding legal decisions issued for the benefit of individuals and the community. In the modern period, however, the term has entered Western languages through the use of *fatwa*s in the Iranian **Shi'ite** clergy's high-profile judgment against the novelist Salman Rushdie and through the use of *fatwa*s as an increasingly popular platform for the political agendas of Islamist ideologues untrained in the intellectual traditions of Islamic legal studies.

Fiqh (1, 2, 9, 10)

Muslim jurisprudence as a field of study and legal practice. **Sunni** Islam has traditionally recognized four major schools of thought *(madhhab)* in this area: the **Hanafi, Maliki, Shafi'i,** and **Hanbali.** The Arabic term *fiqh* literally means "understanding."

Firmach (8)

An organization established in the 1920s to protect the culture and the economic well-being of the Harari ethnic community in eastern Ethiopia. Its name means "signatures."

Fivers (1)
See **Zaydis**

Ge'ez (8)

A Semitic language, now the liturgical language of Ethiopia's Orthodox Christian Church. Though it was widely spoken and used for royal inscriptions in the ancient state of Axum, today, for the most part, it is spoken only by members of the clergy. Its role in Ethiopian life is often compared to that of Latin in the West.

Gey Sinan (8)

The indigenous Harari term for the language that they speak. It literally means "the language of the city."

Gullah (10)

A creole vernacular that began on the western African coast and was developed by slaves on sea islands located off the coast of the U.S. Southeast. It combines elements of both African languages and English. Gullah became the vehicle of a unique culture that includes music, art, storytelling, and more.

Hadith (1, 4, 7, 8)

Traditions or reports of the sayings and doings of Muhammad. Each *hadith* consists of two parts, the *isnad* and the *matn,* that together reflect the early stages of the oral transmission of the material attributed to the Prophet. **Sunni** Muslims have come to accept six collections of *hadith* texts as particularly authoritative, especially the two *sahih*s of al-Bukhari (810–870) and Muslim (817–875).

Hafiz (8)

A person who has memorized the entire text of the **Qur'an** in Arabic. In many Muslim societies, children start learning the Qur'an at a young age, and those who succeed in memorizing it are also recognized in the community by various means, including by parties thrown to mark the occasion of the completion of their studies.

Hajj (1, 10)

The annual pilgrimage to Mecca (in present-day Saudi Arabia) during the month of Dhu'l-Hijja in the **Islamic lunar calendar.** The *hajj* brings Muslims from all around the world to worship together. It is the fifth of the Five Pillars of Islam.

Hanafi (1, 4)

One of the four established **Sunni** schools of Islamic jurisprudence *(fiqh)*. Its adherents trace their origins to the renowned Muslim jurist Abu Hanifa (d. 767).

Hanbali (1)

One of the four established **Sunni** schools of Islamic jurisprudence *(fiqh)*. Its adherents trace their origins to the renowned Muslim jurist Ahmad ibn Hanbal (d. 855).

Hanolato (8)
See **Kulub**

Hijab (2, 10)

Various styles of "modest dress." In many modern Muslim societies, *hijab* in the form of head coverings or even face veils for women has become a prominent focus of public debates over Islamic identity and authenticity. In many places, there has been a sharp increase in the number of women wearing *hijab* over the past three decades, and today many women in different parts of the Muslim world wear *hijab,* even though their mothers and even grandmothers did not. The Arabic term *hijab* literally means "cover" or "screen."

Hijra (1)

The migration of Muhammad and his early followers from Mecca to Yathrib (later renamed Medina) in 622 c.e. The **Islamic lunar calendar** begins its dating from this event. In the modern period, *hijra* has become an increasingly popular metaphor in some Muslim circles for a radical reinterpretation of Islam that advocates withdrawal or "migration" away from the *jahiliyya* of the modern world.

Hui (6)

One of the minority Muslim "nationalities" *(minzu)* within China. However, the Hui are defined not by a common language or geographical origin but by their adherence to Islam. The Hui have been the Muslims who went furthest in accommodating themselves to Han Chinese culture and language.

Hujum (5)

A campaign mounted by the Communist Party in 1927–1929 against religion and traditional ways of life in Muslim Central Asia. The central focus of the campaign was the unveiling of women, but the cultural revival of which the *hujum* was a part also aimed at the dismantling of Muslim institutions such as **madrasa**s and **khanaqa**s and the promotion of modern rationalism over traditional ways of life, which were called superstition.

Ibadis (1)
See **Kharijites**

Ijtihad (1, 3, 7)

The practice of independent jurisprudential reasoning by a qualified Muslim scholar *(mujtahid)*. For **Sunni** Muslims, this is pursued through the established processes of legal reasoning in light of principles derived from the authoritative sources of Islamic jurisprudence *(fiqh)*. In the modern period, agendas for reform have often been cast as exercises in *ijtihad*.

Ikhwan al-Muslimin (1, 2, 9)

Often referred to in English as the Muslim Brotherhood (or Society of Muslim

Brothers), an organization founded by an Egyptian schoolteacher named Hasan al-Banna (d. 1949). The Ikhwan grew rapidly in the 1930s and 1940s and spread beyond Egypt to other Arab countries, where it has founded hospitals, schools, and other social service organizations. The Ikhwan has also actively promoted agendas for the further Islamization of the governments of countries where they are active, sometimes through political activism and at other times through more violent means.

Imam (1, 3, 8, 10)

For **Sunni** Muslims, the leader of Islamic communal prayers *(salat)*, a man often selected for his piety and religious knowledge. "Imam" can also be an honorific title for anyone with sufficient learning and charisma. It is sometimes also used for distinguished religious scholars, including the founders of schools of legal thought *(fiqh)* and of theology *(kalam)*. For **Shi'ite** Muslims, "Imam" refers to the divinely designated familial successors *(khalifa)* of the Prophet, in particular Ali and his male progeny through his wife Fatima, the Prophet's daughter.

Intifada (1, 2)

The uprising of Palestinians against the Israeli occupation of the West Bank and the Gaza Strip. A number of Islamist political and paramilitary organizations have played significant parts in these developments since the 1980s.

Islah (4, 7)

A term used in a number of Muslim societies to refer to various programs of religious and social reform.

Islamic Lunar Calendar (1)

The traditional dating system of most Muslim societies, also referred to as the *hirji* calendar. It takes as its starting point the *hijra* and is a purely lunar system; that is, each month is determined by the actual cycle of the moon. Because this calendar does not use any system of intercalating days, it is shorter than the solar calendar by an average of eleven days a year. Thus, months do not stay associated with any given season and, for example, the festivals held during the month of Dhu'l-Hijja or at the end of Ramadhan in the Islamic lunar calendar will cycle gradually through the solar calendar months.

Isma'ilis (1, 10)

A group, also known as "Sevener" **Shi'ites,** who trace their origins to disputes within the Shi'ite community over determining the successor to the sixth Imam in 765. Since their initial split away from the Shi'ites, they have subdivided into a number of subsects, including the Nizaris, followers of the Aga

Khan. The current Aga Khan, Prince Karim Shah, receives monetary donations from his followers and in turn is the patron of a number of different public institutions, including health clinics and schools.

Isnad (1)

The first part of a **hadith** (a report of a saying of or anecdote about the
Prophet). An *isnad,* which comprises the chain of transmission, is a list of
names of early Muslims who related the material contained in the second part,
the **matn,** of the *hadith.*

Ithna'ashari Shi'ites(1, 3)

The largest subsect of Shi'ism; also referred to as the "Twelvers" or "Imami"
Shi'ites. They follow the teachings of twelve Imams descended from Ali and
Fatima and believe that the twelfth Imam has been in a state of mystical occultation since the tenth century. According to Ithna'ashari doctrine, the twelfth
Imam will appear again as the **Mahdi** to defeat the Antichrist and establish a
righteous community before the end of the world. Since 1979, an Ithna'asharite Shi'ite government has ruled Iran. There are also considerable
populations of Ithna'ashari Shi'ites found in Iraq, Syria, Lebanon, Pakistan,
and some of the Gulf states.

Jadidism (5)

A Central Asian Muslim reformist movement that arose in reaction to the loss
of sovereignty to Russian rule and the perceived threat of cultural and economic marginalization. Jadidism rejected the authority of traditional **ulama** to
interpret Islam, arguing instead for a direct return to the primary textual
sources of Islam.

Jahiliyya (1, 2)

The "Age of Ignorance" in Arabia before the coming of Islam in the seventh
century. In the modern period, some Muslim reformists have come to use the
term rhetorically in their attacks against the perceived "paganism" of the modern world.

Jahriyya (6)
See *Menhuan*

Jakarta Charter (7)

The English rendering of the Indonesian "Piagam Djakarta," referring to a
draft of the preamble to the Indonesian national constitution of 1945. This
document originally included a provision for Muslim citizens to be governed
by the **shari'a,** a provision that was ultimately dropped from the final text of

the constitution. At various times since then, some Islamist groups in the country have struggled for the reimplementation of the Jakarta Charter as a central plank in their platforms for the further Islamization of society.

Jama'at-i Islami (1, 4, 9)
An Islamic revivalist political party founded in 1941 by Sayyid Abu al-A'la Mawdudi. Since the partition of the Indian Subcontinent in 1947, it has played a particularly important role in Pakistan's domestic politics. The party's fundamentalist ideology aims to transform Pakistan into a Muslim theocratic state. Although Jama'at-i Islami has historically never done well at the ballot box, since the end of the twentieth century its profile has increased dramatically. In October 2001, Jama'at-i Islami and a coalition of five other conservative religious political parties made unprecedented gains in the general elections. This alliance now forms the third-largest political group in Pakistan's National Assembly.

Jama'atkhana (10)
The term used by the Nizari **Isma'ili** community to refer to the buildings where they gather for communal worship.

Jihad (4, 7, 8)
A term today often popularly glossed as "holy war." *Jihad* has become one of the most hotly debated words in Muslim societies as well as in the West during the modern period. Some Muslims, basing themselves on **Sufism** and other religious traditions within Islam, have reemphasized dimensions of the inward focus of the "greater *jihad*" as a struggle for self-mastery. However, in popular discourses throughout the world, *jihad* is more often used with reference to armed struggle pursued in the defense of Islam against various perceived threats. The term *jihad* comes from the Arabic root for "exertion."

Kalam (1)
An Arabic term, literally meaning "word," that has come to refer to the field of Islamic theology.

Khalifa (1, 3, 4)
A term literally meaning "successor" that is used in different ways in various Muslim societies. It can refer to the early leaders of the community following Muhammad's death (see **caliph**) or to the successors of the *shaykhs* of Sufi orders *(tariqas)*.

Khanaqa (4, 5)
Sufi lodges or hospices in many parts of the Muslim world, including Central and South Asia. The *khanaqa*s of the South Asian Chishti *tariqas*, for example,

offered intensive spiritual training for their initiates, solace for the local inhabitants who visited them for spiritual blessings, and food and shelter for the wayfarers and mendicants who survived on their charity.

Kharijites (1)

A sect that broke off on its own after becoming disillusioned with the leadership of Ali ibn Abi Talib in the seventh century. Today, some the descendants of this movement, who refer to themselves as Ibadis, make up a small minority of the world's Muslims. **Kharijite** populations are concentrated contemporary Oman and parts of East Africa.

Khilafat Movement (4)

A movement (1919–1924) that crystallized anti-British sentiments among Indian Muslims who rallied behind an attempt to preserve the Ottoman sultan as the spiritual and temporal leader (**caliph**) of Islam. Drawing the support of Mohandas Gandhi and his noncooperation movement, it marked the height of Hindu-Muslim cooperation and the promise of a unified Indian nationalist movement. Its eventual failure, however, furthered the rise of communal politics, which culminated with the partition of India and Pakistan in 1947.

Khufiyya (6)
See *Menhuan*

Kitab Kuning (7)

The traditional corpus of Muslim learning studied in the ***pondok pesantren*** and similar institutions in Southeast Asia. Included among the *kitab kuning* are works in Arabic as well as works in such local languages as Malay and Javanese but written in the Arabic script. The term *kitab kuning* literally means "yellow books" in **Bahasa Indonesia.**

Koran

A common English transliteration of "[al-]**Qur'an**," the name of the primary scripture of Islam.

Kottu (8)

A derogatory term used around Harar, Ethiopia, to refer to the **Oromo** people. In Oromo, it means "farmer" or "peasant" and was originally probably employed by Harari and other peoples to distinguish between pastoral and settled Oromo. It is also sometimes spelled "Qottuu."

Kubrawiyya (6)
See *Menhuan*

Kulub (8)
A political party founded in Harar, Ethiopia, in the late 1940s associated with the Somali Youth League (SYL). Kulub is also sometimes referred to simply as "Hanolato," an abbreviation of the Somali language phrase *Soomaliya hanoolaato,* "Long live Somalia," which was an SYL nationalist rallying cry of the period.

Madhhab (1)
A school of traditional Muslim jurisprudence *(fiqh)*. Since the medieval period, **Sunni** Muslims have recognized the equal validity of four *madhhabs:* the **Hanafi, Maliki, Shafi'i,** and **Hanbali.**

Madrasa (1, 2, 3, 4, 5, 8)
Muslim religious schools in many parts of the world. From their origins in the medieval period until the modern period, they were primarily institutions for the teaching of Islamic law and were financially supported by *waqf.* In the modern period, however, *madrasa* curricula have expanded to take myriad forms in different places, and their funding now more often comes from the government, nongovernmental organizations (NGOs), or the personal support of wealthy Muslim donors of nearly all ideological persuasions.

Mahdi (3, 10)
A figure who Muslims believe will return at the end-time to reestablish a just community before the end of the world. **Ithna'ashari Shi'ites** believe the twelfth Imam to be the Mahdi. Throughout history, **Sunni** Muslims have recognized various figures as the Mahdi, most notably in a series of modern millenarian movements directed at least in part toward the opposition of European colonial control in Muslim countries ranging from the Sudan to Indonesia. The name comes from the Arabic for "the guided one."

Maliki (1)
One of the four established schools of Sunni Muslim jurisprudence *(fiqh)*. Malikis attribute the origins of their legal reasoning methodology to Anas ibn Malik (d. 795).

Marabout (10)
A French term often used to refer to Muslim mystics or **Sufi** "saints" *(awliya Allah)* in parts of northern and western Africa.

Marinñet (8)
The organized friendship groups to which Ethiopian Hararis belong. In the past, individuals usually belonged to only one friendship group, often a neighborhood group that members formed during childhood and that lasted for

the members' lifetimes. Today, with Harari moving to live and work through-out Ethiopia and the world, *mariññet* structures are more flexible.

Marja-e taqlid (3)

The honorific title given to the most learned **Ithna'ashari Shi'ite** cleric—a *mujtahid*, to whom people in the community look for guidance in all *shari'a* rulings. This scholar has the authority to formulate original, unprecedented rulings in law and theology. Because it is forbidden for Twelver Shi'ites to follow the ruling of a dead *marja-e taqlid*, this office is occupied by a succession of scholars who bear the responsibility of providing guidance in matters of Islamic law for the community. The term *marja-e taqlid* is Persian, derived from the Arabic for "source of emulation."

Matn (1)

The second part of a **hadith** (a report of a saying of or anecdote about the Prophet). *Matn* contain the texts of the sayings of or anecdotes about the Prophet that form the basis for Muslim legal rulings and developments in other fields of Islamic religious scholarship.

Menhuan (6)

A Chinese term used to refer to **Sufi** orders. Locally, *menhuan* tended to take the form of groups centered on common descent from a leading Sufi *shaykh*. A list of the most prominent *menhuan* in the history of Muslim China would include the Jahriyya, Kubrawiyya, Khufiyya, and Qadariyya.

Mihna (1)

The theological "inquisition" supported by the Abbasid **caliphs** at Baghdad in the ninth century. The Abbasids' attempt to impose the teachings of one particular school of *kalam* as the official Islamic doctrine of their realms failed in the face of continuing opposition by *ulama* who remained independent of state control.

Minzu (6)

A Chinese term, translated as "nationality," that is the central concept of China's policy of ethnic classification of distinct peoples. The majority *minzu* is Han Chinese. Under a Soviet-influenced policy of managing diverse populations, China also recognizes several minority *minzus*, including the Muslim **Hui** and the **Uyghur**.

Moorish Science Temple (10)

An organization founded by the Noble Drew Ali (1886–1929). It was the first indigenous African American group to claim that blacks were both biologically and historically Muslims, although the contents of its ethical teachings drew more on U.S. traditions of Freemasonry, esotericism, and self-improvement than on foundational Islamic texts and traditions of Muslim piety.

Mufti (2)

A Muslim religious scholar whose knowledge of Islamic law justifies his authority to issue *fatwas.*

Muhammadiyya (7)

An Indonesian Muslim modernist organization founded at Yogyakarta, Central Java, in 1912 by Kyai Haji Ahmad Dahlan (d. 1923).

Mujahidin (1, 2, 4)

A term, literally meaning "those who engage in *jihad,*" used to refer collectively to disparate groups of Islamic militants who fought against the Soviet occupation of Afghanistan in the 1980s.

Mujtahid (3)

A practitioner of independent jurisprudential reasoning *(ijtihad).* For **Ithna'ashari Shi'a**—also referred to as the "Twelvers" or "Imami" **Shi'ites**—law is established by the *marja-e taqlid,* who serves as a living *mujtahid,* deriving his own jurisprudential rulings that are then followed by members of the community.

Mullah (3)

A person learned in Islamic law or other aspects of religious knowledge. In some cases, particularly in **Ithna'ashiri** forms of **Shi'ite** Islam, it is synonymous with *mujtahid.* This Persian term comes from Arabic.

Murid (3, 4)

A disciple of a **Sufi** master in a number of Muslim societies.

Muslim Brotherhood (1, 2, 9)

See **Ikhwan al-Muslimin**

Mu'tazila (1)

A medieval Muslim school of theology whose adherents called themselves "the People of Unity and of Justice." Their rationalist interpretation of *kalam* was forcefully promulgated by the Abbasid **caliphs** during the *mihna* (ninth century). However, since that time it has rarely proved attractive to **Sunni** Muslim thinkers, who have historically tended to favor more traditionalist approaches to Islamic theological issues.

Nahdlatul Ulama (7)

The largest Muslim organization in Indonesia and probably in the entire world. It was founded in 1926 by Javanese *ulama* under the direction of Kyai Haji Hasjim Asjari (d. 1947). Though often considered a traditionalist Muslim organization, since the 1980s it has also produced some of the most innovative and progressive Muslim thinkers in Indonesia.

Nation of Islam (10)

A U.S. organization begun in the 1930s when a Muslim immigrant named W. D. Fard began promoting the idea that Islam was the original religion of "the Blackman." One of his African American followers, Elijah Muhammad, taught that blacks must seek economic and political independence from white America and return to their original religion of Islam. These messages were grounded in a racialized mythology that has been criticized by other Muslims for contradicting what they see as the universality of the teachings of Islam. After the death of Elijah Muhammad in 1975, the movement's teachings were altered under the leadership of his son, Wallace D. Muhammad, who directed his followers to observe **Sunni** Islamic practices. Louis Farrakhan later broke with Wallace Muhammad, reconstituting a version of the old Nation of Islam.

New Order (7)

The political regime of former Indonesian president Suharto, who ruled the country from the bloody 1965 military takeover to his fall in the wake of the social and economic turmoil of the 1997–1998 Asian financial crisis. The English term comes from the **Bahasa Indonesia** name **Orde Baru.**

Nizaris (1, 10)
See **Isma'ilis**

NU (7)
See **Nahdlatul Ulama**

Orde Baru (7)
See **New Order**

Oromo (8)

Probably the largest ethnic group in Ethiopia, numbering 20 million–25 million. They stretch from western Ethiopia throughout the south and into the east, forming the majority ethnic population in much of this huge region. They speak a **Cushitic** language.

PAGAD (9)

The popular acronym for the South African organization People against Gangsterism and Drugs. The organization was ostensibly founded to combat rampant social problems in the Cape, but it eventually evolved as a movement of Islamist opposition to the postapartheid democratic order of South Africa.

Pancasila (1, 7)

The Five Principles that constitute the official state ideology of Indonesia. These are usually rendered into English as (1) belief in one God, (2) humanitarianism, (3) national unity, (4) democracy, and (5) social justice. The first of these is viewed by some as a compromise on the issue of establishing the Indonesian state on an Islamic foundation.

Pembaharuan (7)

The "renewal" of Islamic education, law, theology, and practice in order to make it more meaningful and beneficial for Muslims living in the contemporary world. Since the 1980s, Indonesian Muslim thinkers associated with the *pembaharuan* movement have worked to develop and disseminate interpretations of Islam that emphasize issues of pluralism and social justice. The term is from **Bahasa Indonesia.**

Pesantren (7)

See *Pondok Pesantren*

Pondok Pesantren (7)

Southeast Asian institutions of Islamic learning where the traditional curricula of religious sciences are taught from texts referred to as *kitab kuning*. Since the 1980s, some of these traditionalist Muslim schools have emerged as leading regional centers for the production of progressive interpretations of Islam designed to more effectively address the needs and concerns of contemporary society. This Indonesian term *pondok pesantren* is derived from the Javanese for "place of religious students."

Purdah (4)

Systems of institutionalized gender segregation in Muslim societies in parts of South Asia.

Qadariyya (6)

See *Menhuan*

Qur'an

The primary scripture of Islam. For Muslims, the Qur'an is literally the word of

God as it was conveyed to the Prophet Muhammad over the course of his twenty-two year mission (610–632) in Mecca and Medina. At first delivered in oral recitations, the Qur'an was later written down and arranged into the Arabic text that Muslims around the world use today.

Ramadhan (1)
See *Sawm;* **Islamic Lunar Calendar**

Sabean (8)
The people and language of the south Arabian kingdom of Sheba, which existed for 1,300 years before coming to an end in the sixth century C.E. Its alphabet is widely regarded as the earliest **Semitic** writing system.

Sahih (1)
The term often used to refer to the two major compilations of **hadith,** by Bukhari (d. 870) and Muslim (d. 875). The Arabic term *sahih* literally means "sound" or "reliable."

Salafis (1, 2)
A term usually used to refer to the original companions of the Prophet. "Salafi" has also become the name for a range of movements in modern Islam that promote the further Islamization of society through an agenda of restoring Islamic values and practices to their "pure" state—that is, as they are imagined to have been during Muhammad's lifetime. Since the late nineteenth century, various groups espousing such positions have been active in various parts of the Arab world as well as in more distant Muslim societies. In Arabic, *salaf* literally means "forefathers" or "ancestors."

Salat (1)
The five daily prayers conducted at dawn, midday, mid-afternoon, sunset, and evening. It is the second of the Five Pillars of Islam.

Sasanid Empire (1)
A Persian state that ruled much of the Middle East during the period of late antiquity. It rapidly collapsed after the invasion of Muslim armies in the years immediately following the death of Muhammad.

Sawm (1)
The Muslim practice of fasting during the Islamic lunar month of Ramadhan. From dawn to dusk each day of that month, Muslims refrain from eating, drinking any liquids, smoking, and many other behaviors. *Sawm* is the fourth of the Five Pillars of Islam.

Semitic (8)

A language family that includes a number of major ancient languages, such as Akkadian, and a number of other languages spoken today, including Arabic and Hebrew. However, at present the highest concentration of different living Semitic languages in the world is found in Ethiopia.

Shafi'i (1)

One of the four established schools of Sunni Muslim jurisprudence *(fiqh)*. Shafi'is attribute the origins of their legal reasoning methodology to al-Shafii'i (d. 820).

Shahada (1)

The profession of faith, the first of the Five Pillars of Islam: "There is no god but God, and Muhammad is his messenger."

Shari'a (3, 4, 7, 9)

A term commonly used to refer to Islamic law, broadly inclusive of both commands and prohibitions relating to the proper worship of God and to regulating personal interactions with others. Understandings of the *shari'a* are determined by established schools of law *(fiqh)*, which follow methods of legal reasoning based upon specific disciplines of interpreting the **Qur'an,** *hadith*, scholarly consensus, and reasoning by analogy. **Sunni** scholars generally follow one of the four established schools of law *(madhhab)*: **Hanafi, Maliki, Shafi'i,** and **Hanbali.** **Ithna'ashari** scholars add the teachings of the **Imams** as another source of law, and they stress the need for continual *ijtihad*, maintaining that to correctly follow the *shari'a* each person must follow the rulings of a living *mujtahid*.

In the modern period, popular calls for the implementation of the *shari'a* continue to attract support in various Muslim societies around the world. In most cases, however, these movements tend to conceive of the *shari'a* not as a divine way that must be continually interpreted through the exertions of specially trained scholars but, rather, as a static and formalized code of law with straightforward penalties for various stipulated infractions. In this, they tend to assume a model of law that is more deeply informed by modern Western conceptions of law and society than by classical Islamic ideals.

Shaykh (1, 4, 8)

A term, Arabic for "elder," used in various Muslim societies to refer to men in positions of authority, from tribal leaders to teachers and **Sufi** masters. The feminine form of this word, when used, is *shaykha.*

Shi'a
See **Shi'ite**

Shi'ite (1, 3)

Also Shi'a. A term derived from the Arabic expression for "partisans," referring to the partisans of Ali ibn Abi Talib, the cousin and son-in-law of the Prophet. The Shi'ites, who now constitute about 10 percent of Muslims worldwide, support the claim that Ali and his progeny, through his wife Fatima, are the legitimate religious and political successors *(khalifa)* to the Prophet. Over the centuries, the Shi'ites split among themselves into a number of distinct branches, including the **Zaydis, Isma'ilis,** and **Ithna'asharis,** which differ in certain teachings and in their acceptance of the lineages of their respective **Imams.**

Silsila (4)

The spiritual genealogy that links generations of **Sufi** masters and disciples, leading back ultimately to the authority of the Prophet Muhammad. The *silsila* can be presented as a list of names, which can be chanted as a litany, or it can be rendered visually as a tree or other graphic representation that establishes the proper relationships between the names. The Arabic term, literally meaning "chain," is part of the technical vocabulary of Islamic religious scholarship.

Society of Muslim Brothers
See **Ikhwan al-Muslimin**

Sufism (1, 2, 4, 5, 7, 8, 10)

A wide range of traditions of esoteric piety developed since the rise of Muslim asceticism *(zuhd)* in the seventh century. Practical and intellectual components of this tradition focus on perceiving the unity of God and realizing the perfect model of the Prophet Muhammad. Over the centuries, Sufi teachings have taken on the institutional forms of various organized orders *(tariqa*s) with branches in many parts of the Muslim world. Some of the doctrines and practices associated with Sufism, especially the veneration of *awliya Allah,* have become the focus of intense polemics between different groups of Sufis and Muslim reformists in the modern period.

The English term "Sufism" is often used as a gloss for the Arabic *tasawwuf.*

Sunnis (1, 2, 3, 4, 10)

A term derived from the Arabic phrase *ahl al-sunna wa'l-jama'a,* meaning "people of the way [of the Prophet] and the community," that refers to the majority Muslim community who are neither **Shi'ite** nor **Kharijite.** After the death of the Prophet, the earliest Sunnis were those who supported determining Muhammad's successor *(khalifa)* through community consensus rather than through blood lineage.

Tablighi Jama'at (4, 10)

A modern Muslim organization founded in 1926 by the Deobandi scholar and Naqshbandi **Sufi,** Maulana Muhammad Illyas Kandhlawi (1885–1944). It has rapidly expanded into a global Islamic movement that promotes an agenda of "purifying" Islam through a strict adherence to the *sunna* of the Prophet and the dictates of the *shari'a.* It considers itself to be an apolitical movement whose primary mission is one of *da'wa.*

Tajdid (4, 7)

An Arabic term, literally meaning "renewal," used in a number of Muslim societies to refer to a considerable range of different programs for religious and social reform.

Tanzimat (2)

The reorderings, or reforms, of the Ottoman administration in the eighteenth century. These reforms set the stage for a comprehensive revision in traditional methods of legal and religious training and thus had a considerable impact upon the Middle Eastern lands of the Ottoman Empire.

Tarekat (7)

A **Bahasa Indonesia** term, derived from the Arabic *tariqa,* that in Southeast Asia can refer not only to organized **Sufi** orders but also to mystical dimensions of Islam more generally.

Tariqa (1, 4)

An Arabic term, literally meaning "way," referring to various organized **Sufi** orders. Since the twelfth century, *tariqa*s have proliferated as means to preserve the teachings of revered Sufi *shaykh*s. They have spread throughout the Muslim world, where they have come to play a wide variety of social roles in different Muslim societies.

Tasawwuf (1, 4)
See **Sufism**

Tawhid (3)

The Islamic religious doctrine of the oneness of God. This uncompromising conception of monotheism is perhaps most concisely expressed in the first line of the *shahada,* "There is no god but God."

Taziyeh (3)

The name of the passion plays performed in Iran during the **Ashura** commemorations reenacting the martyrdom of Imam Husayn. The word is Persian, derived from Arabic.

To'y (5)

The feasts traditionally connected with the observance of life-cycle rituals, especially circumcisions and weddings, in parts of Central Asia. During the period of Soviet rule in the region, the *to'y* served both to mark Central Asian Muslims as different from others living in their midst and to affirm status within their own national community. *To'y* is a Turkic term.

Twelvers (1, 3, 10)
See **Ithna'ashari**

Ulama (1, 2, 4, 5, 7)

Muslim religious scholars who, through their studies of Islamic law and other fields of religious learning, have attained authority as spokesmen for the tradition. In medieval Islam, the *ulama* held a virtual monopoly over the interpretation of the tradition. In the modern period, however, they have faced unprecedented challenges to their authority as guardians of Islamic tradition from a number of fronts as innovations in education and communications technology have allowed Muslims from a wide range of occupations to take part in public discourses over religion and its place in contemporary society. *Ulama* is the plural form of the Arabic term *alim*, literally, "one who knows."

Umma (1–10)

A term referring to various configurations of "community" in different Muslim societies, but perhaps most often invoked to refer to the worldwide community of Muslims.

Urs (4)

An Arabic term, literally meaning "wedding," used by some **Sufis** to express the marriage of the soul with the Divine. In such contexts, it has thus come to refer to the ritual commemorations of the death anniversaries of important Sufi masters in their spiritual lineage. On these occasions, *murids* travel from all over Pakistan and beyond, gathering together for several days of communal worship at key Sufi tomb complexes *(dargahs)*.

Usul al-fiqh (4)

The field of Islamic legal studies that deals not with concrete decisions on particular cases but, rather, with the methodology used to reach those decisions. For most **Sunni** Muslims, the methodology includes studies of how to interpret the sources of the **Qur'an,** *sunna,* scholarly consensus, and reasoning by analogy in order to arrive at legal rulings.

Uyghur (6)
The Muslim ethnic group settled on the northwest frontier of China. They

speak a Turkic language and are spread throughout the Xinjiang Uyghur Autonomous Region as well as in a global diaspora.

Velayat-e faqih (3)

The **Ithna'ashari** doctrine that clerics, rather than secular rulers, should have religious and political authority in society while the twelfth Imam is in occultation. In the modern period, Ayatollah Ruhollah Khomeini (1900?–1989) reinterpreted this doctrine in light of modern political institutions. After the 1979 Islamic Revolution in Iran, he established a modern government based upon his own radical reinterpretation of the doctrine of *velayat-e faqih*. This Persian term comes from the Arabic for "guardianship of the jurisprudent."

Wahhabism (1, 8)

A movement of scripturalist reformism initiated in the Arabian peninsula by Muhammad ibn Abd al-Wahhab (d. 1792). He called for a radical reform of society to free Islam from what he viewed as the accretion of ignorance and paganism and to return the faith to what he imagined was its purest form. The Wahhabi movement gained significant political and military support through an early alliance with the Sa'ud clan, and as a result of their occupation of Mecca (a center of scholarship as well as a destination of pilgrimage), Wahhabi doctrine spread beyond the Arabian peninsula to nearly all parts of the Muslim world. Today it is the dominant interpretation of Islam in Saudi Arabia.

Wali (1, 7)

The singular form of Arabic *awliya*, "friends" (see ***awliya Allah***).

Waqf (1, 2, 5)

Endowments of land revenue established for the financial support of religious institutions, such as mosques, schools, and charitable facilities. In the medieval period, *waqf* provided many ***ulama*** with a source of financial support that was independent of state control. Over the course of the nineteenth and twentieth centuries, most Middle Eastern governments encroached to varying degrees on *waqf* institutions by nationalizing the administration of *waqf* properties. These changes have had important implications for traditions of Islamic learning in the modern period.

Yihewani (6)

Chinese Islamic reformists in the twentieth and twenty-first centuries who returned from periods of study in the Middle East bringing agendas for purifying Chinese Muslim practice and Islamic scripturalism. The term *yihewani* is a Chinese adaptation of the Arabic term *ikhwan*, "brotherhood." See **Ikhwan al-Muslimin.**

Zahir (4)

The "outward," or exoteric—as opposed to the "inward," or esoteric (*batin*)—dimension of Muslim piety. The Chishti Sabiri order discussed in Chapter 4 see **Sufism** as a means by which one can find a balance between these two dimensions.

Zakat (1)

The practice of obligatory almsgiving in Islam. It is the third of the Five Pillars of Islam.

Zaydis (1)

Also known as **"Fiver" Shi'ites,** Muslims who split from other groups of Shi'ites over early disputes over the succession of the **imam.** Today they make up a very small minority of the world's Muslims and are centered mostly in North Yemen, which was ruled by a Zaydi **imam** until 1962.

Zuhd (1)

The ascetic movement that developed among some Muslims in the early centuries of Islamic history.

Index

September 11 *(continued)*
  South Asian Islam and, 127–129
  U.S. Muslims and, 284, 298
700 Club (television series), 284
Seveners, African American, 296
Sexism, 284, 304, 305
Sexual Customs, 170
Shadhiliyya, 297
Shadow puppet theater, 210
Shafi'i, 19, 355
Shah, Prince Karim, 296
Shah Wali Allah, 108, 112
Shahada, 5, 355
Shahrur, Muhammad, 70, 71, 72
Shamshatu refugee camp, 110 (photo)
Shanghai Five, 177
Sha'rawi, Hoda, 62
Shari'a, 19, 20, 45–46, 98, 106, 108,
    114, 116, 123, 124, 166, 197, 212,
    248, 262, 264, 271, 273, 277, 283
  as cultural backbone, 112
  described, 355
  ideals of, 196
  implementation of, 31, 213
  precepts of, 295
Shariati, Ali, 87, 88, 89
Shariff, Abdullahi Ali, 241
Shawa Gate, 225
Shawkani, Muhammad ibn Ali al-, 20
*Shaykh*s, 14, 15, 69, 108, 121, 124, 125,
    152, 165, 243
  Chishti Sabiri, 120, 126
  described, 355
  Sufi, 118, 119
The Sheik (movie), 286
Shi'atu Ali, 77
Shi'ism, 83, 289, 356
  Ali and, 12
  forms of, 99
  history of, 80
  teachings of, 75
Shi'ites, 12, 34, 43, 60, 64, 291, 296
  African American, 296
  Imams and, 78
  self-flagellation by, 79 (photo)

  worldviews of, 78, 80
"Shikwa" (Iqbal), 112
Shriners, 286, 292
Shrines, 126, 151
  Sufi, 16 (photo), 117 (photo)
  Uzbek, 153 (photo)
  visiting, 79, 80, 141, 144
Shumburo, Mahdi, 228
SI. *See* Sarekat Islam
Sidamo, 249
Signposts along the Road (Qutb), 55, 56
Silk Road, 173, 178
Silsila, 118, 356
Simmons, Gwendolyn Zoharah, 305
Sinification, 166
Sino-Muslims, 164, 180n1
Sir Sayyid. *See* Khan, Sayyid Ahmad
Sisters in Islam, 19
Slavery, 257, 259, 280, 291
  Asian, 255
  escape from, 246
  freedom of religion and, 255
  Muslim, 255, 289, 290
Social activities, 53, 303
Social attitudes, 188, 260
Social change, 23, 44, 87, 89, 106, 107,
    118, 139, 214, 236, 268
  modernizing, 195
  in Modern Period, 26–27
  positive, 202
Social hierarchies, 44, 225
Socialism, 59, 294
  disillusion with, 56
  Islam and, 87, 139
Social justice, 212, 213, 298
Social life, 51, 91, 109, 246, 264, 304
Social organization, 45, 54, 200
Social problems, 68, 96, 99, 194, 202,
    236
Social services, 53, 70
Social welfare, 21–23, 118
Sodhi, Balbir, 283
Soekarno, 197, 211
  fall of, 198, 199, 201
  Pancasila and, 30

Sufi, 26, 190
Turkmen, 148
Traditionalists, 106, 197, 198, 202, 275
    described, 107–111
    modernists and, 212
Transoxiana, 135
Transvaal, 262, 266
Tri Sakti University, 211
True Islam, 155
Tuan Guru (Abdullah Kadi Abdus
    Salaam), 255
Turabi, Hassan, 34
Turki, 173
Turkish Criminal Code (1926), 51
Turkish Khanate, 173
Turkish Muslims, 174
    Red Crescent and, 291
Turkistan, 174
Turkmen, 148
Türkmenbashï, 148, 152
Turko-Persian Islamic culture, 105
Türköz, Ahmet, 179
Turks, 289
Turpan, 173, 174
Twain, Mark, 290
Twelfth Imam, 77–78, 88, 89, 91, 296
Twelver Shi'ism, 75, 99
    African American, 296
    history of, 77–80
    politics and, 82–84
    teaching, 81
    See also Ithna'ashari
Twelver Shi'ite law, 77

Ulama, 19, 20, 23, 27, 28, 48, 50, 75,
    107, 109, 112, 113, 114, 119, 123,
    136, 137, 139, 149, 193, 194, 195,
    201, 266
    authority of, 116
    described, 358
    influence of, 202
    Sufism and, 116
Ulfah, Maria, 209, 214n1
Ulug'bek, Mirzo, 148
Umayyads, 13, 77, 83

Umma, 4, 54, 164, 358
Umm Assa'd bint Isam al-Himyari, 10
Union of South Africa, Boer republics
    and, 260
Universalism, 107, 295
University of Baghdad, 212
University of Illinois, Muslim Students
    Association of, 294
University of Medina, 294
Unrepresented Nations and People's
    Organization (UNPO), 176
Urdu, 120
Urs, 125, 126, 358
Urumqi, 170, 172, 176, 178
Urwa al-Wuthqa, 28
U.S. Central Intelligence Agency
    (CIA), 86, 93
U.S. Congressional Research Service,
    172
Usul, 82
Usul al-fiqh, 107, 358
Usul-i jadid, 137
Uthman, 3, 13, 219
Uyghur Empire, 173
Uyghur Muslims, 164, 170, 171, 175
    (photo), 358–359
    Chinese society and, 172–174
    Chinese sovereignty and, 174–176
    population of, 163
    rebellions by, 174
    Taliban and, 176
    Tibetans and, 179
Uyghur People's Government, 176
Uyghur separatists, 176, 177, 178
Uyghuristan, 171, 173, 174
Uzbeks, 148, 163
    Uyghurs and, 171, 176

Valentino, Rudolf, 286
Values
    family, 299
    human, 150, 151
    Islamic, 63, 150, 205, 262, 265
    moral, 150
    Western, 114